Why Some Firms Thrive
While Others Fail

Why Some Firms Thrive While Others Fail

GOVERNANCE AND MANAGEMENT LESSONS FROM THE CRISIS

Thomas H. Stanton

OXFORD
UNIVERSITY PRESS

OXFORD
UNIVERSITY PRESS

Oxford University Press, Inc., publishes works that further
Oxford University's objective of excellence
in research, scholarship, and education.

Oxford   New York
Auckland   Cape Town   Dar es Salaam   Hong Kong   Karachi
Kuala Lumpur   Madrid   Melbourne   Mexico City   Nairobi
New Delhi   Shanghai   Taipei   Toronto

With offices in
Argentina   Austria   Brazil   Chile   Czech Republic   France   Greece
Guatemala   Hungary   Italy   Japan   Poland   Portugal   Singapore
South Korea   Switzerland   Thailand   Turkey   Ukraine   Vietnam

Published by Oxford University Press, Inc.
198 Madison Avenue, New York, New York 10016
www.oup.com

Oxford is a registered trademark of Oxford University Press

Library of Congress Cataloging-in-Publication Data
Stanton, Thomas H., 1944–
Why some firms thrive while others fail : governance and management lessons from the crisis /
Thomas H. Stanton.
p.   cm.
Includes bibliographical references and index.
ISBN 978-0-19-991599-6 (cloth : alk. paper) 1. Corporations—United States—Case studies.
2. Industrial management—United States—Case studies. 3. Global Financial Crisis, 2008–2009. I. Title.
HD2785.S65   2012
338.50973—dc23   2011046818

1 3 5 7 9 8 6 4 2

Printed in the United States of America
on acid-free paper

CONTENTS

PREFACE

The Relentless Pattern

On Monday, October 31, 2011, after this manuscript had gone to the publisher, a financial firm called MF Global went into bankruptcy. As the dust settled, investigators found over $1 billion of customer funds unaccounted for. MF Global's CEO Jon Corzine, a former United States senator and former governor of New Jersey, told Congress that he had had no idea the money was missing.[1] At this writing the mystery of the missing funds remains unsolved.

MF Global illustrates many of the themes of this book. According to news accounts, Corzine was a powerful CEO. He led MF Global in making bets on European sovereign debt. When the company risk officer objected, the risk officer was removed; the risk officer's successor was expressly instructed not to analyze risk of the company's European debt exposure. Senior executives also expressed misgivings about the firm's growing bet on European sovereign debt, but to no avail.[2]

When board members suggested that Corzine might limit MF Global's investments in European bonds, Corzine reportedly said that "if you want a smaller or different position [regarding European debt], maybe you don't have the right guy here," and offered to step down. Corzine later told a congressional committee that this was not a threat. And the board, despite knowledge of the company's high leverage and growing concentration of risk, did not prevent the bet from continuing.[3]

Where were the regulators? At this writing, multiple regulators are still sorting out their responsibilities. Corzine personally lobbied one regulator, the Commodity Futures Trading Commission, not to strengthen customer protections by requiring segregated accounts for customer money. The *New York Times* reported:

> Just three months [before its insolvency], Mr. Corzine's firm assured regulators that the proposed rule could cripple the futures brokerage industry by hurting their profitability. In a letter, MF Global told regulators that they were trying to "fix something that is not broken," adding that the firm was not aware of any brokerage firm like itself that was unable to "provide to their customers upon request any segregated funds."

MF Global's clients, including hedge funds, individual investors and agricultural firms, now know a different reality, as the clients struggle to locate their missing funds. And regulators are pushing to again move forward on the rule. But for MF Global, the rule will come too late.[4]

MF Global's bankruptcy fits a pattern. The company's demise shows yet again why it is essential that management should systematically solicit and consider a broad range of feedback such as from the board of directors, company risk officer, employees, and regulators. Regulators should require this of major financial firms and test for it. The alternative all too often is hubris, failure to recognize growing risk, and ruin. While the financial crisis offers the most comprehensive evidence of this pattern, its validity extends beyond the crisis and beyond financial firms to governance and management more generally.

The Financial Crisis: The Pattern Becomes Clear

The pattern became clear to me during my service on the staff of the Financial Crisis Inquiry Commission in 2010–2011, followed by further research to write this book. The crisis raised important issues: If private firms had not been able to protect themselves or the financial system from crisis, and the public sector failed to prevent the crisis, what did this say about the state of our institutions? To try to answer this question I reviewed financial firms including four that had withstood the crisis and eight that had not. My colleagues and I interviewed many present and former officials of government supervisory agencies to get their perspectives. When the Commission finished its work, it put many of those interviews and numerous public documents on the public record.[5] This book builds on that work and those public records. I was fortunate to have participated in many of the interviews and to know where to access recordings and documents that otherwise could consume considerable time before they yield their insights to a researcher.

The Commission operated on a tight budget and an even tighter timetable. When the Commission ended I felt that I still needed to increase my understanding, especially of the influence of organizational design and management on the success of firms. Taking time off to write this book provided opportunity for me to revisit many issues of governance, risk management, and management generally, for which I had been a lead researcher at the Commission, and push to another level. More than a few times I wished for the chance to go back to interviews to ask follow-up questions, now that the larger context had become clear.

Once I thought I understood lessons from the financial crisis, the question became whether these could be applied more generally. Virginia Tech student

Joshua Deal, my capable summer intern, helped me to research governance and risk management at nonfinancial firms. Building on Josh's work, it became clear that even if lines of business were different, there were common aspects of governance, management, and organization with lessons similar to those from the financial crisis.

Recognizing the Pattern: My Background

My professional work over the years includes studying the organizational design, management, and vulnerabilities of government sponsored enterprises (GSEs) such as Fannie Mae and Freddie Mac and their regulator. Based on my research and analysis, I tried to sound the alarm before crisis hit. In 1991 I published my book *A State of Risk: Will Government-Sponsored Enterprises be the Next Financial Crisis?* (HarperBusiness) that analyzed vulnerabilities of the GSE business model. This book, along with my personal lobbying, helped lead to the creation of a new regulator for Fannie Mae and Freddie Mac in 1992.[6] Given determined opposition from the two companies, the regulatory reform was only partially successful; under stress, the GSEs failed because of structural vulnerabilities analyzed in *A State of Risk*.

In *A State of Risk* (see p. 182) I proposed creating a system of what is now known as "contingent capital" (to require financial institutions to issue subordinated debt that automatically converts to equity if the institution begins to fail) as a way to increase the capital cushion of the GSEs and provide some market discipline. Economist Mark Flannery adopted and publicized the idea, and policy makers are now considering requiring contingent capital for large complex financial institutions as part of a pattern of reforms to try to mitigate systemic risk.

I am a fellow of the Center for Advanced Governmental Studies at the Johns Hopkins University, and currently teach courses including the program's core course for the MBA/MA in government and a graduate seminar on the financial system under stress. I served on the board of directors of the National Academy of Public Administration (NAPA), and was chair of the NAPA Standing Panel on Executive Organization and Management for many years. I also served as a member of the federal Senior Executive Service for almost five years at the Federal Trade Commission (FTC). It was in the FTC's Office of Policy Planning that that I first saw the benefits of constructive dialogue, as lawyers and economists brought their different perspectives to bear on decisions about proposed agency actions and learned from one another in the process.

ACKNOWLEDGMENTS

There are many people to thank for this book. Most importantly, I am grateful to my wife Martha Zaslow. She is a wonderful life partner and her encouragement and support mean much to me. I shall never forget Nepenthe and her enthusiasm about the book. Our sons, Benjamin and Joshua, and our daughter-in-law, Mirah, also have been wonderfully supportive over the years and in this effort.

The Financial Crisis Inquiry Commission learned many lessons about governance, management, and the financial crisis that are reflected in this book. The research staff, led by Greg Feldberg, fermented with ideas and discussions. The investigative staff, led by Chris Seefer, taught me much about conducting interviews and eliciting information. Many other members of the staff, including Hillary Allen, Tom Borgers, Brad Bondi, Ron Borzekowski, Al Crego, Vic Cunicelli, Jobe Danganan, Desi Duncker, Mike Easterly, Scott Ganz, Bob Hinkley, Carl McCarden, Joel Miller, Donna Norman, Steve Sanderford, Kim Shafer, Alexis Simendinger, Mina Simhai, Landon Stroebel, and Art Wilmarth, greatly contributed to my thinking and ideas that emerge in this book. It was a wonderful experience. I am deeply grateful to chairman Phil Angelides, Wendy Edelberg, and Tom Greene for bringing me on board. Chairman Angelides worked tirelessly and made a major national contribution with his dedication to place not only the *Final Report* but also important documents and interviews on the public record so that we can better understand the crisis and its causes. Thanks to the Commission, participants in the financial sector—CEOs, traders, risk officers, supervisors, and others—can speak in their own voices in this book.

There have been many reviewers of this book. Friends and colleagues who provided insights about chapters of this book include Gary Cohen, formerly general counsel of the Financial Crisis Inquiry Commission who has returned to Los Angeles to continue his career as a transactions and private funds attorney; Gregory Feldberg, formerly research director at the Commission; Raymond Natter, former senior official of the Office of the Comptroller of the Currency and now a Washington financial services attorney; and Alex Pollock, formerly CEO of the Federal Home Loan Bank of Chicago and now resident scholar at the American Enterprise Institute. Thanks for taking the time and being so thoughtful in your comments! Thanks too to Douglas D. Evanoff, vice president in the economic research department of the Federal Reserve Bank of Chicago, who invited me to present some of my findings and conclusions to the Chicago Fed's Conference on Bank Structure and Competition in 2011. He has been extremely supportive over the years and I am grateful.

I am also very grateful to the many people who have shared friendship and knowledge over the years. These include four giants in the field of public administration, Harold Seidman, Alan Dean, Murray Comarow, and Dwight Ink, and other friends and colleagues at the Standing Panel on Executive Organization and Management of the National Academy of Public Administration. The panel holds a monthly seminar that has taught me an immense amount about the art and science of implementing government policy.

Benjamin Ginsberg, professor of political science and director of the Johns Hopkins Center for Advanced Governmental Studies, has been a friend and mentor for many years. Thanks too to Walter Cohn, John Connor, Michael Kerr, Patrick Lawler, Fernando Montes-Negret, Marvin Phaup, Nicolas Retsinas, David Roderer, Robin Seiler, Ken Stanton, and many others for the sage insights and collegial support you have shared over the years. Some people who provided insight and encouragement continue to work in or with the financial sector and cannot be listed here.

Oxford University Press fielded a strong team for this book. Associate editor Joe Jackson, executive editor Terry Vaughn, production editor Natalie Johnson, project manager Venkat Raghavan Srinivasa Raghavan, marketing manager Jared Wright, and copy editor Anne Sanow all worked to make this effort a success. I plan to continue writing in this field and would welcome comments and insights you might wish to share at tstan77346@gmail.com. All views and any errors or omissions in this book are solely my responsibility. The book would not have been the same without colleagues' willingness to share insights and provide feedback, which indeed was a gift.

Why Some Firms Thrive
While Others Fail

Repairing Our Public and Private Institutions

A NATIONAL IMPERATIVE

I made a mistake in presuming that the self-interest of organizations, specifically banks and others, was such that they were best capable of protecting their own shareholders and the equity in the firms.

—ALAN GREENSPAN, 2008

The United States has experienced the most significant failure of its financial system since the Great Depression. The federal government committed over $3 trillion in spending, loan purchases, loans, and loan guarantees through the Treasury, Federal Reserve System, and Federal Deposit Insurance Corporation (FDIC) to support financial institutions and auto companies among other purposes, and enacted a $787 billion economic stimulus package. The world came close, as Federal Reserve Chairman Ben Bernanke said, to "Depression 2.0."[1]

Princeton professor Alan Blinder and economist Mark Zandi estimated in 2009 that the projected total costs of the financial crisis would exceed $2.35 trillion, or about 16 percent of GDP.[2] These costs included the stimulus package, government support for Fannie Mae and Freddie Mac, the Economic Stimulus Act of 2008, and emergency unemployment benefits, to name the larger items. The economy struggles and the recession catches government in a bind: demand for services such as unemployment and healthcare rises just as tax revenues drop.

Personal costs of the crisis were immense. Perhaps 10 million households may lose their homes to foreclosure.[3] House prices declined to the point where by 2010, almost one-quarter of homes were worth less than the mortgages on the property. Stock prices as measured by the Wilshire 5000 index fell 57 percent from the peak in October 2007 to the deepest point in March 2009, before rising again. Median household wealth fell by 25 percent from 2007 to 2009, for a loss of about $ 17 trillion.[4] The unemployment rate doubled, and millions of people lost their jobs.[5] Real median income fell to $49,445 in 2010, the lowest number since 1997, and the poverty rate rose to its highest level since 1993.[6]

There have been many excellent narratives of the financial crisis, including the *Final Report* of the Financial Crisis Inquiry Commission (FCIC, or Commission) and numerous accounts by financial journalists. Economists also weighed in with detailed analyses of causes of the crisis. This book seeks to continue the process of learning lessons from this expensive debacle. It applies the disciplines of organizational design and management: How did financial firms contribute to the crisis, and why did government fail to prevent it? What can we learn by comparing financial firms that withstood the crisis with those that failed? What do we need to know about the workings of public and private institutions to try to avoid expensive crises in the future?

Former Federal Reserve Chairman Alan Greenspan, no friend of government interference in the workings of private firms, reflected in 2008 that "I made a mistake in presuming that the self-interest of organizations, specifically banks and others, was such that they were best capable of protecting their own shareholders and the equity in the firms."[7]

Chairman Greenspan's statement recognizes institutional failures leading to the crisis: market forces and the best interests of private companies failed to work efficiently and effectively to protect the financial system from calamity. Rather, the untrammeled pursuit of revenues, profits, and market share helped drive major financial firms into ruin, with serious negative consequences for the rest of us as well. While the government's response to the crisis helped to prevent a complete meltdown, government was largely passive before the crisis and failed to prevent it. Repair of our institutions, especially in the financial sector, would seem to be a major national imperative as the country emerges from the crisis and tries to deal with our changing global economic status.

This book focuses on critical elements that helped to determine whether a large financial firm would survive the crisis or fail: governance, management, and business models. Many large financial institutions, including Fannie Mae, Freddie Mac, Countrywide, IndyMac, Washington Mutual (WaMu), American International Group (AIG), Citigroup, Merrill Lynch, Wachovia, Lehman Brothers, and Bear Stearns, failed in the sense that they went out of business, required massive amounts of government aid to stay afloat, or entered into mergers to end their existence as independent companies. Yet other large firms, including JPMorgan Chase, Goldman Sachs, Wells Fargo, and Toronto Dominion Bank (TD Bank), weathered the crisis and emerged stronger than their erstwhile rivals. Some of these firms have had serious problems, reputational and otherwise, but the point here is that they had successful strategies for surviving the crisis.

The crisis damaged even successful firms: The Dodd-Frank Act and other governmental actions imposed restrictions that may or may not help to mitigate effects of a future crisis, but do limit financial firms in significant ways, such as limits on proprietary trading activities by bank holding companies (the so-called Volcker Rule) and regulation of derivatives. Firms that made apparently wise acquisitions during the crisis found that losses mounted unexpectedly. Wells Fargo acquired Wachovia and took losses from Wachovia's large portfolio of pay-option adjustable rate mortgages (a particularly risky mortgage product), while JPMorgan Chase's acquisition of WaMu loan assets generated significant losses.

Otherwise successful firms suffered other negative consequences as well. The Senate Permanent Subcommittee on Investigations reported on Goldman Sachs and Deutsche Bank, two firms that hedged their mortgage market exposures early:

> Throughout 2007, Goldman sold [mortgage] securities to its clients without disclosing its own net short position against the subprime market or its purchase of . . . contracts to gain from the loss in value of some of the very securities it was selling to its clients. . . .
>
> Both Goldman Sachs and Deutsche Bank underwrote securities using loans from subprime lenders known for issuing high risk, poor quality mortgages, and sold risky securities to investors across the United States and around the world. They also enabled the lenders to acquire new funds to originate still more high risk, poor quality loans. Both sold CDO securities without full disclosure of the negative views of some of their employees regarding the underlying assets and, in the case of Goldman, without full disclosure that it was shorting the very CDO securities it was marketing, raising questions about whether Goldman complied with its obligations to issue suitable investment recommendations and disclose material adverse interests.[8]

The subcommittee referred its findings about Goldman to the Justice Department for possible prosecution.[9] As this book went to press, the Federal Housing Finance Agency, which oversees Fannie Mae and Freddie Mac in government hands, announced lawsuits against seventeen major firms for violations of law in connection with the sale of private-label mortgage securities to Fannie Mae and Freddie Mac. In some cases involving firms that weathered the financial crisis (and failed firms whose liabilities they assumed), FHFA alleged that the misconduct involved fraud and was "intentional and wanton," and sought punitive damages. These included JPMorgan Chase, Goldman Sachs, Morgan Stanley, and Deutsche Bank. In short, the financial crisis was damaging to nominally successful firms as well as those that failed. Of relevance here is the contention of this book that because they operate in a financial *system*, where firms depend on one another for their transactions, even firms that exhibit strong risk management have a great stake in protecting the system from such a crisis in the future.

This book seeks to analyze shortcomings in (1) organization, (2) governance, and (3) management, which contributed to the financial crisis, as well as differences in governance and management between the survivors and the others. Even within the flawed organizational framework of large complex financial institutions, some firms successfully navigated the crisis while others failed. What was the difference between winners and losers in organization, governance, and management? This book seeks to understand the differences and lessons that might be learned from the crisis and from the experiences of some nonfinancial firms.

The basic lesson, of course, is that low probability events with devastating consequences do happen. Nassim Nicholas Taleb calls such events "black swans." He argues that they take place much more frequently than people expect.[10] Managers must take the possibility of black swans into account even when times are good; that's one factor that distinguishes survivors from the rest.

Organization

Organizational design refers to the way that the form of an organization affects its development and evolution with respect to critical elements such as its capacity, flexibility, accountability, and life cycle.[11] As with all organizations in our constitutional system, law frames the attributes of private companies. Some firms, such as many state-chartered finance companies, may engage in all activities except where prohibited by law. Other firms, such as commercial banks, thrift institutions, insurance companies, and government-sponsored enterprises (GSEs), may undertake activities only when authorized by law. Some firms are hybrids, such as rating agencies that are free to organize themselves as they wish but with eligibility and functions that are shaped by law. Each organizational form has financial and operational advantages and disadvantages.[12]

A firm's organization shapes its incentives and behavior. Much as occurred with investment banks that converted from partnership form in past decades and began to take more risk as investor-owned companies, in the savings and loan debacle of the 1980s, when thrifts fundamentally changed their behavior after converting from mutual to investor ownership, and as occurred with Freddie Mac when it became an investor-owned company in 1989 and increased its risk-taking, behavior of firms in the financial crisis frequently derived from the form of their ownership and control.

Financial firms often may choose the particular laws that govern their organizations. A commercial bank or thrift institution may select whether it desires a federal or state charter and, if a state charter, where it wishes to locate itself for purposes of selecting the relevant state law. An additional benefit is that this frequently allows firms to select the most amenable financial regulator.

Large complex financial institutions pose special organizational problems. Often consisting of a thousand or more distinct organizational elements, these firms need to devote special attention to managing the company as an integrated unit. Otherwise, as in the case of Citigroup or AIG, one part of the firm may be trying to reduce exposure to a troubled market while another part of the firm increases its exposure.

Governance

Governance is the ability of a firm to guide its activities effectively. Governance relates to the flow of information to appropriate decision makers (both up and down the corporate hierarchy and across the firm), the ability to assess and act on that information, and incentive structures relating to people and units within the firm. Governance thus relates to the distribution of power and authority among different parts of the organization.

Weak governance compounded organizational shortcomings at many firms. Overbearing CEOs too often dominated weak boards that failed to uphold the duty of respectfully challenging management to provide feedback and probe the limitations of proposed management initiatives. Former senior UK Treasury official Paul Myners charged that "the typical bank board resembles a retirement home for the great and the good: there are retired titans of industry, ousted politicians and the occasional member of the voluntary sector." Such people, he noted, are unlikely to have the knowledge needed to provide guidance for a large complex financial institution in today's global economy.

Many firms couldn't provide adequate information to top management or the board to support sound decision making. For example, Martin Sullivan, CEO of AIG, testified to the Commission that he had not realized the financial exposure created for AIG by its London-based subsidiary, AIG Financial Products (AIGFP). From the transcript of the Commission hearing on June 30, 2010:

> CHAIRMAN ANGELIDES: So you had a book of $78 billion of exposure by 2007 and you didn't become aware of it until then?
> WITNESS SULLIVAN: What I was receiving was regular reports from not only [AIGFP CEO] Mr. Cassano on his business, but also from [others] on AIGFP's business in its totality, including the credit default swap portfolio. But to the best of my knowledge, I never recognized that portfolio, and there were no issues raised in the correspondence that would have given me cause for concern.[13]

Better corporate governance is easy to prescribe, but far more difficult to implement. A critical aspect of governance relates to corporate culture—that is, "the unwritten standards and norms that shape mindsets, attitudes, and behaviors."[14] Ability to communicate up and down the line and across organizational units is an essential part of an effective corporate culture. Too many organizations, whether in the public or private sectors, exhibit gaps in information flow between their top levels and subordinate levels of the organization (similar to AIG), and also dissonance of views between top levels and other levels of the organization. Chapter 7 presents similar examples of dissonance between career supervisors and the political level of supervisory agencies, both in the United States and elsewhere. Throughout the book are examples of top leaders both in private firms that failed and in supervisory agencies, who didn't take account of views of people lower in their organizations who had important information to share.

Staff of the Financial Crisis Inquiry Commission conducted interviews of officials and employees of companies and supervisors, and too often found significant dissonance in views and knowledge among people up and down the organizational hierarchy. The point is not whether top management or subordinate levels are correct in their perceptions; rather, it is that effective management requires a flow of information and views across levels of an organization so that top management is not blindsided if risks materialize that were apparent to others in the organization but were not communicated or heard. Effective management depends on a culture that allows a firm's leaders to receive important information promptly from all parts of the organization and to form the judgments needed to recognize changing circumstances.

Management

Management involves building on the firm's resources to meet achievable goals based on a sound assessment of the external environment. At the executive level, management has to do with the way that leaders guide an organization, shape its culture, and ensure sustainable ways of doing business. The cultural gap between well-managed financial firms and those that failed in the crisis was large. Information systems at successful firms captured enterprise-wide risks; those at unsuccessful firms did not. Creating strong and effective systems was expensive and time-consuming for firms, and was essential not only for risk management but for effective management more generally. Moreover, as William Lang of the Philadelphia Federal Reserve Bank observes, major firms allocated skilled people to score risks of assets coming onto the books, but many tended not to allocate similarly skilled people to assess risks that were building across the firm's entire portfolio.[15]

When not tied integrally to a firm's culture, risk management often became a pro forma exercise in which company officials went through the motions without adding value to the company's capacity to address potential risks. Officials of unsuccessful firms complained that they could not have been expected to foresee the nationwide drop in housing prices. But successful firms did not foresee this either; rather, those company leaders took defensive positions by maintaining strong balance sheets or by becoming alert to early signs of a troubled market and reducing risk.

Organization and Management of Financial Supervisors

Organizational structure shapes capabilities and actions of government as well. The United States is perhaps unique in the world in the organizational complexity of financial supervision and regulation. Before the financial crisis firms often could choose not only whether they desired a federal or state charter, but often also which federal regulator they preferred. For firms such as AIG, Washington Mutual, IndyMac, and Countrywide, the Office of Thrift Supervision (OTS) seemed to be the most congenial regulator. The OTS had been reorganized from the old Federal Home Loan Bank Board, an agency that had been mandated by law to promote the industry it regulated; although the Congress dropped that part of the law, the Bank Board's culture of being solicitous of regulated firms seems to have survived.

This created a race to the supervisory bottom. Regulators worried that if they tightened up supervision, a firm would simply leave and place itself under authority of a more lax regulator. The issue of a regulatory level playing field prevented regulators from taking steps they otherwise might have considered appropriate. The problem is, of course, that the playing field never will be sufficiently level. There will always be new ways of doing business that move financial activities from better-supervised firms to those that are not.

While some policy makers and supervisors were alert and concerned, their voices were muffled by organizational complications that made effective financial supervision difficult. Fragmentation of authority among multiple organizations created substantial governance problems for financial supervisors not only with the distribution of authority, but also with the flow of information. Fragmentation made governance difficult among supervisors and even within the Federal Reserve System itself. Impediments to the flow of relevant information can impede effective governance, too. Supervisors described a process of trying to work around those obstacles so that they could do their jobs, but when workarounds are required to be effective, it only indicates that organizational design itself needs attention.

The credit bubble and apparently benevolent economic conditions of the early 2000s also created problems. In her pathbreaking work on the Challenger space shuttle disaster, sociologist Diane Vaughan writes of "normalization of deviance" as a process of reducing standards to unacceptable levels based on past success, without taking proper account of the risks involved in the new low standards.[16] This happened as the housing and credit bubbles inflated. In the pursuit of unprecedented profits, financial firms, including mortgage originators, firms that securitized loans, rating agencies, and investors of all types, deviated sharply from traditional standards of prudence. Increasing asset prices masked risks inherent in those lower standards. Prosperity also created obstacles for government regulatory and supervisory agencies. How does a supervisor tell a company to refrain from activities that appear to be so profitable? Sometimes supervisors would wait until losses appeared before pressing a firm to improve its governance or risk management, but waiting for losses too often meant waiting until mistakes finally crippled a firm.

The Power of Constructive Dialogue

The question then becomes whether from the perspective of organizational design, governance, and management there is any single major recommendation that, if well implemented, could help bring weaker large financial firms up to the level of their more successful peers. The literature on decision making in large organizations yields an answer. Sydney Finklelstein of the Tuck School of Business at Dartmouth and his colleagues analyzed decision making. They found that bad decisions required two key elements: (1) an initial flawed decision that the CEO or another influential person made, and (2) a poorly structured decision process that failed to provide facts and input to correct the mistake. Chapter 9 discusses their findings further. In the felicitous phrase of organizational development expert Jack Rosenblum, "feedback is a gift." Critical input needs to be seen as an offer to rethink a preliminary decision before it potentially causes harm.

One of the critical distinctive factors between successful and unsuccessful firms in the crisis was their application of what this book calls "constructive dialogue." Successful firms managed to create productive and constructive tension between (1) those who wanted to do deals, or offer certain financial products and services, and (2) those in the firm who were responsible for limiting risk exposures. By creating a respectful exchange of views among these divergent perspectives, successful firms freed themselves to find constructive outcomes that took the best from each point of view. Instead of simply deciding to do a deal or not, successful firms considered ways to hedge risks or otherwise reduce exposure from doing the deal. Successful firms created opportunity for constructive dialogue between CEOs and their boards and CEOs and their top managers, and between revenue-producing units and risk officers.

Unsuccessful firms frequently pursued revenue-producing ventures without constructive dialogue with those concerned about risk. Major firms acquired increasing volumes of risky assets, expanded their market share, and avidly pursued profits without regard to risk in 2005–2007, just as house prices peaked and declined. They disregarded input from their risk officers—such as when Freddie Mac's CEO considered his chief risk officer to be unsympathetic to the company's mission and fired him in 2005, just before the company greatly increased its risk-taking. Lehman's CEO sidelined his chief risk officer in 2007.[17] By contrast, because of their application of constructive dialogue and a robust sense of the risk-reward trade-off, successful firms often retained more capital than their competitors and frequently refrained from lucrative but risky types of financial products or transactions that appeared to be making so much money for their competitors.

Senior people need to use their influence to make constructive dialogue work. At successful firms these leaders often were the CEO, or top management more generally. They brought revenue producers together with risk people and ensured that the discussion was constructive and mutually respectful and that it led to positive results. Constructive dialogue was ingrained in company culture.

For firms without effective constructive dialogue in their culture, supervisors will need to require it. The presence or absence of effective constructive dialogue within a company should be a key element for financial supervisors to review in their examinations. In making major decisions (and the supervisor can review these), can the company point to changes it made because of input from the board, from an engaged senior management team, or from risk officers? If not, supervisors likely have found an unsafe and unsound condition in the company's culture that deserves prompt attention from the board, and remediation. This is a test that supervisors can apply long before losses actually materialize from poor decisions the company is likely to make.

Constructive dialogue also should apply to relations between large complex financial institutions and their supervisors. The crisis and its immense costs suggest that companies need to view feedback from their supervisors as a gift. That means listening respectfully and accepting supervisory feedback even before it rises to the level of a formal enforcement action. While regulators may not have the depth of expertise available to large complex institutions, they do have the ability to ask simple questions, such as about the amount of capital a firm has allocated to back potentially risky activities (think of AIG and its hundreds of billions of dollars of credit default swaps the company sold without allocating capital for them) or whether the firm is lowering its standards to meet ambitious goals for growth. This book sounds a theme of the power of simple questions to expose problems before they cause major losses. The search for answers is important, and sometimes more important than the particular answers that emerge. Feedback from supervisors can help to improve decisions sometimes merely by posing the right questions and pursuing the answers.

Constructive dialogue needs to be a two-way street. Supervisors need to be open to input that examiners are engaging in checking-the-boxes compliance drills without understanding the real risks of the company's business, or that there are too many examiners from multiple regulators on site without a focus on the most important issues, or that particular examiners are not open to constructive dialogue. As in successful firms that relied on constructive dialogue to protect themselves in decision making before the crisis, constructive dialogue can improve decision making all around. It can help to improve quality both at supervisory organizations and at the firms they supervise.

A caveat is in order: constructive dialogue between a company and its government supervisor must rest on constructive tension between their perspectives. The supervisor must maintain what some call "principled intimacy" with those it regulates.[18] Without the tension, a supervisor can go the way of the OTS, and essentially be captured by the firms it regulates.

Constructive dialogue is an important alternative to destructive attack. Assaults on the capacity of regulators, such as happened with the Office of Federal Housing Enterprise Oversight (OFHEO), the former supervisor of Fannie Mae and Freddie Mac, and as happens periodically with the Securities and Exchange Commission (SEC) and Commodity Futures Trading Commission (CFTC), are examples of destructive attack. Large complex financial institutions can benefit from recognizing their interest, as chapter 9 argues, in improving rather than diminishing the quality of feedback they can receive from their supervisors.

At this writing, for example, the Consumer Protection Financial Bureau is subject to extreme partisan contention. The Dodd-Frank Act designed the bureau to be funded, similar to the federal bank regulators, from fees and outside of the appropriations process that controls funding of most governmental organizations. Opponents of the bureau seek to withhold approval of any candidate to head the bureau unless the law is changed to subject the bureau to political control through appropriations.

This is the subject matter of destructive attack and can be seen as an effort to weaken the new bureau and subject it to processes and pressures that have prevented many supervisors, and not just OFHEO, from building the organizational strength needed to provide effective input to the parts of the financial system that they supervise or regulate. As the Financial Crisis Inquiry Commission reported, "we conclude widespread failures in financial regulation and supervision proved devastating to the stability of the nation's financial markets. The sentries were not at their posts."[19]

For the new bureau, what would constructive dialogue be? Constructive dialogue would allow the bureau to build capacity with its current funding mechanism, but would push for strong economic analysis to help ensure that any regulations or guidance from the bureau was likely to have benefits that outweighed costs. In other words, constructive political dialogue would insist that the new bureau adopt its own constructive dialogue processes to reduce risk of costly and potentially ineffective interventions into the financial system.

Given the large-scale origination and securitization of low quality mortgages to borrowers without the capacity to repay them, described in chapter 2, one can see how requiring the bureau to adopt high-quality standards could help the financial system to reduce vulnerabilities in the future. Alex Pollock has proposed a one-page mortgage disclosure form that might reflect the kind of high-quality intervention that could benefit the market. Pollock moderated a conference at the American Enterprise Institute and argued that,

> a good mortgage finance system requires that borrowers understand how the loan will work and how much of their income it will demand. The key information should be simply stated and clear. As I say, we can all agree on this. We can also agree that current American mortgage loan documents fail to achieve clarity for borrowers, and that past regulatory efforts to insure detailed disclosure seem to have made things even more confusing.[20]

Pollock pointed to findings of a June 2007 Federal Trade Commission survey of mortgage borrowers

> About a third could not identify the interest rate.
> Half could not correctly identify the loan amount.
> Two-thirds did not recognize that they would be charged a prepayment penalty.
> Nearly nine-tenths could not identify the total amount of up-front charges.[21]

Constructive dialogue between financial firms and the bureau could help to encourage thoughtful interventions such as those Pollock proposes. Destructive attack,of which Washington has seen far too much in recent years, could well lead to the usual high-tension regulatory interventions followed by political assaults on the regulator, with resulting costs to the financial system. Chapter 7 of this book suggests that financial firms often have not represented their own best interests when lobbying in the context of a destructive assault on actions of supervisors and regulators.

Constructive dialogue is not presented as a panacea. Rather, it is a valuable adjunct to other safety and soundness improvements, such as better capital and liquidity standards, transparency, and strengthened supervision. Chapter 9 argues that it is in the best interests of stronger as well as weaker firms to support constructive dialogue. Among other benefits, improving governance and risk management of weaker firms could improve their strength and reliability as counterparties. This would be far superior to having to rely on government once again to bail out the AIGs of the world and, in return, having government impose difficult restrictions on major firms such as are found in Dodd-Frank. Chapter 9 suggests that the Fed chairman or someone of similar stature should work with statesmen in the industry to see whether constructive dialogue might apply to increasing parts of the relationship between major firms and supervisors. This will not be easy, given the current atmosphere in Washington, but would seem well worth the effort.

This book is organized into ten chapters. Chapter 1 is this introduction and overview. Chapter 2 provides background on the financial crisis and how it evolved. There was an inflow of funds into the United States that compressed returns on investments. This made more risky investments attractive, such as subprime mortgages, on which borrowers paid higher interest rates than prime borrowers. This chapter introduces the collateralized debt obligation (CDO), which generated securities that the rating agencies designated AAA even though they were backed by subprime mortgage securities. The chapter describes the financial crisis as a two-step process. When housing prices began to decline and losses appeared in securities labeled AAA and in derivative securities based on them, this threatened major firms that had greatly increased their leverage over the period. Firms became uncertain about their solvency and also about the solvency of counterparties that held these securities. The result was panic and an unwillingness of financial firms to provide credit to one another. Only massive government intervention saved the economy from another Great Depression.

Chapter 3 looks at four firms that successfully withstood the crisis: JPMorgan Chase, Goldman Sachs, Wells Fargo, and TD Bank, including their preparation, their responses to the crisis, and the effects of the crisis on them. These firms dealt in different ways with the period before the crisis and the crisis itself. They possessed (1) discipline and long-term perspective, (2) robust communications and information systems, (3) the capacity to respond effectively to early warning signs, and (4) a process of constructive dialogue between business units and risk managers. Each of the successful firms applied these according to its distinctive culture; unsuccessful firms lacked most or all of these attributes.

Chapter 4 addresses governance and the financial crisis. Successful firms had strong CEOs that invited constructive dialogue from their boards, their management teams, and their risk officers. Good communications were essential for success. The chapter quotes a gentleman at a successful company who said proudly that "the CEO often asks my opinion on major issues," and then added, "but he asks 200 other people their opinions too." Unsuccessful firms often had dominant CEOs, weak boards, and risk managers that they disregarded. Unsuccessful firms were unequipped to deal with early warning signs that the mortgage market was weakening. Their leaders did not seem to have access to feedback that would cause them to ask and reflect on simple questions that could have raised warning flags. Problems were compounded by compensation systems that emphasized short-term rather than long-term financial performance.

Chapter 5 looks at risk management and the financial crisis. Risk management involves balancing risk and returns so that a firm enhances long-term value to itself and its shareholders. Elements of risk management include having people, systems, and processes in place to detect and protect against vulnerabilities, detect potentially risky developments early, communicate across the firm, and respond effectively. The organizational structure of risk management involves a choice between keeping risk management separate from revenue-producing activities, or embedding risk managers in revenue producing units, or some combination. These choices are not nearly as important as having a culture in the firm that respectfully takes risk perspectives into account. Risk officers need support from the CEO and the board. Otherwise, they will not be able to do their jobs in the face of pressures for the company to reap what appear to be easy profits. Judgment is critical. Economist Frank Knight long ago distinguished risk, which can be quantified, from uncertainty, which requires judgment. Successful firms used judgment to add more protection than quantitative modeling would have suggested by itself.

Chapter 6 looks at effects of firms' organization and business models on their behavior and vulnerabilities. Changes in law and advances in technology encouraged increasing consolidation of financial firms. Too many large complex financial institutions, besides being "too big to fail," also became too big to manage. Firms such as Fannie Mae, Freddie Mac, and large mortgage originators such as Countrywide built economies of scale but also vulnerabilities, because of their inability or unwillingness to diversify before the crisis hit. As the former CEOs of Fannie Mae and Freddie Mac both told the Commission, the GSE can be hard if not impossible to manage, especially in a crisis.

Chapter 7 looks at organization and management of financial supervisors. The Gramm-Leach-Bliley Act of 1999 reflected deregulatory sentiment and left serious gaps in the regulatory system. The apparently benevolent period of the early 2000s, when it did not seem easily possible for financial institutions to make serious mistakes, lulled not only financial firms and rating agencies but also policy makers and supervisors into complacency. Supervisors often were unable or unwilling to set limits when firms engaged in regulatory arbitrage, especially to avoid capital requirements. Informal prodding was the approach of choice for supervisors who feared that a supervised firm might move to another supervisor that seemed more congenial.

Chapter 8 looks at the dynamics of the financial crisis and asks: Will it happen again? Economist Hyman Minsky, student of the Great Depression and financial cycles more generally, observed a cyclical pattern. In the first stage, lenders lend based on the ability of the borrower to repay principal and interest. In the second stage they lend based on the ability of the borrower to pay interest and roll over the debt. Then in the third stage, they lend based on future increases in the value of collateral rather than on the borrower's ability to pay. The final stages of the housing bubble fit the Minsky model well; lenders offered money to borrowers based on a belief that home prices would continue to appreciate. If the borrower couldn't repay, that didn't seem to matter—after all, the borrower could always sell the house and repay the loan that way. As Minsky observed, stability in financial markets breeds instability as lenders and borrowers keep pushing the limits.

Minsky saw in the financial system the dynamic of normalization of deviance that sociologist Diane Vaughan identified in the Challenger space shuttle disaster: Under pressure to perform, organizations lower their standards. If that seems to result in success, then they lower their standards yet further. Absent discipline to refrain from increasingly risky behavior, whether imposed by top management or an external supervisor, the cycle of lowering standards and increased risk taking may well end in dramatic failure. Interesting here are the quite different contexts explored by Minsky and Vaughan. Minsky saw the cycle emerge regularly in credit standards when lenders would respond to the lure of profits by taking increasing risks, while Vaughan studied a production-driven government agency, NASA, whose leaders yielded to pressure from the political process to perform without postponing a flight to take account of growing risks. Institutions in both the public and private sectors need to take account of this dynamic.

Chapter 9 summarizes lessons from successful firms and the recommendation that, as discussed above, constructive dialogue be required of all major financial firms as a way to strengthen them and contribute to their safety and soundness. The chapter closes by noting that only effective supervision can help protect financial firms from a race to the bottom, as occurred in 2005–2007 when lenders and borrowers took on increasing amounts of risk without regard to the consequences.

Chapter 10 expands the lessons of this book from financial firms to other types of companies and their nominal regulators. These firms too show the harmful effects of Diane Vaughan's normalization of deviance, the need for constructive dialogue, and the sometimes disastrous problems caused by impeded information flows between front-line employees of an organization and top leaders. The chapter concludes that this book is not only about the financial crisis: It provides lessons about organization, governance, and management of private and public organizations more generally, and the need to strengthen the institutions upon which all of us depend for our safety and economic well- being.

2 }

Dynamics of the Financial Crisis

*After all, you only find out who is swimming naked when the tide
goes out.*
—WARREN BUFFET, 2001

The financial crisis had features that many firms found it difficult to defend
against. A summary of the salient points of the crisis and the buildup of vulnerabilities before the crisis provides context for understanding the quality of
financial firms' governance and risk management. The chapter begins with the
buildup of vulnerabilities before the crisis, moving from the glut of global savings and the unprecedented flow of money into US credit markets and the
mortgage market in particular, to the consequent housing bubble and its
effects on lending standards and borrowers.

Then the credit and housing bubbles peaked and burst. Declining house
prices and asset prices generally led to losses, and especially losses in securities
whose credit attributes had falsely been considered high. These unexpected
losses, especially for highly leveraged financial firms, led to panic in the markets and what can be called a *liquidity crisis*, when firms found themselves
unable to borrow from their usual sources to pay holders of their maturing
obligations.

Building Vulnerabilities

THE GLOBAL SAVINGS GLUT

The most important aspect of years before the crisis was the unprecedented
influx of money from overseas—the "global saving glut," as Federal Reserve
Chairman Ben Bernanke called it.[1] Developing countries increasingly realized the dream of strengthening their economies and lifting large numbers of

their people out of poverty. East Asia, including China, Taiwan, Korea, and Singapore, and then India and Brazil, among others, produced large volumes of goods (and, increasingly, services) that found their way to the United States and Europe. This was in addition to increasing amounts of money that went to oil-producing countries. In the decade from 1996 to 2006, roughly 22–23 percent of the growth in the world economy came from growth in US consumption.[2] Overseas, some countries began to build up large amounts of wealth. Having been buffeted by the 1997 Asian financial crisis, their governments looked to the United States as a source of safety for their investments. One result of the influx of funds to the United States was to reduce yields on treasuries and GSE securities. This was positive for the United States because of the way it reduced borrowing costs. Investors, however, sought higher yields. They searched for safe investments that would have higher yield than treasuries. The trade deficit of the United States grew substantially in the same period. The US savings rate declined and the federal government ran increasingly large deficits in the early 2000s. The United States borrowed increasing amounts of money abroad and had a large and growing current account deficit.

The growth in household debt in the 2000s is seen in figure 2.1, from the Federal Reserve Bank of New York. Household debt almost trebled from $4.6 trillion in 1999 to $12.5 trillion at the peak in 2008. Mortgage debt made up the largest share of total household debt and grew rapidly.

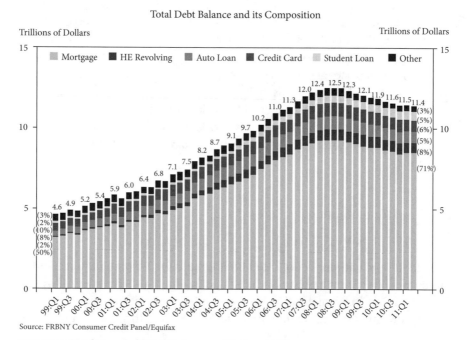

Source: FRBNY Consumer Credit Panel/Equifax

FIGURE 2.1 **Total Household Debt Balance and its Composition**

So much money searching for a combination of safety and yield led to an active market for AAA-rated asset-backed securities, and especially mortgage-backed securities. University of California professor Pierre-Olivier Gourinchas explained the dynamic to the Financial Crisis Inquiry Commission: "As the demand for safe assets outstripped supply (constituted of triple-A corporate bonds, government securities and agency debt backed by the securitized mortgages of low-risk borrowers), this created an irresistible profit opportunity for the US financial system: to engineer 'quasi' safe debt instruments by bundling riskier assets and selling the senior tranches (originate and distribute)."[3]

THE MARKET RESPONSE: CREATING LARGE VOLUMES OF APPARENTLY SAFE FINANCIAL PRODUCTS

Private label asset-backed securities (ABS) and especially mortgage-backed securities (MBS) provided an ideal financial product to satisfy the burgeoning demand for both yield and security. A private label security is one issued by a private financial firm rather than carrying a guarantee from a government agency or government-sponsored enterprise. Figure 2.2, from the Financial Crisis Inquiry Commission, shows the growth of private label mortgage-backed securities in the United States from the late 1990s to 2008. One can see how securitization increased over the period, especially for subprime and alt-A mortgages.

Investors found private-label securities attractive for the reason that Gourinchas pointed out: the AAA-rated part of the security offered both yield and apparent safety. Subprime and alt-A mortgages offered better yields than did prime mortgages; mortgage lenders were able to charge subprime and alt-A borrowers higher interest rates and fees than were charged to prime borrowers with good credit standing. Purchasers of AAA rated mortgage securities

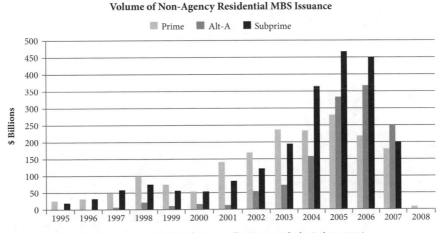

Source: Inside Mortgage Finance (2009). Inside Mortgage Finance reports the data in these categories.

FIGURE 2.2 **Volume of US Private Label Mortgage-Backed Securities Issued 2001–2008**

believed that they were reaping good returns and running only a small chance of taking significant losses. That is true much of the time, but of course sometimes the small probability of a large loss can actually occur. In the case of AAA rated securities based on subprime and other higher risk mortgages, the probability was not as small as investors optimistically believed.[4]

Figure 2.3, published by the Financial Crisis Inquiry Commission, shows how the private-label securitization process worked. A securitizer would assemble mortgages in a pool. These mortgages represented income to the holder from the monthly mortgage payments expected from each homeowner who had taken out one of the mortgages in the pool. The securitizer would divide the pool into tranches, or segments, which represented the right to receive a portion of the cashflows from these mortgage payments. To the extent that the mortgages came from homes in different parts of the country, investors assumed that the risk of default was diversified. The securitizer then would take the pool to a credit rating agency, usually Moody's, Fitch, or Standard & Poor's. The rating agency would apply statistical models and other analyses to determine the credit rating on each of the tranches. Securities in the tranche that would be paid first from the cashflows would receive a higher rating than securities that stood in a lower tranche and would be paid off later.

Residential Mortgage-Backed Securities

Financial institutions packaged subprime, Alt-A and other mortgages into securities. As long as the housing market continued to boom, these securities would perform. But when the economy faltered and the mortgages defaulted, lower-rated tranches were left worthless.

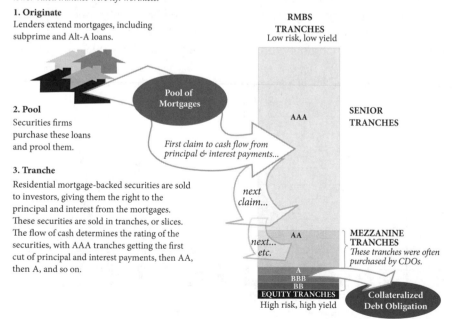

1. Originate
Lenders extend mortgages, including subprime and Alt-A loans.

RMBS
TRANCHES
Low risk, low yield

2. Pool
Securities firms purchase these loans and prool them.

Pool of Mortgages

First claim to cash flow from principal & interest payments...

AAA

SENIOR
TRANCHES

3. Tranche
Residential mortgage-backed securities are sold to investors, giving them the right to the principal and interest from the mortgages. These securities are sold in tranches, or slices. The flow of cash determines the rating of the securities, with AAA tranches getting the first cut of principal and interest payments, then AA, then A, and so on.

next claim...

next... etc.

AA

A
BBB
BB
EQUITY TRANCHES
High risk, high yield

MEZZANINE
TRANCHES
These tranches were often purchased by CDOs.

Collateralized
Debt Obligation

FIGURE 2.3 The Securitization Process

Investors in the junior tranches would bear any losses before investors in the senior tranches. For that reason, the size of the junior tranches was critical to the ratings of the senior tranches.

Despite the high yield on subprime and alt-A mortgages, rating agencies found the bulk of the typical pool to be AAA—that is, of the highest credit quality. Figure 2.4 presents an MBS selected by International Monetary Fund economists to show the process. Noteworthy here is the high percentage of the cashflows that go into AAA-rated tranches even though the underlying mortgages are subprime. The sub-AAA tranches in this example would protect the AAA investors from losses as long as average losses were less than 20 percent; this seemed to be a fair gamble at a time when losses on mortgages were in the low single digits.

Lenders continued to innovate. A major innovation that contributed importantly to the growth of the market was the collateralized debt obligation (CDO). In constructing a CDO, an investment bank would recycle the lower-rated tranches of MBS and other securities to create increasing amounts of AAA-rated CDO securities. This is seen in figure 2.5, again from the IMF. CDOs appeared to carry similar diversification and tranching benefits as did the MBS securities. Also as in the MBS structure, investors in junior tranches of CDOs would bear the losses before investors in senior tranches, affording some measure of protection to senior tranche investors.

There also was the opportunity to recycle the tranches again, into so-called CDOs-squared, thereby adding to the fraction of the original pool that yielded AAA rated securities. The net result of this process was to turn mortgages of lower credit quality into investments that were rated AAA. Indeed, Wall Street firms often marketed the top AAA tranches as "super senior," thereby adding to their cachet with investors. Once a variety of assets went into a CDO, including a remarkable number of securities from other CDOs, companies found it difficult if not impossible to assess what was really backing a particular

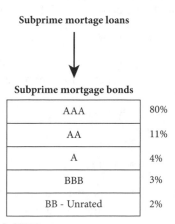

FIGURE 2.4 Rating a Private Label MBS

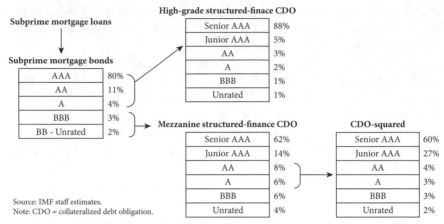

FIGURE 2.5 The Collateralized Debt Obligation (CDO)

security. This led less savvy investors, including major firms, to rely on the AAA rating rather than on a firm's own assessment of the risk of a particular CDO or of the contribution of CDOs to the risk of the firm's overall portfolio. Federal Reserve economist William Lang observes that management at major financial firms might not realize that multisector CDOs, which formerly had been heavily concentrated in corporate securities, had become as heavily concentrated in mortgages as they were.

CDOs were attractive to investors because they offered high yields compared to other obligations:

> Banks create CDOs by bundling together assets ranging from mortgages to loans to high-yield bonds, with income from those assets used to repay investors. The securities are divided into pieces, or tranches, that can offer yields as high as 14%, said Nestor Dominguez, 48, co-head of Citigroup's North American CDO group in New York. Average investment-grade bonds yield 5.1% and junk bonds yield 7.5%, according to Merrill.[5]

They were also profitable for those who arranged CDO transactions:

> CDO fees usually equal about 1.5% to 1.75% of the size of a deal, bankers who arrange such sales say. That's more than triple the average 0.4% that banks charge to sell investment-grade bonds and about the same as fees on junk bonds, traditionally the most lucrative, Bloomberg data show.[6]

INSATIABLE DEMAND FOR MORTGAGES

The other result of this process was to create a virtually insatiable market demand for subprime and alt-A mortgages. Fannie Mae and Freddie Mac purchased most prime mortgages, but they traditionally had declined to purchase

Subprime Mortgage Originations

In 2006, $600 billion of subprime loans were originated, most of which were securitized. That year, subprime lending accounted for 23.5% of all mortgage originations.

IN BILLIONS OF DOLLARS

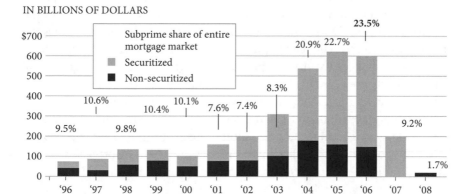

NOTE: Percent securitized is defined as subprime securities issued divided by originations in a given year.
In 2007, securities issued exceeded originations.
SOURCE: Inside Mortgage Finance

FIGURE 2.6 **Securitization of Subprime Mortgages**

most mortgages with lower credit quality. This left the subprime and alt-A mortgage markets largely as the province of non-GSE financial firms.

Figure 2.6, from the Financial Crisis Inquiry Commission, documents the large fraction of subprime mortgages that went into securities.

Market innovations continued. Investor demand for safe assets fostered the emergence of a new type of financial guarantee, called the credit default swap (CDS). The issuer of a CDS would sell protection to an investor against taking a loss on a particular security or group of securities. For reasons that became apparent only after the collapse of AIG, a major issuer of CDSs, the cost of CDS protection to investors was very low, considering the risk. AIG and other CDS issuers believed that they were reaping good returns and running only a small chance of taking significant losses. Partly because of the high credit ratings, they believed that they could take these exposures with little or no capital backing the risk of loss.

These innovations had multiple consequences. One was the growth of the so-called shadow banking sector. Increasing volumes of mortgages were originated and funded not through traditional depository institutions such as banks and thrifts, but rather through nondepository lenders and securitization. While commercial banks and thrifts were subject to regular supervision of safety and soundness, mortgage companies, mortgage banks, investment banks, and other parts of the parallel banking system went largely unregulated as to financial soundness. Chapter 6 discusses the implications of this shift in the financial markets.

THE HOUSING BUBBLE

Another development was a substantial increase in housing prices over many years, as can be seen in figure 2.7, from the Federal Housing Finance Agency. The Case-Shiller index of the top 20 cities doubled from a benchmark 100 in January 2000 to 204.9 percent in the summer 2006. The lower line shows the bubble in mortgages eligible for purchase by Fannie Mae and Freddie Mac; loan size limits kept them from purchasing higher-balance mortgages that were especially prevalent in states where the bubble was greatest.

One reason for the bubble was the increased availability of huge volumes of low-cost mortgage money. Other reasons included new technologies to support mortgage origination and a US cultural predisposition toward homeownership. A 2002 Morgan Stanley analyst report titled "U.S. Mortgage Finance: The American Dream Industry, 2002–2020," explained that:

> Advances in information technology . . . will expand the market through lower processing costs and more flexible underwriting. As a result, mortgage lenders should be able to unlock homeownership opportunities for more immigrants, minorities, and low-income borrowers than they could in the past. The growth of these segments . . . will be an important contributor to household formations and the housing and mortgage markets.[7]

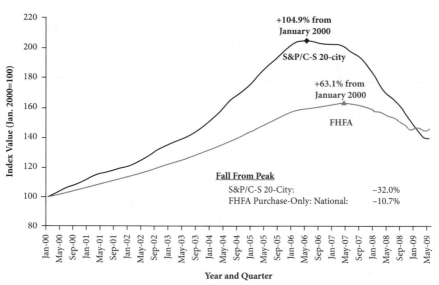

FHFA and S&P/Case-Shiller House Price Indexes
Seasonally Adjusted
January 2000 - May 2009

Note: For purposes of comparison, the FHFA purchase only index has been re-based to January 2000 = 100 (the standard series is set so that January 1991 =100)

FIGURE 2.7 The Housing Bubble

Steady home price appreciation, the availability of large volumes of mortgage money, and declining credit standards all fed on one another. Increasing home prices encouraged lenders to make loans to borrowers who were not creditworthy according to traditional rules: After all, if the borrower defaulted, the lender could simply sell the home and recoup its investment from the increased home price. And for a while it was true: Such lending was safe so long as home prices continued to appreciate.

The volume of subprime and alt-A mortgages in the system grew steadily. In general, the term *subprime* refers to mortgage loans made to borrowers with relatively poor credit histories. These loans are therefore riskier than prime loans, which are made to borrowers with stronger credit. As a result, the marketing, underwriting, and servicing of subprime loans is different than that of prime loans. However, the mortgage industry lacks a consistent definition of the subprime mortgage market. Subprime loans are typically identified in one of three ways: (1) as loans with interest rates above a given threshold; (2) as loans from lenders that have been classified as specializing in subprime loans; or (3) as mortgages that back mortgage-backed securities (MBS) that are marketed as subprime.

It was widely believed that subprime lending could be profitable for lenders if they managed the risks. In 1999 the FDIC issued guidance to that effect:

> Due to their higher risk, subprime loans command higher interest rates and loan fees than those offered to standard risk borrowers. These loans can be profitable, provided the price charged by the lender is sufficient to cover higher loan loss rates and overhead costs related to underwriting, servicing, and collecting the loans. Moreover, the ability to securitize and sell subprime portfolios at a profit while retaining the servicing rights has made subprime lending attractive to a larger number of institutions, further increasing the number of subprime lenders and loans. . . . Institutions should recognize the additional risks inherent in subprime lending and determine if these risks are acceptable and controllable given the institution's staff, financial condition, size, and level of capital support.[8]

One argument for subprime lending was that subprime loans would help to place homeownership within reach of consumers who traditionally might not have had access to mortgage credit. For example, the chairman of the Mortgage Bankers Association spoke against state and local predatory lending laws in 2003:

> The so-called subprime market serves a group of borrowers who would otherwise have little or no access to credit. This is a good and important service. We can make loans to these consumers through innovative financing options that were not available as recently as 20 years ago. This is

an important point, because in the end these laws will hurt those consumers who most need the hand up that access to innovative credit can give.[9]

The term *alt-A* refers to loans generally made to borrowers with strong credit scores but which have other characteristics that make the loans riskier than prime loans. For example, the loan may have no or limited documentation of the borrower's income, a high loan-to-value ratio (LTV), or may be for an investor-owned property. Typically, loans are identified as being alt-A by virtue of backing MBS that are marketed as alt-A.

Many alt-A mortgages allowed the originator to provide less than complete documentation. From the perspective of the financial crisis this is significant, because low-documentation loans—and especially those where the borrower states key information about income, indebtedness, or assets without independent verification by the lender—tend to default at higher rates than other mortgage loans.[10] In retrospect, that should not be a surprise. Bankers have always known that.

Standard or prime mortgages contain numerous provisions that discourage default. They typically require a 20 percent down payment or coverage through mortgage insurance, and amortize the costs of the loan over the course of fifteen or thirty years. The former provision gives the borrower a financial stake in the home and reduces chances that he or she will default on the mortgage, thus giving an incentive to make payments, while the latter keeps payments consistent and affordable; if the borrower can budget for the first payment, later payments are likely to be affordable too.

Lower and moderate-income borrowers typically cannot borrow according to this model. They have little personal wealth, making down payments infeasible. Their incomes are not always documented in traditional ways, such as through the W-2 employment income tax form, and many cannot afford interest payments if the lender accurately adjusts the rate to the risk of the loan.[11]

Subprime mortgages developed to overcome these obstacles. Although they may include provisions such as waivers of documentation or negative amortization schedules (so that the borrower can pay less than a market rate each month until the accrued principal reaches a limit and the borrower must make much higher monthly payments), "the defining characteristic of a subprime mortgage is that it is designed to essentially force a refinancing after two or three years."[12] This operates through the hybrid interest rate structure, under which borrowers pay a lower, fixed rate for two or three years before that rate resets at a much higher variable rate.

A second feature is a prepayment penalty, which appeared much more frequently in subprime mortgages than prime mortgages. This meant that if a borrower chose to pay off the entire mortgage or, more likely, wanted to refinance with a competing firm, he or she would need to pay a substantial fee to the owner of the mortgage.

In practical terms, these provisions are supposed to operate as follows: A risky borrower signs a mortgage, which gives him or her conditional title to the home, subject to payment of the entire mortgage. The mortgage owner permits the borrower to pay interest at a low rate, called a teaser rate in the industry, but this rate generally will increase in two to three years.

If the price of the house rises, the borrower gains equity in the home, which makes him or her a better risk because the equity is a form of collateral. However, if the mortgage interest rate resets and the borrower cannot afford the higher payments, he or she must get a new mortgage, probably again with a teaser rate, to be able to keep the home. Because of the prepayment penalty, the borrower must negotiate with the owner of the mortgage. The mortgage owner collects new fees for the refinancing, which further compensate for the risk of offering a lower initial rate to a less creditworthy borrower.

The most glaring weakness in this arrangement, of course, is the assumption that house prices will always go up. If the house depreciates instead, the borrower does not have enough equity to refinance the mortgage. The borrower also has little incentive to maintain payments on the mortgage, as the mortgage is greater than the home is worth. Rather than sink more money into a bad investment, some borrowers simply walk away. If the law does not allow recourse, the only penalty was the loss of a good credit rating, which by definition a subprime borrower did not have.[13]

The implications of these arrangements depend upon the rate of home price appreciation. Because of the cost of refinancing, house prices must appreciate substantially before the homeowner receives any return on the investment. If the home lacks equity, one might characterize the arrangement as a rental with a mortgage attached.[14]

If house prices appreciate at rates that produce returns well in excess of the prepayment penalties, a borrower can sell a home for a profit. Alternatively, through refinancing, the borrower can extract equity from the home. In either case, the homeowner with a subprime mortgage will not build equity over the long run simply by making regular payments in the manner that is possible with the traditional thirty-year fixed-rate mortgage.

As house prices rose, homes became less affordable to new buyers than before. To deal with affordability, lenders increased the volume of loans that helped to reduce monthly payments, especially in the early year or two of a mortgage. The idea was that borrowers could take out mortgages with teaser rates that were low at first and then jumped to market rates. Figure 2.8 from the FCIC shows the increasing volume of mortgages originated that were interest-only mortgages, option ARMs, or balloon mortgages. Interest-only mortgages grew from only 2 percent of mortgage originations in 2004 to 20 percent by 2007. Option ARMs and balloon mortgages also increased in this period. The most common subprime loan became a 2/28 adjustable rate mortgage—one with a fixed interest rate for two years that would rise to market

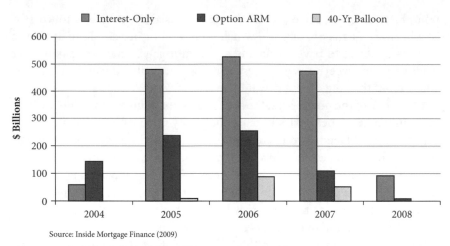

Source: Inside Mortgage Finance (2009)

FIGURE 2.8 **At the Peak: "Affordability" Mortgages**

levels for the last twenty-eight years of the loan; among subprime mortgages, these made up fully 44 percent of subprime originations in 2005.[15]

A 2/28 loan has an initial low interest rate for two years, followed by a reset that results in potentially much higher interest rates for the remainder of the loan. The theory of the loan is that the homeowner can refinance as home prices increase. The problem with the theory becomes apparent if home prices begin to decline; then the borrower either cannot refinance, because the value of the home might drop and the loan-to-value ratio might increase correspondingly, or because refinancing would not be advantageous once interest rates rose.

The shift was especially pronounced for subprime and alt-A loans. While 66 percent of subprime loans in 2003 were traditional fixed-rate loans, that share dropped to 31 percent in 2005 and 26 percent in 2006. The shift away from fixed-rate loans was even more pronounced for alt-A loans.[16]

As home prices rose, loans with teaser rates became increasingly attractive as a way to qualify borrowers for larger mortgages. Lenders frequently deemed borrowers qualified to obtain a mortgage based on the initial rate, even though the borrower might not be expected to make payments the fully indexed rate. The Harvard Joint Center reports that by 2006 a borrower could receive a one-year ARM at a discount of 2.3 percentage points. That allowed a median-income buyer who might be able to obtain a $186,600 mortgage at the fully indexed rate to qualify for a $236,600 loan and a larger home based on the initial teaser rate. However, as the center reports, "when rates on adjustable loans began to reset, the increases in payments were often significant. For example, the owner of a median-priced home purchased in 2003 with 10 percent down and a 3-year adjustable loan would see his or her monthly payments jump from $797 to $1,212 in 2006."[17]

A larger house is good only if the borrower can pay for it. The proliferation of adjustable-rate mortgages or mortgages with teaser rates meant that many lenders, especially if they were originating loans to securitize them, failed to underwrite borrowers as to their capacity to make mortgage payments once the loan reset to a higher rate. The Massachusetts Supreme Judicial Court found that one lender, Fremont Investment & Loan, would underwrite borrowers for up to a 50 percent debt-to-income ratio, but would underwrite the borrower's capacity to pay only at the introductory rate, and not at the rate to which the mortgage would eventually reset.[18] In 2008 litigation, the Attorney General of the State of California brought a case against Countrywide alleging, among other matters, that "Countrywide underwrote 2/28 and 3/27 ARMs based on the payment required while the initial rate was in effect, without regard to whether the borrower could afford the loan thereafter."[19]

This issue was not hidden from investors in the mortgage market. Issuers of mortgage securities put statements in their SEC disclosures about underwriting borrowers at the initial rate. A prospectus for Residential Funding Corporation discloses that:

> For some ARM loans, the mortgage rate at origination may be below the rate that would result if the index and margin relating thereto were applied at origination. Under the applicable underwriting standards, the mortgagor [i.e., the borrower] under each mortgage loan or contract usually will be qualified on the basis of the mortgage rate in effect at origination.[20]

If lenders qualified borrowers at the low initial interest rate, defaults were assured to increase if these borrowers couldn't somehow refinance before higher rates kicked in. These mortgages came in many varieties, and their complexity increasingly meant that borrowers, and especially subprime borrowers who were first-time homebuyers, didn't understand the terms of the mortgages that they took out.[21]

Leverage was a predominant theme of the financial crisis. Here, note how the expansion of mortgage credit increased the potential leverage of the average household. So long as home prices increased, effects of added mortgage debt were minimized. Michael LaCour-Little, Eric Rosenblatt, and Vincent Yao studied the way that borrowers took out equity from their homes from 2000 to 2006. The authors found that "overall, 43 percent of households in our sample chose to take out equity when they refinanced; however, housing appreciation was sufficiently great to actually decrease loan-to-value ratios, on average, over this time period."[22] In other words, so long as home prices kept going up, homeowners could increase their mortgage debt without generally increasing their leverage. On the other hand, if home prices declined, the effects of high debt burdens would make themselves felt.

Appreciating home prices attracted people to buy homes as investment properties. From the perspective of the financial crisis, borrowers who take out mortgages to buy investor-owned properties are more likely to default when their equity turns negative, compared to borrowers with mortgages on their principal residence. Some of these borrower investors took advantage of lenders that increasingly originated loans with low or no documentation (so-called lo-doc and no-doc loans), and other forms of lending that invited fraud and abuse. An official at the Mortgage Bankers Association speaks of the Tucson attorney who took out home mortgages for thirty consecutive days, each time claiming that the mortgage was for his primary residence. Appreciating home prices masked this kind of fraud; the saying in the industry is that "a fraud event occurs only when you have a credit event." If home prices always go up, even the Tucson attorney would be able to pay each mortgage or else cover a default by selling the home and allowing the lender to recoup any potential loss.

The homebuilding industry responded to the bubble by increasing the volume of new homes constructed each year. Figure 2.9, from the U.S. Census Bureau, shows how the volume of new homes jumped from about 1.3 million single family homes annually in 2000 to a peak of some 1.7 million units in 2006. Developments sprang up, especially in California's Central Valley, Nevada, Arizona, and Florida.

For borrowers and their political leaders, the combination of low interest rates, availability of ample mortgage money, and home price appreciation seemed to be the realization of the American Dream. President George W. Bush claimed in 2003 that:

> This administration will constantly strive to promote an ownership society in America. We want more people owning their own home. It is

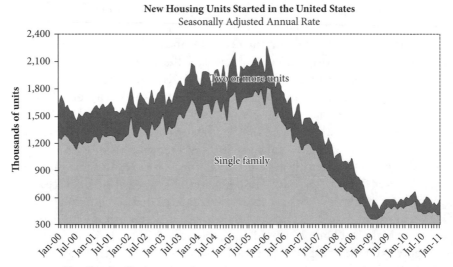

FIGURE 2.9 **New Housing Starts**

in our national interest that more people own their own home. After all, if you own your own home, you have a vital stake in the future of our country.

And this is a good time for the American homeowner. Today we received a report that showed that new home construction last month reached its highest level in nearly 20 years. The reason that is so is because there is renewed confidence in our economy. Low interest rates help. They have made owning a home more affordable for those who refinance and for those who buy a home for the first time. Rising home values have added more than $2½ trillion to the assets of the American families since the start of 2001.

The rate of homeownership in America now stands at a record high of 68.4%. Yet there is room for improvement. The rate of homeownership amongst minorities is below 50%. And that's not right, and this country needs to do something about it. We need to close the minority homeownership gap in America so more citizens get the satisfaction and mobility that comes from owning your own home, from owning a piece of the future of America.[23]

This was not a new sentiment. President William Clinton had made similar remarks when rolling out his Administration's homeownership strategy in 1995.

The national homeownership rate peaked in 2004, as can be seen in figure 2.10, from the Financial Crisis Inquiry Commission. Policy makers kept pushing for increased homeownership. At the end of that year HUD Secretary Alfonso Jackson urged that, "If you don't already own a home, I'd like to suggest that becoming a homeowner in 2005 be among your New Year's resolutions."[24]

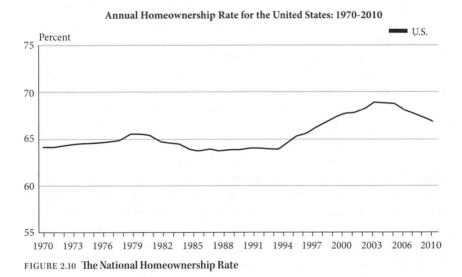

FIGURE 2.10 The National Homeownership Rate

The decline in the homeownership rate from 2004–2008 occurred even as the mortgage market continued to expand, as was seen in figure 2.1. Much of the growth in the mortgage market in 2004–2008 came from existing homeowners taking increasing amounts of equity out of their homes through refinancing.

But even the growing mortgage market was not enough to satisfy investor demand. The expanding CDS market led to yet another innovation, the so-called synthetic CDO. The logic was straightforward: A CDS represented a guarantee that specific MBS or CDO securities would pay investors on time. Cash CDOs were vehicles that invested in actual MBSs, CDOs, and other securities. By contrast, synthetic CDOs contained no actual securities: Rather, firms sold insurance on these securities in the form of CDS so that they would pay off with the same cashflows (from mortgage payments vs. defaults) as the original securities. So Wall Street really didn't need new mortgages and MBSs to create a CDO—a financial company could create a reference pool of specific MBSs and CDOs and use CDS to insure those securities.

The investor in the synthetic CDO was like the issuer of a CDS; it received premium payments from the synthetic CDO that were roughly equivalent to cash payments on the referenced MBS or CDO securities, but bore the risk of loss if the referenced securities failed to make timely payments. The FCIC investigation showed that credit default swaps helped facilitate the CDO and MBS markets by allowing issuers to transfer the risk of mortgage losses in ways that were not well understood by investors, rating agencies, or indeed, in many cases, the issuing banks themselves.[25] The apparently benevolent times fostered other developments as well. One was a range of new solutions to the perennial problem of financial firms trying to lend long and borrow short. Investors tend to prefer shorter maturities so that they have access to their funds. On the other hand, borrowers, who may be trying to finance a home or commercial project, often seek longer term funding. This can be profitable for banks, as short-term rates at which they raise deposits are generally lower than the long-term rates at which they lend. But it was the problem of maturity mismatch, as it is called, that brought down the savings and loan industry in the 1980s. The Fed raised short-term interest rates dramatically in October 1979, making the cost of funds for savings and loans, largely in the form of deposit accounts, substantially more expensive than interest they earned on the mortgages they owned. Thrifts (a remarkable misnomer by that point) had funded long-term home mortgages with overnight deposits. Most thrifts lost their net worth within two years after their maturity mismatches became untenable.

The apparently positive economic and financial climate of the early 2000s again encouraged extreme maturity mismatches. Banks and other lenders created structured investment vehicles (SIVs) that held mortgages and other long-term instruments. Technically, SIVs were independent entities off the balance sheets of the financial firms that sponsored them. SIVs held CDOs and other mortgage securities, commercial mortgages, and other assets. They funded themselves in part by issuing commercial paper—that is, funding with a maturity of 270 days or less. Because SIVs tended to be highly leveraged, they lacked a significant cushion of capital to help buffer against losses if investors declined to roll over their investments. Money market mutual funds frequently purchased the commercial paper, which they funded with money that investors could withdraw at will. Once again the financial system had generated a significant volume of long-term assets, often based on residential mortgages, funded with overnight money.

Another major form of maturity mismatch was the repurchase or "repo" transaction. A financial firm would borrow money by pledging high-quality assets that it would agree to repurchase in a day or a few days, or sometimes longer, at a higher price that reflected the interest paid on the borrowing. Traditionally, repos used high-quality collateral such as US Treasury securities or GSE securities. Over time, as the market relaxed its standards to reflect confidence that the good times had brought, AAA rated mortgage securities also became eligible as collateral for repo transactions. The problem was that once again, overnight borrowing became a way to fund thirty-year mortgage loans. If the market were to lose confidence in the credit quality of AAA securities, much of the repo market could dry up. And the repo market was huge, amounting to perhaps $5–10 trillion in 2008.[26] Like the market for CDSs, the repo market also introduced major linkages among financial firms. Sometimes firms would take repo collateral and lend it in a parallel transaction to another firm. If one part of the daisy chain ever broke, the market was in danger of collapsing.[27]

2005 TO 2007: A PERIOD OF EXCESS RISK AND SPECULATION

Some large financial firms went into overdrive in the period from 2005 to 2007. In the primary mortgage market, WaMu decided to expand its exposure to lower quality mortgages and other loans. A 2005 company strategic plan specified that "in order to generate more sustainable, consistent, higher margins within Washington Mutual, the 2005 Strategic Plan calls for a shift in our mix of business, increasing our Credit Risk tolerance while continuing to mitigate our Market and Operational Risk positions."[28]

The plan called for increasing the firm's exposure to higher risk lending from $32.0 billion in November 2004 to $44.5 billion in 2005, including an increase in subprime loans from $17.0 billion to $28.3 billion.[29]

Lehman Brothers too made a deliberate decision to take on more risk. Anton R. Valukas, the examiner in Lehman's bankruptcy, issued a 2,200-page report on March 11, 2010, that documents the change in business strategy:

> In 2006, Lehman made the deliberate decision to embark upon an aggressive growth strategy, to take on significantly greater risk, and to

substantially increase leverage on its capital. In 2007, as the sub-prime residential mortgage business progressed from problem to crisis, Lehman was slow to recognize the developing storm and its spillover effect upon commercial real estate and other business lines. Rather than pull back, Lehman made the conscious decision to "double down," hoping to profit from a counter-cyclical strategy.[30]

Lehman greatly increased its risk tolerance (called *risk appetite* in the literature) and relaxed transaction limits and other risk-related restrictions. The chief risk officer who had opposed these changes was moved to a less sensitive position in the company. WaMu and Lehman, and other firms such as Fannie Mae and Freddie Mac, ultimately took significant losses from their exposure to the increased risks just as the market was peaking. Chapter 3 discusses this further.

Firms that constructed and sold CDOs began to sell lower-rated pieces but retained the AAA super senior pieces on their own balance sheets. After all, they may have reasoned, the AAA rating was higher than the rating of their company's own obligations. The CDO group at UBS, the large Swiss financial, firm, increased its holdings of AAA-rated CDOs from $5 billion in February 2006 to $50 billion by September 2007. By late summer 2007, Citigroup had accumulated over $55 billion of AAA-rated CDOs.[31] This occurred even though house prices had peaked in mid-2006 and large subprime lenders had begun to fail in late 2006. As it turned out, the company-based ratings, while not ideal, at least were more accurate than the ratings of structured products such as CDOs.

The market generally was heating up. Consider the market for leveraged loans. These are loans sometimes used to fund leveraged buyouts, made to companies that are already significantly indebted. Leveraged loans tend to involve greater risk than loans to less indebted companies and thus offer higher returns to investors. Valukas reports on Lehman and the way that the market for leveraged loans heated up and resulted in a diminution of contract terms that became increasingly unfavorable to investors:

> Because there was so much competition to finance these loans, sponsors were able to negotiate terms that significantly increased the risk to the banks. For example, according to some estimates, covenant light loans— loans that did not include previously standard covenants requiring the borrower to maintain certain levels of collateral, cash flow, and payment terms—increased from less than 1% of all leveraged loans in 2004 to over 18% by 2007 industry-wide. Lenders such as Lehman also abandoned certain contractual protections (e.g., material adverse change provisions ("MACs"), up-front syndication, and joint liability) that were previously standard in the leveraged loan industry.[32]

The feverish pitch of the late bubble years of 2005–2007 reminds Alex Pollock of the warning in Walter Bagehot's nineteenth century book, *Lombard Street*:

> All people are most credulous when they are most happy; and when much money has just been made, when some people are really making it, when most people think they are making it, there is a happy opportunity for ingenious mendacity. Almost everything will be believed for a little while.[33]

Some firms resisted the call to take more risk. Noteworthy among these was JPMorgan Chase. The Federal Reserve Bank of New York issued an annual report of inspection to JPMorgan Chase for the calendar year 2007:

> As our strong assessment of Board and Senior Management Oversight indicates, management's actions were largely responsible for navigating the firm through the volatile markets over the past year. Management's decision-making during 2007 is reflective of its ability to understand the risks inherent in its businesses, take timely actions to reduce exposures where necessary, and is attributable to the firm's recent favorable performance relative to peer. In particular, the effectiveness of the firm's risk committee structure is worth noting.[34]

In the years before the crisis broke, with notable exceptions, vulnerability of individual firms and the financial system increased significantly. This occurred even though firms had taken actions that appeared to reduce or diversify or shed risk. Thus, securitization sought to diversify credit risk by pooling loans and permitting investors to purchase pieces of large diversified loan pools instead of whole loans that embody a concentration of risk in a single house or other asset, and in a single borrower. Banks and other financial institutions could sell pools of loans into a trust and thereby take them off their balance sheets. These trusts were seen as efficient because they could fund loans with relatively little capital and thereby increase the returns to investors. What the designers failed to see was the way that the lack of capital left the securities and their owners vulnerable to loss when the bubble collapsed; the risk was so opaque that each actor in the chain from origination to investment, unless they undertook more careful investigation, had reason to think that someone else might be bearing it. Other devices for spreading risk away from individual firms, such as derivative securities used to hedge risk or quasi-insurance products such as credit default swaps, had the same effect: to increase linkages across the financial system so that when one highly leveraged institution got into trouble, it threatened to bring down its counterparties and even their counterparties.

System-wide vulnerabilities included (1) access to unprecedented amounts of investable funds, (2) a major bubble in asset prices, especially in the housing market, (3) new complex securities (e.g., CDOs) and derivatives (e.g., CDSs) involving risk that many failed to assess and price properly, (4) incentives for individuals and firms that emphasized the short term over the long term, and (5) increasing organizational complexity and concentration of lending in fewer and larger firms that often exceeded a trillion dollars in scope. Then the crisis came. Warren Buffet's aphorism is relevant here: "After all, you only find out who is swimming naked when the tide goes out."[35]

The Crisis Hits in Waves

Because it hit in waves, financial firms and policy makers found it difficult to cope with the crisis. The first wave was an increasing volume of mortgage defaults, especially on subprime and alt-A mortgages. Investors put defaulted mortgages back to the originating lenders, causing large subprime lenders, Ameriquest and New Century, to fail. The remaining lenders suddenly realized that they had exposure to the mortgage market in ways and to a degree that they hadn't understood. Losses on subprime mortgages led to near-collapse of two Bear Stearns hedge funds in 2007. Sudden failure of mortgage securities— and especially CDOs—that had been rated AAA gave rise to the term "toxic asset." For highly leveraged firms, exposure to even a small volume of toxic assets could prove fatal.

Financial firms didn't know their own exposure to toxic assets, much less the exposure of firms with which they did business. This caused the second and most devastating wave of the crisis: a general market panic that threatened to shut down the financial system. The government struggled to contain the crisis as its repercussions expanded from the financial sector to become a general economic recession. In the third wave people are becoming delinquent and defaulting on their mortgages and other credit obligations as they lose their jobs and incomes fall, leading to yet further house price declines in many areas.

THE FIRST WAVE: LOSSES AFTER THE HOUSING BUBBLE BURSTS

The mortgage industry uses early payment defaults as a measure of quality in mortgage underwriting. Most investor agreements provide that a firm that purchases mortgages from an originator may put back to the originator mortgages that default within the first year. This is one of the mechanisms that protect the purchaser from the consequences of improper underwriting. Starting in 2006, early payment defaults spiked. Figure 2.11, from the FCIC, shows this trend. It measures early payment defaults as those mortgages that default within a year of origination.

Two factors were in play. First, housing prices peaked in many parts of the country. Suddenly borrowers who got into trouble couldn't sell their homes to protect themselves and the lender from losses. Second, housing affordability reached its limits. People who bought homes at the peak of the market found that they had bought too much house, with unsustainable debt burdens. In growing numbers, borrowers, and especially people who had bought homes as investments, gave up trying to make their payments.

Figure 2.12, from the Federal Housing Finance Agency, shows the spike in seriously delinquent subprime mortgages that started around 2006. Serious

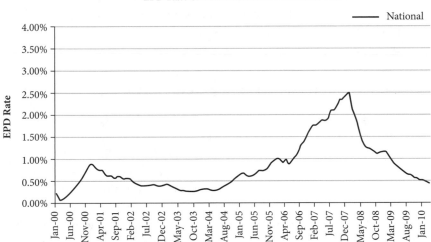

Source: CoreLogic, July 2010

FIGURE 2.11 Early Payment Defaults Spike

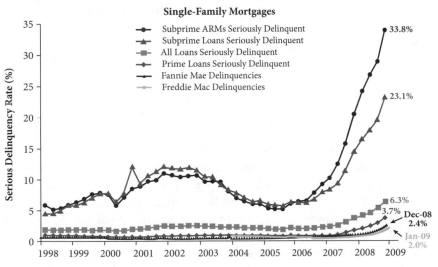

FIGURE 2.12 Serious Delinquencies

delinquencies also rose for prime mortgages, but starting in 2007 and at a much lower level.

Note that in 2007 and 2008, seriously delinquent mortgages (the fourth line from the bottom of the figure) amounted to only about 2–3 percent of mortgages outstanding; 97 percent of American homeowners were paying their mortgages. Federal Reserve Chairman Ben Bernanke opined in May 2007 that "as the problems in the subprime mortgage market have become manifest, we have seen some signs of self-correction in the market. . . . Importantly, we see no serious broader spillover to banks or thrift institutions from the problems in the subprime market; the troubled lenders, for the most part, have not been institutions with federally insured deposits."[36]

Then the second wave hit.

THE SECOND WAVE: THE FINANCIAL MARKETS PANIC

As mortgage losses mounted, especially in AAA-rated mortgage securities and CDOs, financial institutions became uncertain about the volume of losses they were about to suffer. More importantly, lenders suddenly realized that companies with whom they did business, their counterparties, were going to take losses too. The lack of transparency about likely losses meant that institutions could not be sure whether their counterparties might not become insolvent and unable to repay their loans. Lenders stopped lending to one another and to others. The multi-trillion dollar repo market suffered the equivalent of a bank run.[37] The credit markets froze and the housing crisis became a financial crisis.

With firms unwilling to lend to one another, borrowers suddenly were deprived of funding. Worse, rumors flew about investment banks and other financial companies that were suspected of being insolvent. To the extent they could, investors withdrew their funds from those companies and thereby precipitated failures that otherwise might not have occurred. Liquidity—the ability to borrow money at sustainable rates—that once had been plentiful was now virtually impossible to obtain, except through government intervention.

The liquidity crisis struck firms with speed and ferocity. Bear Stearns, which had weathered the near collapse of two hedge funds in mid-2007, again came under stress in early 2008. Figure 2.13, from the FCIC, shows the speed with which Bear lost liquidity as its counterparties panicked and pulled out their funds.

After Bear Stearns, the markets calmed somewhat. Then IndyMac, a large mortgage lender, failed in July 2008 and went into receivership. September 2008 saw a progression of new failures, starting with Fannie Mae and Freddie Mac, which went into government hands on September 7, 2008. Lehman went bankrupt on September 15. The Lehman episode suggested that investment banks would be limited in their ability to access the government's safety net. Bank of America also acquired Merrill on September 15. On September 16, the government provided massive support to AIG to prevent bankruptcy.

Bear Stearns Liquidity

In the four days before Bear Stearns collapsed, the company's
liquidity dropped by $16 billion.

IN BILLIONS OF DOLLARS, DAILY

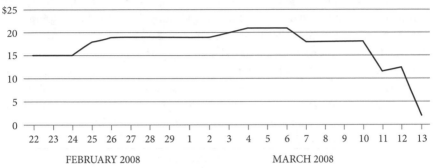

FEBRUARY 2008   MARCH 2008

SOURCE: Securities and Exchange Commission

FIGURE 2.13 The Liquidity Crisis: Bear Stearns Fails

On September 21, 2008, Morgan Stanley and Goldman Sachs, two investment banking firms that had survived the initial liquidity crisis, took their hint from Lehman's failure and became bank holding companies. Market confidence in the two companies increased. Morgan Stanley's chairman John Mack told Commission staff that the conversion sent a signal that the two firms would survive: "I think the biggest benefit is it would show you that you're important to the system and the Fed would not make you a holding company if they thought in a very short period of time you'd be out of business."[38] Then on September 25, the government placed WaMu, the large mortgage lender, into receivership. In October 2008 Wells Fargo acquired Wachovia, which had suffered unsustainable losses after purchasing Golden West, a major lender of nontraditional mortgages.

The government responded with an impressive array of policy tools, often deployed in innovative ways. As will be discussed in chapter 7, gaps in organizational responsibility had allowed risk to accumulate in parts of the financial system that were not subject to the kind of prudential supervision that might have mitigated threats to the larger financial system and economy. Similarly, but to a lesser extent, gaps in organizational authority and available tools also shaped the government's pattern of response.

Major federal organizations involved in responding to the financial crisis included the US Treasury Department and the Federal Reserve System, which includes the Board of Governors, the Federal Open Market Committee (FOMC), and district banks such as the Federal Reserve Bank of New York (FRBNY). Other significant federal actors included the Federal Deposit Insurance Corporation (FDIC), the Securities and Exchange Commission (SEC), the Federal Housing Finance Agency (FHFA), the Federal Housing

Administration (FHA), and the United States Department of Education (ED). Table 2.1 provides an abbreviated timeline of some of the major events relating to responses by the Treasury, Federal Reserve, and FDIC.[39]

By the beginning of the Obama Administration in early 2009, the US government had committed over $3 trillion in spending, loan purchases, loans, and loan guarantees through the Treasury, Federal Reserve System, and Federal Deposit Insurance Corporation (FDIC) to support financial institutions and automobile companies among other purposes, and enacted a massive economic stimulus package. The crisis hit people from multiple directions; millions of households lost money in their retirement and investment funds and millions more faced foreclosure and loss of their homes even before the resulting recession made their jobs insecure.

Table 2.2 shows how the Federal Reserve System increased its involvement in the economy. Note how the volume of assets funded by the Federal Reserve increased by over 150 percent in one year, from year-end 2007 to year-end 2008. If one counts member institutions' stock purchases in the Federal Reserve Banks as capital, then one could say that the leverage of the Federal Reserve System more than doubled, from 23-to-one to 52-to-one in a single year. The rest of the financial sector was deleveraging, and the Federal Reserve stepped in to take up assets and increase its leverage. As AEI's Alex Pollock observes, it is impossible for every institution to deleverage at once; someone must increase leverage to compensate. The Federal Reserve stepped in to allow financial firms to shed assets, increase capital, and otherwise reduce the unhealthy level of leverage in the private part of the financial system.

Was the financial crisis avoidable? The Financial Crisis Inquiry Commission, charged by Congress with investigating this question, reached a split decision. The commission's majority reported that, yes, the crisis was avoidable: "The captains of finance and the public stewards of our financial system ignored warnings and failed to question, understand, and manage evolving risks within a system essential to the well-being of the American public."[40] A minority report opined that, no, the crisis resulted from large forces such as a global savings glut and consequent home price bubble, in the United States and overseas, and poor decisions: "Different types of financial firms in the United States and Europe made highly concentrated, highly correlated bets on housing [and] managers of different types of financial firms in the United States and Europe poorly managed their solvency and liquidity risk."[41] A second dissent, by a single commissioner, pointed the finger at flawed US housing policy and especially at the two government-sponsored enterprises (GSEs) Fannie Mae and Freddie Mac that failed in September 2008 at the height of the crisis.

This book adopts the perspective that improved governance and management could have made a huge difference; successful firms illustrate what the unsuccessful firms should have been doing. Chapter 3 begins by assessing how successful firms coped with the crisis while others failed. Chapter 4 reviews

TABLE 2.1 Timeline of Major Government Actions by the Federal Reserve and Treasury Department (Abbreviated)

December 12, 2007: The Federal Reserve Board announces the creation of a Term Auction Facility (TAF) in which fixed amounts of term funds will be auctioned to depository institutions against a wide variety of collateral.

March 11, 2008: The Federal Reserve Board announces the creation of the Term Securities Lending Facility (TSLF), which will lend up to $200 billion of Treasury securities for 28-day terms.

March 16, 2008: The Federal Reserve Board establishes the Primary Dealer Credit Facility (PDCF), extending credit to primary dealers.

March 24, 2008: The Federal Reserve Bank of New York announces that it will provide term financing to facilitate JPMorgan Chase & Co.'s acquisition of The Bear Stearns Companies Inc.

July 30, 2008: President Bush signs into law the Housing and Economic Recovery Act of 2008 (Public Law 110-289).

September 7, 2008: The Federal Housing Finance Agency (FHFA) places Fannie Mae and Freddie Mac in government conservatorship. The U.S. Treasury Department announces three additional measures to complement the FHFA's decision.

September 16, 2008: The Federal Reserve Board authorizes the Federal Reserve Bank of New York to lend up to $85 billion to the American International Group (AIG) under Section 13(3) of the Federal Reserve Act.

September 17, 2008: The U.S. Treasury Department announces a Supplementary Financing Program consisting of a series of Treasury bill issues that will provide cash for use in Federal Reserve initiatives.

September 19, 2008: The Federal Reserve Board announces the creation of the Asset-Backed Commercial Paper Money Market Mutual Fund Liquidity Facility (AMLF).

September 19, 2008: The U.S. Treasury Department announces a temporary guaranty program that will make available up to $50 billion from the Exchange Stabilization Fund to guarantee investments in participating money market mutual funds.

September 20, 2008: The U.S. Treasury Department submits draft legislation to Congress for authority to purchase troubled assets.

September 21, 2008: The Federal Reserve Board approves applications of investment banking companies Goldman Sachs and Morgan Stanley to become bank holding companies.

October 3, 2008: Congress passes and President Bush signs into law the Emergency Economic Stabilization Act of 2008 (EESA -- Public Law 110-343), which establishes the $700 billion Troubled Asset Relief Program (TARP).

October 7, 2008: FDIC announces, pursuant to EESA, that FDIC deposit insurance temporarily increased from $100,000 to $250,000 per depositor, effective October 3, 2008.

October 7, 2008: The Federal Reserve Board announces the creation of the Commercial Paper Funding Facility (CPFF), which will provide a liquidity backstop to U.S. issuers of commercial paper.

October 8, 2008: The Federal Reserve Board authorizes the Federal Reserve Bank of New York to borrow up to $37.8 billion in investment-grade, fixed-income securities from American International Group (AIG) in return for cash collateral.

October 14, 2008: U.S. Treasury Department announces the Troubled Asset Relief Program (TARP) under the authority of the Emergency Economic Stabilization Act of 2008.

October 14, 2008: FDIC announces a new Temporary Liquidity Guarantee Program to guarantee newly issued senior unsecured debt of banks, thrifts, and certain holding companies, and provide full federal insurance coverage of non-interest bearing deposit transaction accounts, regardless of dollar amount.

October 21, 2008: The Federal Reserve Board announces creation of the Money Market Investor Funding Facility (MMIFF) to facilitate the purchase of assets from eligible investors, such as U.S. money market mutual funds.

November 10, 2008: The Federal Reserve Board and the U.S. Treasury Department announce a restructuring of the government's financial support of AIG.

November 12, 2008: U.S. Treasury Secretary Paulson formally announces that the Treasury has decided not to use TARP funds to purchase illiquid mortgage-related assets from financial institutions.

November 23, 2008: The U.S. Treasury Department, Federal Reserve Board, and FDIC jointly announce an agreement with Citigroup to provide a package of guarantees, liquidity access, and capital.

November 25, 2008: The Federal Reserve Board announces the creation of the Term Asset-Backed Securities Lending Facility (TALF), **to support** recently originated consumer and small business loans. The U.S. Treasury will provide $20 billion of TARP money for credit protection.

(*continued*)

TABLE 2.1 *(continued)*

December 19, 2008: The U.S. Treasury Department authorizes loans of up to $13.4 billion for General Motors and $4.0 billion for Chrysler from the TARP.
December 22, 2008: The Federal Reserve Board approves the application of CIT Group Inc., an $81 billion financing company, to become a bank holding company.
December 29, 2009: The U.S. Treasury Department announces that it will purchase $5 billion in equity from GMAC as part of its program to assist the domestic automotive industry. The Treasury also agrees to lend up to $1 billion to General Motors. This commitment is in addition to the support announced on December 19, 2008.
January 5, 2009: The Federal Reserve Bank of New York begins purchasing fixed-rate mortgage-backed securities guaranteed by Fannie Mae, Freddie Mac and Ginnie Mae.
January 12, 2009: At the request of President-Elect Obama, President Bush submits a request to Congress for the remaining $350 billion in TARP funding for use by the incoming administration.
January 16, 2009: The Treasury, Federal Reserve, and FDIC announce a package of guarantees, liquidity access, and capital for Bank of America.
January 16, 2009: The Treasury Department announces that it will lend $1.5 billion from the TARP to a special purpose entity created by Chrysler Financial to finance the extension of new consumer auto loans.
February 23, 2009: The Federal Reserve, FDIC, OCC, and OTS announce that: "The U.S. government stands firmly behind the banking system during this period of financial strain to ensure it will be able to perform its key function of providing credit to households and businesses. The government will ensure that banks have the capital and liquidity they need to provide the credit necessary to restore economic growth. Moreover, we reiterate our determination to preserve the viability of systemically important financial institutions so that they are able to meet their commitments."
February 27, 2009: FDIC announces an increase in premiums assessed on depository institutions for federal deposit insurance

Note: This is a greatly abridged version of actions by the Federal Reserve, Treasury, and other federal agencies through early 2009, found in the timeline at http://timeline.stlouisfed.org/, accessed September 1, 2011.

TABLE 2.2 Consolidated Statement of Condition of the Federal Reserve System, 2006–2008 Year-end 2006–8

Year	2006	2007	2008
Total Assets	$ 873.9 Billion	$ 893.8 Billion	$ 2.259 Trillion
Total Liabilities	$ 843.2 Billion	$ 856.7 Billion	$ 2.216 Trillion
Total Capital	$ 30.7 Billion	$ 37.1 Billion	$ 42.5 Billion
Leverage (liabilities/capital)	27:1	23:1	52:1

Source: Board of Governors of the Federal Reserve System, Federal Reserve Statistical Releases H.4.1 for December 28, 2006, December 27, 2007, and December 29, 2008.

shortcomings in governance that contributed to the crisis, chapter 5 looks at the risk management function at successful and unsuccessful firms, and chapter 6 explores implications for their behavior of how firms are organized. While the crisis was unexpected in its ferocity, it is likely that many—and probably most—of the unsuccessful firms, with their high leverage and excessive risk-taking, would have collapsed even under lesser stress.

3 }

Coping with the Crisis

Competition may force you to exit a market, but competition should not be viewed as an excuse to take on excessive risk. Competition may be fair or unfair, but a firm is never compelled to compete. A firm chooses to compete and management should be held responsible for that choice.

—ANDREW DAVIDSON, 2011

Leo Tolstoy opens his novel Anna Karenina with the observation that all happy families are alike and each unhappy family is unhappy in its own way. The financial crisis revealed the opposite truth: successful firms each found their own way to withstand the crisis; unsuccessful firms were alike in their inability to cope and in the mistakes they made.

There was a significant disparity in quality of governance and risk management practices among major financial firms in the crisis. Many firms operated with risk management systems and processes that fell far short of known best practices. Four firms in our review that survived the crisis were JPMorgan Chase, Goldman Sachs, Wells Fargo, and TD Bank.[1] Those that essentially failed received massive government infusions of support (Citigroup, Bank of America, Fannie Mae, Freddie Mac, UBS, and AIG), were merged on disadvantageous terms (Bear, Countrywide), or simply went out of business (WaMu, Lehman, IndyMac).

Consider first the four successful firms. JPMorgan Chase and Goldman Sachs are treated at some length; Wells Fargo and TD Bank more briefly. Each of these firms distinguished itself in its operational competence and intelligent discipline, but with different approaches. JPMorgan Chase's story is of preparing the company to be strong enough to take advantage of long-term opportunities. Goldman's is of firm-wide systems and the capacity to react quickly to changes in the environment. Wells is a company with a strong culture of customer focus and restraint. And TD Bank provides the simple lesson: If you don't understand it, don't invest in it. Then this chapter considers failed firms and their problems.

This chapter sets the stage for the following two chapters. Chapter 4 looks at governance of firms and the ways that this contributed to the capacity or inability of firms to cope with the crisis. Chapter 5 discusses risk management and the role of a risk officer. Culture, governance, and management matter more than the role of the risk officer per se. Successful firms built processes of constructive dialogue into their daily practices, while unsuccessful firms tended to subordinate considerations of risk to a determined drive to gain market share, revenues, and profits.

Chapter 6 explores company organization, business models, and the crisis. Failed firms were of all organizational types, including two government-sponsored enterprises, Fannie Mae and Freddie Mac; three investment banks, Bear, Lehman, and Merrill; several commercial bank holding companies, Citigroup, Wachovia, and UBS; one insurance company, AIG; and three thrift holding companies, Countrywide, WaMu, and IndyMac.

The financial crisis was so severe that government backing appeared essential for major firms to survive. This was seen, for example, in the hurried conversion of Goldman and Morgan Stanley into bank holding companies in September 2008. However, many of the major firms that failed—because they were overleveraged, taking excessive risks, insensitive to major risks, and sometimes (e.g., Fannie Mae, Freddie Mac, Countrywide, WaMu, IndyMac, Bear) overly concentrated in a narrow range of assets—likely would have failed even if the crisis had been less severe.

JPMorgan Chase

WITHSTANDING THE CRISIS

In its 2007 annual report of inspection of JPMorgan Chase, cited in chapter 2, the Federal Reserve Bank of New York, Chase's supervisor of safety and soundness, concluded that:

> JPMC's risk management program remains satisfactory ("2") based upon the effective Corporate-wide processes in place to identify, measure, monitor, and control risk. Noteworthy is that the rating for Board and Senior Management Oversight has been upgraded to strong ("1") at this assessment based on management's ability to identify, understand and manage risk during the period of market disruption that occurred in 2007[2]

JPMC had a strategic exposure and limits monitoring system that helped to measure and monitor counterparty risk exposures. The firm's estimates of potential exposures and modeling with stress testing "provided management

with an informed and conservative view of the level of risk in derivative counterparty credit exposures."[3] The firm's liquidity management framework was
effective and strengthened in 2007.

The report also points to shortcomings. While the firm had adopted economic capital as a measure and had developed a comprehensive plan to
improve its processes, work was still under way to strengthen management of
risk capital across business units. Although the firm had sold off its entire 2006
subprime production by year-end 2006, it underestimated losses due to warehouse lines and forward pipeline exposures. However, as indicated by the
supervisor's high rating, these shortcomings were considered limited.

PREPARING FOR THE CRISIS

JPMorgan Chase's CEO, Jamie Dimon, took a long view of his firm's business.
Consider this statement in 2006, *before* the financial crisis broke:

> Go back to 1975, when I had my first job out of high school. Since then
> we've had multiple wars, multiple terrorist attacks, multiple countries
> going bankrupt—three times for Argentina—and multiple recessions.
> We've had interest rates as high as 21 percent and as low as 1 percent.
> These things happen. So when you're running a business, you have to
> run the business maturely, knowing that things are going to happen. The
> only thing that is unpredictable is the timing and, sometimes, where the
> punch is coming from. But you know it's coming, and nobody, in my
> opinion, has ever really picked the inflection points.[4]

In keeping with this outlook, Dimon kept a capital cushion that was larger
than financial supervisors required, which he called the fortress balance sheet.
A 2005 *Business Week* article described the concept as one of "selling off . . .
portfolios and stashing away reserves far beyond what either regulators or the
bank's own targets require [to build] a 'fortress balance sheet' capable of with-
standing rising interest rates and tougher lending markets."[5]

Not all shareholders favored this approach; building up a company's capital
reduces returns on equity. JPMorgan Chase explained in its 2006 annual
report that "our earnings . . . produced with the support of a still-favorable
credit environment, are good, but not excellent. And in some cases, we still
trail our major competitors."[6]

JPMorgan emphasized another fundamental approach that cost funds and
effort. This was an insistence on placing all of the company's far-flung operations onto a common operating platform. Only that way could the large
complex financial firm actually run itself as a single business.[7] As the firm's
CIO put it with respect to integration of the investment business of Bear Stearns, which JPMorgan acquired after that company failed: "One client, one
firm, one view, across all our business lines is the overarching goal."[8] The result

was not only ability of the company to manage itself across multiple business lines, locations, and even countries, but also—of particular relevance here—to take an enterprise-wide view of risks that the firm was incurring.

RESPONDING TO THE CRISIS

This enterprise-wide view, coupled with a flow of significant information to the top, paid off when the crisis began. According to Northwestern University professor Russell Walker, the firm noticed an increase in delinquencies on mortgages that it held and serviced. The retail banking division communicated this information to the firm's leadership and the company's investment banking division. The company used this information to reverse course and sell rather than purchase mortgage-related assets: "When JPMorgan saw signs in its mortgage accounts, it incorporated information on mortgage payments that was unconventional for the evaluation of portfolios of mortgages by the investment bank. Its success came from identifying such novel information and realising that it challenged conventional thinking."[9]

Because it had one of the strongest balance sheets among major financial firms, JPMorgan Chase was able to acquire Bear Stearns and WaMu's assets and network of retail branches in 2008. Unlike WaMu, which had grown through acquisitions that management failed to integrate, JPMorgan promptly integrated operations of the two firms so that remaining employees of the acquired firms worked under a common corporate culture and in the context of a common firm-wide operating system.

EFFECTS OF THE CRISIS

While JPMorgan Chase had shed much of its exposure to the subprime mortgage market starting in 2006, the firm went back into the market in 2008, optimistic that home prices had bottomed out. This misjudgment cost the firm a few billion dollars, still far below losses at firms that had failed to weather the crisis.[10]

The acquisition of Washington Mutual brought its own difficulties. While JPMorgan anticipated losses from WaMu's large subprime mortgage portfolio, the losses appear to have been greater than expected. Perhaps more significant was the damage to JPMorgan's reputation, as the firm foreclosed on households who had defaulted on their mortgages and came under scrutiny from state attorneys general, private litigants, and federal regulators.

That said, JPMorgan Chase emerged from the crisis as one of the strongest financial institutions in the world, with total assets of over $2 trillion at year-end 2010 and reported net revenue and net income for the year of over $100 billion and $17 billion respectively.

Goldman Sachs

WITHSTANDING THE CRISIS

In 1994 Goldman almost went out of business, largely because of operations in its London office. At the time the firm was a partnership; the experience seared itself into the minds of the remaining partners and led the firm to adopt what might be called a culture of risk management. The firm created a parallel structure of traders and revenue-generating businesses on the one hand and an extensive support structure, known in the firm as "the federation," including controllers who oversee the activities of traders and mark their positions each evening. The system of controllers would seem to make it much harder for a rogue trader to accumulate major losses without top management knowing, as brought down Barings Bank in the 1990s and happened at UBS during and after the financial crisis.

While JPMorgan Chase relied upon a fortress balance sheet, Goldman Sachs operated on a different business model. As Goldman officials told Commission staff, the firm operates "as a moving company, not a storage company."[11] This means that the firm monitors assets it holds and firmly encourages traders to sell aged assets out of inventory.

Goldman has a distinctive approach to risk management that involves daily monitoring of the firm's enterprise-wide risk profile on a mark-to-market basis:

> The foundation of Goldman Sachs' approach to risk management is disciplined mark-to-market accounting. This involves the daily practice of valuing the firm's assets and liabilities to current market levels—that is, the value one might expect to find on the open market. Without a transparent and realistic insight into our own financial position, Goldman Sachs would not be able properly to assess or manage our risk. It was mark-to-market accounting that spurred Goldman Sachs to reduce the firm's risk in the residential mortgage market near the end of 2006.[12]

For Goldman, the benefit of strict mark-to-market accounting was twofold: (1) it permitted the firm to maintain an accurate timely picture of its assets and liabilities without the distortions that accompany historical cost accounting, and (2) it provided discipline in making decisions, such as deciding whether to hold or change a position.

PREPARING FOR THE CRISIS

Especially important, senior management were seasoned traders who had experienced the unforgiving and cyclical nature of the markets. Goldman also actively hired people with needed skills. The firm created a specialized mortgage team in the summer of 2006 to review documentation and value CDOs and other complex mortgage products. As the mortgage market turned and became illiquid, this group helped to enforce discipline in the firm's daily valuation of those products.

Without access to a fortress balance sheet, Goldman relied on liquidity management to prepare for unsettled markets. In contrast to other risks such as credit risk or interest rate risk, which a firm is paid to take, Goldman sees liquidity protection as a form of insurance: The firm pays more to borrow, for example, than it might otherwise, in return for obtaining longer-term liabilities that are less susceptible to a run. In the early 1990s, Goldman managed liquidity risk with cash on hand. In 1990–91 Goldman used undrawn bank lines as a backstop. The firm then saw that this was not a good way to raise cash when it needed to. Other firms have pointed out that one sends a strong signal to the market when one draws down a contingency line of credit; this can harm perceptions of the firm's financial strength at just the wrong time. Goldman sought more liabilities for a longer period of time. ("More/longer" is the firm's motto for liability funding.) The firm issued little short-term debt; even though the firm used repos as a tool for collateralized financing, almost all repos had more than a 100-day weighted average maturity. The firm also issues promissory notes for six- to nine-month periods and borrows in the unsecured debt markets at maturities of seven to eight years.

For Goldman, liquidity risk management involves both liabilities and assets. The idea is to borrow long and invest in short-term assets sufficient to weather a period of market disruption. The firm manages the balance sheet on both sides of the ledger. Traders must justify not only maturity but also why they need to hold an asset. Sometimes, as with a hedge or a position held for a client, a position may need to stay open. However, to minimize the storage aspect of the business, the firm uses pricing to discourage traders from holding aged assets.

The company uses quantitative models to calculate the amount of liquidity the firm must keep on hand. Some models might build on Goldman's 1998 experience when liquidity became an issue for financial firms in the aftermath of the Russia debt crisis. CFO David Viniar told Commission staff that the firm adds to the model amounts according to judgment; the final global liquidity core, as the firm calls it, is about 50 percent higher than models alone would suggest.

RESPONDING TO THE CRISIS

The company reported excellent communications within the firm. Information and reports regarding risk metrics and firm exposures flowed up to senior management in a timely manner. Chief Financial Officer David Viniar interacted daily with CEO Lloyd Blankfein and other senior executives. Both senior management and the Goldman board were actively engaged during the crisis.

The firm reported that "Dan Sparks, then head of the mortgage department, [told] senior members of the firm in an email on December 5, 2006, that the 'Subprime market [was] getting hit hard . . . At this point we are down $20mm today.' For senior management, the emergence of a pattern of losses, even relatively modest losses, in a business of the firm will typically raise a red flag."[13]

Chief Financial Officer David Viniar convened a meeting to try to understand what was happening. Goldman's senior management decided, in Viniar's phrasing, "to get closer to home" with respect to the mortgage market. In other words, in its combination of long and short positions, the firm would begin taking a more cautious and more neutral stance. It would reduce its holdings of mortgages and mortgage-related securities and buy expensive insurance protection against further losses, even at the cost of profits foregone on what had looked like an attractive position in mortgages.[14]

In January and February of 2007 Goldman hedged its exposure to the mortgage market. The firm then closed down mortgage warehouse facilities, moved its mortgage inventory more quickly, and reduced its exposure yet further by taking on more hedges and laying off its mortgage positions. This allowed Goldman to avoid taking the substantial losses it would have suffered if it had not reacted so promptly to signs of problems.

Goldman was pleased at the way that its liquidity risk management worked in the crisis:

> As the crisis progressed, our focus on the liquidity of our assets, our relatively limited exposure to distressed asset classes, our discipline of marking virtually all of our assets to market every day, and our policy of funding assets with longer-duration liabilities enabled us to selectively and proactively reduce the balance sheet in a measured and appropriate way to reduce our risk and to protect us against the further weakening of funding markets. Further, because of the duration of our funding book, we raised more liquidity from asset sales than we lost from maturing liabilities, which resulted in increases to the size of our liquidity buffer. Our liquidity buffer averaged $113bn in the third quarter of 2008 and $111bn in the fourth quarter of 2008. As a result of undertaking liquidity-increasing measures, our liquidity buffer increased to an average of $166bn for 2009.[15]

Goldman recognized that market perceptions were critical during the panic. The firm raised cash in a public offering of $5.75 billion and a special $5.25 billion offering to Warren Buffett. The positive "optics" of having Buffet invest in the company at the height of the crisis outweighed the cost of the generous terms that he required. A *New York Times* story from September 2008 states that nonetheless, and especially after the failure of AIG, "jittery investors and clients pulled out of the firm, nervous that stand-alone investment banks—even one as esteemed as Goldman—might not survive."[16] Under pressure, Goldman and Morgan Stanley, the other surviving major investment bank, converted into bank holding companies. At that point, with clear Fed backing, Goldman had weathered the panic and crisis. Herbert Allison, a former senior Treasury official, states that "even they wouldn't have survived without massive actions by government to provide liquidity to them and their borrowers and trading counterparties and to restore public confidence in [their] staying power."[17]

In one major area, Goldman's risk management fell short: reputational risk. This is the risk of erosion of a firm's reputation because of its actions or the perception of its actions. On April 27, 2010, the Senate Permanent Subcommittee on Investigations held a nearly eleven-hour hearing that focused on Goldman's activities, and one particular transaction specifically in which Goldman had failed to inform the purchaser of a CDO that the collateral for the CDO consisted of mortgages selected by a short-seller who wanted the deal to fail so that it could collect on CDS that it had purchased on the transaction.[18] On July 15, 2010, Goldman paid $550 million to settle allegations of the Securities and Exchange Commission that the transaction was unlawful. In the consent agreement, Goldman stated:

> Goldman acknowledges that the marketing materials for the ABACUS 2007-ACI transaction contained incomplete information. In particular, it was a mistake for the Goldman marketing materials to state that the reference portfolio was "selected by" ACA Management LLC without disclosing the role of Paulson & Co. Inc. in the portfolio selection process and that Paulson's economic interests were adverse to CDO investors. Goldman regrets that the marketing materials did not contain that disclosure.[19]

The *New York Times* reported that "the settlement is humbling for Goldman, whose elite reputation and lucrative banking business endured through the financial crisis, only to be battered by government investigations that shed light on potential conflicts of interest in its dealings."[20] The case and its settlement with Goldman's concession was a reminder of the importance of reputational risk in a firm's risk management strategies.[21] One knowledgeable person told Commission staff he believed that this signaled how Goldman had changed from its tradition of being long-term greedy to being short-term greedy—similar to other investment banking firms.

EFFECTS OF THE CRISIS

Goldman emerged from the crisis a strong company. Its Form 10K for 2010 reports total assets of over $900 billion, net revenues of $39 billion, and earnings of over $12 billion. Goldman's conversion to become a bank holding company, subject to the Federal Reserve, along with provisions of the Dodd-Frank legislation, raises issues concerning Goldman's business model going forward. The *New York Times* noted that Goldman's profits had fallen significantly in 2010 and that "clients are shying away from the high-margin products that ran into trouble during the financial crisis, and coming regulation will only crimp [Goldman's] profits further."[22]

In early 2011 the firm published a response to its problems with reputational risk, including a new committee structure for reporting potential conflicts and a code of conduct. Goldman stated that this would be integrated not only into processes of the firm, but also into its culture:

> The firm's culture has been the cornerstone of our performance for decades . . . We must renew our commitment to our Business Principles—and above all, to client service and a constant focus on the reputational consequences of every action we take. In particular, our approach must be: not just "can we" undertake a given business activity, but "should we."[23]

That said, one must wonder, as Herbert Allison suggests, the extent to which a large diversified firm such as Goldman in fact can avoid conflicts with and among its customers without changing its fundamental business model: "In most professions, board members and executives deal with conflicts of interest either by eliminating them or removing themselves from involvement. By doing neither, Goldman and the other megabanks . . . favored some clients above others and the organizations' near-term profitability above all."[24]

Wells Fargo

Wells Fargo's company's vision that "We want to satisfy all our customers' financial needs and help them succeed financially" came from Norwest, when Norwest purchased Wells Fargo in 1998 and took its name.[25] Wells CEO John Stumpf explains that the Wells culture protected the company: "In large part, we avoided the big problems the industry is seeing because of our culture. Our culture puts the customer at the center of what we do. If it's good for the customer, it will ultimately be good for us."[26] The company links the vision to its corporate strategy of cross-selling products to its customers; as customers thrive, and have a good experience with the company, Wells is in a position to furnish them yet more products and services.

The vision did allow Wells to sell subprime mortgages to its customers, but the company stayed away from the most risky mortgage products. Stumpf told the FCIC about Wells's decision not to write option ARMs. These were "hard decisions to make at the time," he said, noting that "we did lose revenue, and we did lose volume."[27] Mark Oman, Group Executive Vice President, Home and Consumer Finance, told FCIC staff that this caution cost the company market share in 2004–2006.

The company also originated alt-A mortgages, but again with caution. Stumpf told an interviewer that "with no documentation, no income verification and at the rate, and frankly, we didn't put mortgages in our books or even a lot of credit in our books a few years ago because there was no return built in for risk. These were viewed as riskless assets, and they're not." Moreover, Stumpf said, the company had a policy of underwriting adjustable rate mortgages at the fully indexed rate, rather than on the basis of the artificially low rate that might exist in early years of a mortgage.[28]

Wells also avoided exposure to commercial real estate lending in 2005–2007 because, Stumpf told Commission staff, it simply made no sense to the company at that point.[29]

Wells's prudence allowed the company to weather the crisis with a strong balance sheet. The *New York Times* summarizes Wells's experience in the crisis as one in which the company's "slow-go approach comes in stark contrast to its rivals. And it is not the only way the bank stands out. Even though Wells Fargo was the nation's biggest lender to consumers, its losses on bad loans (not counting the portfolio it acquired from the acquisition of Wachovia) were lower than the rest of the industry. Wells Fargo officials attribute that to prudent lending standards—like requiring higher down payments—and being quicker to restructure problem loans from the start."[30]

In the end, however, the company, which had avoided negative amortization mortgages in its business, became one of the largest holders of such products in the nation. In October 2008 Wells purchased Wachovia, a large bank holding company that came to grief after purchasing Golden West, a major originator of pay-option ARMs, a negative amortization product. Wells then became embroiled in the foreclosure problems that have affected other large lenders such as JPMorgan, which acquired much of WaMu's large portfolio of troubled mortgages, and Bank of America, which acquired Countrywide. Wells also ran into difficulties with $10 billion of home equity mortgages that it purchased and that became delinquent and defaulted in much higher numbers than expected.

Toronto Dominion Bank

In an investor presentation in September 2007, TD Bank summarized its exposure to difficult assets as seen in table 3.1.:

In the early 2000s, Toronto Dominion Bank was proud of its active international business in structured products. Then, with little explanation, CEO Edmund Clark announced in the company's 2005 annual report that "we . . .

TABLE 3.1 Toronto Dominion Bank Exposure to Difficult Assets September 2007

US subprime mortgages	None
US subprime exposure via CDO's	None
Third party Asset-backed Commercial Paper [2]	No exposure—TDBFG, TD Asset Management Inc., TD Mutual Funds
Corporate Loan Book	Nominal LBO exposure No covenant "lite" exposure
Hedge Funds	No direct lending exposure Nominal trading exposure
Prime Brokerage	Collateralized based on retail (IDA) margin standards

Source: TD Financial Group, "Investor presentation, September 2007," slide no. 15.

made the difficult business decision to exit our global structured products business . . . While the short-term economic cost to the Bank is regrettable, I am pleased that we have taken the steps we have and that we can continue to focus on growing our businesses for the future to deliver long-term share-holder value."[31] The company reported taking significant losses as it unwound its positions in 2005 and 2006.

How did Clark make the decision both to avoid exposure to the US subprime market and to shed the firm's exposure to structured products, including CDOs and interest-rate derivatives? "I'm an old-school banker," Clark told a reporter in May 2008. "I don't think you should do something you don't understand, hoping there's somebody at the bottom of the organization who does."[32]

Clark holds a PhD in economics from Harvard University. He said he spent several hours a week meeting with experts to understand the credit and equity products being traded by the bank's Wholesale Banking unit. "The whole thing didn't make common sense to me," Clark said. "You're going to get all your money back, or you're going to get none of your money back. I said, 'wow!' if this ever went against us, we could take some serious losses here."[33]

Clark recalled that stock analysts did not encourage his long-term perspective:

> [Prudence] does mean that you have to sit in marketplaces, as we did in the US, for a couple of years and grow our loan book less quickly than the market. It did mean that you had to exit structured products in 2005 and 2006 and have analysts write that you're an idiot. . . . But in the end of the day, it means that when the bad times eventually do come, that you don't get rocked by it.[34]

While their approaches differed, all four of the successful firms combined significant qualities: (1) discipline and a longer-term perspective, (2) strong communications and information systems to ensure that top management had access to information needed both to manage the firm and to understand enterprise-wide risks, (3) sensitivity to early warning signs and the capacity to respond quickly and effectively, and (4) a process of constructive dialogue between business units and risk managers. Managers at successful firms solicited feedback continuously.

In looking at the four successful firms, it helps to distinguish among (1) vulnerabilities, (2) behavior in the run-up to the crisis, and (3) capacity to respond as the crisis hit.

REDUCED VULNERABILITY AND THE IMPORTANCE OF CULTURE

Firms that weathered the financial crisis had cultures that supported disciplined restraint. Some firms, and JPMorgan and TD Bank stand out here, kept a capital cushion that was larger than financial supervisors required.

When the successful firms placed all of their disparate operations onto a common operating platform, this allowed them to run their companies—some with tens or even hundreds of thousands of employees, hundreds of affiliates, and, for retail banks, sometimes thousands of retail locations, as a coordinated enterprise.[35] The result was not only the ability of these companies to manage their firms across multiple business lines, locations, and even countries, but also—of particular relevance here—to take an enterprise-wide view of risks that the firm was incurring. Unsuccessful firms such as Citigroup and Washington Mutual expanded in the years before the crisis, but failed to integrate their systems and business platforms to obtain the capacity to manage the entire disjointed company.

PRUDENT ACTIVITIES AND AN ENTERPRISE-WIDE VIEW OF RISKS

Successful firms tended to refrain from offering financial products that they viewed as risky for themselves or their customers. Wells Fargo, for example, decided not to deal in certain kinds of mortgages that could leave borrowers with too much debt. The company gave up market share in the go-go years of 2006 and 2007 while other companies increased lending with such mortgages.

In interviews with the Financial Crisis Inquiry Commission, officials of unsuccessful firms complained that they could not have been expected to foresee the improbable drop of 30 or 40 percent in housing prices that occurred in major market areas after mid-2006. But successful firms did not foresee this either. They simply maintained a disciplined approach to risk-taking and, when they saw that the market was troubled, took a defensive posture until they could figure out what was going on. This was the case at Goldman Sachs and JPMorgan.

Another important ingredient for success was the ability to combine good judgment with good information. Decades ago economist Frank Knight articulated the difference between risk and uncertainty.[36] He explained that risk involves factors that can be modeled statistically, while uncertainty involves factors that require qualitative judgments. Successful firms in the financial crisis combined strong information systems and quantitative analysis with sound judgment about uncertainties that would not be susceptible to quantitative-based understanding alone. Top management at some of the successful firms had weathered earlier financial crises such as the stock-market break of 1987 or the Russia debt crisis of 1998 or, in the case of Goldman Sachs, the experience of nearly going out of business in 1994. As the treasurer of a surviving major firm explained to the present author, it was a major benefit to have seasoned personnel in place to manage adverse events as the panic hit.

On the quantitative side, it was important for the successful firms to draw upon a base of skilled financial modelers who combined sophisticated quantitative skills with practical knowledge of the company's business. When financial modelers possessed good communication skills, this helped too, so that management understood the practical strength of financial models and the limitations of available data and other model inputs that affect virtually all quantitative systems. Unlike firms that relied heavily on flawed models that were unsuitable to capture risks during the housing and credit bubbles, successful firms used their models and data in the context of seasoned judgment.

A third important characteristic of successful firms was good communication, both across business lines and vertically. These firms had a policy of requiring managers to report problems to their superiors: The idea was that top management wanted to hear bad news from subordinates before hearing it from other sources. All four of the successful firms report this approach of requiring managers to report early warnings of potential trouble.

Former Bankers Trust Vice Chairman Eugene Ludwig told FCIC staff about one mechanism he used to bring important information to his attention:

> We had something called the senior control officer. And that was what I could call an out-of-the-box, roaming, risk manager type. So, notwithstanding the formalized risk management structure . . . we had somebody [who would] go everywhere and look at everything and if something simply triggered in his mind—he had small team of accountants—that there was something just wrong; it was growing too fast, they weren't really checking the tickets the way they ought to. Anywhere in the organization—we operated all over the world—his job was to note it and immediately pick up the phone and call me, "Come visit." That was very effective . . . notwithstanding all the organized mechanisms.[37]

Once management received an early warning of possible major issues, more intensive conversations would ensue to try to determine whether the warning signaled impending trouble and, if so, what should be done in response. That happened both at Goldman and at JPMorgan Chase. Northwestern University Professor Russell Walker concludes that "Risk management is really about the identification of key information and its use in the decision-making process. It is not about guidelines or the execution of conventional mathematical models. Preparing for the unknown requires having the best information."[38]

Good communication is also important more generally, in terms of the directions the business is taking and the need for change. A gentleman from one of the successful Wall Street firms proudly told the present author that "the CEO often asks my opinion on major issues," adding, "but he asks 200 other people their opinions too." Managers at the successful firms solicited feedback continuously. While they didn't act on all (or perhaps most) such feedback, they developed a robust understanding of their firm and its environment that otherwise might not have been possible.

Finally, successful firms created organizations and processes that fostered constructive dialogue, as described in chapter 1, to help ensure that short-term returns did not result in decisions that increased the firm's vulnerability to potential failure. For well-run firms, this meant that pricing was appropriate; when the firm buys or sells assets, the price reflects likely risk.

Already years ago successful banks balanced risk and return when financial institutions were much smaller. Top management, often the CEO, would chair a credit committee to determine whether the bank should make a major loan or not. Both the retail or commercial banking side of the organization that wanted to make the loan, and the underwriting side that was concerned about risk of default on the loan, would meet to exchange views. Many times, especially when the process was well managed, the result was to make the loan but perhaps to adjust the terms to provide greater assurances to the bank. For example, the bank might request a guarantor on the loan or additional collateral, or some other form of increased security. This is a classic example of constructive dialogue as a means of making well thought-out decisions to achieve sustainable performance.

In today's large complex financial institutions, this process too has become more complex. Goldman Sachs's system of controllers parallels its traders and ensures a conversation about market values between these two perspectives literally every night and more often when necessary. The firm structures these conversations so that they often involve the valuation of assets and liabilities and traders' market positions.

While TD Bank and Wells Fargo minimized their exposure to the crisis through selective participation in risky activities, JPMorgan Chase and Goldman Sachs had enterprise-wide pictures of risks facing the firms and made disciplined decisions when they detected early warnings that the market might be troubled.

That said, it bears noting that this type of reaction would not have been possible without the company's investment in a culture of risk management, information systems to provide an enterprise-wide view of risk, and the general risk management infrastructure that allowed the company to detect risk early, communicate internally in a robust and open manner, and reach a decision to limit the firm's exposure to the mortgage market.

Firms that Failed

Firms that failed exhibited common shortcomings in management. It is helpful to assess these firms according to some of the hallmarks of successful firms.

LACK OF DISCIPLINE AND LONG-TERM PERSPECTIVE

A distinguishing characteristic of unsuccessful firms was their pursuit of short-term growth and profits without appropriate regard for the risks involved. Herbert Allison points out that,

> "increase profit" . . . has no built-in governor. No result is ever enough. It demands endless broadening and enlarging of activities that, unless checked by other accompanying objectives, will inevitably culminate in excess. It invites executives to stretch the definitions of legality, prudence, and ethics to increase the bottom line.[39]

In 2005, Fannie Mae held a strategic planning meeting for senior officers that included a presentation titled "Single Family Guarantee Business: Facing Strategic Crossroads."[40] The presentation stated that Wall Street firms were playing an increasingly larger role as aggregators of mortgage product; that the growth in private mortgage securities was driven by increases in subprime, alt-A, and adjustable-rate mortgages (ARMs) that were outside Fannie Mae's traditional risk appetite; and that the trend was costing Fannie Mae business with Countrywide, its largest customer.

The presentation argued that the company was at a strategic crossroads and faced two stark choices—stay the course or meet the market where the market is. If Fannie Mae stayed the course, it would maintain its strong credit discipline, protect the quality of its book, preserve capital, and intensify the company's public voice on concerns. However, it would also face lower volumes and revenues, continued loss of market share, and lower earnings, which would affect key customer relationships. Alternatively, Fannie Mae could lower its credit standards, meet the market where it was, and accept higher risk and higher volatility of earnings. That way it could increase growth and slow down the decline in market share. The presentation was candid that the company faced significant obstacles to the meet the market alternative, including a lack of capabilities and infrastructure and a lack of knowledge of the credit risks. Fannie Mae decided to take more risk, as did Fannie Mae's competitor

Freddie Mac.[41] The two companies jumped into the subprime mortgage market just at the point that home prices were peaking.

Former Federal Housing Finance Agency Director James Lockhart told the FCIC that the GSEs wanted to take even more risk:

> Unfortunately, the Enterprises' hubris extended to the whole mortgage market . . . Fannie Mae wanted to expand its Acquisition, Development and Construction lending. We allowed a much reduced AA pilot program and then stopped it. Freddie Mac actually wanted to support the credit default swaps (ABX) on private label subprime securities by buying them as they started to fall. By July and August of 2007 as the private label market fell, they were putting extreme pressure on OFHEO and were backed by members of Congress for us to remove the portfolio caps and 30% extra capital constraints.[42]

Other firms made the decision to take on more risk around the same time, including Lehman and WaMu, as described in chapter 2.

Each of these firms and others took significant losses from its exposure to the increased risks that they incurred through these changes in strategic direction. In some cases, such as Fannie Mae and WaMu, the firm's strategic plan at least called for increased risk management. In other cases, notably Freddie Mac and Lehman, the CEO dismissed the firm's capable chief risk officer just as the company was taking on more risk.[43] Andrew Davidson, a former head of Merrill's mortgage desk and now a Wall Street advisor, notes the governance issue posed by expanding risk-taking merely to defend market share against competitors that are themselves taking too much risk: "Competition may force you to exit a market, but competition should not be viewed as an excuse to take on excessive risk. Competition may be fair or unfair, but a firm is never compelled to compete. A firm chooses to compete and management should be held responsible for that choice."[44]

Almost by definition, one can say that unsuccessful firms operated with excessive leverage compared to their risks. Pushing the limits, especially after 2005, meant that highly leveraged firms could afford to take fewer losses than if they had maintained more of a capital cushion. Fannie Mae and Freddie Mac benefited from unique statutory provisions that allowed them to operate with much higher leverage than their competitors in the mortgage market. The companies fought for high leverage because it benefited their shareholders and managers, at least until the companies failed. Freddie Mac reported returns on equity of over 20 percent in most years since becoming an investor-owned company in 1989, reaching highs of 47.2 percent in 2002 and 39.0 percent in 2000. Fannie Mae reported earnings of almost as much, reaching a high of 39.8 percent in 2001.[45] The two companies fought against higher capital requirements because more capital would have diluted those returns to shareholders.

Many firms played games with their capital requirements, a practice known among regulators as capital arbitrage. Lehman Brothers, for example, used so-called repo transactions to "sell" assets at the end of the quarter so that their capital would look more substantial, only to repurchase these assets once the quarter was over and they had recorded their quarterly earnings. Other firms used this technique as well.[46] At this writing, the SEC is looking into prohibiting this practice.

Firms turned to other devices to conduct business with less capital than was prudent. To take assets off their balance sheets and reduce the amount of capital their regulators would require, Citigroup and other lenders would sell billions of dollars of assets to a trust. A variety of organizational forms facilitated this practice, including conduits that featured so-called liquidity puts and structured investment vehicles (SIVs) sponsored by the lender. The trust then sold securities based on the assets to investors. The problem was that when the market began to panic, these firms often had to repurchase the assets in order to satisfy the terms of their liquidity puts or to reassure their customers who had bought the securities. The assets came back to the company at just the wrong time, with inadequate capital to protect against losses.

Besides failing to maintain a prudent capital cushion, failing firms often also lacked an adequate information technology infrastructure to manage their businesses. Many financial firms had grown during years of prosperity but neglected to update their information systems so that they had a good picture of the risks they were taking across the entire enterprise.[47] This was especially true of firms that had grown through acquisitions without adequately integrating operations into a common information technology platform.[48] Some major financial firms showed their lack of integrated risk management when one part of the firm increased its exposure to the mortgage market while other parts were cutting back, without sharing this information.[49]

Finally, many firms failed to prepare themselves for the market panic and loss of access to funds that finally brought them down. These firms tended to finance their long-term assets with short-term borrowing. The assumption had been that if an individual firm began to fail, it could sell high-quality assets and gain the liquid funds it needed to stay in business. Few foresaw the widespread and systemic nature of the financial crisis. Once the market realized that the AAA rating that traditionally had been a sign of credit quality was not necessarily a sign of credit quality for private mortgage securities, firms began to stop lending to others so that repo transactions became unavailable as a means of raising money. Troubled firms trying to raise cash found themselves unable to sell their assets except at fire-sale prices. The problem was compounded when firms lacked information systems that would reveal the extent of their exposure to mortgages, mortgage securities, commercial real estate, and leveraged loans, among other assets that became hard to price in the crisis.

Even firms that thought they had limited their exposure to mortgages often found that they possessed pipelines of unsold mortgages or had committed warehouse lines of credit to mortgage lenders, or were otherwise exposed to commitments that increased the assets on their balance sheets just when they were trying to reduce their exposures.

LACK OF ROBUST COMMUNICATIONS AND INFORMATION SYSTEMS

Both Fannie Mae and Freddie Mac lacked effective information systems. Both firms had suffered a meltdown of internal controls, which came to light at Freddie Mac in 2003 and at Fannie Mae in 2004. The Financial Crisis Inquiry Commission reported on an interview with officials at the GSE's regulator, the Federal Housing Finance Agency (FHFA), formerly the Office of Federal Housing Enterprise Oversight (OFHEO):

> John Kerr, the FHFA examiner (and an OCC veteran) in charge of Fannie examinations, labeled Fannie "the worst-run financial institution" he had seen in his 30 years as a bank regulator. Scott Smith, who became associate director at FHFA . . ., concurred; . . . To Austin Kelly, an OFHEO examination specialist, there was no relying on Fannie's numbers, because their "processes were a bowl of spaghetti." Kerr and a colleague said that that they were struck that Fannie Mae, a multitrillion-dollar company, employed unsophisticated technology: it was less tech-savvy than the average community bank.[50]

WaMu had similar problems. The company had expanded rapidly, acquiring more than twenty financial institutions and mortgage companies from 1990 to 2002, including American Savings Bank, Great Western Bank, Fleet Mortgage Corporation, Dime Bancorp, PNC Mortgage, and Long Beach Mortgage. The Senate Permanent Subcommittee on Investigations made public a 2004 Report of Examination of WaMu by the Office of Thrift Supervision:

> Our review disclosed that past rapid growth through acquisition and unprecedented mortgage refinance activity placed significant operational strain on [Washington Mutual] during the early part of the review period. Beginning in the second half of 2003, market conditions deteriorated, and the failure of [Washington Mutual] to fully integrate past mortgage banking acquisitions, address operational issues, and realize expectations from certain major IT initiatives exposed the institution's infrastructure weaknesses and began to negatively impact operating results.[51]

While WaMu did try to adopt a common operational platform "to integrate dozens of lending platforms, information technology systems, staffs, and policies, whose inconsistencies and gaps exposed the bank to loan errors and fraud," as the subcommittee reported, WaMu ultimately had to write off the system as a failure.[52]

INABILITY TO RESPOND EFFECTIVELY TO EARLY WARNING SIGNS

Unsuccessful firms were unequipped to deal with early warning signs that the mortgage market was weakening. They did not seem to have the capacity to ask simple questions that could have raised warning flags. There is a power in simple questions, so long as the questioner—as in the case of Edmund Clark at TD Bank—has the discipline and judgment to pursue the answers.

Thus, many witnesses appearing before the Commission contended that the bursting of the price bubble in residential real estate was impossible to forecast. For example, Citigroup CEO Charles Prince testified: "In retrospect it turned out the risk assessment, while widely held, was wrong, given the wholly unanticipated collapse in real estate values across the board, in every community and geographic location nationwide (and across many parts of the world)."[53]

Multiple interviews with firms that failed to anticipate the significant drop in housing prices (or sometimes even a modest drop) confirm the perception that many firms simply missed the risks that such a drop would entail. However, effective risk management should not have depended on this factor alone. That is because highly leveraged firms—including most if not all of the firms that failed in the crisis—can use measures such as the allocation of economic capital to weigh the risks of a particular business activity and the likelihood that, if risks materialize, they could deplete the amount of capital available.[54] So-called toxic assets might be small in volume as a percent of a highly leveraged firm's assets, but could be substantial compared to the firm's capital.

Many firms operated with extreme leverage. A highly leveraged firm has much less margin of error than is available to a better-capitalized firm. This gives rise to a simple risk management question relating to the essential function of capital allocation: For a given activity or line of business, how much can a firm afford to lose before it consumes the amount of capital available to back that activity or business?

If firms had asked that question, and had the discipline to require credible answers, they would have understood when risks would exceed returns even without Prince's "wholly unanticipated collapse in real estate values across the board." Anurag Saksena, who replaced David Andrukonis after the CEO fired Andrukonis as Freddie Mac's Chief Risk Officer in 2005, told FCIC staff that he expressed concern in 2007 and 2008 that Freddie Mac was consuming capital at a higher than expected rate and that "there was a clear knowledge in the firm that, based on the riskiness of our portfolio, we were going to run into a capital deficiency. At the same time, management decided not to raise more capital."[55]

AIG also ran a highly leveraged business. The firm's total capitalization was $95.8 billion at year-end 2007. This backed some $965 billion in liabilities and $2.3 trillion of insurance in force at year-end 2007, plus a notional value of $562 billion in credit default swaps (CDS) outstanding that it had issued.[56] AIG charged little for its CDS business and it does not appear that AIG understood that it needed capital to back the substantial exposure this created.

Another simple question relates to the many firms that took substantial losses on the AAA rated tranches of mortgage securities that they held on their balance sheets. Firms such as Citi that produced CDOs often sold the lower tranches but retained the AAA super senior tranches because they could not sell those at an acceptable price. The perception seemed to be that keeping an AAA-rated security was appropriate, especially if the company itself might have been rated lower than AAA.

This logic contained an important fallacy. If one cannot sell one tranche of a multi-tranche security at an acceptable price, what does this say about the transaction as a whole? One clear implication is that the firm sold the lower tranches too cheaply; if the deal managers had looked at the sale as a unit, they would have seen that the inability to sell one piece at an acceptable price raises a question whether the nominal profits that they booked on the deal were an accurate reflection of the true returns, including appropriate consideration of the market value of the AAA piece. As one financial expert told the Commission, "Your job is to push things out the door, not amass inventory. As everybody in any business knows, if inventory is growing, that means you're not pricing it correctly."

Robert Rubin explained this in testimony to the Commission:

> I first recall learning of these super senior positions in the fall of 2007 during discussions convened by Chuck Prince with the most senior management of Citi to discuss what by then was considerable turmoil in the fixed-income markets. In a presentation on the fixed-income business, I learned that Citi's exposure included 43 billion dollars of super senior CDO tranches. The business and risk personnel involved advised these CDO tranches, related to Triple-A-plus, and had de minimus risk. My view, which I expressed at the time, was that the CDO business was an arbitrage activity and that *I believed, perhaps because of my arbitrage background, that these CDO transactions were not completed until the distribution was fully executed*. (Emphasis added).[57]

In other words, there is a simple question: What is the total value of the transaction—that is, creating and selling CDO tranches—that an alert risk officer could ask? A simple sale of a material amount of the retained AAA tranches, combined with the prices received from actual sale of the other tranches, would quickly reveal whether the company made or lost money on the total CDO transaction. Similar to the pricing model of a credit officer at Fannie Mae that the rest of the company discounted because it indicated that the company was doing unprofitable business, this would signal a difficult business environment and the need for the firm to adopt a more cautious posture.[58]

Another simple question relates to prior experience either of the company itself or of others in the market: what can we learn that has implications for our current business? The excessive acceptance of credit rating agency ratings without doing additional due diligence is a case in point. In the early part of the millennium the manufactured housing (MH) sector underwent a severe downturn. A major finance company, Conseco Finance Corporation, failed after a merger with Green Point Credit, a lender specializing in home equity and mobile home loans:

> The MH sector has been plagued by continued deterioration of delinquencies, foreclosure frequency, and losses. All the major issuers have experienced increasing delinquencies since 1998, with GreenPoint Credit experiencing the greatest increase of 72.0 percent . . . The overall deterioration has been particularly pronounced for loan pools securitized in 1999 and 2000.[59]

Fannie Mae was among the major purchasers of AAA tranches of securitized mobile home loans. In 2003 Fannie Mae's Chief Credit Officer prepared a report on lessons learned from the losses.[60] Among those lessons was: "Avoid undue reliance on the risk-assessment or risk-monitoring capabilities of third parties, including the bond rating agencies." In 2005 the chief credit officer prepared an email for Dan Mudd stating that "the acquisition credit assessment of private label securities investments relies predominately on external ratings. *Although we invest almost exclusively in AAA rated securities, there is a concern that the rating agencies may not be properly assessing the risk in these securities.*"[61] Fannie Mae disregarded this warning and purchased $41 billion of private-label securities in 2005, $58 billion in 2006, and $37 billion in 2007. Indeed, the company proposed to purchase AA, A, and lower-rated tranches of subprime securities, but did not because, FHFA officials stated in interviews, the regulator at the time (OFHEO) prohibited this. In the crisis, Fannie Mae took substantial losses on the AAA rated securities it purchased.

LACK OF CONSTRUCTIVE DIALOGUE BETWEEN BUSINESS UNITS AND RISK MANAGERS

Unsuccessful firms lacked a pattern or culture that fostered respectful dialogue between risk officers and business unit managers. Sometimes this resulted from overbearing CEOs, and sometimes from managers of revenue-producing units.

Moody's, while it is not a financial firm per se, provides a stark example of unmanaged tension between risk managers and revenue producers. Scott McCleskey, a compliance officer for Moody's, told FCIC staff about an interaction with the head of Moody's structured finance unit, Brian Clarkson, at a dinner with the board of directors in late 2006:

> So Brian Clarkson comes up to me, in front of everybody at the table, including board members, and says literally, "How much revenue did Compliance bring in this quarter? Nothing. Nothing." . . . You know, he was not big on compliance with internal policies. But, at any rate, for him to say that in front of the board, that's just so telling of how he felt that he was bulletproof. So I just give this as an anecdote to show that this was the guy that was leading Structured Finance. For him, it was all about revenues.[62]

Clarkson was later promoted to become president and COO of Moody's. McCleskey also reported on other difficulties he faced when trying to carry out his responsibilities:

> I found that my guidance was routinely ignored if that guidance meant making less money or emplacing separation requirements to address conflicts of interest between the ratings side and the business-development side). By early 2008, I was deliberately left out of discussions which had a significant compliance dimension and on which I would have given very strong guidance.[63]

Sometimes corporate leaders gave a double message, requesting that the firm grow and take more risk, but manage it. This happened at Fannie Mae, for example. In 2006 the company hired a Chief Risk Officer, Enrico Dallevecchia. At an off-site strategic retreat for Fannie Mae's senior officers, Fannie Mae's chairman of the board, Stephen Ashley, commented on Fannie Mae's strategic position and Dallavecchia's role:

> Banks are continuing to get bigger, are playing on the global stage, and are marginalizing Fannie Mae in ways that only a few years ago would have been unthinkable. . . .
>   We have to think differently and creatively about risk, about compliance, and about controls. Historically these have not been strong suits of Fannie Mae . . . Today's thinking requires that these areas become active partners with the business units and be viewed as tools that enable us to develop product and address market needs. *Enrico Dallavecchia was not brought on-board to be a business dampener.*[64]

Unfortunately, as was seen in a later email that Chief Risk Officer Dallavecchia sent to his superior, the Chief Operating Officer (recounted in chapter 5), Fannie Mae did not give risk management the priority or resources that Dallavecchia thought it needed.

Many failed firms faced a disconnect between revenue and market share goals on the one hand and professed dedication to risk management on the other. Thus, Countrywide Financial Corporation grew rapidly in the early part of the decade, increasing loans on the balance sheet from $21 billion in 2002 to $50 billion in 2003, $77 billion in 2004, and $107 billion in 2005.[65] A Countrywide report to investors showed an earnings increase from $586 million in 2000 to $4.1 billion in 2005. The company reported its share of originated mortgage loans at 15.7 percent and set a production goal of approaching 30 percent market share for 2010.[66] By 2005, Countrywide had become third in market share in originating subprime mortgages in the United States.[67] In 2005, 2006, and as late as November 2007, Angelo Mozilo emailed Carlos Garcia, CEO of Countrywide Bank, about his concerns about the company's business originating and holding an especially risky form of mortgage known as the pay option ARM. Yet as the Financial Crisis Commission noted in its final report, Countrywide continued to originate these mortgages and hold them in portfolio.

Countrywide was not the only firm where the leadership sent mixed messages. So long as the market continued to grow, it was easy for a CEO to proclaim dedication to managing and controlling risks while continuing to push for increased revenues and market share.

Differences Between Firms that Weathered the Crisis and those that Failed:

- No one saw that house prices would decline precipitously; what distinguished the survivors from the failed firms was that the survivors promptly recognized that the market was moving in ways they did not understand and acted to reduce exposure until they could figure it out.
- Successful firms detected unusual market developments, generally in late 2006 and early 2007 but sometimes earlier, and reacted to them by initiating inquiry as to the origins. They followed this by actively "derisking" (the Deutsche Bank term) or "getting closer to home" (the Goldman term).
- JPMorgan Chase differed from many other firms in the perception of the CEO that a fortress balance sheet was needed not only to protect against risk, but also to provide opportunities to make acquisitions on favorable terms as market cycles caused other firms to become troubled. Effective risk management thus became a strategic strength rather than merely a protective or defensive measure.
- Successful firms reduced their exposure significantly in time to avoid intolerable losses, but failed to detect pockets of risk in the firm that caused losses as the financial crisis played itself out.
- The other firms failed because they were overleveraged (the GSEs, Lehman, Citigroup), took excessive risks at just the wrong time (the GSEs, WaMu, Lehman), and sometimes were overly concentrated in a

narrow range of assets (Fannie Mae, Freddie Mac, Countrywide, WaMu, Bear Stearns). They might well have failed in adverse times even if stresses had not been as exceptionally great as they were in the financial crisis.

- Decision making at successful firms reflected processes to solicit feedback and engage in constructive dialogue as a way for top management to make trade-offs between risks and rewards. Risk-reward decisions involve probabilities rather than certainty, and require good judgment based on a robust understanding of the facts.

4 }

Company Governance and the Financial Crisis

The typical bank board resembles a retirement home for the great and the good: there are retired titans of industry, ousted politicians and the occasional member of the voluntary sector.

—PAUL MYNERS, 2008

Governance is the guidance system that dictates an organization's decision making. More formally, governance is the means by which an organization exercises authority and uses institutional resources to address problems and carry out its affairs. Governance reflects power relationships of stakeholders to an organization and among units within the organization. In the financial crisis, effective governance allowed top managers to prepare for adversity, avoid mistakes, and, when the crisis developed, to respond appropriately.

The Basel Committee on Banking Supervision suggests that corporate governance involves the way that boards of directors and senior management govern an institution, including, to paraphrase slightly, how they:

1. Set the firm's strategy and objectives;
2. Determine the firm's risk tolerance (so-called risk appetite of a firm);
3. Operate the firm's business on a day-to-day basis;
4. Protect the interests of investors, meet shareholder obligations, and take into account the interests of other recognized stakeholders; and
5. Align corporate activities and behavior with the expectation that the firm will operate in a safe and sound manner, with integrity and in compliance with applicable laws and regulations.[1]

Achievement of these objectives requires coordinated or at least complementary action by the CEO and top management, the board of directors, and regulators. The problem, of course, is that power and information are not distributed proportionately among these three groups. Too often, overbearing CEOs held weak boards in thrall while boards failed to uphold the duty of respectfully challenging management to provide feedback and probe the limitations of proposed management initiatives. While this point deserves further exploration, it is not clear whether over the long term, a board of directors can add value to corporate decisions if the CEO does not welcome this.[2] Some institutions lacked the ability to provide adequate information to top management or the board to support sound decision making. Regulators seemed incapable of holding unsafe and unsound practices in check, especially at firms that seemed to be reaping substantial profits. Missing are adequate checks and balances that could help to mitigate poor decision making.[3]

On the other hand, a capable CEO can build relationships with the board and with stakeholders and regulators that help to build in needed checks and balances. CEO Edmund Clark, who successfully led Toronto Dominion Bank through the financial crisis, spelled out his vision that provides almost a textbook description of appropriate relations between the CEO and a board:

> Good executive management teams want a strong board. If they're going to add value they need to ask the tough questions. They need to challenge us on our assumptions. So I tell my Board to wander through the organization; meet the executives; ask for any document you want. And if any executive refuses, tell me and I'll have a conversation with him or her and make sure they know they have to let you have it. Before each Board meeting I go through the agenda item by item. I tell the directors where the problems are and point out where they might want to press for more information on issues.[4]

Paul Myners, a former City of London fund manager who was a nonexecutive chairman of several large companies, makes the same point:

> First, board members should never forget that the most vital part of their job is to challenge executives. My rule of thumb is swiped from Voltaire: judge a person by his or her questions. Are board members asking the right questions and with enough persistence? Simple in theory, but not easy to do in environments where anything more than the occasional mundane query is regarded as bad form.[5]

The Basel Committee on Banking Supervision sets forth fourteen principles of good governance:

- "Principle 1: The board has overall responsibility for the bank, including approving and overseeing the implementation of the bank's strategic objectives, risk strategy, corporate governance and corporate values. The board is also responsible for providing oversight of senior management.
- "Principle 2: Board members should be and remain qualified, including through training, for their positions. They should have a clear understanding of their role in corporate governance and be able to exercise sound and objective judgment about the affairs of the bank.

- "Principle 3: The board should define appropriate governance practices for its own work and have in place the means to ensure such practices are followed and periodically reviewed for improvement.
- "Principle 4: In a group structure, the board of the parent company has the overall responsibility for adequate corporate governance across the group and ensuring that there are governance policies and mechanisms appropriate to the structure, business and risks of the group and its entities.
- "Principle 5: Under the direction of the board, senior management should ensure that the bank's activities are consistent with the business strategy, risk tolerance/appetite and policies approved by the board.
- "Principle 6: Banks should have an independent risk management function (including a chief risk officer or equivalent) with sufficient authority, stature, independence, resources and access to the board.
- "Principle 7: Risks should be identified and monitored on an ongoing firm-wide and individual entity basis, and the sophistication of the bank's risk management and internal control infrastructures should keep pace with any changes to the bank's risk profile (including its growth), and to the external risk landscape.
- "Principle 8: Effective risk management requires robust internal communication within the bank about risk, both across the organization and through reporting to the board and senior management.
- "Principle 9: The board and senior management should effectively utilize the work conducted by internal audit functions, external auditors and internal control functions.
- "Principle 10: The board should actively oversee the compensation system's design and operation, and should monitor and review the compensation system to ensure that it operates as intended.
- "Principle 11: An employee's compensation should be effectively aligned with prudent risk taking: compensation should be adjusted for all types of risk; compensation outcomes should be symmetric with risk outcomes; compensation payout schedules should be sensitive to the time horizon of risks; and the mix of cash, equity and other forms of compensation should be consistent with risk alignment.
- "Principle 12: The board and senior management should know and understand the bank's operational structure and the risks that it poses (i.e., "know your structure").
- "Principle 13: Where a bank operates through special-purpose or related structures or in jurisdictions that impede transparency or do not meet international banking standards, its board and senior management should understand the purpose, structure and unique risks of these operations. They should also seek to mitigate the risks identified (i.e., "understand your structure").

- "Principle 14: The governance of the bank should be adequately transparent to its shareholders, depositors, other relevant stakeholders and market participants."[6]

One can see how some principles (for example, principle 8, relating to risk management or principle 13, relating to complex organizational structure) reflect lessons from the financial crisis. These principles were implicit rather than explicit in the 2006 version of this document, which stated only eight principles. Chapter 9 explores the question of how to help improve the state of corporate governance that the financial crisis revealed.

Herbert Allison argues a board can and should pay careful attention to the firm's culture:

> The board of every financial company should conduct regular, confidential surveys of all employees to elicit their views of the organization's culture—its values (evidenced by day-to-day actions as contrasted with management's proclamations), management's priorities, prevailing attitudes toward risk-taking and compliance, service to clients, and the working environment. Boards should give as much attention to evaluating culture as they give to scrutinizing financial statements and controls.[7]

To anticipate the lessons of the crisis for financial supervisors discussed in chapter 7, supervisors too need to evaluate the quality of a firm's culture along with its financial condition.

Governance and Management at JPMorgan Chase

The composition, organization, and capabilities of the JPMorgan Chase board drew favorable comment in the Nestor Advisors study of governance at six US financial firms:

> JPM is the only bank amongst our peers in which the board had an explicit mandate for risk oversight in its corporate governance guidelines. Moreover, the board set up a separate risk committee in which two important non-executives... with extensive financial industry experience and large ownership stakes reviewed all areas of risk in a consolidated fashion.[8]

The Nestor Advisors report viewed it as a favorable sign that the average tenure of nonexecutive directors was longer than the tenure of the CEO on the board, and also that the average age of nonexecutive directors was lower than almost all of the other firms in the survey. This was viewed as some protection against the problem of directors who might be too acquiescent to the CEO.

Jamie Dimon, JPMorgan's CEO, created both a structure through a top management committee and processes to solicit vigorous feedback:

> Dimon's all-stars who make up the 15-member operating committee are a mix of longtime loyalists, JPMorgan veterans, and outside hires. . . . To make it on Dimon's team you must be able to withstand the boss's withering interrogations and defend your positions just as vigorously. And you have to live with a free-form management style in which Dimon often ignores the formal chain of command and calls managers up and down the line to gather information.[9]

These processes were essential to developing a flow of information, including negative information, to the place in the organization that could use it. JPMorgan had a policy of requiring managers to report problems to their superiors: The idea was that top management wanted to hear bad news from subordinates before hearing it from other sources. In the pithy words of a JPMorgan Chase executive, "Jamie and I like to get the bad news out to where everybody can see it . . . to get the dead cat on the table."[10]

Governance and Management at Goldman Sachs

Nestor Advisors also included Goldman in its study. Looking at the board of directors, Nestor found that

> the GS board of "heavy hitters" contrasted somewhat with its peers, many of which seem to have adopted a policy of seeking out the "good and the great" rather than those with significant and relevant financial industry expertise. . . . Like fellow survivor [Morgan Stanley], the remuneration of its most senior executives was relatively egalitarian, a testament to GS's famous "partnership" culture . . . This, in conjunction with a healthy presence of executives on the board, suggests a balance of power less predicated on the authority of one individual.[11]

Nestor found merit in the Goldman practice of having essentially all nonexecutive directors attend all committees: "From a risk oversight perspective, this practice might be quite effective in providing [nonexecutive directors] with a comprehensive view of key risks and allowing them to have a collective board view on group risk tolerance and risk appetite."[12]

Another important aspect of Goldman Sachs' management is what the firm calls a "culture of over-communication; multiple formal and informal forums for risk discussions coupled with a constant flow of risk reports."[13] As the former head of the Goldman mortgage desk, Dan Sparks told Commission staff, "Part of my job was to be sure people I reported to knew what they needed to know."[14]

Governance and Management at Lehman Brothers

Lehman Brothers provides a contrasting illustration. Anton Valukas, the Lehman bankruptcy examiner, reported that Lehman's management provided ongoing information to the board about the company's levels of risk exposure:

> The directors received reports concerning Lehman's business and the level and nature of its risk-taking at every Board meeting. Although these reports noted the elevated levels of risk to Lehman's business beginning in late 2006, management informed the directors that the increased risk-taking was part of a deliberate strategy to grow the firm. The directors continued to receive such reports throughout 2007, and were repeatedly informed about developments in the subprime markets and the credit markets generally. Management assured the directors that it was taking prudent steps to address these risks but that management saw the unfolding crisis as an opportunity to pursue a countercyclical growth strategy.[15]

So why did the board let Lehman fail? One likely reason for the Lehman board's acquiescence was the lack of financial expertise among directors; another was the strong personality of the CEO:

> The Board of LEH was another "stale," entrenched board with the same individual wielding unchecked power for a long period of time. . . . There was a noticeable lack of [nonexecutive director] financial industry experts . . . on the board—overseeing one of the most complex balance sheets of our peer group.[16]

Even at the end, and unlike the Citi or Merrill Lynch boards, the Lehman board did not obtain the resignation of the company's CEO.

Given the contrast in governance between Morgan and Goldman on the one hand and Lehman on the other, it is appropriate to step back and look at the major actors in governance of a company, starting with the board and the CEO.

Governance and the Board of Directors

Reviews of corporate governance often begin with the board of directors. In functional terms, as recommended by the OECD, a board should (1) select the CEO and monitor the CEO's performance, (2) set compensation, (3) help develop and oversee implementation of the firm's strategy, (4) oversee the quality of management, including internal controls and risk management, and (5) intervene to make major changes in management people, strategies, or activities that may be needed.

According to the OECD Principles of Corporate Governance, the board should fulfill certain key functions, set forth on the following page.

1. Reviewing and guiding corporate strategy, major plans of action, risk policy, annual budgets and business plans; setting performance objectives; monitoring implementation and corporate performance; and overseeing major capital expenditures, acquisitions and divestitures.
2. Monitoring the effectiveness of the company's governance practices and making changes as needed.
3. Selecting, compensating, monitoring and, when necessary, replacing key executives and overseeing succession planning.
4. Aligning key executive and board remuneration with the longer term interests of the company and its shareholders.
5. Ensuring a formal and transparent board nomination and election process.
6. Monitoring and managing potential conflicts of interest of management, board members and shareholders, including misuse of corporate assets and abuse in related party transactions.
7. Ensuring the integrity of the corporation's accounting and financial reporting systems, including the independent audit, and that appropriate systems of control are in place, in particular, systems for risk management, financial and operational control, and compliance with the law and relevant standards.
8. Overseeing the process of disclosure and communications.[17]

These functions reduce to two board functions in normal times, (1) to advise the executive, and (2) to monitor the executive on behalf of shareholders. On occasion, these functions can conflict. To the extent that boards advise the executive, they are likely to become enmeshed in the executive's outlook and unable to achieve the distance needed to be a good monitor. This argument applies to boards the perception of economist Willem Buiter, discussed in chapter 7, that regulators become subject to "cognitive regulatory capture" as they attempt to solve problems of the regulated companies and then adopt the companies' world view. Jonathan Macey points out that Continental European company law seeks to remove the contradiction in function by creating two boards, a board of directors that oversees the company on behalf of stakeholders and an executive board that helps the CEO to manage the company.

Macey also notes that the approach of seating more insiders on a board shows acceptance of the predominance of the advisory function over the oversight function.[18] Thus, views differ between the United Kingdom and the United States as to the appropriate trade-off between director independence and director expertise. Nestor Advisors presents the UK view:

> In principle, boards function better when they include senior key executives in addition to the CEO amongst their members, as stated by the UK Combined Code: "The board should include a balance of executive and non-executive directors (and in particular independent non-executive directors) such that no individual or small group of individuals can dominate the board's decision taking."

In general we strongly support this view because: i) broader executive presence brings more information and different points of view to the board; and ii) more executives are directly accountable to shareholders. In the U.S., the general practice is for boards to include very few executives.[19]

Boards also have responsibilities in unusual times to recruit and select a CEO, dismiss a CEO, and to approve changes in corporate structure—for example by approving a purchase or spin-off of an organizational unit, or, as occurred with the sale of Bear Stearns to JPMorgan Chase in 2008, by approving dissolution of a firm. In the financial crisis boards that exercised the function of accepting the resignation of a CEO, such as occurred at UBS and Merrill Lynch in mid- and late 2007 respectively, took action only after substantial losses had materialized.

In its advisory role, the board is supposed to be the source of feedback and guidance to senior management. Boards should be "strong, high-functioning work groups whose members trust and challenge one another and engage directly with senior managers on critical issues facing the corporation."[20] When it serves as a source of constructive and well-informed feedback, a strong board can help compensate for problems that can arise when an overbearing CEO becomes falsely confident and loses touch with important sources of information.[21]

In fact, many boards failed to live up to this standard, for several reasons: (1) many board members were unqualified and unequipped to provide useful feedback on the complex financial issues that firms faced, (2) many board members were placed on boards at the behest of the CEO and were unprepared to challenge the CEO's judgments, and (3) a weak chairman of the board could prevent a board from developing the climate of respect, trust, and candor necessary to encourage a culture of respectful disagreement.[22]

This is the conclusion of the Walker Report in the U.K:

> The sequence in board discussion on major issues should be: presentation by the executive, a disciplined process of challenge, decision on the policy or strategy to be adopted and then full empowerment of the executive to implement. The essential "challenge" step in the sequence appears to have been missed in many board situations and needs to be unequivocally clearly recognised and embedded for the future. The most critical need is for an environment in which effective challenge of the executive is expected and achieved in the boardroom before decisions are taken on major risk and strategic issues.[23]

Nestor Advisors, in an analysis supported by extensive amounts of data concerning boards and directors of six US financial firms, concluded that "overall, we think that certain patterns of director entrenchment, asymmetric power by one executive leader, non-executive sloth, and inexplicably low levels of expertise in the boards on some of the most complicated business in the world does emerge from our analysis."[24]

The Nestor Advisors study points to the apparent disconnect between perceived responsibilities of the board and the need for board oversight of risk management. It notes that of the six US financial firms in its survey, including Bear Stearns, Lehman Brothers, Merrill Lynch, Morgan Stanley, Goldman Sachs, and JPMorgan Chase, only JPMorgan Chase expressly provides a mandate for the board as a whole to oversee risk management. JPMorgan Chase is also the only firm of the six to have a board committee dedicated exclusively to risk management of all forms of risk in an integrated way. One well-researched board was at Lehman, where the bankruptcy examiner found that management informed the board about the company's increased risk appetite, apparently without challenge: "Lehman's management repeatedly disclosed to the Board that Lehman intended to grow its business dramatically, increase its risk profile, and embrace risk even in declining markets. The Board undoubtedly understood and approved of Lehman's growth strategy."[25]

The relevant governance case law appears to preclude directors acting in their own interests and against the interests of the company, which is known as the duty of loyalty. On the other hand, provided they are acting in good faith, directors need meet only a very low standard for the duty of care. A 2009 Delaware case involving Citigroup, for example, held that directors would be held liable only if: "(a) the directors utterly failed to implement any reporting or information system or controls; or (b) having implemented such a system or controls, consciously failed to monitor or oversee its operations thus disabling themselves from being informed of risks or problems requiring their attention. In either case, imposition of liability requires a showing that the directors knew that they were not discharging their fiduciary obligations."[26] This is a test that virtually insulates directors from consequences of being lax. The FDIC Improvements Act would allow for sanctions against directors of depository institutions for laxness in making major decisions, but it seems that they have been rarely applied, if at all, to directors of large complex institutions.

The Chief Executive Officer

In the years before the crisis CEOs made mistakes that resulted in substantial losses and even the demise of their firms. This is not the first time that previously successful executives have suffered serious lapses in judgment. Dartmouth Business School professor Sydney Finkelstein points, among other factors, to the effects of success on judgment:

> Want to know one of the best generic warning signs you can look for? How about success, lots of it!. . . . Few companies evaluate why business is working (often defaulting the credit to "the CEO is a genius"). But without really understanding why success is happening, it's difficult to see why it might not. You have to be able to identify when things need

adjustments. Otherwise you wake up one morning, and it looks like everything went bad overnight. But it didn't—it's a slow process that can often be seen if you look.[27]

This observation helps to relate the credit bubble to governance and risk management: In years when house prices were appreciating and the economy displayed the great moderation, financial firms grew and reaped generous returns, regardless of whether they had the people and systems and processes in place to ensure effective risk management. The problem was exacerbated as financial firms consolidated and became larger and more complex. Only some firms—and JPMorgan Chase stands out here among the largest firms—took care to build the infrastructure needed to integrate information about operations of each part of the firm. Then housing prices dropped and governance, risk management, and infrastructure shortcomings became apparent. TD Bank's Edmund Clark provides his view of how the CEO should deal with the risks of complacency:

> I'm constantly saying to people: "Bring forward the bad news, the good news will surface soon enough. What I want to hear about is what's going wrong. Let's deal with it." . . . It's about no surprises. Any number of problems we've had to deal with could have been solved if the person had only let us know early on . . . In fact [employees] joke that I'm only happy when the world's falling apart and that I'm a total pain when everything is going well.[28]

Another example of communications between the CEO and staff comes from JPMorgan Chase. Former Fed governor Mark Olson told FCIC staff of a conversation he had had with a member of the JPMorgan Chase audit and risk committees. In that person's view, Olson said, "It was all [CEO] Jamie [Dimon . . . he] would walk around and he would talk to people in the mortgage originators and he would talk to people on the investment side and he said, 'We're not buying any of this crap. Keep it off our balance sheets.'" Concludes Olson, "It was that idiosyncratic. The difference between the quality of a leader made that much difference."[29]

At the other end of the spectrum, the absence of effective risk management may not have been apparent to executives unless they were looking for it. Thus, the CEOs of both Citigroup and AIG told the Financial Crisis Inquiry Commission that they had been unaware of the risk exposures that ultimately brought down their firms. Martin Sullivan, AIG's CEO, told the Commission that he first became aware of the company's exposure to $78 billion in multisector CDSs sometime in 2007.[30] Citigroup CEO Charles Prince told Commission staff that in early 2007 he had no knowledge of the CDO tranches that Citigroup held on its books; he first learned of the holdings as an issue in September 2007.[31]

The Citigroup and AIG pattern is symptomatic of a major problem confronting CEOs and other top managers of large complex financial institutions: Many firms lacked the capacity to integrate risk management from an enterprise-wide perspective. For instance, the UBS report to shareholders on the firm's losses notes an absence of strategic coordination. While the various risk functions relating to market risk, credit risk, and finance came together to assess individual transactions, "it does not appear that these functions sought systematically to operate in a strategically connected manner."[32]

The risk management system at Citigroup suffered from business lines separated into silos without cross-cutting communication. Citigroup had multiple exposures to subprime mortgages, including through CitiFinancial, a subprime lender, the company's residential mortgage backed securities desk, and the company's CDO desk. These organizations did not communicate well with respect to the deterioration in the subprime mortgage market and its potential consequences. This had major consequences for the company since the CEO, top management, and the board of directors all lacked timely information about the company's growing exposure to subprime mortgages to be able to fashion a consistent company-wide response when early warning signs emerged.

Finally, there is the problem of the overbearing executive who brooks little opposition, even at the cost of performance of the company. This was the Lehman experience:

> [CEO Richard] Fuld commanded the highest pay premium over his senior executive colleagues. In 2007, he earned almost three times more than the four most senior executives beneath him did on average. This is one more indication of the enormous amount of power that Fuld wielded within the firm. It might explain, to a degree, his unquestioned authority in at least two failed merger negotiations that could have saved the firm during the last months of its existence. After all, he had been the boss of the board for more than 13 years and a long-term shareholder at that. Nobody could really challenge his devotion to the firm.[33]

FCIC staff gained an impression that the problem of overbearing CEOs is widespread on Wall Street. The Commission heard repeated statements that pressure from chief officers to increase market share was a problem—for example at Moody's Investors Services, which came under pressure to please issuers with its ratings, and at numerous financial firms including AIG Financial Products, Lehman, Countrywide, and WaMu.

Stakeholders

Effective governance involves managing risks that may arise with respect to a range of stakeholders.

1. SHAREHOLDERS

Shareholders are the owners of the company and the primary subject of corporate governance. Shareholders expect returns on their investment and often expect short-term returns.[34] The Walker Report found that this was true of institutional investors as well as shareholders more generally:

> Before the recent crisis phase there appears to have been a widespread acquiescence by institutional investors and the market in the gearing up [i.e., leveraging] of the balance sheets of banks (as also of many other companies) as a means of boosting returns on equity. This was not necessarily irrational from the standpoint of the immediate interests of shareholders who, in the leveraged limited liability business of a bank, receive all of the potential upside whereas their downside is limited to their equity stake, however much the bank loses overall in a catastrophe. The environment of at least acquiescence in and some degree of encouragement to high leverage on the part of shareholders will have exacerbated critical problems encountered in some banks (and other entities).[35]

When Jamie Dimon became CEO of JPMorgan Chase at the end of 2005, he brought with him his philosophy of the fortress balance sheet. As noted earlier, not all shareholders favored Dimon's approach; building up a company's capital reduces returns on equity. By 2008 tables had turned. The fortress balance sheet allowed the company to make favorable acquisitions of Bear Stearns and WaMu's assets and operations.

This pattern can be generalized. Researchers analyzed returns for a sample of large banks in the United States and overseas and found that banks with the highest returns in 2006 had the worst returns during the crisis. More specifically, the banks in the worst quartile of performance during the crisis "had an average return of-87.44 percent during the crisis but an average return of 33.07 percent in 2006. In contrast, the best performing banks during the crisis had an average return of 16.58 percent but they had an average return of 7.80 percent in 2006. . . . Banks that had a higher Tier 1 capital ratio and more deposits generally performed better during the crisis."[36]

Herbert Allison points out that large fund managers "abetted the banks' excessive risk-taking and shoddy practices" both by neglecting issues of governance and by "pressing the banks to grow earnings or else lose share among the funds' holdings."[37] This occurred because of the fund managers' own interests:

> Many of the large fund families have an obvious, disturbing motive to avoid confronting megabanks about their business practices and governance: They too have conflicts of interest. The funds' sponsors derive substantial revenues from providing investment services (such as 401(k) plans) to the megabanks, and many rely on the banks to distribute their funds to the public.[38]

In the case of Fannie Mae and Freddie Mac, stakeholder pressure, including concern about needing to satisfy shareholders, led both companies to increase their market presence and risk exposures in 2005–2007 even after house price appreciation peaked and then dropped. The Fannie Mae experience has already been recounted; the same dynamic applied to Freddie Mac. A strategic plan document presented to Freddie Mac's board in March 2007 highlighted "pressure on the franchise" and the fact that "We are at risk of falling below our return aspirations."[39] The plan suggested that a major opportunity existed to improve earnings by expanding into adjacent markets: "We have an opportunity to expand into markets we have missed—subprime and alt-A."[40]

Several former Moody's officials pointed to the company's transition to a stand-alone, shareholder-owned company as a cause of increased emphasis on revenues at the cost, as they perceived it, of the quality of the ratings that Moody's assigned. Jerome Fons, Moody's managing director for credit policy, testified that:

> Following the 2000 "spin" from Dun & Bradstreet, in which Moody's became a stand-alone public company, management's focus increasingly turned to maximizing revenues. Stock options and other incentives raised the possibility of large payoffs. Managers who were considered good businessmen and women—not necessarily the best analysts—rose through the ranks. Ultimately, this focus on the bottom line contributed to an atmosphere in which . . . rating shopping could flourish.[41]

There is similar evidence that Freddie Mac's appetite for risk-taking increased after the GSE became a shareholder-owned and controlled company in 1989.[42]

Finally, there is a growing literature on the way that institutional investors exhibit short-term time horizons. Fund managers tend to be compensated on performance, often measured quarterly against peers. Thus, their interests are not tied to the longer term welfare of a company in which they might invest. Governance authority Ben Heineman observes that "there is plenty of anecdotal evidence that many CEOs or CFOs are appalled by the pressure for very short-term results placed on companies by powerful institutional holders."[43] A short time horizon prevents companies from making the kind of investments in people and systems and other elements of risk prevention and mitigation that might better serve the long term interests of a firm. A good counterexample of this tendency is the way that Wells Fargo, one of the successful firms, obtained a long-term equity investment from Warren Buffett as a way to permit the company to take a longer view of its business.

2. DEBT HOLDERS AND OTHER COUNTERPARTIES

As was seen in the liquidity crises of August 2007 and September 2008, holders of short-term debt can and will flee a company that they perceive to be in financial difficulty. One form of protection against this pressure is to maintain a fraction of liabilities in the form of longer term debt; unlike investors in repos or other short-term instruments, holders of longer term debt are locked in until the debt obligation matures.

Goldman Sachs was sensitive to this issue. The Goldman Sachs 2006 annual report articulated the company's policies with respect to maintaining excess liquidity, which it calls "global core excess," sufficient to meet stressful conditions: "We maintain Global Core Excess and other unencumbered assets in an amount that, if pledged or sold, would provide the funds necessary to replace at least 110 percent of our unsecured obligations that are scheduled to mature (or where holders have the option to redeem) within the next 12 months."[44]

By contrast, firms that lacked appropriate liquidity management, especially if they were highly leveraged, were vulnerable to runs if the market began to question their solvency. Lehman, which relied on a business model that depended on management of liquidity risk, is a case in point:

> Lehman maintained approximately $700 billion of assets, and corresponding liabilities, on capital of approximately $25 billion. But the assets were predominantly long-term, while the liabilities were largely short-term. Lehman funded itself through the short-term repo markets and had to borrow tens or hundreds of billions of dollars in those markets each day from counterparties to be able to open for business. Confidence was critical. The moment that repo counterparties were to lose confidence in Lehman and decline to roll over its daily funding, Lehman would be unable to fund itself and continue to operate.[45]

In a crisis, problems of liquidity can hit hard; being able to avoid or defer a perception of illiquidity can go a long way to reassure investors about the solvency of a firm. Chapter 5 discusses this issue in more detail. Thomas Fontana, chief risk officer of Citigroup's global transactions businesses, told FCIC staff there is a saying at Citi that "financial institutions die of a heart attack; corporates die of cancer," explaining that "financials tend to be more sudden. Loss of confidence is the biggest factor."[46]

3. EMPLOYEES

Especially in the fast-moving Wall Street environment, employees are an important stakeholder group. To the extent that compensation practices at one firm are perceived as less generous than those at others, for example, a firm risks losing its employees to competitors. The problem is more acute when a firm faces a decision whether or not to enter or withdraw from a particular activity or line of business. Former Citigroup CEO Charles Prince, for example, explained his statement that the firm would "keep dancing," in terms of his employees:

My belief then and my belief now is that one firm in this business [leverage lending] cannot unilaterally withdraw from the business and maintain its ability to conduct business in the future. Running a securities business is a lot like running a baseball team where none of the players have contracts, and people can leave any day and go to another team. And if you are not engaged in business, people leave the institution. And so it's impossible, in my view, in the leveraged lending business, for you to say to your bankers, we're just not going to participate in the business for the next year or so until things become a little more rational. You can't do that and expect that you'll have any people left to conduct business in the future.[47]

4. THE POLITICAL ESTABLISHMENT

Members of Congress and senior members of the executive branch play important roles in enacting the laws and setting policies that govern the benefits and burdens of a government charter such as a national bank, thrift, or GSE charter. Policy makers are an important constituency of financial firms.[48]

Laws establish the framework within which financial institutions operate, including conditions of entry, permitted activities, and conditions of exit in case of failure. Laws also establish the regulatory framework, including the mandate, authority, and capacity of each regulator. Finally, congressional oversight is a tool that can be applied with respect to the activities of virtually any financial firms or financial regulators. For all of these reasons, the political establishment constitutes an important group of stakeholders for the leadership of financial companies. The financial sector is the largest source of campaign contributions to federal candidates and parties. Chapter 7 explores these issues and their implications.

5. GOVERNMENT REGULATORS

The law authorizes the establishment of each regulator, whether at the federal or state level, specifies the regulator's organizational structure, relationship with the rest of government, capacity, authority, and powers. The ability of financial firms to choose their regulators or, in the case of the SEC's consolidated supervised entity program, to threaten that business would become subject to European rather than US regulation, put pressure on some regulators to lower their standards. When Countrywide shifted financial regulation from the Federal Reserve and the OCC to the Office of Thrift Supervision, that was a sign of this dynamic. Another sign of the dynamic was the willingness of some regulators, notably the OCC and OTS, to preempt state consumer protection and predatory lending laws, and thereby create a more favorable environment for the institutions they regulated, who therefore would not need to adapt business practices to the different requirements of the different states. Chapter 7 discusses the regulatory framework of financial institutions.

6. CUSTOMERS

In the financial services industry, customers are the people or firms to whom one sells products and services or from whom one buys them. The financial crisis was marked by sometimes significant disparities in market power or sophistication between some firms and their customers. The result was increased risk to both firms and their customers as the disparities weakened market forces that might otherwise have helped to keep risky practices in check. As Lew Ranieri, father of the private mortgage-backed security, asked, if one party lacked the right skills and information, "Who was defending the deal?"[49]

Among the less sophisticated customers were many borrowers and some investors. Many borrowers took out mortgages that they ultimately could not afford. The result was not only default for the borrower, but also an accumulation of risk on the books of investors. Borrowers were the customers of primary lenders, and the primary lenders in turn were customers of the secondary market. Freddie Mac and Fannie Mae, suffering after 2003 and 2004, respectively, from the need to devote many resources and much management attention on rebuilding their internal controls to be able to issue financial statements, faced pressure from their larger customers to purchase mortgages that did not meet traditional credit standards. Consolidation of firms in the primary market gave these customers market power that they had not traditionally possessed. A concern for the two GSEs also was that the customers would turn into competitors; their largest customer, Countrywide, was building a vertically integrated chain from origination to securitization for the ultimate investor. Wall Street firms such as Merrill Lynch and Bear Stearns vertically integrated forward to the loan origination market as well.

The rating agencies faced pressure from their customers, the large issuers of mortgage-related securities, to provide favorable ratings of mortgage securitizations and CDOs. With the rating agencies, too, pressure from customers with the ability to play one firm against another meant pressure to lower standards.

The need to attend to customers as stakeholders also relates to reputational risk of a firm. Long ago, Walter Wriston, former Chairman of Citicorp, pointed out that "it is inconceivable that any major bank would walk away from any subsidiary of its holding company. If your name is on the door, all of your capital and assets are going to be behind it in the real world. Lawyers can say you have separation, but the marketplace . . . would not see it that way."[50]

Citigroup rediscovered this truth in 2007 when the company decided to take financial responsibility for the structured investment vehicles (SIVs) that it had sponsored and that were legally separate from Citigroup and its

balance sheet. Other Wall Street Firms, such as Bear and Goldman, also protected investors in their asset management funds for fear of the consequences
to their reputations.

In summary, then, financial firms faced the need to juggle a broad range
of stakeholders. Inability to deal with any particular stakeholder, such as
shareholders, customers, or government, could result in an accumulation of
risk. The paradox is that while strength of some stakeholders such as Countrywide could lead firms such as Fannie Mae and Freddie Mac to make risky
decisions, weakness or unsophistication of other stakeholders—some mortgage borrowers, investors in mortgage-related securities or SIVs, rating
agencies, and regulators—fostered a relaxation of standards and the accumulation of risk, both at particular financial firms and in the financial system as
a whole.

Distracted Management

In several cases, including Fannie Mae, Freddie Mac, AIG, and Citigroup, top
management was distracted by the need to remediate major problems. It is
likely that in some cases, distracted management focused on what were perceived to be major problems rather than expanding their attention to include
other possible problems on the horizon. The failure of internal controls at
Freddie Mac and Fannie Mae, discovered in 2003 and 2004 respectively,
required the GSEs to dedicate literally billions of dollars and thousands of outside contractors to restoring the ability file timely financial statements. FCIC
staff interviewed acting FHFA director Edward DeMarco, who observed that
"it would be fair to say that the opportunity cost for the restatement was that
the GSEs did not spend as much time looking at other things including the
changing markets." DeMarco added that it would be reasonable to say that the
remediation effort also distracted the regulator from focusing on other safety
and soundness issues.[51]

AIG's Martin Sullivan told the Commission that when he assumed his
position as CEO in 2005, "the company was in crisis" after its auditors informed
management that they could not rely on management's certification. This
meant that AIG would need to delay filing its form 10-K annual report and that
"I was meeting regularly with our key state and federal regulators, and working
with senior management to strengthen and enhance AIG's overall financial
reporting and internal control environment."[52]

Citigroup's Charles Prince told FCIC staff that after he became CEO in
2003, "almost immediately we got diverted into . . . regulatory problems"
relating to improprieties in the US consumer business after Citi's acquisition of
the Associates Corporation, a subprime lender, actions of Citi in Japan, and a
controversy in Europe.[53]

While such management distractions were not a necessary precondition for a firm to fail, they did provide opportunity for badly managed firms to compound their vulnerability to the financial crisis.

Compensation for Short-Term Gains

Another vulnerability arose from the short time horizons of individual actors in the financial system. Firms at all levels of the financial system frequently compensated their loan officers, brokers, traders, and others on the basis of loan production and revenues generated. The Senate Permanent Subcommittee on Investigations concluded with respect to Washington Mutual Bank, a depository institution with $307 billion in assets and 43,000 employees, and its affiliate Long Beach Mortgage, that:

> The Long Beach and Washington Mutual compensation systems [involved] misplaced incentives that encouraged high volumes of risky loans but little or no incentives to ensure high quality loans that complied with the bank's credit requirements. Long Beach and Washington Mutual loan officers, for example, received more money per loan for originating higher risk loans and for exceeding established loan targets. Loan processing personnel were compensated according to the speed and number of the loans they processed. Loan officers and their sales associates received still more compensation if they charged borrowers higher interest rates or points than required in bank rate sheets specifying loan prices, or included prepayment penalties in the loan agreements. That added compensation created incentives to increase loan profitability, but not loan quality.[54]

Mortgage lenders increasingly turned to mortgage brokers to originate mortgages. The mortgage broker required little overhead and provided flexibility for a lender's payroll. The lender paid the broker only when a loan was closed, rather than needing to pay monthly compensation to an in-house loan officer. As the mortgage market expanded or contracted from year to year, the lender could reduce or increase the number of brokers more easily than trying to change the size of its in-house staff. Lenders frequently compensated their brokers with a so-called yield-spread premium, based on the yield of mortgages the broker originated:

> Yield spread premiums are paid from lending institutions to mortgage brokers. A number of factors influence the setting of yield spread premiums, but the most significant is the rate of interest on the borrower's loan.... The more an interest rate charged on an above par loan exceeds the rate for a comparable par loan, the greater the yield spread premium payment to the mortgage broker.[55]

This meant that brokers made greater returns on high-yielding mortgages. As an analysis of broker-originated loans for New Century found:

> We find evidence consistent with broker market power that is greater for more complex mortgages and for borrowers who may be less informed. We relate the estimated broker profits to future loan delinquency and find that after controlling for other factors, loans associated with higher broker profits have a greater risk of future delinquency. This establishes a link between broker incentives and delinquency risk in the mortgage market.[56]

Moreover, brokers had an incentive to increase loan production regardless of the quality of information about risk:

> The broker has little incentive to worry about whether the information presented in the mortgage application is accurate, so long as the information gathered is sufficient to cause the mortgage banker to fund the loan, and trigger the payment of the broker's fees. Lacking a long-term interest in the performance of the loan, the broker is immune from many of the adverse consequences of failing to match the borrower with the best available mortgage or providing accurate data needed for loan underwriting to assess the probability that the loan will default or otherwise prepay faster than anticipated.[57]

The problem of short-term incentives extended up the financial chain to major financial firms and their top officers. Former Citigroup CEO Charles Prince expressed to the Financial Crisis Inquiry Commission his concern about this issue: "The compensation structure on Wall Street is—is one that many people have criticized over the years. It is for—for traders, for bankers and so forth, a compensation model that is based on revenue growth, not even profit growth."[58]

Some firms provided compensation on the basis of revenues brought in (i.e., commissions) rather than longer-term profits. One witness, Joseph St. Denis, told FCIC staff that this was the case at AIG Financial Products, which rewarded its people on the basis of a bonus pool consisting of 30 percent of revenues that the unit brought in.[59] That form of compensation is essentially a sales commission on the new business coming into the unit, with no accounting for the amount of risk inherent in that business.

Compensation practices at firms that generated CDOs also fostered a short-term perspective. The CDO group at UBS, for example, had greatly increased the firm's CDO holdings even after housing prices peaked and other parts of the firm sought to reduce its exposure to the subprime market:

> None of this mattered to the UBS CDO group. For every $1 of super senior securities held, it booked the premium as immediate profit. And for every dollar of current "profit" booked, the members of the CDO group received correspondingly high bonuses. The members of the

group had every incentive to increase the quantity of CDOs on the balance sheet as much as possible, since their own bonuses were tied to instant profits with no recognition of any risk.[60]

The problem of misaligned incentives between managers and employees of a firm on the one hand, and the need to protect the financial system on the other, operates at two levels. First is the problem of misaligned incentives between employees and the firm; to the extent that compensation practices foster risk taking without due consideration of the longer term interests of the firm, employees may benefit while taking unacceptable levels of risk for their firms.

The second level involves an inherent conflict of interest between employees and shareholders on the one hand, and the interests of the financial system as a whole. This issue, discussed earlier, relates to the interest of shareholders and of employees who are compensated through stock-related awards, to increase leverage of the firm so that the up-side benefits are greater. Increasing leverage may help shareholders make profitable bets on future earnings while exposing the financial system to greater risk.[61] Thus, Freddie Mac refused to issue new equity stock in 2008 despite the risks that high leverage posed to the company and ultimately to the financial system and taxpayers.[62]

Nestor Advisors, in its survey of executive compensation practices at six US financial firms, highlights this issue:

> But, contrary to previous governance crises, management does not seem to have short changed shareholders—or, in terms of governance theory—agents did not expropriate principals. Top executives seem to have aligned with long-term owners, especially so in the case of the departed [i.e., firms in the survey that failed]. . . . Regulators, like everyone else, seem to have forgotten that, when it comes to firms that are by definition highly geared [i.e., leveraged] due to their maturity transformation function, full alignment with shareholder interest might be the riskiest of all alignments.[63]

Often the rewards for risk taking could be substantial. Professor Lucian Bebchuk and colleagues undertook a study of compensation of the top five company officers at Bear Stearns and at Lehman Brothers and argue that although the company officers lost significantly on their stock holdings when their firms failed, they had sold enough stock beforehand and had received enough in cash from bonus payments to create incentives to take excessive risks in the period from 2000 to 2008.[64]

The problem was compounded when firms provided compensation on the basis of revenues brought in rather than profits, such as happened at AIG Financial Products. The AIG Financial Products risk officer was among the employees compensated this way.[65] WaMu achieved a similar result when it assigned 35 percent of the compensation of its senior vice president and chief risk officer for home loans, the factor with greatest weight, on the company's *growth.* The company weighted the CRO's performance in risk management as a factor worth only 25 percent.[66]

Anthropologist Karen Ho suggests that traders and other employees at a firm have a fundamental dedication to high returns because this helps to compensate for the risk that, in a downturn or for other reasons, their tenure at a firm may be short:

> In the context of rampant insecurity negotiated through compensation, Wall Street's pay-for-performance bonus system "incentivizes" bankers to compete by doing more deals, bringing in more revenue, finding more profitable trades, convincing more people to invest in funds and the stock market, and so on. Not only are their bonuses tied directly to the amount of deals and revenues that they are able to generate for the bank, but bonuses are also seen as symbols of coming to terms with the riskiness of their jobs . . . Bankers are structurally primed to generate as many deals as possible whether or not these deals are ultimately "good" for the company.[67]

By contrast, Goldman Sachs has sought to retain the culture of a partnership in its compensation practices:

> The process is at the heart of Goldman's culture, a way for the firm to reward and retain top talent. Goldman was one of the last of the big Wall Street partnerships to go public, selling shares in 1999. When it was private, the partners were the owners, sharing in the profits, and in some cases having to put in money to shore up losses. To retain that team spirit as a public company, Goldman continued to name partners. In 1999, there were 221.[68]

One question to consider is the extent to which incentive structures or the firm's culture, or some combination of both, shape the company's aversion to taking on uncontrolled or excessive risk.[69] Brian Leach, who became chief risk officer of Citigroup in 2008, discussed Citigroup's post-crisis efforts to relate risk to compensation and culture:

> There is, in fact, a year-end scorecard review process where, in fact, we go through several assessments about whether we believe someone has done the right approach to risk, whether they understand risk, whether they've taken hedging actions to deal with risk, whether they, in fact, have a holistic view of risk. And we assess people against those. And then based upon that, it has a compensation impact, so . . . So I felt in '08 we had a really effective process where I went through and reviewed people and the items that I thought we could work on . . . I was able to have a conversation with the managers and get behavior pattern changes that I thought were appropriate. In '09, we did it, but with a tighter link to comp. And I'm not sure which one is more effective.[70]

George Washington University professor Robert Van Order has suggested a way to recreate some of the incentives of a partnership. He would have the firm issue contingent capital—that is, debt that would automatically convert into equity if the firm became troubled. Then he would pay bonuses to firm employees in the form of contingent capital that would vest when the employee retires. This would help to align the incentives of employees with shareholders without creating an incentive for management to increase the company's leverage. The question then becomes whether, as Karen Ho's research would suggest, such a restriction on compensation would merely drive employees to firms with less restricted compensation practices.

Compensation created incentives that played a major role in the crisis. Most firms paid those who generated significant revenues with bonuses based on success during the year (AIG, Lehman, Moody's). Compensation incentives were important in distinguishing successful from unsuccessful firms; note, however, that successful firms also paid their traders based on revenues generated. Firms' cultures and operating environments were much more important than compensation alone.

Finally, the functional relationship of a firm's compensation practices to its risk management practices deserves careful consideration. One seasoned Wall Street observer told Commission staff that once a system was in place that rewards people on the basis of the deals they do, "there is no stopping them. No one knows enough to stop them."[71]

But good processes and a strong culture can make a difference. David Viniar of Goldman Sachs believes that:

> You can't have a compensation structure that will cause you to have good risk management. You have to have a risk management structure that will cause you to have good risk management. You can have a compensation structure that could negatively affect your risk management, but I think it is very hard to make it positive. It is very hard for your compensation to cause you to have good risk management. You need to have good risk management to have good risk management.[72]

Unqualified Managers in Key Positions

Rapid growth often led to firms outgrowing the capabilities of their people and systems. As the size of the financial sector burgeoned, firms often failed to recognize that people and systems needed greater capabilities just to keep up. Managers might be seasoned from their time with the organization when it was smaller, but simply lack skills needed to manage a large complex organization. Adverse effects of outgrowing internal control systems and people have been well documented at Fannie Mae and Freddie Mac. The two GSEs benefited

TABLE 4.1 Growth of Fannie Mae and Freddie Mac, 1975–2008 (Year-end Mortgage Holdings Plus Mortgage-Backed Securities Outstanding)

1975	1980	1985	1990	1995	2000	2005	2008
$ 37.3 billion	$ 77.6 billion	$ 263 billion	$ 740 billion	$ 1.3 trillion	$2.3 trillion	$ 4.0 trillion	$ 5.3 trillion

Source: Federal Housing Finance Agency, *2010 Annual Report*, tables 4, 4a, 13, and 13a.

from numerous tax, regulatory, and other benefits, including statutory authority to operate at high leverage, that allowed them to grow rapidly for many years. As can be seen from table 4.1, Fannie Mae and Freddie Mac grew rapidly, both in their portfolio businesses and in the outstanding mortgage-backed securities that they guaranteed.

This growth reflected less the financial acumen of the two companies and their managers and systems and more the size of government subsidies they received, compared to benefits that the government provided to their competitors. Thus, in January 2003, Freddie Mac announced that it would need to restate its financial results for 2002, 2001, and possibly 2000. In June 2003 Freddie Mac announced the termination, resignation, and retirement of the CEO and other principal officers of the company. In December 2003 the regulator, OFHEO, published an extensive report on Freddie Mac's internal control failures.

Problems at Freddie Mac prompted OFHEO to launch a special examination of Fannie Mae. In September 2004, OFHEO produced an interim report on numerous irregularities. That month, pursuant to an agreement with OFHEO, a board of directors' special review committee at Fannie Mae retained former United States Senator Warren Rudman and his law firm, Paul, Weiss, Rifkind, Wharton & Garrison LLP, to investigate. On February 23, 2006, Senator Rudman and his firm reported on many improprieties, substantiating OFHEO's findings. Both the Rudman Report and the OFHEO Freddie Mac Report document how officials rose within both organizations and reached major positions inappropriate for such large and complex organizations. The Rudman Report shows, for example, how Fannie Mae promoted an internal candidate to become Senior Vice President for Internal Audit despite having had no prior training or experience as an auditor.[73] At Freddie Mac, the Chief Financial Officer, also promoted from within, "had little knowledge of GAAP, financial accounting, or disclosure rules."[74] That was a problem of too-rapid growth, beyond the ability of management to keep up; people who might have been qualified to perform a function for a small firm were not qualified for a trillion dollar firm.

The problem of skill level was especially acute at the GSEs, which often hired senior officers and selected their boards based on ability to manage political risk rather than the operational risk associated with managing trillions of dollars of mortgages that the GSEs either held in portfolio or guaranteed in MBSs.[75]

Rapid growth also caused serious staffing problems at mortgage originators. In 1997 Patricia Lindsay, an experienced real estate professional, joined
New Century Financial Corporation first as a wholesale underwriter and then
as an official responsible for fraud detection for the company. New Century
was a mortgage company that failed in 2007. Lindsay told the Commission
that in contrast to earlier years, New Century began to hire less qualified loan
originators. In her view, lack of professional qualifications combined with a
revenue-based incentive structure to reduce the credit quality of the mortgages that New Century originated before its demise:

> Account executives, who were New Century employees who brought
> loans in from brokers, were primarily compensated on commission of
> closed loans that they brought in . . . Many of the sales managers and
> account executives lacked any real estate or mortgage experience. They
> were missing the depth of experience necessary to make an informed
> lending decision. These same sales mangers had the ability to make
> exceptions to guidelines on loans, which would result in loans closing
> with these exceptions, at times over the objections of seasoned appraisers,
> underwriters or risk personnel.[76]

Other times, the lack of capable officials in professional positions resulted
from an apparent pattern of shifting senior officers according to considerations other than skills and training. That happened in late 2007 at Lehman,
when the firm replaced Chief Risk Officer Madelyn Antoncic with the CFO
Chris O'Meara and replaced O'Meara with Erin Callan, who had headed
hedge fund investment banking for the firm. O'Meara was an experienced
CFO but lacked the background in risk management that Antoncic possessed;
and Callen lacked O'Meara's experience as a CFO.[77]

Competence is an essential element for risk officers in particular. To take an
example from the province of financial modeling, the present author asked
one vice president, responsible for aspects of risk management at an unsuccessful firm, what his assumptions had been about house price declines. He
responded that he had used varying house price assumptions and attached
varying probabilities. I asked, "Oh, you mean a Monte Carlo simulation?" He
replied yes, in a tone that conveyed surprise that the present author knew the
term. Later I asked a top-flight risk officer from another firm whether she used
a Monte Carlo simulation. She replied (almost indignantly) of course not,
because that assumes a normal distribution of risk. Her argument implicitly
recognized the need to structure models to capture the possibility of black
swan events, or tail risks, which may occur more frequently than a normal
distribution would assume. It would seem to be difficult at best to bring the
former risk person up to the sophistication of the latter.

Other forces were also in play. Rating agencies lost capable staff to hedge
funds and investment banks. Henry Tabe observed that "in addition to assigning

ratings that allowed SIVs continuous access to the credit markets, the rating agencies served as nurseries for some SIV analysts and managers." He found that "SIV analysts at the agencies were typically poached by banks and management companies" with more generous compensation packages; more senior analysts and managers of rating agencies would leave and "join forces with sponsoring banks and asset managers to launch new SIVs."[78]

This removed critical knowledge from rating agencies, which were potential gatekeepers, and transferred it to firms that structured SIVs and used the rating agencies to bless the structure.

Governance and the Financial Crisis

The review of governance and risk management at twelve firms provides useful lessons. Even though many of the firms had governance structures and risk management systems in place that superficially appeared to be sophisticated and effective, many of them proved themselves not to be.

Some firms did not live up to even a semblance of sound governance and risk management. AIG, Bear Stearns, Fannie Mae, and Moody's (although the latter is not a financial firm), stand out in this regard. Problems of an overbearing CEO and a supine board can make the risk officer's job impossible. Problems of a board with too few financially informed members can lead to the same result. Robert Rubin told the Senior Supervisors' Group, "as financial engineering became more complex, it exacerbated rather than reduced complexity."[79]

Complexity is a serious problem. Some of it, as in the case of Lehman's use of repos at the end of each quarter or Citi's creation of SIVs and provision of liquidity puts, relates to regulatory avoidance and a desire to increase leverage beyond recognized limits. As these cases show, complexity and higher leverage can create vulnerabilities and reduce a firm's ability to deal with volatile markets. In addition, especially for large complex financial institutions, but also for smaller ones, competence of key personnel may also be an issue. Effective risk management—to say nothing of management generally—requires capable leadership and employees in key positions who can exercise good judgment to deal with the uncertainties that have become commonplace in an increasingly complex financial services industry.

Chapter 3 recounts several relative success stories. JPMorgan Chase had leadership that emphasized a fortress balance sheet, construction of infrastructure to ensure the flow of information across the organization, and effective risk management. Goldman Sachs emphasized a rapid flow of information and ability to respond rapidly to early signs of emergent risk. The experience of these two firms demonstrates that "too big to fail" need not mean "too big to manage," even though that was the case with other large firms such as Citigroup, AIG, and Fannie Mae.

Goldman Sachs built a system of controllers that parallels the organization's traders and ensures a conversation about market values between these two perspectives literally every night and more often when necessary. Whatever risk management system a financial firm adopts, it would be wise to ensure that such conversations take place regularly among competent and independent parties on both sides, based on high-quality information. Then the conversation needs to expand, so that traders and controllers across the organization, and especially across a large complex financial institution, have access to that information and those judgments.

Once again, however, poor governance can swamp even the best risk management structure. Lehman Brothers is a case in point. The company created a strong risk management process involving the type of deliberations needed for effective risk decisions. Yet as the company decided to increase its size and market presence and risk appetite, those deliberations turned into vehicles for top management to implement decisions greatly to increase the company's risk appetite and exceed important risk limits.[80]

There is a large question about the extent that regulators can add value to governance and risk management practices. In an interview with FCIC staff, one supervisor of a major financial firm that failed used the word "prod" to describe his efforts to get the firm to improve its risk management processes. Interviews with officials responsible for supervising Fannie Mae indicate a similar approach, perhaps because the political strength of the GSE made it difficult to force more rapid changes on the company. Can regulators overcome information asymmetries to understand the actual and not merely formal circumstances at a regulated firm? A number of the firms in this review reaped generous returns just before they failed. Can a regulator intervene—and not merely prod—an apparently profitable firm that is taking unacceptable risks? Can a regulator in fact add value to the governance and risk management processes at major financial institutions? That question deserves exploration. If the answer is in the affirmative, this would be helpful; the regulator would be a natural ally of the risk officer of a financial firm. Chapter 7 explores these issues.

The issue of executive compensation and incentives that it creates is a difficult one. Clearly, as the UBS report found, and as can be seen in the experience of AIG Financial Products, some forms of compensation fail to align the incentives of employees, and especially traders and revenue producers, with the long-term interests of the firm. On the other hand, it would be unwise to align incentives too directly with shareholders, given the returns that shareholders gain from a firm that is excessively leveraged or otherwise imposes costs or risks on external stakeholders or the financial system. These considerations need to be weighed in an environment where top producers are likely to have considerable bargaining power and credible opportunities to move to firms offering more congenial compensation.

That relates to another issue: the race to the bottom, in terms of risk taking, that the housing bubble encouraged. Many firms—UBS, Citi, Fannie Mae, and Bear—lowered their standards as they raced to catch up with the accelerating financial markets. Shareholders penalized firms such as JPMorgan Chase and TD Bank that maintained discipline.

In the end, it seems that the single most important factor in sound governance and effective risk management may be a firm's culture. Policy makers, regulators, CEOs, and boards of directors need to be sensitive to culture as something to be developed and nurtured. Karen Ho's work would seem to indicate the difficulty of transforming cultures, especially with respect to compensation and a short-term orientation to risk taking. But expensive and embarrassing lapses such as occurred at most of the firms reviewed for this book may provide a good starting point for the emergence of improved cultures of governance and risk management to supplement the formalities of promising practices suggested here.

Differences in Governance Between Firms that Weathered the Crisis and those that Failed:

- At some firms (JPMorgan Chase, TD Bank) the CEO was actively involved in the decision to reduce risk; at another (Deutsche Bank) the head of a major business unit began the process; at a third (Goldman) the CFO led the top management team, working with the mortgage desk, to reduce the company's risk profile.[81]
- Governance at the successful firms depended on the company's culture, especially as it relates to risk management, and good judgment of the CEO and senior company officials. Successful firms had a culture, nurtured from the top, that promoted constant communication between business units and risk or control units and up the line.
- When firms had had the experience of nearly going out of business (e.g., Goldman Sachs in 1994 or Lehman in 1998), this provided the impetus for renewed emphasis on effective risk management. At Lehman, this emphasis lasted only until 2006, when management began to take increased risks. Lehman replaced its chief risk officer with an inexperienced risk person in 2007.
- Successful firms possessed information systems that permit a timely enterprise-wide view of risk and changes in risk.
- Perhaps the greatest governance problem facing financial firms is pressure from shareholders, or surrogates such as fund managers, to deliver short-term results. This creates disincentives to invest in effective risk management systems and business strategies that take account of long-term risk-return trade-offs.
- Governance at firms that failed exhibited significant flaws, such as (1) an overbearing CEO whose bad judgment went unchecked by the board of directors and (2) management processes that failed to respond to the increased risk of a changing market environment.

- While the Commission's research on this point was not extensive, firms that survived seemed to possess high quality boards of directors that helped management think through decisions; however, the quality of those boards reflected the quality of the firm's culture and judgment of its CEO. Even those boards that finally replaced CEOs because of excessive risk-taking (e.g., at Citigroup or Merrill) waited too long, until losses had actually materialized and it was too late to turn the company around.
- Effective risk management requires expenditures and also discipline to refrain from profits that other firms may be making from risky practices. Support from the CEO, and preferably the board as well, is essential.
- Implications concerning incentives created by compensation systems:
  - Actors throughout the financial system operated on the basis of compensation systems that encouraged them to take short-term risks.
  - Firms that insisted on tight controls, to help offset the effects of short-term compensation, found that some employees, including some who generated high revenues, preferred to migrate to firms that offered more freedom and unfettered returns.
  - Some firms (AIG stands out here) failed to appreciate the consequences of incentives created by compensation of their employees and business units based on short-term results.

5 }

Risk Management and the Financial Crisis

You can't have a compensation structure that will cause you to have good risk management. You have to have a risk management structure that will cause you to have good risk management. You can have a compensation structure that could negatively affect your risk management, but I think it is very hard to make it positive. It is very hard for your compensation to cause you to have good risk management. You need to have good risk management to have good risk management.

—DAVID VINIAR, 2010

While flawed risk management was one of the fundamental causes of the financial crisis, the roles of the chief risk officer and risk managers were only part of the larger culture, governance, and management that distinguished successful firms from those that failed.

Risk management refers to the process by which an organization identifies and analyzes threats, examines alternatives, and accepts or mitigates those threats. In its current form, risk management is a new discipline, both in terms of organization of the risk management function and in terms of ways to assess risks. Firms differed whether they kept the risk management function separate from revenue-generating operations, merged risk management into line units, or adopted a hybrid approach. Successful firms such as JPMorgan Chase, Goldman Sachs, Wells Fargo, and Toronto Dominion managed risk in different ways. What they had in common was a respect for the risk function and the importance of managing risk-return trade-offs on a firm-wide basis. Unsuccessful firms frequently dismissed (Freddie Mac), sidetracked (Lehman), isolated (AIG), layered their risk officers far down in the firm (Countrywide), or otherwise disregarded them (Fannie Mae). At many firms, enterprise risk management expert Stephen Hiemstra explains, risk management was a compliance exercise rather than a rigorous undertaking.[1]

What Firms Needed to Weather the Crisis

When it broke, the financial crisis hit firms from multiple directions. Firms without risk-sensitive cultures were simply unequipped either to protect themselves beforehand or to respond adequately as the crisis broke. The experience of successful firms leads to a fairly clear picture of the risk management policies and practices that a large complex financial firm needed if it was to have a chance of surviving the crisis.[2] Risk management involves balancing risk and returns so that a firm enhances value to itself and its shareholders. Elements of risk management include having people, systems, and processes in place to:

- Detect emerging risks promptly, including identification of multiple risks and risks affecting the firm as a whole;
- Convey appropriate information about risks and returns to senior management and the board of directors;
- Promptly make appropriate decisions about risk and uncertainty, including risk avoidance, risk reduction, risk sharing and risk acceptance;
- Set the firm's risk appetite and relate the firm's risk decisions to that risk appetite;
- Monitor allocation of the firm's capital to support activities and their risk;
- Make appropriate decisions about risk and adjust those decisions on the basis of new information.

Consider here preparation, detection of early warning signs, and the ability to respond.

Preparation for the crisis meant that a firm had awareness that the financial business is cyclical with frequent emergence of serious shocks. That awareness would lead successful firms to build more resilient organizations than their peers. Resilience consisted of (1) a strong balance sheet and asset-liability management to take account of liquidity risk, (2) pricing of assets to include an assessment of risk both when purchasing an asset and when deciding to dispose of it, and (3) an infrastructure that enabled bad news to flow to the top of the organization rather than being bottled up at a lower level where the full implications might not be realized. Information systems at successful firms captured enterprise-wide risks; those at unsuccessful firms did not. Creating strong and effective management systems was expensive and time-consuming, to say nothing of the cost of maintaining a top quality risk organization as well.

Detection of early warning signs meant that a firm was constantly questioning the basis for lines of business, and especially successful lines of business. That might include performing due diligence, for example, on new complex securities that the firm purchased or carefully monitoring counterparty risk, or on detecting changes in the environment that could affect lines of business. That could have occurred once firms understood that the national homeownership rate peaked in 2004 and the Case-Shiller House Price Index peaked in late 2006.

Then a firm needed to understand the implications of what it found. If due diligence on mortgage pools backing residential mortgage-backed securities revealed that mortgages were of lower quality than stated in the originator's representations and warranties, what did that mean for the investing firm? What was the implication of particular legal covenants in complex securities or derivatives, or the absence of particular legal covenants, to the firm? Why would it matter to the firm and its investments if home prices had stopped appreciating? One can see that these questions, simple but important, could not easily be answered in firms that lacked strong analytical capacity as well as processes to ensure that information flowed to places in the firm where it could be analyzed and addressed.

Information flow depends both on a strong enterprise-wide infrastructure and on a company culture that requires bad news to flow promptly up the line. Citigroup illustrates the problems that can occur absent such infrastructure and communication. The Financial Crisis Inquiry Commission published notes from a senior supervisors' group interview with Citigroup senior management:

> Management believed that it had taken effective actions to prevent exposures to "exotic" sub-prime risks in its consumer bank [but there was] Poor communication across businesses: decentralized nature of the firm created silos. For example, despite perception of increased risk of sub-prime borrowers by consumer bank, credit packaging was designated a growth business and established sizeable unhedged positions. Risk appetite increased in pursuit of earnings late in the credit cycle. Leverage loan limits doubled in early 2007 to accommodate then-increasing and expected volumes. Limits also increased in the CDO warehouse business.[3]

In other words, even while one part of the firm recognized and acted on its analysis that the subprime and CDO markets were becoming troubled, other parts of the firm increased their exposure. This is a direct contrast to JPMorgan Chase, discussed in chapter 3, which cut its exposure to subprime mortgages when the consumer retail part of the bank reported increased mortgage defaults and risks.

Then, if its preparation was good, and if a company acted in time to detect changes in its environment, the company needed to respond effectively. That included de-risking by removing risky assets from its balance sheet and hedging. De-risking needed to be timely; if it began too late, as at Lehman, which began to de-risk only in 2008, the results still might not be sufficient to avert catastrophe. De-risking also needed to take account of linkages across the firm. Many large complex financial firms (and again Citi provides a good illustration) failed to recognize the exposure they had to the subprime mortgage market from the warehouse lines of credit they provided to subprime originators or from their own pipelines of mortgages waiting to be securitized.

As the crisis hit the panic stage, when financial firms realized they could not properly assess the value of assets that they or others held, the burden of implementing a response fell to corporate treasurers.[4] In responding, seasoned treasurers realized the value of perceptions as well as reality. This was the functional equivalent of a bank run in the days before deposit insurance and, now as well as then, optics mattered.[5] Again, preparation paid off. Treasurers would reassure their investors by pointing to their balance sheets and their asset-liability matches. Goldman Sachs improved the optics of its position by securing a major investment from Warren Buffett, someone known for his financial acumen. If Warren Buffet would buy an equity stake at the height of the crisis, why should other investors worry? Other firms turned to sovereign wealth funds to strengthen their balance sheets with equity investments as a way to reassure their investors. In the end, which came with the peak of the crisis in September 2008, the two surviving investment banks—Goldman Sachs and Morgan Stanley—needed to convert to bank holding companies. Investor perceptions of that organizational form for a large complex financial institution had been so colored by the failures of Bear, Lehman, and Merrill that the survivors needed an offsetting perception of strength that only the Fed could give.

Consider first the role of the risk management function and risk officer; then the types of risk that affect financial firms; and, finally, recommended best practices for organizing and implementing the risk management function at a financial firm.

Risk Management at Financial Firms

The financial crisis shows how, while fortune does favor the well prepared, even successful organizations may find preparation, detection, response, and complete implementation to be a challenge. Looking at successful firms may give an impression that when properly understood, risk management is reproducible science. This would be a misimpression. In fact, risk management should be understood as an art, backed up by sophisticated metrics when available, and sometimes not. Judgment is as important as any metrics.

It is helpful to separate the risk function into parts: (1) risk oversight, which is the province of the board of directors and includes setting the firm's risk appetite, and (2) risk management, which includes both the risk management framework and the risk management process, which are the responsibility of a firm's management. The following section considers the organization and process of risk management. The role of the board vis-à-vis management was covered in chapter 4 and is discussed further below, in the section on promising practices in risk management.

Role of the Risk Officer

Increasing numbers of firms have created a risk management function, often under supervision of a chief risk officer (CRO) to facilitate the flow of risk-related information and assist top management to make appropriate risk-return decisions. There exists a tension in the risk management literature between recommending an enterprise-wide CRO and trying to embed the risk management function in each major business unit. Some firms have both a CRO and embedded risk officers who report to the head of the business unit, but with a dotted-line reporting relationship to the CRO. This tends not to work as well as the converse: having a dotted line relationship with the business unit but direct reporting responsibility to the CRO. Michael Power summarizes the problem:

> Like all organizational control agents CROs walk a tightrope between being a "captured" insider and a disenfranchised outsider, between appropriation by operational units and marginalization by them. They are responsible for selling new "regulatory" ideas internally, ideas which may threaten existing patterns of work. In this respect the position is an inherently unstable one in terms of the role conflicts that are hidden by official blueprints.[6]

The advantage of an enterprise-wide CRO is that this person can take a view of risk across the entire firm; also, the CRO then may be of high enough stature to command respect from business unit heads. The advantage of embedded risk management officers is that they may become more attuned to the business decisions facing line managers and may be able to fashion more appropriate responses than someone could who lacked that kind of familiarity. But embedded risk managers may become susceptible to cognitive capture, again a phenomenon similar to what Willem Buiter sees with respect to the relationship between firms and their regulators. As Buiter explains, "cognitive regulatory capture" contributed to the current debacle by bringing financial regulators into the cognitive mindset of the institutions that they regulate. Cognitive capture is not a product of corruption, but rather a process by which regulators, and by extension other parts of the control function such as risk officers, may internalize "as if by osmosis, the objectives, interests, and perception of reality of the vested interests they are meant to regulate and supervise."[7] That can happen to boards of directors, as discussed in chapter 4, and also to risk officers.

Madelyn Antoncic, a well-regarded chief risk officer at Lehman before CEO Richard Fuld sidelined her to a lesser position, told Commission staff that the relationship between an embedded risk officer and the business unit needed to be a careful one that the chief risk officer should supervise:

> There shouldn't be conflict, but they shouldn't be too cozy. There has to be an intellectually independent, intellectually honest person who's mature enough not to drink the Kool Aid and become part of the trading desk. He knows where he's getting paid from—he's getting paid from me. The whole concept of his job is to steer the business out of trouble, but at the same time, do the risk reporting and analytics and ensure that the business didn't blow up.[8]

One widespread problem concerns the authority and stature of risk officers. As the senior supervisors group reported, "within firms, the stature and influence of revenue producers clearly exceeded those of risk management and control functions."[9] This relates to the perception that existed at many firms that the risk management function consumes resources and seeks to set limits that impede a firm from reaching its full growth potential.[10] The supporting infrastructure for risk management may be weaker than a firm needs as well. According to the senior supervisors group: "Firms need to reexamine the priority they have traditionally given to revenue-generating businesses over reporting and control functions."[11]

The low status of the risk function can be found when companies set budgets. In 2006 Enrico Dallavecchia, chief risk officer at Fannie Mae, attended a board meeting at which the company told directors that Fannie Mae was going to take on significant new credit risk and manage it. Dallavecchia returned to his office and found that he was slated to take a 16 percent budget cut. Dallavecchia emailed to his superior, the chief operating officer:

> I got no say and no input in building of the budget I was given. And I can only assume that those that built it were knowledgeable of the build up state of CRO and of the fact that last year CRO took a 25pct headcount reduction. when the company avererage 10 percent . . . Doing the budget for nxt year of my forecast and with a 16pct further reduction in budget is at best being ill informed or maybe I sdue to malice. I find it offesive to my intelligence and that of my staff. The company has one of the weakest control processes I ever witness in my career. We have barely started to work on it, we took significant costs out of the company while during our job and we still get a 16pct reduction this year?[12]

More subtle reasons also can make it difficult to be a chief risk officer or embedded business unit risk officer. While the head of a business unit will have data available about potential gains from a particular decision, the risk officer may be limited to providing judgments about probabilities of potential risks. This can make it difficult for a risk officer to present the kinds of data that may be needed to persuade a senior company official about the nature of the risk-return trade-off.[13]

Even when data are available, they may depend on assumptions that cannot be verified. A Fannie Mae official told Commission staff that his unit produced pricing models showing that Fannie Mae was not appropriately pricing the mortgages that it purchased. The official recounted that the executive vice president to whom he reported asked, "Can you show me why you think you're right and everyone else is wrong?"[14] There is also the tendency of company top management, and indeed of people generally, to neglect the implications of low probability events, even if they might have significant effects.

Top management must promote constructive dialogue between the risk officer and business units and then make informed and disciplined decisions:

> Internal controls, such as those represented by an effective Internal Audit function and Risk Management function, are critical to ensuring that business line management operate in a controlled environment where risk/reward decisions can be made in a fully informed fashion. *The fundamental issue is the ability of the independent control functions to successfully challenge management.* (Emphasis added).[15]

Karen Ho notes the status of risk officers in the investment banking firms she studied:

> It is important to recall that at most investment banks, risk management is a middle-office function, not part of the prestigious revenue-generating front office; as such, until the meltdown, traders and bankers in structured finance and mortgage-backed securities were lionized for profiting on both sides of the trade. Unlike conventional risk managers, who were seen as dampening profitability, front-office bankers and traders were able to sell their version of risk management as products.[16]

Ultimately, a risk officer must be ready, as a former risk official at a major financial firm said in an interview, to "walk the plank." Alex Pollock adapts the famous saying by Keynes: "The market can stay irrational longer than you can stay employed." The risk officer must be willing to get fired, because there are simply too many constituencies who want to keep the game going.

Another former chief risk officer similarly stated that, "I think a chief risk officer can never be afraid to be fired." This may be the only option if major risks appear on the horizon and are disregarded by a company's leadership; otherwise risk officers face the dilemma of choosing between becoming pain in the neck of senior management or alternatively, if they are docile and risks then materialize, being known as the chief risk officer at a firm that blew itself up.

Stated differently, the chief risk officer needs support:

> CEOs must play an active role in advocating the importance of risk and risk management. By witnessing the CEO's interest in risk, subordinates will be compelled to follow suit. Such engagement fosters a healthy exchange of risk information, ideas, and strategies throughout the company. The CEO must ensure that risk management is the responsibility of every employee. Allowing abdication of that responsibility to the Chief Risk Officer is a recipe for failure.[17]

If the CEO fails to support the risk function, and especially given the pattern of failed institutions with overbearing CEOs, one former risk officer pointed out that a risk officer "has got to be able to stiff the CEO." That means strong board support for the risk function, with the risk officer reporting directly to the board and preferably to a capable risk committee of the board. This is not an easy role to play for any length of time if the CEO is not supportive.

Successful firms provided the needed support for their risk officers. At Goldman Sachs, the parallel system of controllers and traders provides a framework for ensuring information flow—literally daily—to the CFO and others charged with monitoring the firm's risk. In interviews with FCIC staff, Goldman officials repeatedly stated that promotions and other important career benefits accrued to controllers and other members of the "federation" as well as to traders. Indeed, Goldman told FCIC staff, there can be a pattern of shifting from the revenue side of the firm to the controller side and back again as a person advances in his or her career at the firm.

Wells took a different approach. Wells CEO John Stumpf told Commission staff that "we believe at the company that risk is best managed as close to the customer as possible with strong oversight from independent bodies within the company."[18] Michael Loughlin, Wells Fargo's chief risk officer, provided FCIC staff with several examples of how oversight from his office helped detect risk shortcomings in major business units and led to remediation, and in some cases, changes in business unit management.[19]

The Power of Simple Questions

To provide meaningful input to a firm's business decisions, risk officers and other managers (and board members, as discussed in chapter 4) require a clear understanding of the firm's business sufficient to ask important questions, either with or without the application of models to assess pricing and allocations of economic capital in the company's lines of business, and other fundamentals of the risk-reward trade-off.

The most basic question is: Can I understand what's going on here? Dan Sparks, former head of the Goldman mortgage trading desk, told commission staff that unexpected market-value losses on the mortgage portfolio in late 2006 precipitated a conversation within the firm: "If you can't explain it, then you need to be careful." The result of those conversations was that the firm decided to become neutral ("flat") in its mortgage exposure far before others in the market responded to changing circumstances.[20]

As was seen with the approach of Edmund Clark and TD Bank, perhaps the simplest question of all is: Do we understand this financial product and its characteristics? Another nice example came from Kevin Blakely, president of the Risk Management Association:

> For example, when I was a Chief Risk Officer, I was presented with the opportunity to enhance earnings through the use of a U.S. Dollar-Denominated Inverse-Floating French Franc—Deutsche Mark Indexed Amortizing Swap. This struck me as an earnings tool so difficult to understand that it was functionally useless, built by a group of "quants" trying to see how creative they could be—much like those who built today's collateralized debt obligations.[21]

This is not to dispute the value of risk models in making judgments. But models, like any other tool, have strengths and limitations:

> Risk models are a tool, not a crutch. The roots of the crisis are not in the structure of risk models, but in an undue reliance placed upon them to the detriment of qualitative assessments. Risk models can be useful if their limitations and assumptions are well understood, but they are not substitutes for board and management judgment.[22]

Bennett Golub and Conan Crum make a similar point:

> In order to be tractable and useful, risk models necessarily must simplify the characteristics of a very complex and fast changing world. However, that simplification comes at the cost of accuracy and structural integrity under stress. Hence, given their known limitations, risk models and financial analytics always need to be monitored for their effectiveness and relevance. The underlying assumptions residing in models should be constantly assessed to see if they still hold true, and, if not, what the impact will be for the models that use those assumptions.[23]

Here, simple questions alone are not enough. It is not easy for a firm, and especially the board of directors, to decide how much tail risk the firm should take. Corporate officers and directors must be capable of having a dialogue about models with technical people whose knowledge may be deep, but who may not be practiced in explaining the implications to generalists who do not possess the same technical training.[24]

Judgment is also critical. Thus David Viniar, Goldman's chief financial officer, explained that the company used its model of maximum liquidity outflow to calculate the amount of liquidity that the firm needed to keep available and then, as the treasurer and CFO considered the data, each added further liquidity requirements until the final result was perhaps 50 percent higher than the model had originally suggested.[25]

Another example concerns so-called reverse stress testing. This starts with a question: If this institution incurs a large multibillion dollar loss, what would cause that?

> The analysis would then work backward to identify how such a loss could occur given actual positions and exposures prevailing when the stress test is conducted. If the assumed loss were truly large, it is highly likely that the possible sequence of events producing such a loss would have to entail elements of contagion or systemic forces. Thus, the reverse stress test is likely to require institutions to address issues that are not normally captured in stress tests. Done properly, the conduct of such a reverse stress test would be a very challenging exercise, requiring the engagement of senior personnel from both the income-producing and the control functions in a context in which the results of such exercises would be shared with senior management.[26]

A working group of the Bank for International Settlements points out the benefits to a firm of reverse stress testing for a major, systemic event:

> It is correct that the precise timing, triggers and development of a systemic shock are hard to exactly predict; however, accurately predicting specific market events is not necessary to incorporate systemic risk in to a scenario. Thorough analysis and understanding of the economic and financial environment, coupled with predictions on further environmental evolution, the identification of how different risk factors could potentially play out, the identification of the drivers of potential market dislocations, the ways in which contagion may spread, and the firm's own behaviour during these events, will increase financial conglomerates preparedness and robustness to manage through these turmoil events.[27]

As Jamie Dimon said in an interview before the crisis broke, "it's one thing to say to your shareholders, 'We had a really, really, really bad day.' But it's another thing to say, 'We filed for chapter 11 last night.'"[28]

One of the most important results of reverse stress testing may be the way that it reveals events that cut across silos, either on the revenue-producing or risk management sides of the firm. For example, similar to Fannie Mae, does the firm separate the credit risk function from management of other risks? Such risk management silos can prevent management from obtaining an enterprise-wide view of types of risk that might bring the company down.

Many firms separate management of liquidity risk, often the province of the CFO or company treasurer, from other types of risk. Reverse stress testing by emphasizing the importance of liquidity risk can foster improved communications at firms with such silos—including, for example creation of cross-cutting risk committees that include both perspectives. It can also increase the firm's sensitivity to second order effects, as when other firms or the firm itself take actions in response to stresses.

The question then becomes how a firm can create a culture that is responsive to risk management and input from capable risk officers.

Promising Practices in Risk Management

An increasing number of US companies have adopted an approach to risk management known as enterprise risk management (ERM). In contrast to risk management functions at many financial firms before the crisis, ERM is intended to be integral to a firm's strategy as it is actually implemented; it is more than a set of models and quantitative measures that may or may not relate to the firm's actual behavior. Douglas Webster, President of the Association for Federal Enterprise Risk Management, provides a useful definition of ERM: "Enterprise Risk Management (ERM) is the management of all key risks across the enterprise in order to optimize the opportunity for achieving enterprise goals and objectives."[29]

Webster sees ERM, as distinguished from risk management more generally, as having two key components:

- Consistency of policy and process accomplished through a centralized risk management oversight process, typically led by a CRO, which seeks to ensure consistency of risk management practices across the enterprise (but does not take ownership of those risks, which remain with business managers); and
- Comprehensive identification of risks and risk treatments between functional domains (i.e., silos), to ensure an understanding of how risks and risk mitigation actions in one functional area or line of business may impact other functional areas or lines of business.

This fits well with the original definition of ERM, by the Committee on Sponsoring Organizations of the Treadway Commission (COSO):

> Enterprise Risk Management is a process, effected by an entity's board of directors, management and other personnel, applied in strategy setting and across the enterprise, designed to identify potential events that may affect the entity, and manage risks to be within its risk appetite, to provide reasonable assurance regarding the achievement of entity objectives.[30]

ERM is especially necessary for far-flung organizations consisting of disparate units that have the potential to generate sufficient risk to threaten the well-being—or even survival—of the larger company. The ERM framework encompasses key elements, including (1) aligning risk appetite with the company's strategy, (2) rigorously identifying and selecting among alternative risk responses (i.e., risk avoidance, reduction, sharing, and acceptance); (3) reducing operational surprises and losses; (4) identifying and managing multiple and cross-enterprise risks; (5) considering a full range of potential events so that management positions itself to identify and proactively realize opportunities; and, for financial firms, (6) effectively assessing overall capital needs and enhancing capital allocation.[31] Those principles are clear and appropriately general. The problems come in application and ensuring that risk management is more than a pro forma exercise.[32]

The basis of effective ERM is a series of conversations among top managers, supported by information from across the firm. The conversations focus on two key questions: (1) What are risks facing our firm that could prevent us from achieving our mission goals? And (2) How can we mitigate the impact of the most serious risks? Once the conversations take place, firms can make informed and cost-effective decisions about areas where they need to enhance risk management. A special focus of ERM is to ensure that the conversations take place across organizational units so that risks are managed consistently and with an understanding of how risks in one area affect the others.[33] Goldman Sachs and its system of controllers backed by the firm's use of market value accounting to price trading positions daily and roll them up to a firm-wide overview reflected an especially sophisticated form of ERM.

By contrast, AIG was a classic case of a financial firm where these conversations did not happen, most notably between the corporate CRO and AIG Financial Products. The situation at AIG deteriorated so badly that PwC, AIG's outside auditor, wrote to the chairman of AIG's board on February 6, 2008, urging major changes in the company's governance and management. Included was a statement of the need to shore up AIG's risk management. With respect to ERM, PwC wrote that "there are two key skill sets that we would expect an ERM head to have—the first being the ability to understand, assess and evaluate risk (i.e., risk appetite) and second the ability to build an infrastructure to manage and monitor risk throughout a company like AIG."[34] PwC's warning came too late to save AIG.

Following the crisis, in 2009 the Senior Supervisors Group (SSG) requested that twenty major global financial firms conduct self-assessments of their current risk management practices. From these, supplemented by interviews with fifteen of the firms and its review of major risk management studies, the SSG presented a collective view of critical areas for continued improvement. While the SSG did not discuss ERM as such, many of its observations relate well to the ERM concept. Together with recommendations from other studies, the

SSG's observations provide a good basis for articulating ten promising practices in risk management.

1. STRENGTHEN BOARD DIRECTION, SENIOR MANAGEMENT OVERSIGHT, AND THE RESOURCES, STATURE, AND AUTHORITY OF RISK MANAGEMENT

A major element in improving governance involves the need to increase technical expertise of board members to understand the firm's business, and especially risk management. The best-managed firms developed a firm-wide culture that facilitates the flow of risk-related information and enables management to make sound risk-return decisions for particular lines of business as well as for the firm as a whole. Only a strong culture can help to prevent the risk management function from turning into a compliance exercise with attention to the mechanics rather than to important issues of judgment. This shortcoming can be exacerbated by excessive reliance on models to deal with complexities of a firm's business, rather than supplementing the use of models with sound judgment and the search to answer simple driving questions, as suggested above.

One major issue is reflected in the well-known comment of Citigroup CEO Charles Prince with respect to Citigroup's leverage lending business: "When the music stops, in terms of liquidity, things will be complicated. But as long as the music is playing, you've got to get up and dance. We're still dancing."[35] Only with capable and informed top management and directors can a firm maintain the discipline to resist potentially dangerous decisions because of a herd mentality ("cognitive herding," Alex Pollock calls it), especially when such decisions involve giving up short-term returns that other firms reap. Both the board and top management need to understand the environment in which the firm and its people are operating and the forces at play.

While firms differ on the appropriate relationship of the chief risk officer to the board, it is clear that the chief risk officer requires the ability to report directly to the board and to nonexecutive members of the board.[36] Within the firm, it now appears that a promising reporting structure is to have embedded risk staff report directly to the CRO and through a dotted-line relationship to the head of the business unit where they are located.

Issues of appropriate competence, resources, and supporting infrastructure for the risk function are matters of judgment and hard to specify in guidelines. Firms such as Goldman Sachs, that underwent an experience in 1994 of nearly going out of business, tend to weight the allocation of resources more toward effective risk management, compared to firms that did not recently have such experiences. On the other hand, Lehman CEO Richard Fuld worked intensely to save the firm from catastrophe in 1998 but then led the firm to bankruptcy only ten years later.

2. ENSURE THAT THE BOARD ARTICULATES THE RISK APPETITE OF THE FIRM, SPECIFIES APPROPRIATE METRICS, AND MONITORS THE FIRM'S ADHERENCE TO THE ARTICULATED AMOUNT OF RISK APPETITE

To paraphrase the SSG report, firms should compile for their boards and senior management (a) relevant measures of risk (e.g., based on allocation of economic capital or on stress tests), (b) a view of how risk levels compare with limits, and (c) the level of capital needed to sustain a loss of the magnitude of the risk measure. A board must be able to articulate risk appetite in the context of the business lines of the firm, both separately and firm-wide.

This again puts a premium on the qualification of board members and their ability to deal with the complexities of the firm's business, both quantitatively and as a matter of informed judgment. As the SSG notes, "a key weakness in governance stemmed from . . . a disparity between risks that [firms] took and those that their boards of directors perceived the firms to be taking."[37]

Kevin Blakely of the Risk Management Association makes a similar point:

> Boards of directors should ensure they have individuals within their ranks who understand financial risk. In the United States, we have laws that mandate Audit Committees to have individuals conversant in financial statements. Yet we have no such mandates for board expertise in risk management, whose absence poses a far greater threat than most accounting errors do.[38]

3. ALIGN FIRM COMPENSATION WITH THE RISK APPETITE OF THE FIRM AND THE RISK-ADJUSTED NATURE OF GENERATED REVENUES

The issue of firm compensation, discussed in chapter 4, continues to evolve. One recent work poses the problem in blunt terms: "What are the odds that people will make smart decisions about money if they don't need to make smart decisions—if they can get rich making dumb decisions?"[39]

One approach should be to involve the company's chief risk officer in structuring compensation at the firm. Under its post-crisis CEO, Vikram Pandit, Citigroup has adopted this approach. Brian Leach, who joined Citigroup in 2008 as chief risk officer, told FCIC staff that setting compensation involves considerable judgment:

> There is no doubt that . . . in a trading organization, any organization which is an incentive-based organization, compensation is designed to, in fact, encourage a particular behavior pattern. I mean, by definition, that's what an incentive compensation structure does. And in a trading environment, you want people to take the appropriate amount of risk. That's the artwork. And I'm really stressing the word, "appropriate."

Because you clearly want the organization to find the right—the optimal risk reward that is appropriate.[40]

That said, the application of compensation practices cannot be easy. A major limiting aspect is the fear that employees skilled at bringing in high revenues would migrate from firms with risk-related compensation practices to those that offer compensation in less restricted forms. The race to the bottom, in terms of risk-sensitivity, appears in many forms.

4. DEVELOP AND MAINTAIN AN INFORMATION TECHNOLOGY INFRASTRUCTURE THAT ALLOWS FIRMS TO AGGREGATE AND MONITOR EXPOSURES ACROSS COUNTERPARTIES, LINES OF BUSINESS, RISK ELEMENTS, AND OTHER DIMENSIONS

The problem of inadequate risk management infrastructure is greater than merely a lack of resources that many firms made available to the risk management function. Many of the largest firms involved in the financial crisis grew through consolidation with other firms. The resulting firms often found it difficult to integrate their business processes—to say nothing of risk management—across the organization. It is not easy to develop an integrated view of risk across a thousand or even hundreds of diverse subunits of a large complex financial institution.

5. ENSURE CAPACITY TO IDENTIFY RISK CONCENTRATIONS, FOR EXAMPLE BY COUNTERPARTY, PRODUCT, AND GEOGRAPHY

Given the speed with which markets shift, the SSG recommends that firms be able to aggregate their gross and net exposures to institutional counterparties "in a matter of hours." This is nimbleness seen in few firms in the financial crisis. Even if they do not yet possess the ability to identify risk concentrations so quickly, firms must overcome limitations such as a fragmented infrastructure or the need to compile data manually. The SSG concludes that firms must construct technology platforms "to handle unexpected spikes in volumes and . . . effectively produce aggregated data and appropriate management information for credit, liquidity, market, and other risk metrics."[41]

6. USE STRESS TESTING TO CONVEY RISK TO SENIOR MANAGEMENT AND THE BOARD OF DIRECTORS

Ideally, a firm should be able to conduct both robust forward-looking stress testing with a range of scenarios, as well as so-called reverse stress testing to identify scenarios and risks that can cause a significant stress event for the firm or a particular line of business. The SSG points out that infrastructure limitations have impeded the ability of firms to develop more than short-term or tactical stress tests in response to requests from senior management and firms' boards of directors.

Citigroup's Brian Leach explains the importance of reverse stress testing:

> If you've got a scenario that you can think of, and that scenario would cause a life-threatening problem to an institution, then you've got to shut that off. You've got to cut it off. And so what we've been doing a lot on our risk limits, is to make sure that we don't have a situation where, whether it's CDOs or whether it's another flavor, that you put the institution at risk for that. And . . . that is what I refer to as "risk appetite," and different institutions will have different risk appetites.[42]

7. DEVELOP CAPACITY TO MANAGE COUNTERPARTY RISK AND RESPOND TO CHANGES IN EXPOSURE AS MARKET CONDITIONS CHANGE

Here the SSG emphasizes the ability to "drill down" to understand how company risk exposures react to market changes. This involves understanding specific "risk drivers" within particular exposures.[43] Once a firm understands potential changes in exposure, it can hedge or limit risks proactively. The SSG points out that only some firms demonstrated this capacity in the current crisis.

8. DEVELOP A RIGOROUS VALUATION FUNCTION THAT INCLUDES ENFORCEMENT OF UNIFORM PRICING ACROSS THE FIRM AND TIMELY RECOGNITION OF LOSSES

Some firms found that multiple systems and valuation models impeded their ability to maintain consistent pricing policies across the firm. The finance department and areas of the firm responsible for carrying out key valuation processes must be independent, with sufficient stature and influence within the firm. Valuation disputes need to be surfaced and addressed promptly through constructive dialogue. Timely loss recognition can allow a firm to dispose of assets, perhaps at a loss, but with potentially less loss than otherwise could be the case.

9. STANDARDIZE PRACTICES, REDUCE UNCONFIRMED OTC DERIVATIVE POSITIONS, AND IMPROVE COLLATERAL MANAGEMENT TECHNIQUES

Over the counter (OTC) derivatives are contracts that two firms negotiate and trade privately, without going through an exchange or other intermediary. With respect to OTC derivative positions, firms need to streamline business processes so that they can achieve same-day matching. (Undoubtedly this time frame will shrink as markets innovate yet further.) Firms also need to adopt and implement standard technology platforms and reduce notional amounts of derivatives transactions outstanding to the extent that they do not make sense from an enterprise-wide perspective. Collateral management techniques include improvements in contracts so that conditions that trigger collateral calls are known to management and are appropriate to protect each party if an adverse event occurs.[44]

10. IMPROVE FUNDING AND LIQUIDITY RISK MANAGEMENT PRACTICES

Firms must improve coordination and interaction among the treasury function, risk management function, and the relevant business units and must enhance liquidity reporting and other communication across the firm. Coordination is especially important because of the way that liquidity risk management requires consideration of both assets and liabilities. One useful metric concerns the number of days a firm wishes to remain liquid: this can be translated into asset-liability matching to limit the amount of short-term funding to which the firm is exposed. Given the stresses to which a firm may be exposed, robust stress testing is also needed. This can prompt development of defensive measures such as risk-based pricing that takes account not only of credit quality but also liquidity risk, improved contractual provisions to take account of emergency situations, and setting of higher standards for acceptable collateral for repos and other short-term transactions. As the SSG itself notes, these promising practices continue to evolve as firms and supervisors understand more fully the lessons of the crisis.

Types of Risk

Risk management involves an array of types of risk that evolve with circumstances and innovations. Firms are paid to take some of these risks, such as credit risk and interest rate risk. These must be assessed and, when they exceed the firm's risk appetite, contained or hedged against. Other risks must be minimized. These include operational and reputational risks. Reputational risk must be addressed almost without regard to cost; otherwise, a firm's customers can lose confidence in the firm. Finally, some risks—and liquidity risk was paramount for many firms in the crisis—must be protected against. One company treasurer likened protection against liquidity risk as being similar to purchasing insurance; one judges the risk and pays to reduce it to prudent limits. The complexity of risk management is seen in studying both how successful firms implemented it and the costs those firms bore from risks that they misunderstood or imperfectly addressed.

There are many different types of risk and various commentators may categorize them differently. Thus, the discussion of mismatched duration of assets and liabilities is presented here as part of the discussion of market risk while others might characterize that as liquidity risk. New forms of risk—such as model risk—emerge as markets or ways of doing business change.[45] Consider five kinds of risk: liquidity risk, credit risk, interest rate risk, market risk, and operational risk. A critical factor in assessing these risks is risk velocity, or the speed at which a risk can materialize. As was seen in chapter 2, loss of liquidity (i.e., ready access to funding) can drive a firm out of business in very few days. By contrast, losses from credit risk tend to take longer to have an impact. It is risk velocity that explains why so many managers of failed firms testified that their gambles had not failed: Credit risk, which takes some time to materialize, had not yet caused substantial losses at the point when loss of liquidity drove their firms into insolvency.

1. LIQUIDITY RISK

Liquidity is the ability of a financial firm to fund its assets and meet obligations as they come due, without incurring unacceptable losses.[46] As market panic spread starting in August 2007, firms suddenly found that they could not raise the funding that they needed for ongoing operations. On the liability side, as obligations matured, firms found that they could not be rolled over to replace funds that investors withdrew. On the asset side, firms faced price dislocations that sometimes compelled sales at fire sale prices. When AIG sold approximately $25 billion of CDS protection to Goldman Sachs, the documents provided for collateral calls by Goldman in the event that the value of the underlying collateral, protected by the CDS, declined. It was the inability of AIG to meet increasing collateral calls (i.e., a liquidity problem) that caused the demise of AIG regardless whether paying on the CDS protection for credit losses in fact would have cost the company that much in the end.

Markets had become complacent about liquidity risk. This was an era where numerous firms showed an optimism that was not supportable once the market began to panic. The brief 1998 disruption caused by the Russia debt crisis prompted little change in firm behavior with respect to liquidity. The lesson has now been learned:

> The Credit Crisis demonstrated unequivocally that it is folly to assume that markets will always be available to provide required liquidity. Just as it would be highly imprudent to run a critical care medical facility without a backup electrical generator, it is imprudent bordering on malfeasant to run a financial institution in a manner dependent on the continuously available liquidity from the markets. Many investors, who grew complacent because market liquidity was assumed to always be available, learned this lesson the hard way.[47]

Liquidity risk is probably the most difficult risk to protect against, given the way that it depends on matching both the asset and liability sides of the balance sheet and on market reactions whose concatenations may be hard to predict. The terms of contractual provisions and also power relationships between firms suddenly may come into play in unexpected ways, such as when counterparties demand collateral. When counterparties began to fail, all firms, including JPMorgan Chase and Goldman Sachs, became vulnerable. At some point government support may be the only option once markets freeze up for any length of time.

2. CREDIT RISK

Credit risk is the risk of loss due to the inability of a counterparty such as a borrower to meet its obligations as they come due. Financial firms of all kinds failed to recognize the credit risk inherent in subprime and other nontraditional mortgages and the mortgage-related securities that derived from them. This relates to the extensive reliance by purchasers on untested risk models that contained overoptimistic assumptions about patterns of changes in home prices. Purchasers also relied extensively on AAA ratings assigned by the credit rating agencies to the top tranches of private-label mortgage securities and CDOs. Even assuming that firms were appropriately prudent in accepting a rating without conducting independent due diligence, excessive dependence on ratings violated well known principles of risk management:

> Even if large financial firms were convinced of the rating's accuracy, it does not explain a decision to have excessive concentrations of mortgage related assets in a portfolio. [A] central tenet of modern financial risk management is the need to analyze portfolio risk and to guard against the unexpected. Just as we would not expect a large sophisticated firm to have all of its securities investments in AAA rated firms within a small group of firms or within a specific industry, we would not expect such a firm to be so concentrated in a sector that a severe tail event in that sector threatens the solvency of the firm.[48]

Some firms also took unexpected losses from counterparty risk. Countrywide was by far Fannie Mae's largest customer. Because Countrywide was Fannie Mae's largest provider of home mortgages, Fannie Mae charged Countrywide lower fees than it charged other originators. Yet witnesses told the FCIC that loans purchased from Countrywide generated a disproportionate amount of seriously delinquent loans. After going into government hands, Fannie Mae applied the recourse provisions of its mortgage purchase contracts to put mortgages back to Bank of America, which acquired Countrywide, to the extent that those mortgages violated representations and warrants.

This highlights a major counterparty problem that the financial crisis revealed: Firms that bought mortgages that turned out to be fraudulent or otherwise in violation of representations and warrants have recourse only against firms that have not gone out of business. Major subprime mortgage originators such as Ameriquest and New Century, for example, went bankrupt, leaving mortgage purchasers without recourse; other firms such as Lehman went out of business as well, thereby leaving their creditors with claims that often take time to resolve and that may not be settled at near their original value.

3. INTEREST RATE RISK

Interest rate risk played a major role in the savings and loan debacle of the 1980s. By contrast to that crisis, which was triggered by a massive asset-liability mismatch in the thrift industry, the generally low level of interest rates in the 2000s created an unusual form of risk. Because returns on many investments were so low, firms had especially strong incentives to go for yield—to invest in more risky assets in order to enhance returns. This would explain the popularity of subprime mortgages and subprime securities, for example, in contrast to traditional prime mortgages of greater credit quality but also less yield for the investor.

As often happens, one form of risk could translate into another. Homeowners who took out variable-rate mortgages, and especially mortgages with teaser rates that kept payments low for the first two or three years of a mortgage, faced the prospect (which did not materialize to the full extent expected) that they could not repay their mortgages once they reset to a higher rate. In that way interest rate risk would transform into credit risk.

4. MARKET RISK

Market risk is the risk of loss due to changes in market prices. Market risk can be especially harmful for firms with serious mismatches in the terms of their assets and liabilities. Disruption in the market in 2007–2008 had significant effects, among other reasons, because of the frequent tendency of financial firms to fund long-term assets with short-term liabilities. An extreme example of this practice occurred in the asset-backed commercial paper (ABCP) market. ABCP is commercial paper with a maturity of 270 days or less. Yet ABCP conduits purchased mortgage-related securities with potential maturities of many years' duration. That permitted a run on ABCP as investors stopped rolling over their investments. This occurred in July 2007 as investors became concerned about the credit quality of investments backing ABCP of a German bank IKB. The bank did not support its ABCP conduit and a public-private bailout was arranged. The ABCP market immediately came under stress as investors withdrew from other ABCP investments in early August. Billions of dollars fled the ABCP market and especially from mortgage ABCP programs with assets from just one issuer (single-seller programs).

Another example of maturity mismatch occurred in the auction-rate securities market which allowed state and local governments to lower their borrowing costs by borrowing long-term at variable rates that reset at regular intervals, usually less than a month. When the financial markets came under stress, panic spread to the auction-rate securities market. As investment banks came under financial pressure, they stopped bidding to provide funds to allow state and local governments to roll over their debt. That meant that the auction failed, and this triggered clauses in the borrowing agreements so that interest rates for states and localities jumped substantially.

The practice of lending long and borrowing short that had been paying off for many years suddenly threatened the viability of firms and even some local governments when the markets became turbulent.

5. OPERATIONAL RISK

Operational risk is the risk that a firm's processes and systems do not work as intended. For a mortgage originator or secondary mortgage market firm, operational risk may include the failure of automated underwriting systems to screen mortgages appropriately and price them according to risk.

Dan Sparks, former head of the mortgage desk at Goldman Sachs, told Commission staff that Goldman had tried to grow its mortgage business by acquiring a mortgage originator. In addition to price, operational risk was a significant factor in the decision not to acquire a firm. One criterion was whether there could be integration of systems of the acquired firm to Goldman's integrated systems. "Some wouldn't fit," Sparks said. "You've got to run that company too." He added that he saw managing a mortgage originator, an operational business, as quite different from Goldman's trading business.[49]

Model risk is one part of operational risk:

> Financial firms' overreliance and overconfidence on untested risk models led to an underestimation of risk . . . Market participants greatly underestimated the potential downside risk in the mortgage market . . . This overreliance on statistical analysis led firms to ignore more qualitative judgments on the nature of the housing boom, irrational exuberance, and the increasing problems associated with moral hazard and adverse selection. . . .
>
> Most firms relied on a relatively short history of data that did not contain periods of severe economic stress. Modelers typically had to choose between building models covering longer time periods but with fewer data elements and lower data quality versus building models with more data elements of higher quality covering a shorter time period.

Typically, firms chose to use more sophisticated models with higher quality data covering a shorter time period.[50]

Another aspect of operational risk concerns the distorted incentives that a firm may create for its traders. This includes incentives to game the risk models that firms use. The following example concerns the ubiquitous VaR, or value-at-risk models:

> [Former JPMorgan banker Til] Guldimann, the great VaR proselytizer, sounded almost mournful when he talked about what he saw as another of VaR's shortcomings. To him, the big problem was that it turned out that VaR could be gamed. That is what happened when banks began reporting their VaRs. To motivate managers, the banks began to compensate them not just for making big profits but also for making profits with low risks. That sounds good in principle, but managers began to manipulate the VaR by loading up on what Guldimann calls "asymmetric risk positions." These are products or contracts that, in general, generate small gains and very rarely have losses. But when they do have losses, they are huge. These positions made a manager's VaR look good because VaR ignored the slim likelihood of giant losses, which could only come about in the event of a true catastrophe. A good example was a credit-default swap, which is essentially insurance that a company won't default. The gains made from selling credit-default swaps are small and steady—and the chance of ever having to pay off that insurance was assumed to be minuscule. It was outside the 99 percent probability, so it didn't show up in the VaR number. People didn't see the size of those hidden positions lurking in that 1 percent that VaR didn't measure.[51]

Ineffective risk management systems are another form of operational risk. This is especially a problem if top management believes that a risk management system offers more protection than it actually does. Even as one part of Citigroup was tightening criteria for mortgages that it would purchase for securitization, another part of the firm continued to expand CDO operations. Similarly, at AIG, one part of the company was reducing its exposure to the subprime market while other parts continued to increase their exposure.[52] An effective enterprise-wide risk management system could have helped firms to avoid such results or at least reduce their exposure.

Legal risk is a part of operational risk. When Goldman Sachs inserted well drafted provisions into its contracts to purchase CDS protection from AIG, it protected itself against legal risk; senior officials of AIG, by contrast, including the CEO, CFO, and chief risk officer, did not understand until mid-2007 at the earliest that the company had sold billions of dollars of CDSs that contained covenants pledging to provide collateral to CDS purchasers in the event that the there was a decline in market value of the CDSs. As AIG's chief risk officer told FCIC staff, there was considerable consternation at the company when management became aware of the covenants at the time that Goldman, which had purchased many CDSs, made its first collateral call on AIG in July 2007.[53]

AIG's failure is an important illustration of the need to perceive risk in detail and then draw important inferences. The covenants allowing CDS purchasers to make collateral calls were linked not only to deterioration of performance of the securities covered by the CDS, but also to market prices of the securities. This transformed credit risk on the securities into liquidity risk; that was fatal for AIG because of the lack of information at the AIG holding company level about the firm's enterprise-wide liquidity needs and the company's failure to prepare a liquidity position to be able to meet the calls. Liquidity risk materializes suddenly compared to credit risk; the company's failure to understand the nature of covenants that AIG Financial Products wrote meant that AIG lost the time that it thought it had to meet any deterioration in credit quality of the securities on which it wrote CDSs.

6. REPUTATIONAL RISK

This is the risk of erosion of a firm's reputation because of its actions or the perception of its actions. Technological and media developments have made reputational risk of more consequence to firms than ever before.[54] Wall Street firms that enjoyed substantial profits before failing and becoming the recipients of government funds are especially vulnerable to reputational risk, for example.

Reputational risk has other consequences as well. Perhaps most importantly, firms found themselves under pressure to satisfy the needs of customers and other counterparties even without a legal requirement to do so, for fear that failure to deal responsibly with these counterparties would cause a loss of market confidence that could be more costly than the losses incurred by making counterparties whole. As the market began to experience disruption, pressure grew on firms to protect their reputations to try to reassure counterparties so that they would not panic and flee from doing business with them.

A classic example of the effects of reputational risk occurred when Citigroup felt obligated to stand behind its off-balance sheet structured investment vehicles (SIVs) so as to preserve its reputation. This also occurred with a number of other firms including Bear Stearns and Goldman Sachs, which felt themselves compelled to bail out their asset management funds despite having no legal obligation to do so. In the case of Bear's multibillion dollar bailout of investors in one of its hedge funds, one analysis (without mentioning Bear by name) recounts the pressure on the firm:

> First, the action may have avoided a precipitous liquidation of the assets by the other creditors that could have adversely impacted the already stressed CDO market. Second, the other creditors may have used "moral suasion" insomuch as they had relied, in part, on the securities firm's name

and reputation in lending to the hedge funds it managed. Finally, the firm may have calculated that the further harm to its reputation resulting from its simply walking away could have ultimately been more harmful than the potential losses that may arise from taking over the financing. However, it should be pointed out that the second fund was, in fact, allowed to fail without the firm providing relief to the secured creditors.[55]

A Wall Street analyst observed about the Bear fund that "if they walked away from it, investors would have lost all their money and lenders would have lost all of the money, [but] if they did that to everyone in the financial community, the financial community would have shut them down."[56]

Over the long term reputational risk can mean as much to a firm as do the more traditional kinds of risk. One analyst traces the growth of reputational risk as reflecting the change in investment banking from being a relationship-based business with clients, as it was when investment banks were partnerships, to being a transaction-based business.[57]

Differences in Risk Management Between Firms that Weathered the Crisis and those that Failed:

- Risk Management is a subset of effective management more generally. A strong information infrastructure is needed both to manage the company and to obtain an enterprise-wide view of risks.
- Risk management can become a formality rather than an effective process. This was seen in UBS, which in 2006 published an extensive description of its risk management system and processes but in 2008 published a letter to shareholders in which it described extensive failings of that same risk management system.
- It is not easy to be a risk officer at a firm that decides to disregard risks; a risk officer must be ready to tell the truth to those in power at the firm and be ready to be fired as a consequence. Interpersonal skills can be essential for a CRO.
- As markets, processes, and products become more complex, simple questions remain critical to making good judgments. For example, if the market reveals anomalies, companies must ask: What is going on here that we don't understand?
- Pricing models at many firms signaled that the market had become overheated. Reactions at the surviving firms included intensive conversations about the implications. Reactions at failed firms included disregarding the information, impugning the judgment of the credit officer who produced the information, or removing the risk officer.
- Model risk was a significant issue at many firms. Surviving firms used an array of models as tools to inform judgment but did not rely blindly on them. Surviving firms also did not rely blindly on rating agency ratings, but did their own due diligence.

- Liquidity risk is the ultimate risk that brings financial firms down; no one wants to lend them money. In an age of large-scale use of overnight funding, repos, and complex derivatives, it is not clear that most firms have the capacity to manage liquidity risk, especially at a time of market panic such as occurred in August 2007 and September 2008. Here again, successful firms showed their sophistication and strength vis-à-vis those that failed.
- Reputational risk proved vexing and costly for firms such as Goldman Sachs. Management of reputational risk calls for processes that are different from other risk management systems. Here, cultural values can be of special importance in dissuading managers from doing deals that may be legal but do not appear to be fair or legitimate to stakeholders outside the firm.

6 }

Company Organization, Business Models, and the Crisis

I would advocate moving the GSEs out of No Man's Land. Events have shown how difficult it is to balance financial, capital, market, housing, shareholder, bondholder, homeowner, private, and public interests in a crisis of these proportions. We should examine whether the economy and the markets are better served by fully private or fully public GSEs.

—DANIEL MUDD, 2008

Organization played a major role in the financial crisis. A firm's organization defines the rules by which it must operate. Managers either work within those rules to create favorable circumstances or change their organizational status. Changes in organizational form occurred before the crisis, for example, when Wall Street firms converted from partnerships into investor-owned companies, and during the crisis when Goldman Sachs and Morgan Stanley converted into bank holding companies backed and supervised by the Federal Reserve.

This chapter considers first the formal structure of various types of financial firm and then implications for the business models that these firms adopted before the crisis. Among the most important business models were portfolio lending, popularly known as the *storage business*, and transaction-based finance, popularly known as the *moving business*.

From an organizational perspective, competition among financial firms takes place on anything but a level playing field. Three major factors are (1) a firm's size and complexity, (2) the charter or other legal framework under which it operates, and (3) whether it is a partnership or investor-owned.

Size and Complexity: Consolidation, Vertical Integration, and Conglomeration

The industrial organization of the mortgage industry changed significantly in the years before the crisis. Starting in the 1990s a combination of technology and changes in the law helped to drive substantial consolidation in the mortgage industry and among financial firms generally. Technology developments increased the economies of scale of servicing loans and large servicers such as Countrywide grew to service over a trillion dollars of mortgages. On the loan origination side, technology meant that a mortgage broker or loan officer with a laptop could travel to customers, input loan application information, and quickly obtain an "accept" or "refer" decision from a lender's central database. In the case of an accept, the acceptance was conditional on verification of loan documents; a refer—which for purposes of fair lending laws was not a denial of mortgage credit—meant that the loan application would receive added scrutiny before it might be accepted.

For Fannie Mae and Freddie Mac, the advent of technology in the mid-1990s was an opportunity to increase the value added, and commensurate profits, that the GSEs would receive compared to primary lenders that sold mortgages to them. The shift in underwriting function from automated underwriting systems that the GSEs adopted is seen in figure 6.1.

Technology also was a driving force for securitization and increasingly complex types of securitization. As computing power increased, it was possible to build technology platforms that could monitor the complicated cashflows for a Collateralized Debt Obligation (CDO), for example, from monthly payments of mortgage borrowers ("mortgagors," in industry parlance) to mortgage backed-securities, to the particular tranches of the MBS, and then to the holders of particular tranches of the CDO. (See figure 2.5, in chapter 2.) It is not clear that a derivative security such as a CDO would have been technically possible in the 1990s, merely from the standpoint of ensuring that payments all went promptly to the right place.

Legal changes also came into play. The Riegle-Neal Interstate Banking and Branching Efficiency Act of 1994 resulted in consolidation of the banking industry by eliminating geographic restrictions that previously had helped to keep many banking organizations operating only within individual states. When combined with the growing advantages and scale economies associated with new technologies, the result was significant consolidation of financial services firms, including those serving the mortgage sector. Mortgage originators grew in size, as did the market share of the largest companies. In 1995 the top twenty-five originators had a market share of 39 percent; by 2007 this grew to 90 percent of a market that had almost quadrupled in size.

One other change occurred in industry structure. This was the effort by firms at both ends of the mortgage market to integrate vertically, so that they

THE EFFECT OF AUTOMATED UNDERWRITING ON THE
ENTERPRISES' ROLE IN THE LOAN ORIGINATION PROCESS

Traditional Role of the Enterprises in Underwriting a Loan

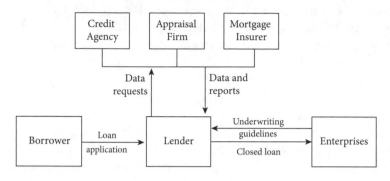

Alternative Enterprise Role Using Automated Underwriting

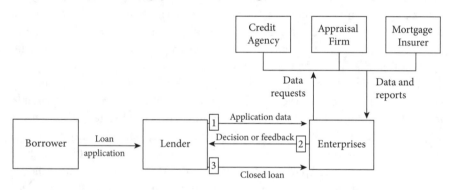

SOURCE: Office of Federal Housing Enterprise Oversight, *1995 Report to Congress* (Washington, D.C.: Government Printing Office, 1995), fig. 1, p. 4.
NOTE: Lender has the option to do business directly with appraisal firms and mortgage insurers.

FIGURE 6.1 **Effect of Automated Underwriting o0n the Mortgage Origination Process**

served the entire range of functions. Thus, Countrywide created a fast-growing firm, Countrywide Securities Corporation, which securitized some $72 billion in subprime and other nonprime loans in 2004. By 2005, Wall Street investment banking firms—Bear Stearns, Lehman Brothers, and Merrill Lynch, among others—established or acquired major mortgage originators. As the mortgage market grew and home prices appreciated, major firms sought to capture an increasing share of the value.

Countrywide Financial Corporation (CFC) probably benefited most from consolidation and vertical integration. By 2007 the company had total assets of $212 billion and a total mortgage servicing portfolio of $1.48 trillion. It was the largest mortgage originator in the United States from 2004 through 2007 and ranked third in subprime origination in those years. Countrywide had the largest market share of mortgage servicing in 2004, 2005, and 2007.

Countrywide operated five business segments: Mortgage Banking, which originated, purchased, securitized and serviced mortgages; Capital Markets, which operated as an institutional broker-dealer that specialized in trading and underwriting of mortgage backed securities (MBS); Insurance, which offered property, casualty, life, and credit as both an underwriter and independent agent; Banking, which operated an insured depository institution, Country-wide Bank, N.A., and later Countrywide FSB (reflecting Countrywide's shift from a bank holding company to a thrift holding company, discussed in chapter 7), originating mortgage loans through CFC's mortgage banking operations; and Global Operations, which performed both corporate administrative functions and loan servicing.

The combination of increased capacity and relaxed statutory restrictions such as the Gramm-Leach-Bliley Act of 1999, that ended the restrictions imposed during the New Deal by the Glass-Steagall Act, helped to encourage the growth of large complex financial institutions (LCFIs). Using Bank of England criteria for determining whether an institution was a large complex financial institution (LCFI), Herring and Carmassi found that by year-end 2007 each of the LCFIs had at least several hundred subsidiaries, eight had over a thousand, and Citigroup had almost 2,500 subsidiaries. While these figures are instructive, they must be used with caution; many subsidiaries were small, with neither significant revenues nor significant risks in their activities.

As table 6.1 shows, LCFIs included major subsidiaries engaged in providing a multitude of financial services.[1]

Large Complex Financial Institutions and the Financial Crisis

Major firms that failed were of all organizational types, including two government-sponsored enterprises, Fannie Mae and Freddie Mac, two investment banks, Bear and Lehman, two commercial bank holding companies, Citigroup and UBS, one insurance company, AIG, and two thrift holding companies, Countrywide and WaMu. This suggests that perhaps the major organizational issue for the financial sector is the tendency of major US financial firms to increase in size and complexity. Herbert Allison argues that, "in acquiescing to the calls for diversification and synergy, the megabanks' boards tolerated accumulation of vast assortments of businesses across the globe that directors and executives were hard-pressed to understand, let alone manage."[2]

From 2000 to 2006, the largest financial firms more than doubled their size, as can be seen from figure 6.2, from the Bank of England.

TABLE 6.1 Breakdown by Industry of Subsidiaries of Large Complex Financial Institutions (Year-End 2007)

LCFIs	Banks	Insurance Companies	Mutual & pension funds nominees trusts / trustees	Other financial subsidiaries[1]	Nonfinancial subsidiaries[2]
ABN AMRO Holding NV*	50	7	129	204	280
Bank of America Corporation	30	24	396	282	673
Barclays Plc	49	21	309	239	385
BNP Paribas	88	74	102	433	473
Citi	101	35	706	581	1009
Credit Suisse Group	31	4	91	63	101
Deutsche Bank AG	54	9	458	526	907
Goldman Sacha Group, Inc	7	4	48	151	161
HSBC Holdings plc	85	30	245	381	435
JPMorgan Chase & co	38	17	229	145	375
Lehman Brothers Holdings Inc.	9	3	84	210	127
Merrill Lynch & Co., Inc.	16	9	85	89	68
Morgan Stanley	19	22	225	170	616
The Royal Bank of Scotland Group Plc	31	29	188	450	433
Societe Generale	81	13	93	270	387
UBS AG	29	2	121	66	199
TOTAL BY INDUSTRY	720	310	3490	4263	6729
% by industry	5%	2%	22%	27%	43%

Source: Bankscope Majority-owned subsidiaries. For methodology see footnote for figure 1.

* See footnote for figure 1.

1 "Other financial subsidiaries" include private equity subsidiaries.

2 "Nonfinancial subsidiaries" include all companies that are neither banks nor insurance companies nor financial companies. They can be involved in manufacturing activities but also in trading activities (wholesalers, retailers, brokers, etc). We have allocated foundations and research institutes to this category as well.

Source: Herring, Richard and Jacopo Carmassi, "The Corporate Structure of International Financial Conglomerates: Complexity and its Implications for Safety and Soundness," chapter 8 in Berger, Allen N., Phillip Molyneux and John O.S. Wilson, eds, *The Oxford Handbook of Banking*, Oxford: Oxford University Press, 2010, figure 8.2.

Financial services firms also became more complex. Table 6.2 below shows the size, number of subsidiaries, and other elements of the sixteen large complex financial institutions they survey based on criteria from the Bank of England.[3] Large complex firms often are seen as "too big to fail." This perception allows them to borrow money more cheaply than their smaller competitors. Investors in the debt of large financial institutions gain comfort from the belief that government is likely to protect them in case of a crisis. They then are

LCFIs' total assets

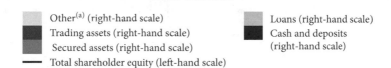

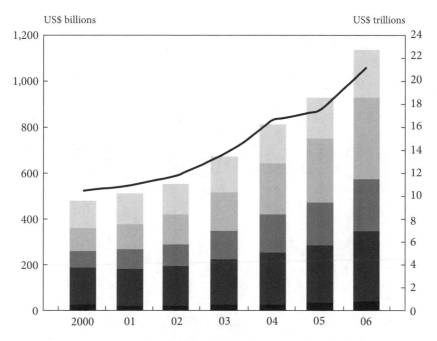

Sources: Bloomberg, SEC fillings, published accounts and Bank calculations

(a) Other includes (among other items) receivables, investments, goodwill and property

FIGURE 6.2 **Loan Assets of Large Complex Financial Institutions (LCFIs)**

willing to accept lower returns on their investments in debt obligations of those favored firms. Lower borrowing costs then factor into scale economies that permit large complex firms to dominate key functions such as securitization.

Virtually all of these firms had dozens of subsidiaries in foreign countries and earned a large fraction of their revenues from international operations. This list could be supplemented by addition of other names, such as the American International Group (AIG) that, until its failure, comprised at least 223 companies had operations in 130 countries, and 116,000 employees.[4] While the individual boxes are too small to read, figure 6.3 shows the complexity of the AIG structure, which is small compared to a Citi or Morgan or any of the others listed below in table 6.2.[5]

Failure of many large complex firms in the financial crisis, including Bear Stearns, Lehman, Citigroup, AIG, WaMu, and Fannie Mae and Freddie Mac, suggests that most firms that are too big to fail may also be too big to manage.

TABLE 6.2 Overview of Large Complex Financial Institutions*

1	2	3	4	5	6	7	8	9
LCFIs	Total assets (billions of $, year-end 2006)[1]	Total subsidiaries[1]	% of foreign subsidiaries	% of foreign net income before taxes(2006)[2]	HHI—business lines revenues (2006)[3]	Number of countries[4]	Subsidiaries in OFCs, number[5]	Subsidiaries in OFCs, %[5]
UBS AG	1,964	417	96%	62%	2,903	41	38	9%
Barclays Plc	1,957	1,003	43%	44%	2,179	73	145	14%
BNP Paribas	1,897	1,170	61%	51%	1,843	58	62	5%
Citi	1,884	2,435	50%	44%	4,122	84	309	13%
HSBC Holdings Plc	1,861	1,234	61%	78%	3,945	47	161	13%
The Royal Bank of Scotland Group Plc	1,711	1,161	11%	34%	1,966	16	73	6%
Deutsche Bank AG	1,483	1,954	77%	80%	3,931	56	391	20%
Bank of America Corporation	1,460	1,407	28%	12%	4,256	29	118	8%
JPMorgan Chase & Co.	1,352	804	51%	26%	2,086	36	54	7%
ABN AMRO Holding NV**	1,300	670	63%	77%	1,381	43	37	6%
Société Générale	1,260	844	56%	46%	4,128	60	64	8%
Morgan Stanley	1,121	1,052	47%	42%	4,476	46	203	19%
Credit Suisse Group	1,029	290	93%	71%	3,868	31	53	18%
Merrill Lynch & Co., Inc.	841	267	64%	35%	4,089	25	23	9%
Goldman Sachs Group, Inc.	838	371	51%	48%	5,391	21	29	8%
Lehman Brothers Holdings Inc.	504	433	45%	37%	7,807	20	41	9%

* Year-end 2007 (unless otherwise specified).

** After the most recent list of LCFIs (Bank of England 2007b) was published, a consortium of three banks (RBS, Forits and Santander) acquired ABN AMRO.

1 Sorce: Bankscope. Data on subsidiaries refer to majority-owned subsidiaries for which the LFCI is the ultimate owner with a minimum control path of 50.01%.

2. Source: Annual reports for each LCFI Net income before taxes with five exceptions: net income after taxes for Citi and net revenues for Barclays plc, BNP Paribas, Lehman Brothers Holdings Inc., Merrill Lynch & Co Inc.,

3 Source: Oliver Wyman. The Herfindahl-Hirschman Index ranges from 0 to 10,000 and it is calculated on the percentage of revenues per business line. Higher values indicate a higher degree of specialization. Lower values imply a higher degree of diversification.

4 Number of countries in which the LCFI has at least one majority-owned subsidiary.

5 Offshore Financial Centers identified by the Financial Stability Forum (2000). We exclude Swiss Subsidiaries for Credit Suisse and UBS and Hong Kong subsidiaries for HSBC Four subsidiaries were allocated to OFCs on the basis of locations designated in their names even though Bankscope did not specify a home country.

Source: Herring, Richard and Jacopo Carmassi, "The Corporate Structure of International Financial Conglomerates: Complexity and its Implications for Safety and Soundness," chapter 8 in Berger, Allen N., Phillip Molyneux and John O.S. Wilson, eds, *The Oxford Handbook of Banking*, Oxford: Oxford University Press, 2010, figure 8.1.

In the years before the financial crisis, large complex financial institutions such as WaMu, Citigroup and AIG had grown into collections of separate organizations located around the globe that performed a huge variety of functions. They were hard to manage, especially since they had grown rapidly through acquisitions that displayed differing cultures and practices. Only a few firms, and JPMorgan Chase stands out here, troubled themselves to force all of their activities into a common operating platform. Firms also failed to create common cultures across their sprawling empires; Citigroup CEO Charles Prince used to joke that Citigroup had not one good culture, but rather five or six good cultures. JPMorgan, Goldman Sachs, and Wells Fargo provide good counterexamples.

The Legal Charter

Sometimes the government charters a firm for special purposes. This is a major difference between federally insured depository institutions and GSEs on the one hand, and investment banks and the so-called shadow banking system of mortgage companies and securitization conduits on the other. An investment bank or mortgage company simply files articles of incorporation in a state of its choice. By contrast, when government charters a bank or thrift or GSE, it transforms into a governmental decision business matters that, in ordinary businesses, are the province of the market place. The government charter and associated legal framework determine a broad range of issues:

- Entry to the market: Unlike the ordinary corporation that can simply file articles of incorporation and enter the market, a chartered institution must receive permission to enter the market. Thus, the Office of the Comptroller of the Currency (OCC) charters national banks, the Office of Thrift Supervision (merged into the OCC by the Dodd-Frank Act) chartered federal thrift institutions, the Fed approves charters of bank holding companies and, after enactment of Dodd-Frank, thrift holding companies, and state regulators charter state banks, thrifts, and insurance companies. The most selectively issued charters are those granted directly by the Congress, as in the case of Fannie Mae and Freddie Mac. These charters are especially valuable because the Congress is unlikely to grant a similar charter to anyone else, even if they might be valuable additions to the secondary mortgage market. That serves as a significant barrier to entry from potential competitors.
- Exit from the market: Under the bankruptcy laws creditors may force exit of a firm from the market if it defaults on its obligations. In the case of banks, thrifts, and GSEs, a government regulator must close them down through a receivership. Sometimes, as in the case of Fannie Mae

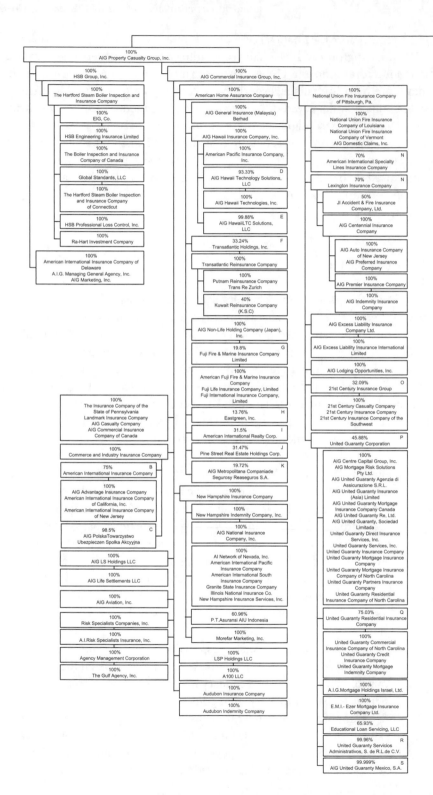

FIGURE 6.3 **AIG: A Large Complex Financial Institution, Organization as of December 31, 2008**

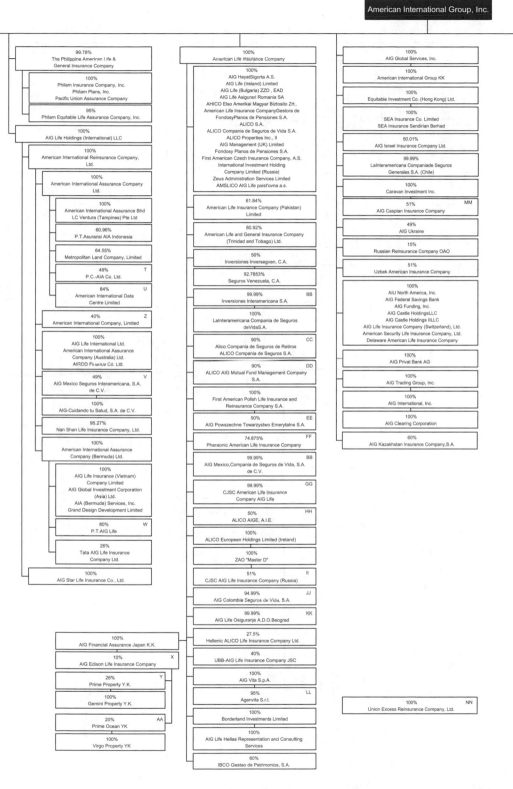

American International Group, Inc.

99.78%
The Philippine American Life & General Insurance Company

100%
Philam Insurance Company, Inc.
Philam Plans, Inc.
Pacific Union Assurance Company

95%
Philam Equitable Life Assurance Company, Inc.

100%
AIG Life Holdings (International) LLC

100%
American International Reinsurance Company, Ltd.

100%
American International Assurance Company Ltd.

100%
American International Assurance Bhd
LC Ventura (Tampines) Pte Ltd

60.96%
P.T.Asuransi AIA Indonesia

64.55%
Metropolitan Land Company, Limited

49% T
P.C.-AIA Co. Ltd.

84% U
American International Data Centre Limited

40% Z
American International Company, Limited

100%
AIG Life International Ltd.
American International Assurance Company (Australia) Ltd.
AIRCO Finance Co. Ltd.

49% V
AIG Mexico Seguros Interamericana, S.A. de C.V.

100%
AIG-Cuidando tu Salud, S.A. de C.V.

95.27%
Nan Shan Life Insurance Company, Ltd.

100%
American International Assurance Company (Bermuda) Ltd.

100%
AIG Life Insurance (Vietnam) Company Limited
AIG Global Investment Corporation (Asia) Ltd.
AIA (Bermuda) Services, Inc.
Grand Design Development Limited

80% W
P.T.AIG Life

26%
Tata AIG Life Insurance Company Ltd.

100%
AIG Star Life Insurance Co., Ltd.

100%
AIG Financial Assurance Japan K.K.

10% X
AIG Edison Life Insurance Company

26% Y
Prime Property Y.K.

100%
Gemini Property Y.K.

20% AA
Prime Ocean YK

100%
Virgo Property YK

100%
American Life Insurance Company

100%
AIG HayatSigorta A.S.
AIG Life (Ireland) Limited
AIG Life (Bulgaria) ZZD , EAD
AIG Life Asigurari Romania SA
AHICO Elso Amerikai Magyar Biztosito Zrt..
American Life Insurance CompanyGestora de FondosyPlanos de Pensiones S.A.
ALICO S.A.
ALICO Compania de Seguros de Vida S.A.
ALICO Properties Inc., II
AIG Management (UK) Limited
Fondosy Planos de Pensiones S.A.
First American Czech Insurance Company, A.S.
International Investment Holding Company Limited (Russia)
Zeus Administration Services Limited
AMSLICO AIG Life poist'ovna a.s.

61.84%
American Life Insurance Company (Pakistan) Limited

80.92%
American Life and General Insurance Company (Trinidad and Tobago) Ltd.

50%
Inversiones Inversegven, C.A.

92.7853%
Seguros Venezuela, C.A.

99.99% BB
Inversiones Interamericana S.A.

100%
LaInteramericana Compania de Seguros deVidaS.A.

90% CC
Alico Compania de Seguros de Retiros
ALICO Compania de Seguros S.A.

90% DD
ALICO AIG Mutual Fund Management Company S.A.

100%
First American Polish Life Insurance and Reinsurance Company S.A.

50% EE
AIG Powszechne Towarzystwo Emerytalne S.A.

74.875% FF
Pharaonic American Life Insurance Company

99.99% BB
AIG Mexico,Compania de Seguros de Vida, S.A. de C.V.

99.99% GG
CJSC American Life Insurance Company AIG Life

50% HH
ALICO AIGE, A.I.E.

100%
ALICO European Holdings Limited (Ireland)

100%
ZAO "Master D"

51% II
CJSC AIG Life Insurance Company (Russia)

94.99% JJ
AIG Colombia Seguros de Vida, S.A.

99.99% KK
AIG Life Osiguranje A.D.O.Beograd

27.5%
Hellenic ALICO Life Insurance Company Ltd.

40%
UBB-AIG Life Insurance Company JSC

100%
AIG Vita S.p.A.

95% LL
Agenvita S.r.l.

100%
Borderland Investments Limited

100%
AIG Life Hellas Representation and Consulting Services

60%
IBCO Gestao de Patrimonios, S.A.

100%
AIG Global Services, Inc.

100%
American International Group KK

100%
Equitable Investment Co. (Hong Kong) Ltd.

100%
SEA Insurance Co. Limited
SEA Insurance Sendirian Berhad

50.01%
AIG Israel Insurance Company Ltd.

99.99%
LaInteramericana Companiade Seguros Generales S.A. (Chile)

100%
Caravan Investment Inc.

51% MM
AIG Caspian Insurance Company

49%
AIG Ukraine

15%
Russian Reinsurance Company OAO

51%
Uzbek American Insurance Company

100%
AIU North America, Inc.
AIG Federal Savings Bank
AIG Funding, Inc.
AIG Castle HoldingsLLC
AIG Castle Holdings IILLC
AIG Life Insurance Company (Switzerland), Ltd.
American Security Life Insurance Company, Ltd.
Delaware American Life Insurance Company

100%
AIG Privat Bank AG

100%
AIG Trading Group, Inc.

100%
AIG International, Inc.

100%
AIG Clearing Corporation

60%
AIG Kazakhstan Insurance Company,S.A.

100% NN
Union Excess Reinsurance Company, Ltd.

(*Continued*)

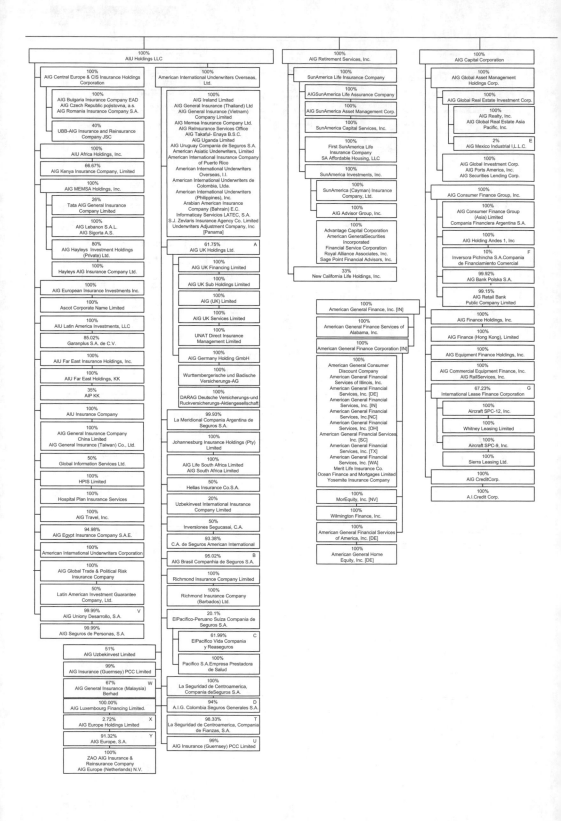

100% AIU Holdings LLC

- **100% AIG Central Europe & CIS Insurance Holdings Corporation**
  - 100% AIG Bulgaria Insurance Company EAD / AIG Czech Republic pojistovna, a.s. / AIG Romania Insurance Company S.A.
  - 40% UBB-AIG Insurance and Reinsurance Company JSC
- 100% AIU Africa Holdings, Inc.
- 66.67% AIG Kenya Insurance Company, Limited
- 100% AIG MEMSA Holdings, Inc.
  - 26% Tata AIG General Insurance Company Limited
  - 100% AIG Lebanon S.A.L. / AIG Sigorta A.S.
  - 80% AIG Hayleys Investment Holdings (Private) Ltd.
  - 100% Hayleys AIG Insurance Company Ltd.
- 100% AIG European Insurance Investments Inc.
- 100% Ascot Corporate Name Limited
- 100% AIU Latin America Investments, LLC
- 85.02% Garanplus S.A. de C.V.
- 100% AIU Far East Insurance Holdings, Inc.
- 100% AIU Far East Holdings, KK
- 35% AIP KK
- 100% AIU Insurance Company
- 100% AIG General Insurance Company China Limited / AIG General Insurance (Taiwan) Co., Ltd.
- 50% Global Information Services Ltd.
- 100% HPIS Limited
- 100% Hospital Plan Insurance Services
- 100% AIG Travel, Inc.
- 94.98% AIG Egypt Insurance Company S.A.E.
- 100% American International Underwriters Corporation
- 100% AIG Global Trade & Political Risk Insurance Company
- 50% Latin American Investment Guarantee Company, Ltd.
- 99.99% AIG Uniony Desarrollo, S.A. [V]
- 99.99% AIG Seguros de Personas, S.A.

- 51% AIG Uzbekinvest Limited
- 99% AIG Insurance (Guernsey) PCC Limited
- 67% AIG General Insurance (Malaysia) Berhad [W]
- 100.00% AIG Luxembourg Financing Limited.
- 2.72% AIG Europe Holdings Limited [X]
- 91.32% AIG Europe, S.A. [Y]
- 100% ZAO AIG Insurance & Reinsurance Company / AIG Europe (Netherlands) N.V.

- **100% American International Underwriters Overseas, Ltd.**
  - 100% AIG Ireland Limited / AIG General Insurance (Thailand) Ltd / AIG General Insurance (Vietnam) Company Limited / AIG Memsa Insurance Company Ltd. / AIG ReInsurance Services Office / AIG Takaful- Enaya B.S.C. / AIG Uganda Limited / AIG Uruguay Compania de Seguros S.A. / American Asiatic Underwriters, Limited / American International Insurance Company of Puerto Rico / American International Underwriters Overseas, I.I. / American International Underwriters de Colombia, Ltda. / American International Underwriters (Philippines), Inc. / Arabian American Insurance Company (Bahrain) E.C. / Informaticay Servicios LATEC, S.A. / S.J. Zevlaris Insurance Agency Co. Limited / Underwriters Adjustment Company, Inc [Panama]
  - 61.75% AIG UK Holdings Ltd. [A]
    - 100% AIG UK Financing Limited
    - 100% AIG UK Sub Holdings Limited
    - 100% AIG (UK) Limited
    - 100% AIG UK Services Limited
    - 100% UNAT Direct Insurance Management Limited
  - 100% AIG Germany Holding GmbH
    - 100% Wurttembergische und Badische Versicherungs-AG
    - 100% DARAG Deutsche Versicherungs-und Ruckversicherungs-Aktiengesellschaft
  - 99.93% La Meridional Compania Argentina de Seguros S.A.
  - 100% Johannesburg Insurance Holdings (Pty) Limited
  - 100% AIG Life South Africa Limited / AIG South Africa Limited
  - 50% Hellas Insurance Co.S.A.
  - 20% Uzbekinvest International Insurance Company Limited
  - 50% Inversiones Segucasai, C.A.
  - 93.38% C.A. de Seguros American International
  - 95.02% AIG Brasil Companhia de Seguros S.A. [B]
  - 100% Richmond Insurance Company Limited
  - 100% Richmond Insurance Company (Barbados) Ltd.
  - 20.1% ElPacifico-Peruano Suiza Compania de Seguros S.A.
    - 61.99% ElPacifico Vida Compania y Reaseguros [C]
    - 100% Pacifico S.A.Empresa Prestadora de Salud
  - 100% La Seguridad de Centroamerica, Compania deSeguros S.A.
  - 94% A.I.G. Colombia Seguros Generales S.A. [D]
  - 98.33% La Seguridad de Centroamerica, Compania de Fianzas, S.A. [T]
  - 99% AIG Insurance (Guernsey) PCC Limited [U]

100% AIG Retirement Services, Inc.

- 100% SunAmerica Life Insurance Company
- 100% AIGSunAmerica Life Assurance Company
- 100% AIG SunAmerica Asset Management Corp.
- 100% SunAmerica Capital Services, Inc.
- 100% First SunAmerica Life Insurance Company / SA Affordable Housing, LLC
- 100% SunAmerica Investments, Inc.
- 100% SunAmerica (Cayman) Insurance Company, Ltd.
- 100% AIG Advisor Group, Inc.
  - 100% Advantage Capital Corporation / American GeneralSecurities Incorporated / Financial Service Corporation / Royal Alliance Associates, Inc. / Sage Point Financial Advisors, Inc.
- 33% New California Life Holdings, Inc.

- 100% American General Finance, Inc. [IN]
- 100% American General Finance Services of Alabama, Inc.
- 100% American General Finance Corporation [IN]
  - 100% American General Consumer Discount Company / American General Financial Services of Illinois, Inc. / American General Financial Services, Inc. [DE] / American General Financial Services, Inc. [IN] / American General Financial Services, Inc.[NC] / American General Financial Services, Inc. [OH] / American General Financial Services, Inc. [SC] / American General Financial Services, Inc. [TX] / American General Financial Services, Inc. [WA] / Merit Life Insurance Co. / Ocean Finance and Mortgages Limited / Yosemite Insurance Company
  - 100% MorEquity, Inc. [NV]
  - 100% Wilmington Finance, Inc.
  - 100% American General Financial Services of America, Inc. [DE]
  - 100% American General Home Equity, Inc. [DE]

100% AIG Capital Corporation

- 100% AIG Global Asset Management Holdings Corp.
  - 100% AIG Global Real Estate Investment Corp.
    - 100% AIG Realty, Inc. / AIG Global Real Estate Asia Pacific, Inc.
    - 2% AIG Mexico Industrial I,L.L.C. [E]
    - 100% AIG Global Investment Corp. / AIG Ports America, Inc. / AIG Securities Lending Corp.
- 100% AIG Consumer Finance Group, Inc.
  - 100% AIG Consumer Finance Group (Asia) Limited / Compania Financiera Argentina S.A.
  - 100% AIG Holding Andes 1, Inc
  - 10% Inversora Pichincha S.A.Compania de Financiamiento Comercial [F]
  - 99.92% AIG Bank Polska S.A.
  - 99.15% AIG Retail Bank Public Company Limited
- 100% AIG Finance Holdings, Inc.
- 100% AIG Finance (Hong Kong), Limited
- 100% AIG Equipment Finance Holdings, Inc.
- 100% AIG Commercial Equipment Finance, Inc. / AIG RailServices, Inc.
- 67.23% International Lease Finance Corporation [G]
  - 100% Aircraft SPC-12, Inc.
  - 100% Whitney Leasing Limited
  - 100% Aircraft SPC-9, Inc.
  - 100% Sierra Leasing Ltd.
- 100% AIG CreditCorp.
- 100% A.I.Credit Corp.

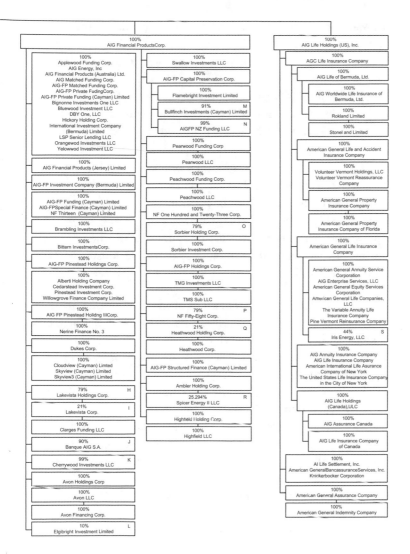

100% AIG Financial ProductsCorp.

- **100%**
  Applewood Funding Corp.
  AIG Energy, Inc
  AIG Financial Products (Australia) Ltd.
  AIG Matched Funding Corp.
  AIG-FP Matched Funding Corp.
  AIG-FP Private FudingCorp.
  AIG-FP Private Funding (Cayman) Limited
  Bignonne Investments One LLC
  Bluewood Investment LLC
  DBY One, LLC
  Hickory Holding Corp.
  International Investment Company (Bermuda) Limited
  LSP Senior Lending LLC
  Orangewod Investments LLC
  Yelowwod Investment LLC

- **100%** AIG Financial Products (Jersey) Limited
- **100%** AIG-FP Investment Company (Bermuda) Limited
- **100%** AIG-FP Funding (Cayman) Limited
  AIG-FPSpecial Finance (Cayman) Limited
  NF Thirteen (Cayman) Limited
- **100%** Brambling Investments LLC
- **100%** Bittern InvestmentsCorp.
- **100%** AIG-FP Pinestead Holdings Corp.
- **100%** Alberti Holding Company
  Cedarstead Investment Corp.
  Pinestead Investment Corp.
  Willowgrove Finance Company Limited
- **100%** AIG FP Pinestead Holidng IIICorp.
- **100%** Nerine Finance No. 3
- **100%** Dukes Corp.
- **100%** Cloudview (Cayman) Limted
  Skyview (Cayman) Limited
  Skyview3 (Cayman) Limited
- **79%** Lakevista Holdings Corp. **H**
- **21%** Lakevista Corp. **I**
- **100%** Clarges Funding LLC
- **90%** Banque AIG S.A. **J**
- **99%** Cherrywood Investments LLC **K**
- **100%** Avon Holdings Corp
- **100%** Avon LLC
- **100%** Avon Financing Corp.
- **10%** Elgibright Investment Limited **L**

- **100%** Swallow Investments LLC
- **100%** AIG-FP Capital Preservation Corp.
- **100%** Flamebright Investment Limited
- **91%** Bullfinch Investments (Cayman) Limited **M**
- **99%** AIGFP NZ Funding LLC **N**
- **100%** Pearwood Funding Corp
- **100%** Pearwood LLC
- **100%** Peachwood Funding Corp.
- **100%** Peachwood LLC
- **100%** NF One Hundred and Twenty-Three Corp.
- **79%** Sorbier Holding Corp. **O**
- **100%** Sorbier Investment Corp.
- **100%** AIG-FP Holdings Corp.
- **100%** TMG Investments LLC
- **100%** TMS Sub LLC
- **79%** NF Fifty-Eight Corp. **P**
- **21%** Heathwood Holdlng Corp. **Q**
- **100%** Heathwood Corp.
- **100%** AIG-FP Structured Finance (Cayman) Limited
- **100%** Ambler Holding Corp.
- **25.294%** Spicer Energy II LLC **R**
- **100%** Highfleld Holding Corp.
- **100%** Highfield LLC

100% AIG Life Holdings (US), Inc.

- **100%** AGC Life Insurance Company
- **100%** AIG Life of Bermuda, Ltd.
- **100%** AIG Worldwide Life Insurance of Bermuda, Ltd.
- **100%** Rokland Limited
- **100%** Stonel and Limited
- **100%** American General Life and Accident Insurance Company
- **100%** Volunteer Vermont Holdings, LLC
  Volunteer Vermont Reassurance Company
- **100%** American General Property Insurance Company
- **100%** American General Property Insurance Company of Florida
- **100%** American General Life Insurance Company
- **100%** American General Annuity Service Corporation
  AIG Enterprise Services, LLC
  American General Equity Services Corporation
  American General Life Companies, LLC
  The Variable Annuity Life Insurance Company
  Pine Vermont Reinsurance Company
- **44%** Iris Energy, LLC **S**
- **100%** AIG Annuity Insurance Company
  AIG Life Insurance Company
  American International Life Asurance Company of New York
  The United States Life Insurance Company in the City of New York
- **100%** AIG Life Holdings (Canada),ULC
- **100%** AIG Assurance Canada
- **100%** AIG Life Insurance Company of Canada
- **100%** AI Life Settlement, Inc.
  American GeneralBancassuranceServices, Inc.
  Knickerbocker Corporation
- **100%** American General Assurance Company
- **100%** American General Indemnity Company

and Freddie Mac, the law prohibits a regulator from terminating the
charter without obtaining an act of Congress.
- Powers: While operating in the market, the asset powers and other
authority of a bank, thrift, or GSE are determined by law, as interpreted
and applied by the institution's regulator. This relates to the fact that
specially chartered institutions are considered to have a public purpose;
limits on powers are intended to focus the institution on serving their
purposes.
- Special benefits: To help institutions serve their public purposes, the
law grants them special benefits such as deposit insurance for banks or
thrifts, privileged access to facilities of the Federal Reserve, and implicit
federal backing of obligations and MBSs issued by GSEs.
- Special responsibilities: These include the Community Reinvestment Act
for federally insured depository institutions and affordable housing goals
for Fannie Mae and Freddie Mac.

The relative benefits and burdens of different kinds of charters affected firms'
actions before and during the financial crisis. Benefits for commercial banks
include access to federally insured deposits, which are a source of stability for
many banks. In the panic phase of the crisis, when many investors sought to
withdraw their investments from financial firms, insured depositors had no
reason to flee; federal deposit insurance gave them confidence that, even if the
insured bank went down, their deposits would be fully protected. Even unin-
sured depositors provide stability because they withdraw retail deposits more
slowly than do wholesale purchasers of a firm's debt. The presence of a solid
depositor base provided stability for banks that was unavailable to investment
banks.

Benefits for member banks of the Federal Reserve System include access to
a variety of services from the Federal Reserve System, including clearing
checks and processing interbank payments. Depository institutions also can
access the Fed's discount window for emergency borrowing. In the crisis this
was a source of considerable comfort for investors; both Goldman Sachs and
Morgan Stanley converted to bank holding companies in September 2008,
just after the failures of Fannie Mae, Freddie Mac, and Lehman triggered
widespread panic.

The law may provide for competitive advantages by firms chartered under
one set of laws compared to others. Investment banks regulated by the SEC
had lower capital requirements than banks and thrifts. Major banks and
LCFIs sought lower capital requirements under the international agreement
known as Basel II, compared to smaller institutions. The argument was that
supervisors could validate the quality of an institution's risk management
system and that the institution then could use that system to set its own capital
standards according to Basel II requirements. Fortunately, Basel II was not yet

implemented for banks in the United States at the time of the financial crisis. On the other hand, capital requirements imposed on banks and thrifts encouraged securitization and other off-balance sheet activities to reduce the capital an institution was required to hold.

Tax requirements may also differ across institutions; credit unions, another form of insured depository, operate under preferential tax treatment compared to competing banks and thrifts. Firms of all types might move assets off of their balance sheets to reduce tax consequences.

Another important issue is the extent that the charter provides for prudential supervision and regulation. Chapter 7 discusses how the law gave supervised institutions considerable latitude to select a congenial regulator. That said, supervision of some institutions was much more stringent than others. The difference became especially pronounced when firms in the so-called shadow banking sector, including mortgage companies, securitization conduits, and other nondepository institutions, competed with banks, thrifts, and GSEs.[6]

Authorizing legislation may provide for other forms of burden levied on an institution such as the Community Reinvestment Act and affordable housing goal requirements that apply to federally insured depositories and Fannie Mae and Freddie Mac, respectively, but not to securitization activities of mortgage companies and investment banks.

Status as a commercial bank or financial services holding company brings restrictions too. Institutions with federal backing through the FDIC and Federal Reserve are subject to rules and limitations imposed by law and federal regulation. Until passage of the Gramm-Leach-Bliley Act (GLBA) in 1999, for example, banks and bank holding companies were limited in the financial activities that they were authorized to undertake. These limitations included those of the Depression-Era Glass-Steagall Act that, although eroded over the years by increasingly liberal regulatory interpretations, continued to separate investment banking from commercial banking activities. Even after GLBA, banks are limited; GLBA encouraged the development of large complex financial institutions by limiting the commercial activities in which banks may engage. However, by permitting a broad range of activities in the holding company, as contrasted to the bank itself, GLBA encouraged the development of large complex financial institutions that included banks among the affiliates that they controlled.

Fannie Mae and Freddie Mac, chartered directly by federal law, operated in an organizational form that provided extensive benefits as well as restrictions. Among the benefits of their GSE status were a perception of government backing of their obligations and MBSs and statutory capital standards that allowed them to maintain leverage of two-to-three times the permitted leverage of banks and thrifts that purchased and held mortgages. Moreover, the quality of GSE capital was illusory. The law permitted the two GSEs to count deferred tax assets as capital. This was dubious at best; a deferred tax asset is a future tax benefit, similar to prepaying taxes in return for a reduction later. The problem, of course, is that capital is needed to stave off failure of a firm; yet deferred tax assets become worthless when the firm fails because it no longer has any tax liability.[7] Another major benefit of a congressional charter was that it served as a barrier to entry by competitors; it was virtually impossible for other firms to obtain the same charter that was so favorable for Fannie Mae and Freddie Mac for so many years.

Among the disadvantages of GSE status were restrictions in the GSEs' charters that largely limited Fannie Mae and Freddie Mac to dealing in residential mortgages rather than in the broad range of assets that a commercial bank or thrift could originate or service. This prevented the GSEs from diversifying their portfolios. The GSEs were further limited to purchasing mortgages rather than directly originating them with the borrower. Moreover, the law limited the size of mortgage that the GSEs could purchase. For single-family mortgages, this limit was set at $417,000 for 2006 and 2007, for example.

By limiting the size of single-family mortgage to $417,000, the law helped to prevent Fannie Mae and Freddie Mac from loading up on even greater volumes of mortgages than they did in the major housing bubble markets of California, Nevada, Arizona, and Florida. It was only in 2008 that, as the GSEs had long sought, the Congress raised their loan size limits; fortunately this came too close to the peak of the crisis for the GSEs to be able to adjust their operations and accumulate even more mortgage volume from those states before the bubble burst and housing prices plummeted there. The GSEs were pursuing a political goal that would merely have compounded their losses.

The government-sponsored enterprise is an organizational form that fosters governance problems because of the way that it forces chief officers to balance contending stakeholders in the political realm as well as the marketplace. Former Fannie Mae CEO Daniel Mudd testified that "I would advocate moving the GSEs out of No Man's Land. Events have shown how difficult it is to balance financial, capital, market, housing, shareholder, bondholder, homeowner, private, and public interests in a crisis of these proportions. We should examine whether the economy and the markets are better served by fully private or fully public GSEs."[8] In his interview with FCIC staff, former Freddie Mac CEO Richard Syron concurred in this conclusion, saying about the GSE organizational form that "I don't think it's a good business model."[9]

It has long been argued that the organizational form of financial institutions shapes not only their activities and competitive position, but also their life cycles. Writing in 1994, I suggested that GSEs, banks, and thrifts were "mercantilist" institutions, in the sense that their success depended as much on the political process, to expand their asset powers or other aspects of the balance between their benefits and burdens, as on the marketplace:

Mercantilist institutions thus have quite a different kind of market risk than other companies. They may enjoy oligopoly profits undisturbed for years, only to be confronted suddenly with new technologies that permit nonmercantilist companies rapidly to take away key portions of their customer base. . . . Unlike such companies, the management risk of a mercantilist institution may jump dramatically when it runs into the limits of its enabling legislation and managers feel themselves forced to take greater risks within their permitted markets.[10]

This happened to Fannie Mae and Freddie Mac. CDOs and other securitization products suddenly created a market where the all-in cost of securitizing through the GSEs was greater than it was for subprime and alt-A mortgages through private-label securitization and CDOs that investors bought at low prices because they failed to understand the risk and thought they were purchasing high quality AAA securities. Fannie Mae and Freddie Mac suddenly found themselves losing market share as mortgage originators securitized an increasing volume of loans through channels other than the GSEs. That loss of market share, in turn, led the two GSEs to take greater risks in 2005–2007, just as the housing bubble reached its limits and burst.[11]

The two GSEs lacked the ability to manage those risks. A report by the Office of Comptroller of the Currency on Fannie Mae and Freddie Mac just before they went into government hands in 2008 concluded that "given the role of the GSEs and their market dominance, they should be industry leaders with respect to effective and proactive risk management, productive analysis, and comprehensive reporting. Instead they appear to significantly lag the industry in all respects."[12]

Banks, thrifts, and other portfolio lenders also found their portfolio businesses losing market share to securitization. This occurred because securitization offered larger businesses an opportunity to borrow in the credit markets at lower rates than were available from banks. The distinctive competence of banks, to judge the creditworthiness of borrowers before extending credit, evaporated as companies became larger and more transparent to investors. This increasingly limited banks, and especially smaller banks, to lending to smaller borrowers who had not yet established themselves in the market. Large parts of consumer lending also migrated to securitization-based funding, including credit cards, student loans, and auto loans, that made up growing parts of the asset-backed securities markets, to say nothing of the private-label mortgage-backed securities market. Securitization appealed to investors as well, who found that they could obtain better returns from securitization services such as mutual funds or money market funds than from federally insured deposits.[13]

Among other benefits, besides capital and tax advantages, securitization allowed a financial firm with an AA rating or less to originate and package loans into MBSs or asset-backed securities that carried the AAA rating and thus had much greater acceptance in the market. Another apparent advantage of securitization, which many failed to recognize at the time, was the way that the AAA rating allowed for the sale of structured products at prices that failed to reflect the true risk to investors.

Mispricing of risk allowed private-label securitization to outcompete portfolio lending as the decade progressed. Figure 6.4, from the Bank of England, shows the growth of revenues for large complex financial institutions from 2002 to 2007. While interest income, the traditional source of bank revenues, was flat, trading profits, for investment banks and commissions and fees for all institutions rose substantially.

While interest income represents returns from longer-term activities, trading profits, commissions and fees, all represent short-term revenues. The Bank of England found that US investment banks "tended to focus growth on riskier products, such as subprime RMBS [i.e., residential MBSs] and collateralized debt obligations (CDOs)."[14] It was in these products that mispricing of risk was most substantial.

16 LCFIs' revenue sources

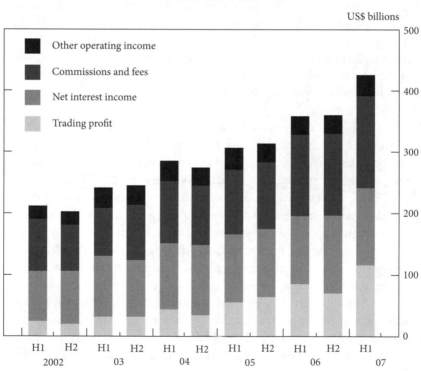

Sources: Bloomberg and Bank calculations

FIGURE 6.4 **Sources of Revenue for Large Complex Financial Institutions (LCFIs)**

Ownership and Control: Partnership vs. Investor-Owned

One other organizational distinction deserves attention here: that is the difference in structure and incentives between the partnership and the investor-owned company. FCIC staff interviewed numerous officials of investment banks. There seemed to be a consensus that partnerships tended to be more cautious and prudent than investor-owned companies. Partners can lose not only their stake in the enterprise, but also have personal liability to creditors if the partnership fails. People who had been members of partnerships talked of the way that partners would watch one another's activities constantly for fear that an unwise decision might trigger losses.

Incentives of investor-owned companies are different. Managers of investor-owned companies do not have the same personal liability if the firm fails. If they are rewarded in company shares that vest within a few years, risk-taking may provide them short-term profits that offset any personal exposure to losses from those risks. The simplest example is a company's decision to increase leverage. Managers who make this decision can reap additional returns on equity, perhaps for years before high leverage turns to ruin, as it did for Fannie Mae, Freddie Mac, Lehman, and other firms in the financial crisis.

The choice of organizational form also has implications for the way that managers are compensated and the problem of risk-taking that short-term compensation can foster. Brian Leach, who became chief risk officer of Citigroup in 2008, told the FCIC about his experience watching the evolution of the trend toward shorter-term compensation after Morgan Stanley became an investor-owned company:

> When I first started in Morgan's family, it was a private company. When you're a private company, you don't get paid until you retire. I mean, you get a good, you know, year-to-year compensation. But in terms of the retained earnings that's multiplying inside the company, the exit is retained—is when you retire.
>
> Morgan Stanley went public in the mid-eighties, and I started there in '81, so just to give some perspective on it. And they tried to maintain that partnership structure. And the idea was that you were—that you then got paid, but you got paid in very long dated, vested stock. And then a few years later, you know, frankly the rest of the street was paying in shorter dated stock and shorter dated stock and shorter dated stock. And the next thing you know, you get down to a very brief window. And I don't know where they were at the time, when I finally left. I can't remember, but I want to say it's closer to two years at that time, but I really don't know.[15]

That said, investor ownership has one major advantage over the partnership: the ability to raise investor capital allows firms to become much larger than a partnership ever could. David Viniar, Goldman's CFO, told FCIC staff that Goldman's decision to convert from a partnership and become investor-owned resulted from extensive debate within the firm. "What it really came down to was culture versus capital," he said. "Could we operate as a global financial institution with partnership capital versus would our culture be diminished if we went public?"[16]

Especially after Goldman suffered a crisis in 1994 and many partners retired, the firm's capital base shrank to uncomfortable levels. To be a global firm, Goldman decided to convert to investor ownership. Viniar added that Goldman believed that its culture did not diminish after the conversion. Moreover, there was an unexpected benefit from the conversion in the effects of stock ownership on the many Goldman employees who had not been partners: "It really energized people to be owners of the firm."[17]

Business Model

To what extent were shortcomings in risk management related to particular business models rather than merely to practices at individual firms? Put another way, to what extent did flaws in particular business models contribute to the financial crisis?

Consider three basic business models: (1) a trading or investment banking business based on transactions rather than long-term holding of assets on the balance sheet, (2) lenders that hold a diverse portfolio of assets on the balance sheet, and (3) specialized lenders or guarantors that guarantee or hold a narrow class of asset on the balance sheet.

Management of financial firms, including all three of these business models, must include similar governance and risk management practices, as were discussed in chapters 4 and 5. Where business models make a difference is in the added tools that some models offer to manage risk, compared to others.

Probably the most flexible business model involves the trading or investment banking business where the financial firm does not intend to hold assets on the balance sheet for any significant period of time—the so-called moving business. The moving business is flexible because it allows a firm to select a position in the market that is either long or short with respect to particular financial products, according to the firm's view. As markets become volatile, these firms have the option of "getting closer to home," as Goldman Sachs' CFO David Viniar puts it, thereby riding out the turbulence without significant exposure on either side of a neutral position, either with respect to the firm's position as to particular financial products or with respect to the firm's position overall.[18] Derivatives, which allow a firm to take a shorter position than its assets would otherwise allow, are a major instrument for hedging risk in this way.

The second model involves a commercial bank or other lender or a financial holding company that invests in a variety of assets. This kind of institution is in the storage business, which holds many of those assets for a considerable period of time. Because of a significant balance sheet commitment in key financial products—such as mortgages, leveraged lending, or commercial or sovereign loans, for example—these firms must manage the risk of a long position. One alternative is to sell off specified asset classes, such as subprime mortgages, to reduce risk exposure and to continue holding other preferred kinds of assets. In addition, it may be possible to hedge some of the risk, recognizing that no hedge is as perfect as actual divestiture of the asset. CDSs were an increasingly popular form of financial protection in the run-up to the financial crisis, but this involved counterparty risk and the chance that, in a panic, the issuer of the CDS protection couldn't pay up.

Portfolio lending also requires careful management of a company's asset-liability mix. Lending long and borrowing short is what brought down the savings and loan industry in the 1980s. SIVs, which were securitizations from the perspective of banks that sponsored them, were also portfolio lenders, in the sense that they held CDOs and other securities based on long-term assets and funded these often by issuing shorter term commercial paper. Securitization trusts that held that commercial paper, in turn, often funded their portfolios with overnight money from money market funds. This extreme maturity mismatch and the resulting liquidity risk that exceeded stresses contemplated in SIV models, helped to bring down SIVs during the crisis. By September 2008 all independent SIVs had failed, and almost all bank-sponsored SIVs had been supported by their sponsoring banks.[19]

Finally, there is the third model of the specialized lender that is also in the storage business. As has long been recognized, managing risk of a monoline company is much more difficult than managing risk of a financial firm that takes a variety of assets onto its balance sheet. Anurag Saksena, chief enterprise risk officer of Freddie Mac, told Commission staff about his company:

> We are a firm which is really concentrated in one segment of the entire financial services industry—mortgage product. Unlike Jamie Dimon [CEO of JPMorgan Chase, a diversified financial services company operating largely on the second type of business model, above], I cannot say hey, Mr. CEO, we are way too concentrated in this product, let's diversify it.[20]

In other words, a specialized lender such as Fannie Mae, Freddie Mac, or a thrift institution specializing in mortgages such as WaMu or IndyMac may purchase protection, (e.g., through a financial guarantee) and may hedge with derivatives, but lacks the ability of a diversified firm to disinvest in a potentially volatile type of asset and invest instead in other preferred asset classes. Moreover, a large specialized lender such as Fannie Mae or Freddie

Mac constitutes such a large part of the mortgage market, holding or guaranteeing literally trillions of dollars of residential mortgages, that it can be difficult or impossible to hedge the inherent risks. In the case of Fannie Mae and Freddie Mac, their statutory charters require that mortgages above an 80 percent loan-to-value (LTV) ratio be protected by private mortgage insurance for the amount above 80 percent, and that helps mitigate credit risk. On the other hand, an increasing incidence of so-called piggyback mortgages—those that separated the first mortgage with an 80 percent LTV from a second mortgage that added to the combined LTV—reduced the amount of this coverage.

Indeed, the GSE business model may create more difficult risk management issues than exist for other monoline firms. According to Saksena of Freddie Mac: "You have dueling objectives between public policy and shareholders. As a CRO you are trying to maximize the risk-return balance. . . . From a risk management perspective, this duopoly of the two objectives is very difficult to deal with."[21]

One answer to this problem would be to require a monoline company such as a GSE to hold a larger capital cushion than would be required of a more diversified company or of a company in the moving business. Instead, Fannie Mae and Freddie Mac were permitted to hold less capital than other companies in their markets. In the decade 1998 to 2007 Freddie Mac, for example, operated with capital that ranged between 1.34 and 2.08 percent of total MBS that it guaranteed plus total assets. Consequently, Freddie Mac's shareholders obtained returns on equity that ranged from 20.2 percent to 47.2 percent in the years from 1998 to 2002, the last full year before the company reported the failure of its internal controls and the need to restate its financial statements. Higher capital requirements, which would have reduced returns to shareholders, also would have increased the company's ability to withstand the impact of losses on its business activities.

Another aspect of the business model, reflected in the discussion of liquidity risk, concerns the funding sources for a financial firm. Nondepository mortgage originators, for example, depended heavily on warehouse lines used to fund mortgages as they were being assembled to be securitized; these lines could be and were withdrawn by lenders on short notice when the mortgage market became turbulent. On the other hand, GSEs, with their access to borrowings with the perception of an implicit government guarantee, possessed a more stable form of funding, at least until the markets began to question the financial viability of Fannie Mae and Freddie Mac.

Firms in the moving business or diversified firms in the storage business could use sound risk management to save themselves from failure, and by extension, avoided contributing to the financial crisis. The case is less clear whether the business model of monoline firms, and especially GSEs, was such that even with good risk management, they would have failed anyway unless they had significantly increased their capital cushions, even for this business model with its more limited options, it would seem that prudent risk manage-ment, and especially reduced leverage, might have prevented failure. The need for greater capital protection can be seen in comparing failure of the GSEs with the survival, albeit with difficulty, of monoline private mortgage insurers despite their concentration of risk in mortgage assets, but which held signifi-cantly more—and higher quality—capital than the GSEs maintained.

Political strength and financial soundness

The experience of the GSEs, which operated under favorable charters until the end, raises an issue that deserves mention here. That is the matter of political strength of financial institutions and the relationship of that strength to their financial soundness.

The GSEs were especially skilled at the Washington political game. Because a GSE would live or die according to the provisions of its charter, GSEs spent considerable effort dealing with their legislative and regulatory environment. Fannie Mae and Freddie Mac selected board members, CEOs, and other top company officers on the basis of their skills at dealing with that environment. Professor Jonathan Koppell of the Yale School of Organization and Manage-ment studied the GSEs and found that "Fannie Mae and Freddie Mac rosters boast numerous alumni of the executive and legislative branches. . . . Further-more, there is an impressive history of GSE executives crossing back into government service, giving the company advantages in terms of access, and sympathy, at the highest levels."[22]

A favorable charter gave Fannie Mae and Freddie Mac increasing market power over the 1990s and ability to protect their interests in the political arena. Fannie Mae was especially active: "Builders, real estate brokers and bankers across the country rely so heavily on Fannie Mae for mortgage funds that they live in fear of offending the firm and routinely defend it in Washington."[23]

The GSEs retained a roster of respected economists and former govern-ment officials. Fannie Mae hired the services of former Federal Reserve Chairman Paul Volcker, who argued against applying capital standards to Fannie Mae comparable to those that applied to commercial banks.[24] Fannie Mae also commissioned a paper from Nobel Prize winner Joseph Stiglitz, Jonathan Orszag, and Peter Orszag defending the low capital requirements of Fannie Mae and Freddie Mac.[25] Freddie Mac commissioned work by former OMB Director James Miller III defending the value of the government subsidy provided to the GSEs.[26] In addition, the GSEs issued their own policy statements.[27]

Former HUD Secretary Mel Martinez recalls the impact of GSE lobbying on the ability of OFHEO to supervise Fannie Mae and Freddie Mac:

It became clear to me immediately that OFHEO [the safety-and-soundness regulator of Fannie Mae and Freddie Mac] was underfunded and undermanned and their mission was very limited. And it became clear to me that that's exactly how Fannie and Freddie wanted it and they had the power and wherewithal in the Congress to keep it that way.[28]

Other financial firms also actively defended their franchises and charters. Organizational form and especially charter authority make a major difference to financial firms. That, along with the desire to limit regulatory and supervisory involvement in their businesses, discussed in chapter 7, leads financial firms to exert political power to fashion a favorable balance of benefits and burdens, especially vis-à-vis their competitors.

The Center for Responsive Politics, which tracks and tabulates campaign contributions and lobbying expenditures each year and in each election cycle, reports that "the financial sector is far and away the largest source of campaign contributions to federal candidates and parties, with insurance companies, securities and investment firms, real estate interests and commercial banks providing the bulk of that money."[29] The question, again as illustrated by failure of the GSEs on the basis of favorable charters that they lobbied to get and to keep, is whether those expenditures ultimately helped or hurt financial firms as they sought the lowest common denominator with respect to capital standards, prudential supervision, and charter advantages.

7 }

Supervision and Regulation of Financial Firms

The status quo: Walk softly and carry no stick.

—PATRICK HONOHAN, *GOVERNOR OF THE CENTRAL BANK*
OF IRELAND

On paper, federal financial regulators seemed to possess extensive authority to deal with shortcomings in governance and risk management at financial firms. Bank supervisors' powers included authority (with some variations) to charter financial institutions after reviewing capability of the charter applicants, examine their financial condition, set capital standards, prohibit unsafe or unsound practices or conditions, bring enforcement actions, require prompt corrective actions with respect to institutions that begin to lose their capital strength, and place a failing institution into conservatorship or receivership. (In a conservatorship, the goal is to restore an institution to sound financial condition; in a receivership, the goal is to wind up the institution's affairs by paying creditors and liquidating assets.)

There are many variations on this pattern. For example, the FDIC and the Federal Reserve supervise state-chartered banks, among other institutions, while the Office of Comptroller of the Currency (OCC) supervises only institutions that it charters, national banks.

Fragmentation of the US System

The US financial system is fragmented into many more institutions of varying sizes and types than in Canada or Europe. Similarly, supervision of the US banking system is fragmented, with responsibilities divided among federal and state authorities. At the federal level, supervisory responsibilities are divided among a multiplicity of federal agencies and instrumentalities. Much of the fragmentation derives from historical circumstances in the United States and especially the populist antagonism to the power of the nation's first central banks, the First and Second Banks of the United States, chartered in the eighteenth and nineteenth centuries respectively. This antagonism, heightened with Andrew Jackson's famous veto of the charter of the Second Bank of the United States in the 1830s, also reflected itself in the long time it took to create the Federal Reserve System as the nation's central bank and, of relevance here, the fact that the Fed was a decentralized system rather than a single powerful central bank.

The fragmented regulatory structure meant that multiple agencies examined the activities of various components of a large complex financial institution, as can be seen in figure 7.1. Relevant agencies include the Commodity Futures Trading Commission (CFTC), which is supposed to regulate derivatives; the Securities and Exchange Commission (SEC), charged with enforcing the securities laws and protecting investors; the Office of Comptroller of the Currency, which regulates national banks; the Office of Thrift Supervision (OTS), which regulated thrift institutions (savings and loan associations) and their holding companies; the FDIC, which supervises the majority of state-chartered banks and thrifts; and the Federal Reserve, which supervises bank holding companies, branches, and agencies of foreign banking organizations, and state-chartered banks that are members of the Federal Reserve System. (Since enactment of the Dodd-Frank Act in 2010 and elimination of the OTS, the Fed now also supervises thrift holding companies and the OCC also supervises federal savings associations.) In addition, there are consumer finance companies that are largely unregulated and served as profitable affiliates of many large banks.

Fragmentation of the US financial regulatory system was seen also in the division of responsibilities between the Securities and Exchange Commission (SEC) and the Commodity Futures Trading Commission (CFTC). While the SEC regulates securities, the CFTC regulates most derivatives: "The world of derivatives is thus divided between the two, with the SEC having jurisdiction over options, while still a third category of derivatives—swaps—was placed by Congress in 2000 largely beyond the reach of both agencies. No other nation does anything like this."[1]

There is also a variety of self-regulatory organizations (SROs) and state regulators. Regulation of insurance is a state function; the law expressly precludes federal agencies from exercising jurisdiction over the business of insurance, except at the margins.

Before enactment of Dodd-Frank, federal regulators, notably OTS and the OCC, adopted rules preempting state efforts to impose consumer protection regulations on national banks and federally chartered thrift institutions, including regulations aimed at abusive mortgage lending practices. One motivation was to make the federal charter, which the OCC and OTS supervised, more attractive than state charters. The OCC issued a press release in 2002 touting that the "Comptroller Calls Preemption a Major Advantage of National Bank Charter."[2]

Preemption allowed an institution to conform to a single set of national requirements rather than to requirements that would vary across the country, depending on laws enacted by particular states and localities.

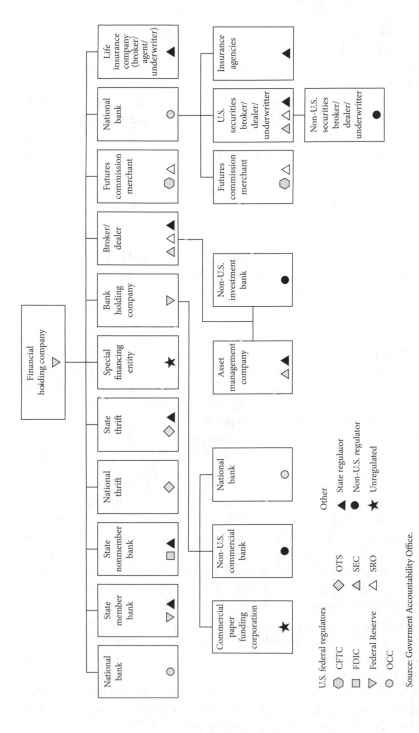

FIGURE 7.1 **The Fragmented US Financial Regulatory System**

Source: Goverment Accountability Office.

Regulation and Supervision

To understand what these agencies and instrumentalities do, it helps to distinguish between regulation and supervision. In regulating, a federal agency establishes rules that the regulated institutions are required to follow. These rules, which must be authorized by law, deal with a plethora of matters such as the range of permissible activities that an institution may engage in, required capital levels and the nature of assets that may be counted as capital, and prohibited conduct. Some laws and regulations also specify consumer protections, obligations of institutions to conform to the Community Reinvestment Act, and other requirements.

An agency may also issue supervisory guidance to firms and their examiners. Examiners may check whether institutions comply with the guidance, much as they may review an institution's compliance with laws and regulations. While guidance is technically not binding, as a practical matter it is viewed by both the agencies and the regulated financial companies as a mandatory instruction, with repercussions for noncompliance.

The role of examiners relates to the task of supervision. Julie Dickson, Supervisor of Financial Institutions Canada, provides a useful definition:

> In short, supervisors are the people on the front lines who identify risk management problems at individual institutions and decide what to do about them. They decide whether to tell an institution to stop growing its business in certain areas until problems are fixed, or require an institution to do more stress testing, or require an institution to raise capital, or require that an institution hire expertise in a particular area to manage risk, or push an institution to spend money on their data systems so they can more clearly see what risks they have taken on. These are critical functions and they help make institutions safer and limit losses.[3]

In other words, supervision is the task of examining an institution and its activities, evaluating its financial condition, assessing its governance and risk management, ensuring compliance with laws, rules, and less formal requirements, and evaluating the institution in these dimensions in a report presented to the institution's board and management. This book uses the terms "regulatory agency" and "financial supervisor" interchangeably, even though the terms formally have different nuances. The distinction is especially significant with respect to an agency such as the SEC, which has power to write regulations and bring enforcement actions but which traditionally has not exercised an examination function except in a limited way with respect to investor protections.[4]

While regulators seemed strong on paper, the practice was quite different. First, the laws were weaker than they seemed. The idea of prompt corrective action, for example, was a product of the 1991 FDIC Improvements Act

(FDICIA). This law gave supervisors power to take specified actions to deal with a bank or thrift with capital that began to drop below specified levels. The intent was not necessarily to forestall problems beforehand, but rather to give the regulator an opportunity to apply corrective measures before the institution actually failed at cost to taxpayers. The problem was that capital is a lagging indicator; troubled firms may be slow to recognize credit problems that would lower their capital ratios and, by the time losses emerge, it can be too late to apply preventative measures to forestall failure. Further, capital provides protection against credit risks, but does not protect against liquidity risk. A well-capitalized institution that does not have sufficient liquid assets can fail if it cannot meet demands for cash payments, even if the institution is holding high levels of capital. This was seen in the financial crisis when liquidity evaporated and caused "severe and rapid declines in the financial condition of well or adequately capitalized institutions that were precipitated by an inability to meet rapid, sustained deposit outflows or other cash and collateral demands."[5]

Misplaced faith in market efficiency

Another problem, in the words of a Federal Reserve Bank of New York (FRBNY) document, was a belief that "markets will always self-correct."[6] In other words, similar to Chairman Greenspan's views before the crisis, "regulators have long assumed that a bank's board of directors will act in the best interests of the shareholders to assure the long-run profitability and viability of their firm."[7] These basic assumptions, the FRBNY report later concluded, were wrong: "A deference to the self-correcting property of markets inhibited supervisors from imposing prescriptive views on banks."[8]

Other countries also placed great faith in the markets to keep excessive financial risks in check as well. The Turner Report in the United Kingdom, reporting on shortcomings of the UK's Financial Services Authority (FSA), concluded that there had been a "dominant philosophy of confidence in self correcting markets" that had impeded the ability or willingness of the FSA to require banks to take corrective actions.[9] A postmortem on the Irish banking crisis found that the financial supervisor would "walk softly and carry no stick."[10]

The prevailing theory was that market forces provided stronger protection than a regulator could. Moreover, markets would act efficiently and not stifle innovation the way that excessive regulation and supervision might. Testifying in 1994 on proposals to create a single financial regulator, Federal Reserve Chairman Alan Greenspan stated his opposition:

> A consolidated single regulator would deprive our regulatory structure of what the Board considers to be the current invaluable restraint on any one regulator conducting inflexible, excessively rigid policies. Laws on

bank regulation and supervision must be drawn very generally, leaving the specifics to agency rulemaking. This vests the agencies with a broad mandate and a not inconsiderable amount of discretionary power. . . . We must avoid a regulatory structure that inhibits economic growth.

The current structure provides banks with a method . . . of shifting their regulator, an effective test that provides a limit on the arbitrary position or excessively rigid posture of any one regulator. The pressure of a potential loss of institutions has inhibited excessive regulation and acted as a countervailing force to the bias of a regulatory agency to overregulate.[11]

Greenspan argued against a consolidated regulator on economic grounds:

Indeed, a single regulator with a narrow view of safety and soundness and with no responsibility for the macroeconomic implications of its decisions would inevitably have a long-term bias against risk-taking and innovation. It receives no plaudits for contributing to economic growth through facilitating prudent risk-taking, but it is severely criticized for too many bank failures. The incentives are clear.[12]

He urged that the Congress adopt principles for federal supervision of financial institutions, including the provision that "first, there should not be a single monolithic federal regulator," and "second, every bank should have a choice of federal regulator."[13]

Gramm-Leach-Bliley and Supervisory Gaps

In 1999 Congress enacted the Gramm-Leach-Bliley Act (GLBA) as part of an effort to further deregulate the financial services industry and reduce influence of government on the markets.[14] Among other changes, the act removed the remaining New Deal restrictions on combining investment banking and commercial banking in the same financial services holding company. Previously, the Federal Reserve Board used its regulatory authority to permit such affiliations, but subject to certain quantitative limitations. GLBA, enacted at the urging of the Clinton administration, completed the task of removing restrictions on the affiliation of banks, investment firms, and insurance companies.

To pass GLBA, Congress and the administration had to satisfy various interests. The Federal Reserve insisted that the affiliation of banks, securities, and insurance companies had to be done under its supervision through the use of a bank holding company structure. The OCC, which regulated national banks, argued for an alternative structure that would authorize such affiliations through bank subsidiaries. The final GLBA legislation permits the use of bank subsidiaries, but under such stringent conditions that it was not a practical option for companies engaged in securities or insurance under-writing. Thus, for all intents and purposes, the Fed was successful in requiring the use of a bank holding company structure.

The other major stumbling block for the legislation related to the deep-seated fear in the insurance and securities industries of Fed regulation. Insurance companies had a long history of largely congenial state regulation, and did not want a new federal regulator overseeing their activities. Securities firms were comfortable with the SEC and other securities regulators, and did not want to become subject to the regulatory strictures of a potentially powerful federal agency. Both industries also were concerned that the Fed would subject them to more stringent bank-like capital requirements.

The Federal Reserve supported a compromise that allowed the bill to pass and be signed into law by President Clinton. Under the compromise, limita-tions would be placed on the supervisory and regulatory powers of the Federal Reserve Board over companies that were subject to the regulations of a State insurance regulator, the SEC, or the CFTC. This compromise was known as "Fed-Lite": The Fed would be an umbrella supervisor of bank holding com-panies but it would largely avoid examining holding company subsidiaries, notably insurance and securities firms, which were subject to oversight by other regulators.[15] The Senate Banking Committee Report on GLBA made this clear:

> For functionally regulated subsidiaries, the Board is required, to the greatest extent possible, to rely on reports required by and examinations conducted by the functional regulator. Thus, the Board must generally defer to regulation by the State insurance commissioners, the State and Federal banking agencies, the Securities and Exchange Commission (the "Commission"), the State securities commissioners, and appropriate self-regulatory organizations.

Moreover, the Fed would be careful not to try to supervise parts of the shadow banking system that affiliated with banks in the new holding com-panies. Both the Fed and the OCC focused on the safety and soundness of insured depository institutions rather than allocating their resources to deal with systemic risk more broadly. The Fed grounded this approach, once again, on faith in the effectiveness of market forces:

> In addition, since market discipline operates more effectively with nonbank activities not subject to the moral hazard of the safety net, regulators should also avoid diminishing this market discipline in the new financial holding companies. Thus, the act discourages the extension of bank-like regulation and supervision to the nonbank affiliates and subsidiaries.[16]

Former comptroller of the Currency Eugene Ludwig told Commission staff that there was a "historic vision, historic approach, that a lighter hand at regulation was the appropriate way to regulate. After all, when you look at the Gramm-Leach-Bliley itself, the Fed's regulatory purview over the nonbank-affiliated activities was affirmatively characterized—I think in the statute, but certainly in all the literature—as Fed-Lite. That I think is endemic of what was a viewpoint from Gramm-Leach-Bliley forward of appropriate regulation of financial activities."[17]

Richard Spillenkothen, director of the Federal Reserve Board's Division of Banking Supervision and Regulation during this period, believes that GLBA and Fed-Lite "precluded a robust and integrated hands-on evaluation of enterprise-wide risk management and controls by a single regulator and contravened fundamental principles of effective and comprehensive consolidated supervision."[18]

GLBA also affected the OCC. Ludwig told FCIC staff that

> under Gramm-Leach-Bliley you had functional regulation enshrined, and the historic enthusiasm of regulators like the comptroller to view their responsibility as bank-organization centric became cut back to bank-centric so that the examination and supervision of the non-bank affiliates was restrained, and of course it's the SIVs and the off-balance-sheet activities that are not in the bank and therefore were not getting bank supervision. It was assumed that they were getting supervision by their regulators, the regulators of those non-bank-affiliated activities, sometimes the SEC, sometimes the Fed, something else, but not the bank regulator.[19]

A 2009 OCC lessons-learned document recognizes that looking at the bank alone was not enough:

> As we have seen, in times of stress, the entities outside of the national bank can severely affect the bank, whether through exposure and subsequent losses that come through the "back door" as we saw with certain CDOs; through heightened liquidity pressures on the bank arising from the need to shore up various off-balance sheet conduits; acquisitions by the holding company of significant nonbanks engaged in banking activities; etc.[20]

While GLBA rested on a theory that the bank regulators would cooperate with one another, serious gaps existed. Regulators were even reluctant to share supervisory information with one another. This could keep information compartmentalized among the multiple regulators of the entities within a single holding company so that no one had a complete picture. In addition to these turf issues, regulators also perceived legal issues:

> The most significant barrier to disclosure is that if a regulator discloses confidential supervisory information to another regulator, the disclosure could lead to further, unintended disclosure to other persons. Disclosure

to another regulator raises two significant risks: the risk that information shared with the other regulator will not be maintained as "confidential" by that regulator, or that legal privileges that apply to the information will be waived by such sharing.[21]

Financial institutions skillfully exploited gaps in supervision. They could shop for the most attractive charter, which meant being able to select the most favorable regulator. This happened when Countrywide shifted from supervision by the Federal Reserve and OCC to supervision by OTS. OTS, widely seen as the most congenial regulator, supervised major institutions that failed (Countrywide, AIG, WaMu, IndyMac).

As Eugene Ludwig told FCIC staff, "the fact of the matter is that . . . a number of institutions change charters because they wouldn't even really articulate it themselves that they—many of them, that they were looking for the most lax regulator, but they were looking for a regulator that was most understanding or appreciative of their particular way they did business."[22]

The Fed acknowledged that it had a fundamental mission to promote financial stability.[23] But it did not feel it could step on toes of other regulators to accomplish this, especially after enactment of GLBA and application of Fed-Lite. Federal Reserve Vice Chairman Janet Yellen told FCIC staff that the Fed in fact did not believe it had the mandate to use its supervisory powers to protect the financial system against systemic risk:

> I think we were focused on the banking system and I don't think we were sufficiently looking at the risks throughout the entire financial system and I don't think that we or anyone else in the government really had a financial stability mandate. . . . I don't think we were tasked in some sense with doing the kind of analysis of the financial sector as a whole and explicit responsibility for identifying broad risks in the financial system that for example the new FSOC [Financial Stability Oversight Council] is charged with doing.[24]

The Fed's problem was compounded by gaps within the Federal Reserve System itself. Following long tradition, the Federal Reserve Board has delegated its supervisory responsibilities to the twelve regional Federal Reserve banks, among which the Federal Reserve Bank of New York has always played a leading role. The Federal Reserve Board would set policy for the twelve Reserve banks, but largely relied on the supervisory staff of the Reserve banks to be "the eyes and ears" of the Federal Reserve Board's supervisory staff, as Sabeth Siddique, formerly assistant director and head of credit risk supervision at the Federal Reserve Board, told FCIC staff.[25]

Out of 2,622 supervisory staff in the Federal Reserve System in 2007, only 283 were located at the Federal Reserve Board; the other 90 percent were employees of the Federal Reserve banks.[26] Moreover, because the Federal

Reserve banks are privately owned by their member commercial banks, while the Federal Reserve Board is a government agency, staff of the larger Federal Reserve banks are paid more handsomely than their counterparts at the Board. The difference is material enough that it makes it difficult for the Board to attract skilled Federal Reserve Bank supervisors to Washington while, conversely, the Board may lose some of its better people to the banks.

Coordinating between the Federal Reserve banks and the Board could be difficult. For example, as a way to strengthen the information available to supervisors of large complex financial institutions, Federal Reserve Governor Susan Bies created a horizontal review process that would allow supervisors of each major holding company to share information and best practices with one another. Siddique attributes the inability of this innovation to make a significant difference before the financial crisis to bureaucratic opposition within the Federal Reserve system:

> There are strong cultures that are in place in the Reserve Bank system that were hard to overcome, and that culture includes not giving Washington the information that they're looking for. So it's always been very, very difficult to get information out of the Reserve Banks throughout the years. And the responsibility for supervision has been delegated to the Reserve Banks, so invariably when we would ask questions for information or data, they would say, "everything's fine, don't worry about it." We would get tremendous pushback when I would try to get data.[27]

There was another problem at the Fed. It is a long-standing principle of organizational design that when an organization has two missions, one important and the other considered less important, that the less important mission may atrophy or be disregarded. Economists at the Fed supported the Fed's primary function, which was to set monetary policy. Supervision ranked as important, but not nearly on a level with monetary policy and the associated macroeconomic analysis. Thus, when Chairman Bernanke stated publicly in May 2007 that problems in the subprime mortgage market were largely contained, as recounted in chapter 2, he received this analysis from staff economists at the Fed who projected aggregate direct loan losses on bank balance sheets and determined that the numbers were unpleasant but tolerable.[28]

By contrast, supervisors at the Fed have said that they actively warned that the crisis indeed could be catastrophic. They based this view on impressions gained from reviews of major institutions rather than on quantifiable data. Culturally, supervisors didn't speak the quantitative language that the Fed's leadership could hear, which meant that the supervisors' views were disregarded in Bernanke's speech. Moreover, no one at the Fed seems to have thought to create a constructive dialogue between macroeconomists and senior supervisors to try to tease out why there were such profound differences between the two perspectives.

The SEC's Consolidated Supervised Entity Program

The Securities and Exchange Commission, created in 1934 as part of the New Deal, had as its primary responsibility the protection of retail investors through disclosure, securities registration, and other measures. In 2002 the European Union ramped up its supervision of financial holding companies, including investment bank holding companies, except if a financial regulator in another country supervised their holding companies. This created an incentive for investment banks in the United States, other than those whose holding companies were already supervised by the Fed or OTS, to seek a new option for supervising their holding companies that would be more congenial.

In 2004 five major broker dealers (i.e., investment banks) that the SEC oversaw for purposes of the securities laws requested that the agency also assume responsibility for overseeing their holding companies and set their capital standards. The SEC agreed to set up a voluntary program called the Consolidated Supervised Entity (CSE) program, to supervise investment bank holding companies.[29] The program was voluntary; an investment bank could enroll or not, as it determined. One of the attractive features of the CSE program for investment banks was that they would be permitted to calculate their own capital levels pursuant to the Basel II capital standards. The SEC allowed this even though Basel II capital regulations were still being hotly debated by the Federal banking agencies, and final regulations had not been issued. Thus, while no US bank had permission to use the Basel II framework, and detailed regulations had not been finalized, the SEC authorized the five largest securities firms to use this new capital framework.

Five investment banks enrolled in the SEC's CSE program: Bear Stearns, Lehman Brothers, Goldman Sachs, Morgan Stanley, and Merrill Lynch. While the SEC had required a debt-to-net capital ratio of less than 15 to 1 for broker-dealers before the CSE program, the application of Basel II standards allowed broker-dealers to significantly increase their leverage. Bear, for example, had gross leverage of about 33 to 1 before its collapse.[30]

Another benefit of the CSE program for enrolled companies was that it was not burdensome. The SEC initially staffed the program with less than a dozen people to oversee five of the largest complex financial institutions in the world. Dedicated CSE staff later increased to about two dozen people, still far below resources available to the Fed or other supervisors. Moreover, they tended to be skilled quantitative people rather than experienced safety and soundness supervisors. Cynthia Glassman, an SEC commissioner at the time the SEC established the program, had been a long-time veteran of the Federal Reserve Board and the Federal Reserve Bank of Philadelphia before joining the SEC. She recalls requesting that SEC staff develop the needed expertise to supervise safety and soundness and that they consult with the Fed and OCC, which dealt with larger institutions.[31]

The SEC failed to develop the necessary supervisory capacity. Moreover, the organizational complexity of the five major investment bank holding companies was so great that the SEC lacked authority over most of them. SEC chairman Christopher Cox (who had not been a member of the SEC when the agency began the CSE program) testified that:

> The holding company in the case of Lehman Brothers . . . consisted of over 200 significant subsidiaries. The SEC was not the statutory regulator for 193 of them. There were over-the-counter derivatives businesses, trust companies, mortgage companies, and offshore banks, broker-dealers, and reinsurance companies. Each of these examples I have just described falls far outside of the SEC's regulatory jurisdiction. What Congress did give the SEC authority to regulate was the broker-dealers, investment companies, and investment adviser subsidiaries within these conglomerates.[32]

Chairman Cox pointed to the voluntary nature of holding company regulation under the SEC program as a fundamental flaw: "It was a fateful mistake in the Gramm-Leach-Bliley Act that neither the SEC nor any regulator was given the statutory authority to regulate investment bank holding companies other than on a voluntary basis."[33] Even when SEC CSE staff found problems, the agency failed to react. A later Inspector General report found that:

> Although [it] was aware, prior to Bear Stearns becoming a CSE firm, that Bear Stearns' concentration of mortgage securities was increasing for several years and was beyond its internal limits, and that a portion of Bear's mortgage securities (e.g., adjustable rate mortgages) represented a significant concentration of market risk, [the SEC] did not make any efforts to limit Bear Stearns' mortgage securities concentration.[34]

Former SEC Commissioner Harvey Goldschmid states that it was incompetence at best that prevented the SEC from looking closely at Lehman after Bear failed in March 2008, "once you understood the problem."[35] The CSE program, in chairman Cox's words, "did not work."[36] Of the five firms nominally supervised under the CSE program, three (Bear, Lehman, and Merrill) failed and two (Goldman and Morgan Stanley) became bank holding companies supervised by the Fed.

Splintered Responsibility and Cumbersome Processes

Splintered responsibility among federal regulators and with state regulators prevented supervisory agencies from acting even after they perceived problems. In an interview with FCIC staff, Federal Reserve Vice Chairman Janet

Yellen, who had been president and CEO of the Federal Reserve Bank of San Francisco from 2004 to 2010, confirmed the issue, using the example of growth of concentration of commercial real estate (CRE) assets on the books of many banks that her reserve bank supervised.

By 2005 it had become clear that CRE values were becoming inflated. However, the Federal Reserve Bank of San Francisco felt itself precluded from imposing greater prudential requirements on financial firms in the San Francisco district because that would have been inequitable compared to less restrictive requirements for banks headquartered in other Federal Reserve districts:

> We felt that we in San Francisco . . . operate under the guidelines on supervision that are given to us by the board of governors. And those guidelines in turn are typically negotiated through inter-agency . . . processes . . . So in some sense, it required, I think, an inter-agency process to issue guidance that would enable examiners throughout all of the institutions to take a tougher line on some practices we were seeing.[37]

Yet when the federal banking agencies finally issued commercial real estate guidance in 2006, it was late and unhelpful. Yellen said, "I felt when this guidance came out you could take this, and rip it up and throw it in the garbage can; it wasn't a tool that was of any use to us in controlling this risk."[38]

But as a practical matter, there seemed little or no option for a regulator to go it alone. According to Yellen:

> Could we, if we had insisted, have done something in our own supervision in the institutions that we supervise to crack down in a way that was in some sense, San Francisco Fed discretion? I honestly don't know if we could have done that. I don't think we felt empowered to do it. If you're asking me, is it conceivable that we could have used our own discretion to be tougher than our colleagues were in other reserve banks or Comptroller of the Currency or the Office of Thrift Supervision or what was allowed for in policy coming out of an inter-agency process, I don't think my supervisors felt they had the power to do that.[39]

In other words, an individual supervisory organization such as the Federal Reserve Bank of San Francisco was unwilling to move alone to correct problems within its jurisdiction unless this was backed by interagency guidance—guidance that came far too late and, after going through a long consensus-driven process, was too bland to be helpful: "This kind of process that I think we have had where it takes six different regulators in the FFIEC to negotiate in what I gather is an excruciating process over many years, to do something in the end that is probably too little, too late. To my mind, that process fails."[40]

Fear of political influence

In the US political system, supervisors may feel the influence of legislators who have authority to adjust the legislation governing a supervisor's authority or to diminish the agency's funding. Thus, even the Federal Reserve Board, the most autonomous of the US financial regulators, can feel pressure, according to former Fed Governor Mark Olson: "When the Congress decides to move aggressively to curtail a regulator they can very directly narrow the focus of what a regulatory entity can do. . . . Congress had a lot of weapons one way or the other that they could use."[41] Governor Olson mentioned calls for Government Accountability Office reviews, changes in authorizing language, and other forms of influence that members of Congress could bring to bear on financial supervisors, including the Fed.

The problem was even more significant at oversight agencies that, unlike the bank supervisors, were subject to the appropriations process such as the SEC, CFTC, and the former GSE regulator, the Office of Federal Housing Enterprise Oversight (OFHEO). For these agencies, regulated entities can use the political process to seek to curtail their oversight, especially in times such as the early 2000s that reflected a deregulatory tone in Washington. Former SEC commissioner Harvey Goldschmid told Commission staff that understaffing was a chronic problem at the SEC and that "we never had enough people. The history of the SEC is almost adequate but never adequate resources, and then starvation."[42] Former OFHEO director Armando Falcon told the FCIC that his agency "was starved of resources for many years."[43] Falcon attributes this directly to the political influence of Fannie Mae and Freddie Mac. He also pointed to legislation by a Senate appropriations subcommittee to prevent the agency from spending $10 million of its appropriated funds until he was removed from office. While that language was absent from the final appropriations bill, the message had been sent.[44]

The problem was compounded if congressional committees or subcommittees declined to exercise restraint in applying pressure to regulators. On September 14, 2006, the Subcommittee on Financial Institutions and Consumer Credit of the House Committee on Financial Services summoned federal regulators to a hearing focused on implementation of draft Basel II capital standards and guidance on commercial real estate (CRE) that the federal bank and thrift regulators had proposed earlier that year.

Concern for competitiveness permeated the hearing. Subcommittee members saw Basel II as a way to improve the competitive position of the United States vis-à-vis Europe unless, as the FDIC was insisting, it was accompanied by a potentially higher minimum capital requirement. On the other hand, other committee members said they saw the Basel II proposals as a source of unfair advantage for large banks, which then could calculate their own capital levels based on risk models compared to smaller banks, which would not be in a position to invest in the models needed to implement Basel II.

With respect to the commercial real estate (CRE) guidance, subcommittee chairman Spencer Bachus expressed concern that the proposed guidance would be "unfairly burdensome for community banks that do not have opportunities to raise capital or diversify their portfolios like larger banks." Moreover, Bachus said, the guidance was too rigid; the supervisory agencies should leave it to individual examiners to determine on a case-by-case basis whether particular kinds of commercial real estate lending done by individual banks were risky or not.[45]

Three of the supervisory agencies tried to hold their ground. Federal Reserve Governor Susan Bies reiterated her position that the European version of Basel II was inadequate. Moreover, she said, "I think we are very proud that in the United States we consider our capital standards to be the strongest in the world, and we're not going to weaken them. . . . And this has not disadvantaged our banks."[46]

Fed Governor Bies, Comptroller of the Currency John Dugan, and FDIC Chair Sheila Bair also defended the guidance on commercial real estate. Governor Bies explained the need for lenders to underwrite commercial real estate loans carefully, because repayment depends on a flow of rental or other income to pay the mortgage that can be threatened by competition from other projects in the locality:

> A bank can do a great job of underwriting, but if projects in their market are getting funded and create excess capacity so there are a lot of vacancies or they're poorly underwritten for cash flow, so the maintenance and the property values go down, it can negatively affect the bank because those other projects could, through rent concessions and other things, attract tenants to competitive projects. . . . unlike other types of credit, bad lending can really affect their good credits.[47]

One regulator decided to backtrack. OTS Director John Reich claimed that he didn't agree with a joint letter that the four regulators had sent to Representative Barney Frank in which they expressed concern about CRE concentrations of risk and defended the proposed guidance, even though he had signed it:

> REPRESENTATIVE BARNEY FRANK. . . . Let me ask any of the regulators.
> MR. REICH. Well, Mr. Frank, I would plead guilty to signing onto a letter that I didn't necessarily agree with everything in it. I agreed with—
> MR. FRANK. The letter to me?
> MR. REICH. I believe that's the letter that you're referring to. That letter.
> MR. FRANK. Mr. Supervisor, that is very odd behavior.

Finally, industry representatives contended that the commercial real estate (CRE) guidance could cause significant harm to lenders and to the nation's communities. Thus, according to the Independent Community Bankers Association (ICBA):

> ICBA believes that the proposed commercial real estate guidance is seriously flawed, and we have strongly urged banking agencies not to go forward with its current form. Nearly 1,000 commenters filed letters with the agencies expressing grave concerns. Many community banks see it as a call to cut back on CRE lending. If a community bank must cut back, it means cutting back on one of its more profitable business lines, but we fear that it will also lead to an artificial credit crunch in the CRE sector, with less money being available to support community growth.[48]

In December three of the regulators, the Fed, OCC, and FDIC decided to issue CRE guidance somewhat weaker than the proposed guidance had been. Even so, the pressure did not abate. Representatives Barney Frank and Spencer Bachus issued a press release beforehand expressing their "disappointment" that the three-agency guidance "may unduly discourage lending."[49] The OTS went it alone and issued yet weaker guidance for the institutions that it supervised. The final result, as Janet Yellen told Financial Crisis Inquiry Commission staff, was CRE guidance that one could rip up and throw "in the garbage can."

This had real consequences. The FDIC reported in early 2011 that "of the 322 insured institutions that failed [since the start of 2008], more than 86 percent exceeded the CRE concentration levels that were defined in the December 12, 2006, Joint Guidance on CRE Lending. This is more than twice the proportion of banks with elevated CRE concentrations observed in the industry as a whole."[50] As the FDIC concluded, "in retrospect, it is clear that the bank regulatory agencies could have been more aggressive in their approach to institutions with the riskiest CRE exposures, especially in real estate development lending."[51]

Once again, it was not clear that industry was lobbying in its own best interests or that members of Congress who helped industry to apply pressure actually helped those constituents. Other examples can be found, such as the letter from the American Bankers Association objecting to the supervisors' proposed guidance on nontraditional mortgage products and arguing, among other objections, that the proposed categorization of stated-income loans (for which the borrower was allowed to declare rather than verify his or her income) as generally inappropriate was "overly prescriptive and inflexible."[52]

Difficulty of detecting risk when bank management didn't

There was another problem. The banking system had grown substantially between 2001 and 2008. The Federal Reserve Board released information showing that total assets at institutions that it supervised as the primary regulator or consolidated supervisor had almost doubled from $9.3 trillion in 2001 to $17.5 trillion in 2007, while total supervisory staff diminished over the period.[53] As they grew in size, major financial institutions also became more complex. Many firms grew through multiple acquisitions of companies whose operations they failed to integrate into a single management system, as was discussed in chapter 5. The lack of an integrated view of enterprise-wide risk was compounded by an increasing number of innovations in the financial markets. Because the innovations by definition were fairly new, risk managers too often lacked an understanding of the risk inherent in new lines of business such as manufacture of CDOs or sale of CDS protection; however sophisticated relevant financial models might be, many firms simply lacked adequate data points, collected from bad times as well as good, sufficient to make the models useful.

A major example was the inability of OTS to detect and address risk taking at AIG, which owned AIG Federal Savings Bank, a thrift institution, and thus was a thrift holding company. Despite its systemic importance, supervision of AIG at the holding company level was essentially nonexistent. OTS had a dedicated examiner team of only ten to fifteen people to supervise the $1 trillion financial conglomerate. Joseph Gonzalez, Examiner-in-Charge of AIG, commented that OTS was "overwhelmed" in their attempts to supervise AIG. With regard to AIG Financial Products (AIGFP), the part of AIG that sold over half a trillion dollars of CDS protection to investors and ultimately brought AIG down, he noted that "we had no cooperation from [AIGFP CEO Joseph] Cassano [and he] questioned our authority to examine FP," and further, that "we spent our time trying to get our hands around the company." He told Commission staff that "a big focus was just understanding AIG. I can't emphasize that enough. It was new to us, a very large organization . . . A lot of our focus was just understanding the interrelationships of these [AIG] entities worldwide."[54]

John Reich, former OTS Director, saw OTS vis-à-vis AIG as "like a gnat on an elephant."[55] AIG's size and complexity and OTS's insufficient resources and lack of clarity about its mandate with respect to AIGFP, all contributed to OTS' failure to recognize the extent of AIG's financial exposure and its virtual absence of risk management.

If a bank or bank holding company failed to perceive the extent of risks in its financial position, a supervisor was even less likely to be able to detect the risk; regulators did not seek out additional areas of risk that a company's internal audit or compliance had not already flagged. A FRBNY interview concluded that "supervisors often looked into areas a bank judged as risky rather than making an independent judgment of risk across the bank."[56] Richard Spillenkothen, former director of banking supervision and regulation at the Federal Reserve Board, summarized two of the regulators' beliefs: (1) "Risk management and controls in large financial firms, while not perfect, were good overall and getting better with time," and (2) "regulators' risk focused supervision programs and techniques, particularly those for large firms, while continuing to evolve, were generally effective and expected to continue to improve."[57]

Spillenkothen concluded that these rosy assumptions were widely enough held by policy makers and supervisors, and were reiterated by agency leaders, so that they affected "the perceptions, findings, and conclusions of examiners and supervisors in carrying out day-to-day supervisory responsibilities."[58]

Some institutions didn't take risk management seriously. Roger Cole, another former director of bank supervision at the Federal Reserve Board, told FCIC staff:

> Key people in the industry were throwing risk management out on the table as kind of a diversion. You've got those supervisors in the Basel committee really focused on talking about risk management and good practices and governance and whatever. And that's fine. But we're in the business of product, and we've got to sell, we've got to make money—it's all about marketing.[59]

In practical terms, excessive reliance on financial firms' perceptions of risk meant that supervisors often missed serious concentrations of risk. Supervisors often relied "on the supervised institution's internal management information system (MIS) and the output from models, as opposed to requiring data provided according to standardized regulatory reports."[60] They generally reviewed reports submitted to bank management and looked at them at that point in time. Supervisors did little trend analysis, especially with data outside that which was provided by the firm in the format that the firm had provided. Many times too regulators succumbed to the false precision that a model could provide, and failed to appreciate the nature of catastrophic exposures that might be inherent in a firm's business.[61]

To the extent that the regulators perceived risk management weaknesses mostly after losses had become manifest, it is not clear how well federal supervision promoted improved risk management. The Federal Reserve Bank of New York (FRBNY) issued annual reports of inspection for the holding companies that it supervised. In the reports for the years 2006, 2007, and 2008 on Citigroup, FRBNY gave increasingly negative ratings for Citi's overall risk management, declining from a 2 ("satisfactory") for 2006 to a 3 ("fair") for 2007 and a 4 ("marginal") for 2008. The pattern of decline in ratings that FRBNY assigned to Citigroup is seen in table 7.1.

The 2007 report, issued in early 2008, is candid in its recognition that FRBNY's downgrade in ratings followed rather than led the revelation of Citigroup's losses.[62] The company had reported record profits in 2005 and good returns in 2006, recognized significant losses in 2007, and received billions of dollars of federal support in 2008. It appears that the supervisor, and not only

TABLE 7.1 Supervisory Risk Management Ratings for Citigroup, 2006–2008

	12/31/06	12/31/07	12/31/08
Overall Risk Management Rating	2 (i.e., "Satisfactory")	3 (i.e., "Fair")	4 (i.e., "Marginal")
Component Ratings:			
Board and Senior Management Oversight	2	3	4
Policies, Procedures, and Limits	2	3	4
Risk Monitoring and MIS	2	3	3
Internal Controls	2	3	3

Calculated from Federal Reserve Bank of New York, "Summary of Supervisory Activity and Findings, Citigroup, Inc.," transmitted April 15, 2008, and Federal Reserve Bank of New York, "Summary of Supervisory Activity and Findings, Citigroup, Inc.," transmitted January 14, 2009.

Citigroup management, succumbed to the problem of too much success that Dartmouth Business School professor Sydney Finkelstein highlighted as a potential harbinger of failure.

As the Government Accountability Office summarizes:

> In the years leading up the financial crisis, some regulators identified weaknesses in the risk management systems of large, complex financial institutions. Regulators told us that despite these identified weaknesses, they did not take forceful action—such as changing their assessments—until the crisis occurred because the institutions reported a strong financial position and senior management had presented the regulators with plans for change. Moreover, regulators acknowledged that in some cases they had not fully appreciated the extent of these weaknesses until the financial crisis occurred and risk management systems were tested by events. Regulators also acknowledged they had relied heavily on management representations of risks.[63]

The draft FRBNY study concluded that "it is difficult to inspect a risk management division to determine if it is effective in helping the bank manage those risks. On paper, an area may look independent and have reporting lines that go to the bank's top managers, but these managers may not listen to the risk management area. . . . The risk management function was often marginalized within the banks."[64]

In retrospect, senior supervisors say that they could and sometimes did detect major deficiencies. Once again, as with boards of directors and risk managers at firms, there was a power of simple questions that could have unlocked answers about areas where supervised firms were taking on too much risk. The Fed's Roger Cole explains that examiners need to follow the money when they look at firms:

Supervisors going forward, especially, have to really be focused on where is the money coming from, where are they making their money? And that—it's those centers of big profits that have to have some risk because the competition is fierce. And you're not going to make big dollars without getting into some risk. And so it's understanding those risks associated with the big dollar revenue generators. And these firms have huge overhead expenses to cover; they have to make huge profits. And the question is how do they do that with competition so ferocious?[65]

Cole also believes that simple questions can help to flag deficiencies in financial products such as CDOs and other mortgage securities:

[There was] an asymmetry of knowledge, that somebody was willing to pay a lot more than these very, very knowledgeable bankers and investment bankers thought that they could get just on a standalone loan product basis. And right off that's kind of a red flag: What's going on here and who's likely to be right in terms of the buyer versus the seller of these bundle [sic] products?[66]

In short, just as was true for firms' boards and management, the process of disciplined inquiry can make a big difference in whether or not a supervisor detects risks in time.

Difficulty of taking action against a profitable firm with deficiencies

Even when a supervisor identified deficiencies at a large complex financial institution, it was difficult to persuade management to take prompt action to correct the deficiencies. To some extent this related to faith in the markets rather than regulation:

Regulators faced and often shared skepticism that regulators could push for more effective practices than those required by the market for controlling firm risk. After years of record profits, low and declining price volatility and minimal losses during 2003–2007, supervisors faced an up-hill battle to challenge banks' appetite for risk or their business practices.[67]

Roger Cole reported his perception that there was

a lot of complaining from the industry in terms of, "Oh, this is too much capital," and, "It's going to kill us," blah-blah, and, "There's too much involvement of the board of directors—you're always telling the board of directors they have to do this, that, or even have to understand the risk profile of the company. How can you ask a board member to do that? How are we going to get anybody to serve on the board?"

Cole concluded that "I have this just innate feeling that . . . we spent too much time trying to work acceptable deals with the industry."[68]

Moreover, as the Fed's Sabeth Siddique told FCIC staff, "a bureaucrat is not paid to take risks," and can get his or her "head chopped off."[69] A draft 2009 FRBNY report found that supervisory staff often feared to speak up. It lists the following responses to interviews of its staff:

> No one feels individually accountable for financial crisis mistakes because management is through consensus.
>
> Grow up in this culture and you learn that small mistakes are not tolerated.
>
> Don't want to be too far outside from where the management is thinking.
>
> No opportunity to earn enough merit from ten right policy decisions to compensate for one wrong decision.
>
> The organization does not encourage thinking outside the box.
>
> After you get shot down a couple of times you tend not to "go there" any more.
>
> Until I know what my boss thinks I don't want to tell you.
>
> Members of the vetting committee fight their way through a giant document rather than risk prioritizing and being wrong. People are risk-averse, so they include everything.[70]

The report states that supervisory staff were deferential to the banks they supervised: "Regulators were reluctant to be prescriptive in exam findings. Beyond not wanting to impose their judgment on an outwardly successful business model, supervisors were concerned that their recommendations might be wrong and would be faced with ongoing criticism from the bank."[71]

The OCC Examination Handbook of May 2001 indicated that OCC examiners would focus on the quality of a bank's risk management rather than trying to limit risks:

> The OCC recognizes that banking is a business of taking risks in order to earn profits. . . . Large banks assume varied and complex risks that warrant a risk-oriented supervisory approach. Under this approach, examiners do not attempt to restrict risk-taking but rather determine whether banks identify, understand, and control the risks they assume.[72]

This attitude resulted in examiners trying to use informal persuasion rather than taking formal actions that might have achieved a more prompt response from the supervised firm, its management, and board of directors. Words such as "prod" appeared in FCIC interviews with supervisors, most memorably in an interview with a senior OTS supervisor responsible for examining AIG.

Thus, although Washington Mutual (WaMu) failed in 2008, OTS examined WaMu annually and rated WaMu with a high a composite 2 from 2001 through

2007. Further, in the area of asset quality, OTS rated WaMu a 2 through February 2008. OTS supervisors commented during an Inspector General investigation into WaMu's failure that "even though underwriting and risk management practices were less than satisfactory, WaMu was making money and loans were performing."[73] The Inspector General's final report on OTS supervision of WaMu found that although OTS knew of significant shortcomings at WaMu and "had formal enforcement authority to compel WaMu to correct deficiencies, OTS never took such action."[74]

The problem of information gaps between career supervisors and top officials

Among other shortcomings, the OTS had a problem of cultural dissonance, between the perspectives of examiners on the ground and the agency's top officials. The Senate Permanent Subcommittee on Investigations reported on "demoralization" of OTS examiners. As James Vanasek, formerly chief risk officer at WaMu testified:

> My opinion is that the OTS Examiner-in-Charge during the period of time in which I was involved . . . did an excellent job of finding and raising the issues. Likewise, I found good performance from . . . the FDIC Examiner-in-Charge. They were both there the entire time that I was there.
>   What I cannot explain is why the superiors in the agencies didn't take a tougher tone with the banks given the degree of findings, negative findings. My experience with the OTS, versus with the OCC, was completely different. So there seemed to be a tolerance there or a political influence on senior management of those agencies that prevented them from taking a more active stance. By a more active stance, I mean putting the banks under letters of agreement and forcing change.[75]

Vanasek suggested that top levels of the OTS were more inclined to be lenient with WaMu than examiners because of the large fraction of thrift industry assets that OTS represented, and "so I think they had a very strong mutual interest in the company succeeding."[76] OTS funded itself on fees based on the asset size of institutions it was supposed to supervise. Top OTS officials failed to engage in constructive and respectful dialogue with examiners who raised so many warnings about WaMu.

The problem of organizational dissonance also existed at the Federal Reserve. Some career officials, such as Sabeth Siddique, were more attuned to impending systemic risks than some top officials in the Federal Reserve System. Siddique made a presentation in 2005 about growth in nontraditional mortgage loans, declining underwriting standards, and growing risk from lo-doc and stated income loans.[77] Susan Bies, then a Fed governor, recalled,

I don't recall anybody saying that they didn't believe the presentation that was put together wasn't credible. I mean, I think everybody thought it was credible. But there were some people on the board and regional presidents who just wanted to come to a different answer. So they did ignore it, or the full thrust of it. . . . Well, there's just some regional presidents that, you know, have more of a, "Let the banks and free market view prevail."[78]

The problem of political levels failing to take appropriate account of warnings by supervisors is not restricted to the United States. In Spain, a union of bank examiners, the Association of Inspectors of the Bank of Spain, wrote on May 26, 2006 to top officials of the Ministry of Economy and Housing warning of the housing bubble in that country and the impact if it would burst (as it later did), and objecting to "the well-intentioned optimism" of the governor of the Spanish central bank.[79]

Failure to consider the larger financial organization or the financial system

GLBA created segmented supervisory relationships that reduced the ability of regulators to take an organization-wide perspective on risks to financial institutions. Multiple witnesses told FCIC staff about the segmentation that GLBA created. The OCC didn't look at external threats to a national bank from other places in the holding company, much less from places outside the regulated banking system. GLBA even placed wholly owned subsidiaries of national banks such as broker/dealer and registered advisers off- limits to the OCC. The Federal Reserve found itself hampered by its commitment to Fed-Lite, despite its responsibility for supervising holding companies. Supervisors looked at particular nodes of the financial system—individual banks and holding companies—and often neglected the linkages.

The focus on individual institutions had multiple consequences. First, supervisors generally tested whether a bank or holding company could absorb a shock directed at the individual institution; they generally failed to look at the potential impact of problems arising in the larger conglomerate organization. The OCC recounted that failure to take a systemic perspective had serious results for many national banks: "Even though national banks were not as significantly involved in originating subprime and payment option products . . . subprime-related exposures came back into the national banks through CDOs that had been arranged and structured by nonbank holding company affiliates. This failure to see and aggregate comparable risks arising in different parts of the entire banking organization is an issue that supervisors and firms must address."[80]

Or, when monitoring liquidity risk, supervisors focused on events affecting a single institution and failed to anticipate what actually happened: a market-wide failure to be able to sell assets that previously had been considered to be highly saleable. If the shock had hit only a single institution, it could have sold its AAA rated securities to another firm; the system wide shock involved calling into question the credit quality of AAA private label securities across the financial system and making them unsalable except at fire-sale prices. Ronald Marcus, an OTS examiner, told FCIC staff, "banks die because of liquidity issues."[81] As noted in chapter 4, when the markets panicked, it was lack of liquidity that suddenly brought down many large institutions.

The Essential Role of Supervision

The literature on governance and risk management suggests many good ideas for improving management at major financial firms.[82] But if an institution in fact does not improve, or adopts the trappings of good governance and risk management but not the actual practice, the literature does not propose how to deal with this. The only answer seems to be to impose discipline and improved governance and risk management from the outside. This was supposed to be the theory of Basel II; yet while large complex institutions invested in risk management systems to justify lower capital standards, regulators never perceived that they possessed the mandate, and never developed sufficient capacity to deal effectively with poor governance and risk management that nonetheless persisted at many major firms.

Collective action through government appears to be the only solution to the kinds of excessive competitive pressures that existed before the crisis, and especially in 2005–2007. Citigroup CEO Charles Prince made the argument for supervisory intervention at a dinner with then-Treasury Secretary Henry Paulson on June 26, 2007. Paulson recounts that Prince asked with respect to leveraged loans "whether given the competitive pressures there wasn't a role for regulators to tamp down some of the riskier practices," and "isn't there something you can do to order us not to take all these risks?"[83]

Successful firms in the financial crisis largely managed to take care of themselves. But, as Prince noted, only a regulator could help to set a floor on conduct and prevent less successful firms from undertaking risky practices that have cost our country so much in so many ways. A draft FRBNY report concludes with an insight that supports Prince's view:

> The most fundamental of the lessons learned during the crisis is that banks cannot be relied upon to protect themselves adequately against systemic risk. This shakes a basic foundation of regulation. It turns out that risk management systems were far less robust than had been imagined.

Not only were the models flawed, but risk managers were not empowered. They appeared to be doing their job, but much evidence after the fact suggests that they had little power to challenge or stop transactions during the boom. The transactions were apparently very profitable and the business side of the bank in most cases was unwilling to slow down because of risk concerns.[84]

What is reassuring about the Federal Reserve and OCC lessons-learned documents and the Commission staff's interviews with numerous supervisors at all of the federal supervisory agencies is their forthright analysis of supervisory shortcomings in the period leading up to the financial crisis; the regulators deserve credit for this frank recognition. In the end, effective supervision and regulation is essential to try to protect the financial system against failures of governance and risk management at banks, especially at large complex financial institutions—and, if possible, in the shadow banking sector. Chapter 9 seeks to address this issue.

Conundrums of Supervision

That said, difficulties of organizing and managing supervision must be recognized. The first problem relates to Stanton's Law, the precept that "risk will migrate to the place where government is least equipped to deal with it."[85] The capital markets found numerous places where supervisors could not monitor and deal with major risks, including the shadow banking system: structured investment vehicles of commercial banks, money market funds, the repo market, commercial paper programs, private securitization conduits, and collateralized debt obligations that were virtually unregulated except by the vagaries of the rating agencies and exuberance of the market during the housing bubble. Huge volumes of subprime, alt-A, interest-only, and other toxic mortgages went to these parts of the market. Even when shadow banking organizations were parts of bank holding companies, regulators did not feel empowered to check on them, both because of their limited mandates under GLBA and also because of resource constraints.

The problem of systemic risk originating outside of the system of supervised depository institutions is not a new one. On January 20, 1931, during the Great Depression, the Senate Banking and Currency Committee, as it was then known, heard testimony from George Harrison, the head of the Federal Reserve Bank of New York. In his testimony Harrison pointed to borrowing that fueled excessive stock market speculation in 1928 and 1929. The Federal Reserve tried to dampen speculation, Harrison said, by raising rates it charged on loans to stock brokers and dealers. However, the Fed action affected only regulated institutions; lenders in what he called the "bootleg banking system," outside of the Fed's purview, only increased their lending as the Fed's actions raised the costs of bank loans:

> At one time over half the total volume of money borrowed by brokers and dealers was money advanced in that fashion. It was money that was totally outside of the control of the banking system; It was money loaned by lenders who had no responsibility to the money market or to the banking system. It was money loaned without any responsibility on their part to maintain reserves of any character.[86]

Another concern about differential regulation for different kinds of organizations grew more pronounced over the years. Similar to Countrywide, a regulated holding company could simply migrate to the OTS where supervision was considered more congenial. This raises the issue of regulatory shopping and the pressure this places on supervisory agencies. Former Federal Reserve Governor Susan Bies remembered concerns raised within the Fed, even after problems became apparent in the mortgage industry:

> Based on the data that I saw back then, I think it was—and this is off of memory; I could be off—but I want to say two-thirds of the more troublesome forms of mortgages were being originated by non-commercial bank lenders. Now, some of those were subsidiaries of bank holding companies. And there was some real concern about if the Fed tightened down on non-bank subs of bank holding companies, whether that would create an unlevel playing field between bank holding company mortgage lenders and stand alone mortgage lenders, who the Fed did not regulate.[87]

This dynamic continues even after the financial crisis. For example, the Basel Committee on Banking Supervision is seeking to improve the international supervisory framework for addressing liquidity risk. One of the concerns that may limit the extent of such measures is the fear that, as JPMorgan Chase's treasurer explained in 2011, burdensome requirements might "direct traditional banking activities away from regulated financial institutions, into market sectors that are less regulated."[88] In other words, fear of migration of functions from the regulated financial sector to the unregulated or underregulated shadow banking sector, deters supervisory agencies and regulated institutions from proposing the kind or extent of preventative measures they otherwise would. The extent that this is wise or not would seem to depend on the balance between benefits and burdens of particular regulatory proposals. Alan Greenspan was not completely wrong: Unfettered regulatory prescriptions, enacted without regard to burdens on financial institutions' efficiencies, effectiveness, and innovation, would be a mistake. Chapter 9 revisits this issue.

One other fear was that financial firms might change their domicile to countries with more congenial supervisory frameworks. The UK's Lord Adair Turner is adamant that this concern is misplaced:

A lot of what the industry tells us on that is often nonsense, I think, because they would say that, wouldn't they. That's their game. And a lot of it, of course, is often to do with tax, to which the regulator replies, "That's not my job," right, "that's Treasury's job." Right? You know, so issues about whether people move to Switzerland from London for tax, that is for the Chancellor of the Exchequer to decide. That's not a regulatory issue.

On the regulatory side, I'm pretty confident that there's—that the Swiss National Bank are going to be as tough as us on capital and there's going to be no sense to move to Switzerland for capital, nor, by the way, to Singapore or—the emerging markets, let's be blunt, have tighter capital requirements than the developed economies. So if banks tell you they're going to move to Singapore or Hong Kong because our capital requirements are too high, that is nonsense, absolute nonsense.[89]

That said, differences among rules on matters relating to particular transactions or compensation of traders may well encourage migration of parts of a business to other jurisdictions.[90] In other words, processes of regulation and supervision would seem—almost inevitably—to drive transactions from regulated institutions to those that are less well regulated. This would seem to be an ongoing dynamic that, as is discussed in chapter 9, requires enhanced authority of the Fed or another federal agency, to monitor risks that arise in the less-regulated sector and, when necessary, to devise ways to protect regulated institutions from the impact of those risks when they acquire systemically important dimensions.

Rules versus Discretion

The legal literature is replete with discussions of rules versus application of discretion on a case-by-case basis.[91] The choice of applying rules, with their nominal clarity, versus discretion, and the desire to tailor application of principles on an individual basis, is at the core of government oversight of private financial firms.

In the financial context, practical issues tend to shape the choice. On the one hand, regulated companies may favor regulations to obtain greater certainty about what they may or may not do, and under what conditions. Perhaps most vigorous in seeking hard-wired requirements were the two GSEs, Fannie Mae and Freddie Mac. Thus, only three months before the company failed, Fannie Mae CEO Daniel Mudd asked that capital standards be largely prescribed by law, as reported by *American Banker*:

> Mr. Mudd urged lawmakers to be as specific as possible about the powers they grant to the new regulator [now FHFA], including its ability to

enforce capital requirements. "The more that that's elaborated in the legislation, the better," he said. "The whole mortgage finance market is built around how much capital we hold."[92]

The Housing and Economic Recovery Act of 2008 (HERA), signed into law July 30, 2008, reflected this position. It required the new housing GSE regulator, the Federal Housing Finance Agency, to conduct an estimated 25–30 rulemakings to implement key provisions of the act, including any increases in capital requirements. The GSEs sought the certainty of largely favorable legislative language that prescribed regulations to be far superior to the vagaries of a process that would have given their regulator greater discretion.

On the other hand, where there is discretion, the supervisor opens itself up to pressure—such as a large complex financial institution can apply—to be lenient. This pressure may be rooted in jurisdictional considerations, as when a supervisory agency fears losing authority over a large financial institution such as Countrywide that decided to switch supervisors, or that credibly threatens to shift from a federal to state charter or to move operations overseas or otherwise shift to another supervisor.

Large and complex financial firms can also exert influence directly on the examiners who are supposed to exercise discretion, or on others higher up the examiners' chain of command. Influence can come in many forms. One is Willem Buiter's "cognitive regulatory capture," discussed in chapter 4, in which the examiner becomes enmeshed in the regulated firm's world view by helping the firm to resolve problems. This type of cognitive capture reflects an ambiguity in the examiner's role. On the one hand the examiner is supposed to advise the regulated institution how it should improve; on the other, the examiner is supposed to detect shortcomings and direct the institution to take corrective action. This is similar to the complexities of the role of a board of directors, also discussed in chapter 4. For both examiners and boards, it is far more comfortable to play the advisory role rather than trying to be an auditor and adverse force.

The problem is compounded for examiners (and boards of directors too) by information asymmetries; management simply knows more than either the examiner or the board. That is especially true in a fast-moving realm such as financial services when complex innovations constantly come into play.

Many years ago, just after the savings and loan debacle and the New England financial crisis, James Pierce wrote a book called *The Future of American Banking*. He too examined the supervisory process:

> Government supervisors who interrogate bankers earn maybe sixty thousand dollars a year; the people they question often make ten or twenty times that and operate out of offices that make a regulator's quarters look like a shelter for the homeless. How can regulators second-guess the management of these multinational corporations . . .? Can they

evaluate how [a particular] loan fits into the entire loan portfolio or how it adds or deducts from the riskiness of the entire banking organization? How are they going to evaluate the risks of the bank's securities trading . . . or its bewildering array of off-balance sheet activities . . .? What about hedging strategies . . .? The answer is clear: regulators cannot substitute their judgment for a bank manager's."[93]

The financial crisis showed a similar dynamic, except that disparities in compensation, office infrastructure, and training to understand financial complexities have widened dramatically in the interim. Little wonder, as the Commission learned in multiple interviews, that examiners preferred to flag demonstrable compliance violations rather than more nuanced concerns such as whether a board was adequately involved in robust decision making or whether the chief risk officer had adequate influence in a supervised firm. One senior supervisor pointed out how losses occurred at a large complex financial institution and he tracked them back to flawed decisions and poor governance processes. Of course, once losses appear it may be too late to prevent substantial harm to an institution, especially under the circumstances that occurred in the financial crisis. Not only private firms but also the financial supervisors exhibited inability to deal effectively with governance and risk management.

Hyman Minsky

WILL IT HAPPEN AGAIN?

Over an expansion, new financial instruments and new ways of financing activity develop. Typically, defects of the new ways and the new institutions are revealed when the crunch comes.

—HYMAN MINSKY

Underlying the bubble and its collapse was a dynamic that had been predicted several decades ago by a little-known economist, Hyman Minsky. He observed that financial boom-and-bust cycles, such as he studied from the Great Depression, were a natural consequence of the financial markets. Understanding these cycles helps to place governance and risk management into context. In the aftermath of a crisis, lenders and borrowers both become cautious. At that point, governance and risk management, whatever their quality, are unlikely to lead to overlending and systemic risk. Problems arise largely as memories fade, the economy enters a period of apparent prosperity, leverage increases, and lending standards become more lax. That is when good governance and strong risk management count most. Badly managed firms can fail in strong economic times, but the chances of systemic risk are smaller then. The key is to manage firms well during good times so that they can survive when circumstances change.

For Minsky, there are three types of lending: (1) loans based on the ability of the borrower to repay them, (2) loans based on anticipated cashflows from assets, sufficient to make timely interest payments but not the original principal, and (3) loans based on future increases in the value of collateral. As prosperity flourishes, banks and other lenders take on greater leverage as a way to increase their returns to shareholders, and to the managers who are rewarded with stock options.

Because asset values such as the value of homes securing mortgage loans increase, lenders begin to relax their standards. They move away from loans based on the borrower's ability to repay, or even on ability to repay interest, to loans based on the value of the underlying asset. In other words, as memories of the last crisis fade, lenders begin to believe that loans can profitably be made to borrowers who are not creditworthy according to traditional rules: after all, if the borrower defaults, the lender can simply sell the asset and recoup its investment from the increased asset price. In the case of home mortgages and mortgage-backed securities, lenders masked their reduced lending standards with econometric models that purported to show the safety of such lending. This was true so long as home prices were increasing. Figure 2.7 in chapter 2 shows the bubble in house prices.

But the growth in asset values eventually stops. Borrowers default on their loans in growing numbers. Defaults result in forced sales as borrowers sell to get out from under their loans, forcing further declines in asset values, and the cycle spirals downward. Declining asset values force increasing defaults, and highly leveraged lenders begin to fail as their collateral drops in value below the amounts loaned. They are forced to sell better quality assets to try to stay in business, and these sales further depress asset prices. The culmination of all the forced sales at fire-sale prices has become known as a "Minsky moment." The downward spiral of asset prices, similar to the upward spiral that preceded it, continues to reinforce itself. It was this downward spiral that the Federal Reserve and Treasury tried to block with their multiple interventions during the crisis.

Minsky's model reveals the paradoxes that underlie the recent financial crisis. At the systemic level, there is tension between interventions to prevent crises from breaking out and the advent of a Minsky moment when, precisely because of prior interventions to forestall financial crises, the market gains unbounded confidence in financial system stability and creates a massive credit bubble followed by catastrophic collapse. In the early 1980s the US government intervened to prevent major insolvent banks from closing because of losses from unwise petrodollar lending. In the late 1980s the United States resolved the savings and loan debacle and numerous bank failures without greatly troubling the larger economy. And in the 1990s, the Federal Reserve arranged for liquidation of the failed hedge fund Long Term Capital Management, again without disturbing the larger economy. Little wonder that regulators and financial firms alike believed in their power to control the worst excesses of financial folly.

Understanding Minsky cycles helps to understand why systemic risk is so hard to contain. As happened in 1989 and 1998, government interventions to forestall financial crises can give the markets confidence in financial system stability and help to encourage a major bubble followed by collapse. That is especially true after the recent crisis, given the way that the Treasury and Fed provided massive taxpayer support for insolvent financial institutions such as AIG, Bank of America, Citigroup, Fannie Mae, and Freddie Mac, and even for insolvent auto companies.

Such intervention, while helpful in mitigating the crisis of the moment, has serious behavioral consequences. The most serious consequence is the way that such rescues protect debt holders from loss. Monitoring by debt holders has traditionally been a strong source of market discipline. As a firm's risk profile increases, debt holders require increased rates of return and also shorten the maturity of the firm's obligations they are willing to hold. At some point a debt holder will require the firm to post collateral or other protection against default and, finally, debt holders may decide that they simply won't invest in the firm under any conditions.

That's fine if a single firm gets into trouble. The problem becomes greater when solvency of many major firms is called into question at once and debt holders begin pulling their money out of many firms at once. That occurred in the panic stage of the financial crisis. Then the Treasury and Fed, throwing free market principles overboard (except with respect to Lehman's bankruptcy), had to intervene drastically to stop the panic from cascading even deeper into the financial system.

This was not the first time the government helped preserve insolvent institutions. In the Great Depression, the government used the Reconstruction Finance Corporation, a government agency, to provide preferred stock to shore up the balance sheets of otherwise insolvent institutions. In actions echoed in the TARP program and the infusion of Treasury stock into Fannie Mae and Freddie Mac, the government examined institutions that had reopened after the "bank holiday" of 1933 and pronounced them qualified to do business.[1] As Jesse Jones, chairman of the RFC board, later wrote: "In literally thousands of cases, in those feverish days and nights, it was difficult to decide whether a bank was truly sound . . . A great many unsound banks were allowed to resume business."[2]

In the 1980s, the government also refrained from requiring write-downs of delinquent or nonperforming loans, this time to protect large money-center banks from insolvency from losses on large portfolios of sovereign loans they had made the previous decade as they recycled petrodollar investments from oil-producing countries. Former FDIC Chairman William Seidman later wrote that regulatory forbearance was needed because seven or eight of the ten largest US banks might have been considered insolvent in 1982, which could have precipitated a crisis.[3] Only after 1987, five years after the crisis broke, did banks begin to take large write-downs of their troubled assets. As Seidman concluded:

> In the case of Latin American loans, forbearance gave the lending banks time to make new arrangements with their debtors and meanwhile acquire enough capital so that losses on Latin American loans would not be fatal. Like medicine and the other healing arts, bank regulation is an art, not a science.[4]

The FDIC review similarly concluded that forbearance proved successful then because banks were eventually able to increase their loss reserves and take charge-offs and "no money-center bank failed."[5] Hyman Minsky would have appreciated the logic and the second-order effects that can occur when authorities intervene to protect major banks from their serious mistakes.

Many years ago Walter Bagehot, the father of central banking, had articulated principles of what a central bank should do in a crisis. In his book *Lombard Street*, named after the street on which the Bank of England was located in London, Bagehot tried to distinguish financial firms that were illiquid (i.e., had a positive net worth) but couldn't meet demands from debt holders to pay maturing obligations in a liquidity crisis from those that were insolvent (i.e., had a negative net worth).[6] He developed a rule that prescribed for the central bank to lend to solvent but illiquid banks to help them meet their short-term demand for cash. The central bank should lend at "a very high rate of interest" based on good collateral, so that firms would not take advantage of the opportunity too often to borrow money that way.[7] By contrast, insolvent banks would close. As in a bankruptcy, creditors would simply sell the firm's assets and recoup what they could from the proceeds. As investors saw that they could lose money from an insolvency, they gained added incentive to be cautious about investing in a financial firm without conducting due diligence first.

This time around, policy makers felt pressure to act to save the financial system from calamity even if this meant bailing out debt holders in insolvent banks. One Treasury official said afterward, in words reminiscent of Jesse Jones, "we knew we were dealing with insolvent companies, but we didn't know which ones they were." As the Fed and Treasury strove mightily to avert another Great Depression, there was no time to worry about second-order effects such as the complacency that debt holders would gain if they saw that large complex financial firms were indeed too big to fail and government could be expected to protect debt holders when the firms got into trouble.

President Bush explained the pressure to act:

> I was in the Roosevelt Room and Chairman Bernanke and Secretary Paulson, after a month of every weekend where they're calling, saying, we got to do this for AIG, or this for Fannie and Freddie, came in and said, the financial markets are completely frozen and if we don't do something about it, it is conceivable we will see a depression greater than the Great Depression. So I analyzed that and decided I didn't want to be the President during a depression greater than the Great Depression, or the beginning of a depression greater than the Great Depression. So we moved, and moved hard.[8]

The result was to prevent calamity, but with consequences for market discipline. According to former comptroller of the currency Eugene Ludwig:

> The use of governmental largess, flooding the market with liquidity, bailouts and/or safety net extensions in a time of crisis, is necessary but costly. In addition to the more easily measurable short-and intermediate-term

costs, they have serious long-term costs, including the buildup of moral hazard. I fear what we have done in this past cycle is to privatize the profits and to socialize the risks. This then sets the framework for less risk-averse behaviors in the future.[9]

In other words, absent corrective actions by policy makers, market discipline, the next time around, is likely to be even weaker than it was this time. If the markets do not provide the necessary discipline, then an alternative source of discipline might be government supervision and regulation. However, as was seen in chapter 7, the fragmented nature of bank supervision makes it difficult for regulators to take necessary steps even if they do detect problems in time. As Ludwig states:

> In my country, where we have a cacophony of regulatory bodies, serious regulatory consolidation must take place. Whether or not there should be a single consolidated regulator in the U.S. or elsewhere is an open question. . . . Having one regulator makes a great deal of sense from the standpoints of equivalency and efficiency, but large bureaucracies come with their own challenges.[10]

Senator Chris Dodd sought to strengthen the regulatory framework by consolidating supervisory powers of the four federal bank and thrift regulators, the OCC, OTS, FDIC, and the Fed into a single safety-and-soundness regulator. The proposal immediately ran into what the *New York Times* called a "phalanx of industry opposition."[11] When Senator Dodd brought his bill to the floor the regulatory consolidation feature failed passage by a 91-to-8 Senate vote. Community banks, state chartered banks, and regional Federal Reserve Banks all weighed in against the idea of supervisory consolidation even though by the time of the vote, Senator Dodd had modified it to try to accommodate smaller banks while still precluding banks from shopping for a congenial regulator. One consequence of the Senate vote against consolidation, Senator Dodd pointed out, was to give large national banks an incentive to move from OCC regulation to less expensive, and less onerous, state regulation:

> Since the OCC depends on assessments from the banks it regulates to fund its operations, the agency may go to great lengths to keep its banks from converting to State charters. We have seen what happens when depository institutions exploit these weaknesses in our bank regulatory system and when agencies compromise their supervisory integrity to maintain companies within their domain. If this happens, we could have another race to the bottom—just like the competition and regulatory arbitrage that led to the financial crisis.[12]

Although the final Dodd-Frank Act makes progress on some of these issues (by subsuming the OTS into the OCC, for example), the fragmentation of financial institution supervision and regulation remains. The federal organization responsible for monitoring systemic risk, the Financial Stability Oversight Council, consists of the disparate bank supervisory agencies and others who have diverse agendas and lack of a common focus on systemic issues. In one positive—if limited—development, Dodd-Frank reinforced the mandate of the Fed to supervise nonbank affiliates of holding companies. But Senator Dodd's vision of preventing banks from shopping for their regulator was not included in his final legislation. Indeed, many observers believe that enactment of Dodd-Frank at all was a very close call.

The danger, of course, is that both market discipline and feedback from government will be inadequate to stem the powerful forces that flawed organizational structures and incentive systems unleash when inadequately constrained. That is true both for large systemically important institutions with debt holders that now have clear evidence that government will protect them from losses, as well as the many smaller institutions that are concentrating in commercial real estate and other types of lending with risks that are both hard to assess and cyclical in nature.

Other dynamics also merit consideration. As was seen in chapter 2, high leverage, excessive borrowing, and a major asset bubble preceded the financial crisis of 2008. Carmen Reinhart and Kenneth Rogoff, in their book *This Time is Different: Eight Centuries of Financial Folly*, observe that these are frequent preconditions to a financial crisis:

> If there is one common theme to the vast range of crisis . . ., it is that excessive debt accumulation, whether it be by the government, banks, corporations, or consumers, often poses greater systemic risk than it seems during a boom. Private sector borrowing binges can inflate housing and stock prices far beyond their long-run sustainable levels, and make banks seem more profitable and stable than they really are . . . Debt-fueled booms all too often provide false affirmation of a government's policies, a financial institution's ability to make outsized profits, or a country's standard of living. Most of these booms end badly.[13]

The problem with bubbles or booms, they note, is that they foster complacency. Governments take credit for a "great moderation," financial institutions look much more profitable than is ultimately sustainable, and regulators (and other gate keepers such as rating agencies and accounting firms) begin to believe that a "light touch" is superior to restrictions that could curtail growing prosperity.

Complacency also grows within financial firms. Risk officers lose sway as firms reap unprecedented revenues year after year. So long as the CEO is at least minimally capable, firms become consistently profitable whether the board is alert or helpful or not. Losses from poor lending become minimal; the rising tide seems to lift all loans.

A particular problem concerns leverage. In boom times losses diminish dramatically, and leverage becomes increasingly attractive as a way to enhance earnings without taking perceptibly more risk. Many of the most significant innovations before the financial crisis helped firms to increase their leverage. A classic case was AIG and its use of credit default swaps (CDSs). The firm issued hundreds of billions of dollars of these financial guarantees that were not subject to AIG capital requirements, to help other institutions reduce their needed capital. The company reported that "approximately $379 billion of the $527 billion in notional exposure on AIGFP's super senior credit default swap portfolio as of December 31, 2007 were written to facilitate regulatory capital relief for financial institutions primarily in Europe."[14]

Capital arbitrage was also at the root of other innovations such as SIVs and conduits, which removed assets and liabilities from the balance sheets of Citigroup and other firms and thus reduced capital that the firms needed to hold. Citi structured its off-balance sheet conduits to provide liquidity puts, which added contractual obligations to the reputational stake that it had to ensure that its sponsored securitization vehicles would not fail and harm customers of the parent firm. Once the SIVs and conduits began to fail, Citi and other firms needed to bring them back onto their balance sheets—at just the wrong time. Only then did Citi need to hold capital to back those assets, again at just the wrong time, when the firm was hemorrhaging losses and couldn't raise enough private capital to cover the decline in its balance sheet.

It is not clear that supervisory agencies can write capital rules that are immune to balance sheet arbitrage. Citigroup's liquidity puts and AIG's poorly written CDS contracts that required the firm to post collateral if CDOs became unmarketable rather than if they failed to perform, as discussed in chapter 5, were arcane technical contractual provisions that few in or outside the affected firms really understood. It is not yet known what the next generation of financial innovations will produce to help firms to avoid the impact of the next generation of capital requirements.

Bubbles also affect the relationship of financial firms to their supervisors. Many years ago there was a senior supervisor at the Federal Reserve Bank of Boston. He saw that banks in New England were underwriting increasing volumes of commercial real estate loans. As a bank made a commercial real estate loan it would book handsome fees and begin to collect interest payments. The supervisor understood that this could be a profitable business for one bank or even several. However, he realized that it was unsustainable for the numerous banks that all were all underwriting commercial real estate projects in the same small geographic area. Even worse, he saw the appraised value of projects rise as each successful project caused an increase in land prices for the next project. He saw that the trend was unsustainable and tried to use his supervisory authority to restrain banks from joining the bubble and taking ever-greater amounts of risk.

The banks complained to the president of the Federal Reserve Bank of Boston. They pointed to their income statements and balance sheets and the fact that they were booking unprecedented profits. Why was this stubborn bureaucrat trying to stand in the way? The Federal Reserve Bank acted: The supervisor lost his position as vice president and head of supervision and became vice president and advisor. Within a short time the New England commercial property bubble burst and the former supervisor watched as dozens of New England Banks, including the Bank of New England, failed because of unsustainable losses on their previously profitable commercial real estate loans. As the FDIC later reported:

> The problems of the northeastern banks arose to a large extent because they had been aggressive participants in the prosperous real estate markets of the 1980s. Between 1983 and 1989 the median ratio of real estate loans to assets rose from approximately 25 percent to 51 percent ... The increase in the median commercial real estate loan concentration is widely held to have been a primary reason for the asset-quality problems and eventual failure of many of the region's banks in the late 1980s and early 1990s.[15]

I spoke with the former supervisor just before his retirement. The man was still bitter about the way he had been blocked from trying to prevent the carnage. The combination of political influence from the regulated firms and a bubble mentality had defeated him, and ultimately defeated the regulated firms as well.

Because a bubble allows even poorly managed firms to reap generous returns, the role of other gatekeepers is weakened as well. Boards of directors find they have little reason to question high profits. In 2005, for example, AIG Financial Products, the part of AIG that brought the firm down, was generating 17.5 percent of the company's total profits. Its profit margin was 83 percent of revenue that year.[16]

On the one hand, following Roger Cole's precept in chapter 7 that one should follow the money, one would expect some risk officer or board member or rating agency or accounting firm to ask how the firm (or in this case AIG Financial Products) was making its money. On the other hand, who wants to look a gift horse in the mouth?

There is a growing body of behavioral literature on the way that dependence makes it difficult if not impossible for a gatekeeper to remain impartial and resolute. Max Bazerman and coauthors published a paper asserting, for example, "the impossibility of auditor independence."[17] They conducted research that indicated how subjects adopted a clear pattern of first determining their self-interest, and only then seeking to decide the issue presented to them for judgment:

> When presented with identical information, individual perceptions of a situation differ dramatically depending on one's role in the situation.

People first determine their preference for a certain outcome on the basis of self-interest and then justify this preference on the basis of fairness by changing the importance of attributes affecting what is fair. Thus the problem lies not in our desire to be unfair, but in our inability to interpret information in an unbiased manner. Self-serving biases exist because humans are imperfect information processors. One of the most important non objective influences on information processing is self-interest. People tend to confuse what is personally beneficial with what is fair or moral.[18]

The result, they conclude, is that the auditor's dependence on clients makes the gatekeeper role difficult at best: "In addition to economic incentives that may bias an auditor's judgment in favor of the client who pays the fees, the relationship that auditing firms strive to develop with the clients may add to the auditors' psychological difficulty to make truly independent judgments."[19]

The behavioral research is consistent with Lawrence White's analysis of why the rating agencies performed so badly with respect to mortgage securities compared to their ratings of corporate and government debt. White begins, as do many, by pointing to the growth of the system of having issuers rather than investors pay for ratings. He then observes that because the market for corporate and government debt was both fairly transparent and occupied by numerous issuers, the long-term interest of a rating agency in maintaining its reputation outweighed the harm to the rating agency's bottom line if a particular bond issuer—representing only a fraction of the number of issuers in the market— tried to take its business elsewhere.

The balance shifted when rating agencies turned to the growing market for asset-backed securities, and especially mortgage-backed securities. First, these securities were much less transparent than were corporate or government bonds. Second, the rating agency, which had to review extensive details of securities' structures, received much greater financial returns from rating an asset-backed security than from rating any particular corporate or government bond. Third, and potentially more important, only a few firms dominated the asset-backed securities market:

> The market for rating mortgage-related securities involved only a handful of investment banks as securitizers with high volumes. An investment bank that was displeased with an agency's rating on any specific security had a more powerful threat—to move all of its securitization business to a different rating agency—than would any individual corporate or government issuer.[20]

The balance between a gatekeeper's long-term interest in reputation versus interests deriving from dependence upon a revenue source can be complicated, and can shift over time. This was especially true, the Commission heard in numerous interviews, when the investment banking industry shifted from a partnership model based on a significant fraction of compensation that would be paid to partners only upon retirement, and with substantial individual downside risk if a partner took losses that affected the firm, to a shareholder/ investor model, with stock prices dependent upon quarterly earnings reports. This greatly shortened the relevant time horizon for the leadership and traders at financial firms.

Financial complexity complicates matters even more. As Minsky observed, "over an expansion, new financial instruments and new ways of financing activity develop. Typically, defects of the new ways and the new institutions are revealed when the crunch comes."[21] Henry Hu and others have highlighted the way that derivative securities can obscure even basic elements of transparency.[22]

A particularly striking example was the way that Wall Street firms used specially structured currency swap transactions to circumvent leverage limits that the EU had sought to impose on euro zone countries to help prevent a debt crisis as occurred in Greece. Even though it represented a pledge of revenues in the future, the borrowing never appeared on countries' balance sheets.[23]

Or consider the Dodd-Frank requirement that firms securitizing certain kinds of mortgages should retain a fraction of the value on their balance sheets. With derivative transactions such as purchases of CDSs, a firm can hedge an asset position by shorting the relevant market. While the required fraction of the mortgage security remains clearly on the firm's balance sheet, the firm's hedges, and especially any connection to particular asset positions, may be much less transparent.

The problem is compounded when decisions of a gatekeeper such as a risk officer or a bank examiner or a rating agency whether to flag a particular practice may depend on a combination of complex factors and ultimately on judgment rather than certainty. Take away the punch bowl when the party is still going strong? At what point? How much punch should be allowed? At what cost? While it may be easy to see a bubble, no one really knows when the bubble may burst. Little wonder that bank supervisors felt much more comfortable flagging compliance shortcomings of large institutions, or raising governance issues after losses had resulted, rather than addressing intangible issues such as whether governance was adequate even before losses materialized.

Another complexity deserves mention here. The years 2005–2007 saw a remarkable expansion of risk taking at many major firms. In almost all of these cases the articulated driver for risky actions related to market share. Fannie Mae and Freddie Mac feared losing market share to the private label securities market that had learned how to fund huge volumes of mortgages and bypass the GSEs. Both GSEs feared that they were lagging in their traditional ability to price more advantageously than competitors. They could, a Fannie Mae document suggested, find themselves "irrelevant" in the mortgage market or, as Fannie Mae Board Chair Stephen Ashley warned, turned into mortgage industry utilities, available at the behest of firms with greater market power: "The company is at risk of becoming a utility—a commodity company if you will. Here when somebody needs us, but at their option; not ours."[24]

Other firms, including Countrywide and WaMu, were driving to increase their market share. Even as chairman Angelo Mozilo warned management about risks of some subprime and alt-A mortgages the company was originating, Countrywide continued to push to meet Mozilo's announced goal of a 30 percent market share of mortgage originations by 2008.[25] Citigroup continued to expand its CDO business. And yet other firms, like Lehman, saw the general pullback of other market participants in areas such as commercial real estate to be a golden opportunity to reap great rewards by taking yet more market share. Risk officers at all of these firms had been fired, set aside, submerged in the organization, or otherwise neutralized. Regulators were weak or largely absent. It was as if top management was racing with gas pedals to the floor but without brakes and guardrails. One more feature: the cars were equipped with ejector seats and parachutes so that the drivers emerged largely unscathed, even though bystanders took a hit.

The race for market share at the cost of taking on substantial risk was only one of many examples of a race to the bottom that was unleashed by flawed incentive structures and lack of internal or external constraints. Covenants in securitization documents also underwent a race to the bottom as investors jostled to obtain ever-greater amounts of mortgage product and other securitizable assets. And, as home prices continued to rise in the years 2004–2006, and later in parts of the country such as California, the quality of mortgage underwriting dropped with increasing origination of "affordable" products such as mortgages with teaser rates and negative amortization mortgages. The volume of no-documentation and low-documentation mortgage loans also continued to rise. So long as investors had money with which to make their purchases, the mortgage machine was ready to supply anything the market would buy. The Commission noted the observation of one witness, a former fraud specialist at New Century, a subprime originator: "The definition of a good loan changed from 'one that pays' to 'one that could be sold.'"[26]

Then Minsky's moment arrived: Housing prices peaked, borrowers began to default in growing numbers, early payment defaults reached unsustainable levels, and firms in all parts of the financial system, starting with giant mortgage originators such as New Century, Ameriquest, and Countrywide, began to fail.

The political process, over which financial firms exercised considerable influence, failed to stop the boom as it became a bubble. Indeed, one could argue that the political process helped to exaggerate the boom part of the cycle significantly. Consider the dynamics.

There is little question that financial firms are influential in the US political context. The Center for Responsive Politics reports that in the election cycle 2007–2008 alone the finance-insurance-real estate sector provided some

$468 million in federal campaign contributions.[27] This stakeholder strength occurs as part of what a World Bank report considers exceptional stakeholder influence over governmental decisions in the United States, compared to many other developed countries.[28]

One significant way that the sector used its influence relates to the supervisory process, as was recounted in chapter 7. Regulators came under constant pressure to be reasonable, to defer to apparently beneficial forces such as innovation and market efficiency, and—above all—not to interfere with business decisions of firms that were reaping immense profits. The concerns of a senior supervisor such as Sabeth Siddique were disregarded by his more market-oriented superiors in the Federal Reserve System; it seemed that the higher one went in the political hierarchy, the less willing that officials were to give serious feedback to financial firms during the boom times.

Then, when regulators in fact did stand up to insist that matters were getting out of hand, the Congress itself might intervene, as a Financial Services subcommittee did with respect to guidance on commercial real estate or as the Congress did frequently when the Office of Federal Housing Enterprise Oversight tried to restrain the untrammeled ambitions of Fannie Mae and Freddie Mac. A particularly memorable example of political interference occurred when the Commodity Futures Trading Commission (CFTC) announced in May 1998 that following significant losses and examples of misuse of derivatives, the agency would reexamine its approach to regulating the over-the-counter derivatives market. The reaction was swift and effective. First, senior Clinton administration officials objected to the CFTC review and called for a moratorium on CFTC action. Then in October 1998, the Congress enacted the administration's requested moratorium. It followed this with enactment of the Commodity Futures Modernization Act of 2000, which largely deregulated derivatives and ended oversight by the SEC and CFTC.

To some extent, turf issues were involved; some Washington insiders contend that the CFTC, which reported to the congressional agriculture committees, had encroached on the turf of the banking committees when it sought to expand its role in overseeing derivatives. But industry pressure played a role as well. Former Treasury Secretary Robert Rubin said that he personally shared concerns about the OTC derivatives market, but that "I think they were very strongly held views in the financial services industry in opposition to regulation. And I think that they were not overcomable . . . not surmountable at that point . . . The industry had very strong views on this and it wasn't going to be something that we could do."[29]

Rubin added that prevailing deregulatory sentiments were not the reason for Congress's actions: "I don't think when you got into the political arena that that really was what this was about. I think this was more about the interests of those who were involved and their ability to effect those interests."[30]

The same dynamic operated to discourage protection of consumers from abusive practices. Thus, a 2003 House hearing on abusive lending practices was titled "Protecting Homeowners: Preventing Abusive Lending While Preserving Access to Credit." The subcommittee chairman opened the hearing by making clear that, while he was opposed to predatory lending practices, "the Financial Services Committee is challenged with preventing abusive lending without denying consumers access to credit." After all, he said, "Subprime lending is a legitimate and valuable part of our Nation's credit markets. Millions of Americans rely on subprime lending for everything from their children's education to health care. Placing onerous new restrictions on access to subprime credit will be devastating for consumers and our Nation's economy."[31]

The hearing began with industry statements, continued with statements from consumer advocates, and ended inconclusively. One of the consumer advocates took issue with the way that the subcommittees had positioned the hearing; the issue was not homeownership but overlending and a growing number of subprime defaults:

> We who represent low-income consumers and consumers actually believe there is too much credit. There is especially too much home credit. This is a push market. People are too often being pushed into mortgages . . . essentially for reasons that do not benefit them . . . Between the years 1980 and 2001 we have seen an increase in homeownership of 3.4 percent. That is an important increase. But we have seen an increase in foreclosures of 250 percent. This we blame on the subprime mortgage market.[32]

That was in 2003, before the mortgage market went into overdrive. The advocate's focus on growing defaults was consistent with the position of the FDIC, that overlending could be a problem: "It is almost as serious, from the standpoint of ultimate losses, to lend a sound financial risk too much money as it is to lend to an unsound risk. Loans beyond the reasonable capacity of the borrower to repay invariably lead to the development of problem loans."[33]

The agency also noted that loans may be high risk to an institution if they are based on collateral value but that "involve a borrower with limited or unassessed repayment ability."[34]

As the crisis reached its crescendo, it is not clear how much members of Congress appreciated developments in the mortgage or finance markets. Former Senate Banking Committee member Mel Martinez recalled that the housing bubble was not a subject of discussion on the committee: "Don't forget we're there to legislate and if there was not a piece of legislation dealing with those issues . . .," adding that the only relevant piece of legislation to draw the committee's attention was the effort to strengthen the regulatory framework for Fannie Mae and Freddie Mac. The committee became aware of the precarious state of the financial markets only when Secretary Paulson and Fed

Chairman Bernanke came to Capitol Hill warning that the markets had frozen and asking for the legislation that became TARP.[35]

But what about Dodd-Frank and the recognized need to act after the financial crisis occurred? Analysts with a historical perspective note the backward-looking nature of major financial legislation that the Congress enacts after a crisis:

> First, reform has frequently been crisis-oriented. Despite an awareness of the structural defects in the financial system or in the monetary authority, little effort is directed toward reform until a crisis has occurred or is about to occur. . . . Second, related to the crisis-orientation of reform, financial reform is frequently myopic and backward-looking. It is designed to deal in *ad hoc* fashion with an immediate set of problems usually within a specific sector of the financial system.[36]

This pattern of patchwork reform reflects political realities. Ronald Moe, former senior analyst with the Congressional Research Service, has noted three levels of possible governmental response to a crisis. First, Washington tends to concern itself with the interpersonal level of government: Who did what to whom? Congressional committees summon leaders of failed financial institutions and their supervisors to grueling hearings to vent anger about public losses. Then, second, if the crisis was serious enough, Washington may debate policy: What should the new rules for derivatives, for example, look like? Only third—and rarely—will the political process take issues to a deeper level to ask what our institutions should look like to avoid another crisis in the future. Senator Dodd took the debate to the deepest third level when he proposed a new financial regulatory structure that sought to mitigate many problems of the current structure. He lost that vote 91–8. It was only after Senator Carl Levin went back to the first level and brought Goldman Sachs officials to Washington for a nearly eleven-hour hearing that the political process could personalize the issue—and mobilize public anger—that the compromise Dodd-Frank bill became law.

Given the political compromises that occurred in enacting Dodd-Frank, it is likely that the legislation represents a significantly sub-optimal solution: imposing sizable burdens on many firms in the financial sector without adequately addressing fundamental issues of systemic risk. JPMorgan Chase's Jamie Dimon challenged Fed Chairman Ben Bernanke in 2011, charging that regulators implementing Dodd-Frank were imposing heavy burdens on the industry, including capital requirements that were too stringent.[37] And implementation of Dodd-Frank has not gone well. Treasury Secretary Timothy Geithner charged in June 2011 that opponents of financial reform were undermining regulators' efforts to implement the law:

> We face two new risks in [implementing Dodd-Frank]. One is the effort by politicians and groups that oppose financial reform to starve the regulatory agencies of the resources they need to carry out their new responsibilities. The second is to use the confirmation process to block appointments.

Those in the U.S. financial community who are supporting these efforts to block resources and appointments are looking for leverage over the rules still being written. There is a long tradition of similar efforts. They will not be successful in undermining the core elements of reform, but . . . over time, they will make it less likely that there will be enough capable people in the regulatory bodies to bring the care and judgment necessary for the new rules to work . . . We can't allow loopholes, gaps, and weaknesses to take hold and undermine the fundamental strength of our reforms. We've been down that road before, and it led us to the edge of the abyss.[38]

For the moment, one can expect that prudence will emerge from the current debacle and the spectacle of major institutions that disappeared because of insolvency or forced merger, all in a context of significant popular anger at Wall Street and lenders in general. Indeed, the next few years could bring targeted congressional enactments, supervisory stringency, and lender caution. Markets and policies tend to overcorrect on the way down after the bubble has burst, and not just on the way up. But in the end, unless we improve our public and private institutions, it is likely that we will go through yet other cycles in the future as Hyman Minsky's moment appears, disappears, and reappears over the years.

9 }

Governance and Management

LESSONS LEARNED

A bad decision starts with at least one influential person making an error of judgment. But normally, the decision process will save the day: facts will be brought to the table that challenge the flawed thinking, or other people with different views will influence the outcome. So the second factor that contributes to a bad decision is the way the decision is managed: for whatever reason, as the decision is being discussed, the erroneous views are not exposed and corrected.

—SYDNEY FINKELSTEIN, JO WHITEHEAD, ANDREW CAMPBELL, *THINK AGAIN*, 2008

How can the financial system be strengthened to reduce the incidence and costliness of financial meltdowns? Consider lessons learned about the model of successful governance and management, especially risk management, and then possible ways to increase their quality at all large complex financial institutions. The focus is on large complex financial institutions because they tend to pose greater systemic risk than smaller institutions, even if the smaller institutions act in a herd, as happened in the savings and loan crisis of the 1980s.

Depending on the definition one uses, large complex financial institutions would include the nineteen largest bank holding companies in the United States, with assets over $100 billion, which the Fed selected for its Supervisory Capital Assessment Program in 2009. Together these nineteen firms held two-thirds of the assets and more than half of the loans in the US banking sector that year.[1] Besides bank holding companies, other large complex institutions might include major insurance companies (think of AIG) or large investment funds or the Federal Home Loan Bank System, a GSE with a trillion dollars of assets.

Eight Lessons from Successful Firms

Lessons from successful firms relate to (1) culture, (2) preparation, (3) processes, and (4) response to a crisis.

CULTURE

Culture appears to be the critical element in effective governance and risk management. It distinguishes firms that address risk well and those that merely go through the motions. Some firms may use a credo or code of values or, as in the case of Wells Fargo, a vision and values statement, as a first step in helping risk sensitivity to pervade the organization and its actions from top to bottom and across its many organizational units. As the firm infuses its decisions with a balance between rewards and risks, cultural values can take on concrete meaning to line managers and help inform their actions.

1. Encourage a Robust Approach to Decision Making

It was striking how CEOs exercised judgment in the run up to the financial crisis and made decisions that either protected firms or hastened their demise. Both Jamie Dimon of JPMorgan Chase, which succeeded, and Richard Fuld of Lehman Brothers, which did not, can be characterized as strong leaders. The essential difference in decision making between the two firms relates to processes that Dimon uses to solicit vigorous feedback:

> At the monthly all-day operating-committee meeting of the top 15 executives, the atmosphere is variously described by the participants as "Italian family dinners" or "the Roman forum—all that's missing is the togas." Dimon will throw out a comment like "Who had that dumb idea?" and be greeted with a chorus of "That was your dumb idea, Jamie!" "At my first meeting, I was shocked," says Bill Daley, 60, the head of corporate responsibility and a former Secretary of Commerce. "People were challenging Jamie, debating him, telling him he was wrong. It was like nothing I'd seen in a Bill Clinton cabinet meeting, or anything I'd ever seen in business."[2]

While this particular style may be a bit strong for some firms, the underlying principle is sound. Robust decision making with plenty of feedback before reaching closure on major issues is essential for sustained success of nonfinancial as well as financial firms.[3] Professor Sydney Finkelstein of the Tuck School of Business at Dartmouth has analyzed public and private organizations and their decisions.[4] He and his colleagues found that decision makers may be hampered by misleading experiences in their backgrounds (fighting the last war), misleading prejudgments, inappropriate self-interest, or inappropriate attachments, all of which can lead to flawed decisions. Finkelstein and his colleagues point to two factors that must be present for an organization to make a major mistake: (1) an influential decision maker makes a flawed decision, for any number of reasons, and (2) the decision process lacks capacity to provide feedback to expose errors and correct the decision.

The remedy, they found, lies with improved decision processes. First, design the decision process to enlist additional experiences and data relevant to major decisions. This can help to offset tendencies toward groupthink. Second, encourage group debate and challenge to ensure that opposing points of view have been heard and understood. Third, possibly separate decision-making bodies, with one group submitting the proposed decision to a higher "governance" group for approval. Professor Finkelstein reports he has become a strong supporter of the idea of separating the role of CEO from that of board chair. Dividing the roles allows the board to exercise more independent judgment than may be possible if the CEO also exercises authority as the board chair. Finally, implementation of a decision should be carefully monitored to ensure that each major decision is yielding the promised results.

When a bank credit committee conducts a mutually respectful dialogue between bankers who want to consummate a deal and underwriters who fear the downside risks, this helps to create a balanced decision that considers both upside gains and downside risks and helps to shape a well-rounded decision. In other words, risk management is an essential ingredient in a robust decision process and an important component of what this book calls constructive dialogue. Successful financial firms built constructive dialogue into their decision making.

Either company CEOs or their firms' cultures must be strong and self-confident to create a robust decision process such as Finkelstein and other governance experts recommend. The cost of lower quality decision making, as became painfully clear in the financial crisis, can be substantial harm to an organization and its future.

2. Incorporate Risk Management into Major Decisions

Proposed courses of action have risks as well as potential benefit. This was seen during and after the crisis when firms made major acquisitions. Consider two examples, one that brought its firm to grief and one that succeeded in adding value. Wachovia acquired Golden West and its immense book of negative amortization mortgages in May 2006, just as house prices were peaking, for $25.5 billion. Wachovia saw this acquisition as a way to expand its geographic coverage and gain several hundred new branches. As house prices declined and defaults jumped, however, especially on negative amortization mortgages, the company suffered billions of dollars in unexpected losses that caused its demise. Wells Fargo bought Wachovia in 2008 for $15 billion in stock and also benefited from a special new tax break that allowed Wells to utilize Wachovia's losses to offset its own profits in the year of acquisition.[5]

By contrast, when JPMorgan Chase acquired Bear and assets of WaMu, the acquisitions seemed based on more careful due diligence and analysis than Wachovia had exercised. In the case of Bear, which JPMorgan acquired at the request of the Treasury, the firm hedged its downside risk with government guarantees. In the case of WaMu, JPMorgan acquired the bank's assets, while leaving liabilities of the holding company to the FDIC's receivership process. JPMorgan paid $1.9 billion to acquire $307 billion in combined assets, $188 billion in total deposits (plus other liabilities) and some 2,200 branches, which greatly expanded Morgan's reach, especially to markets in California and Florida. Morgan said it would write down some $31 billion in expected losses from the loan portfolio.[6] Observers later characterized JPMorgan's purchase as reaping a windfall, although credit losses exceeded Morgan's original estimates.[7] The Bear and WaMu acquisitions confirmed CEO Jamie Dimon's reputation as a tough, detail-oriented banker.

As these contrasting examples show, risk management needs to become an integral part of corporate decision making. Only that way will firms be able to incorporate consideration of downsides as well as upsides when they consider their business strategies, financial vulnerabilities, and major activities.

3. Build Risk-Awareness into the Organizational Culture

Building risk-awareness into the firm's culture is an important step toward more robust decision making. Leaders need to integrate (1) the firm's strategy, (2) sensitivity to risk management, and (3) compensation and personnel incentives into a culture that balances the need to detect potential risks early against the need to make important decisions and move forward.

The essential part of risk-awareness is to build in a process of constructive dialogue concerning risks and rewards. The constructive dialogue would not necessarily lead to a yes-or-no decision whether to take an action. Rather, it might lead to a constructive synthesis. When JPMorgan Chase looked at the Bear acquisition, for example, the firm calibrated how much risk it was willing to take from a shaky portfolio and obtained government guarantees to hedge against greater risk. To be successful, constructive dialogue requires the following:

1. *Support for the process from top management.* In the case of Jamie Dimon and the acquisition of Bear, JPMorgan's top management was an integral part of the process of ensuring careful due diligence, judging the benefits, risks, and uncertainties of the acquisition, and making a proposal to the government (which had asked JPMorgan to make the acquisition) about how much risk the government would absorb.

2. *A mutually respectful process.* In working out the Bear acquisition, the JPMorgan people recognized that they all were on the same side: their job was to assess the benefits and risks, identify the parts of Bear's

business that posed the greatest risks, and decide how to limit that risk. Goldman has created a similarly respectful process of constructive dialogue between traders and controllers to allow the firm to establish credible market values for each trading position every evening.

3. *A fact-based process.* JPMorgan used active due diligence to gain facts needed to reach a sound conclusion about risks and rewards of the Bear acquisition. Goldman uses skilled and experienced controllers to estimate market values based on comparables when available and, if necessary, based on selling some assets whose market value is in doubt.

4. *A process based on capable participants.* One of the most important— but difficult to measure—attributes is competence. If the constructive dialogue is to succeed, there must be competent people on all sides of the discussion. When Freddie Mac's internal controls failed in the early 2000s, management had created an artificial distinction between revenue-producing parts of the business and overhead parts of the business such as accounting and internal controls. A 2003 report on Freddie Mac found that the company constrained resources needed for accounting and internal controls. Senior management treated the accounting and financial reporting parts of the company as "second class citizens."[8] It took years to for Freddie Mac to remediate problems caused by the firm's disregard, and disrespect, of the internal control function.

Capability also means that all sides of the constructive dialogue must have access to the same high quality information. Goldman does this by making market value information the province of the controller rather than the trader; if a trader wants to challenge a controller's assessment of market value, it is on the basis of mutually available data.

Constructive dialogue should be a continuous process. Lessons learned from each discussion can help to inform revenue producing units and risk managers about each other's perspectives. Over time the process can contribute to translating the firm's general commitment to risk-awareness into understanding by operating units of the implications of that awareness for decisions they make.

PREPARATION

4. Check for Vulnerabilities and Especially Mission-Critical Vulnerabilities

Companies have different goals, strategies, environments, and internal organizations. At each level, risk-aware managers should develop sensitivity to potential risks. Perhaps the best systematic approach is to engage in so-called reverse stress testing. In a reverse stress test, the manager asks: What problems—whether internal or external—could bring my firm or line of business to a halt?

In this kind of exercise it is impossible to figure out all of the different kinds of risks that could materialize and cause to disruption. On the other hand, the exercise could bring some fundamental issues to management's attention. Are information systems adequate for the workload? Does the firm possess adequate accountability over third parties such as mortgage brokers, who are essential for success? If accountability is weak or sporadic, what are the major areas that require prompt attention?

To address special kinds of risk such as cybersecurity issues, some organizations may use a "red team" approach. If a firm has a critical information system, possibly containing information essential to carrying out its activities, how long does it take a vendor, commissioned for the purpose, to penetrate the system from outside and extract information?

The OCC recognizes that model risk is another subject, both important and technically difficult, that deserves a process of effective challenge: "A central principle for managing model risk is the need for 'effective challenge' of models: critical analysis by objective, informed parties who can identify model limitations and assumptions and produce appropriate change." The OCC guidance goes on to explain the types of incentives, competence, and influence, needed to make challenge effective.[9]

Sometimes an organization will detect vulnerabilities that it cannot remedy alone. There are no easy answers to such a problem. To take an example from financial supervision, in the several years before the financial crisis, the Office of Federal Housing Enterprise Oversight (OFHEO) had the daunting responsibility for supervising safety and soundness of Fannie Mae and Freddie Mac, two government-sponsored enterprises (GSEs) that funded, between them, some $5.3 trillion of mortgages. OFHEO was subject to appropriations constraints that greatly limited its capacity. OFHEO chose a wise if ultimately unsuccessful course: The agency annually reported on safety and soundness problems at the two GSEs and OFHEO's director regularly urged the Congress to enhance OFHEO's statutory mandate, authority, and capacity. When Fannie Mae and Freddie Mac failed in September 2008, some two months after OFHEO was reconstituted to obtain many of the powers it had sought, no one in Washington could claim that they hadn't been warned.

5. Build Capacity to Respond to Unforeseen Events

This idea relates to what has come to be known as the "resilient organization." Especially when risks concern physical events with potential to disrupt the workplace, an issue that gained particular salience after 9/11, firms have undertaken continuity of operations planning as a regular course of doing business.

But resilience means more as well. Resilience is an organizational quality that allows people to undertake new changes in mission promptly and effectively. Toronto Dominion Bank showed this kind of resilience when, in the space of two years, it stopped purchasing subprime mortgage assets and sold them off. Goldman similarly showed great resilience when the firm decided to go short on the mortgage market and hedge its long positions. It takes great organizational discipline, supported by an appropriate compensation system, for a firm to be able to drop lines of business or at least hedge them without its employees who depended on those lines of business becoming seriously disgruntled. Citi, a less resilient firm, remained in a line of business—leveraged loans—even though CEO Charles Prince knew they posed significant risk.

PROCESSES

6. Build a Process for Flow of Information that Promptly Surfaces Risk-Related Information and Important Changes in the Environment

Without the right information, managers can't manage. Firms need to design and operate systems and processes that bring risk-related information to the right level of decision maker. Information needs to be surfaced in a useful form.

The most successful financial firms built information systems and processes to ensure that information, for example about the early effects of increased subprime mortgage defaults, was transmitted up the organization and across to those parts that could most use it. The examples of JPMorgan Chase and Goldman Sachs were noted in chapter 3. Ideally, employees ought to be able to trust that if they bring problems to the attention of senior management, there will be an effort to investigate and reduce risk rather than to assign personal blame.

Information systems are expensive and difficult to implement across large complex financial institutions with many lines of business. Too often firms build add-on systems rather than trying to integrate disparate systems into a single system. The result has been systems that may not talk to one another or that cannot be rolled up into an enterprise-wide view of operations. This was the case at Fannie Mae, for example:

> Most of the Enterprise's IT back-end and accounting applications are aging platforms and legacy business applications, which have significantly contributed to an ineffective internal control environment. The systems are able to provide stable performance for traditional loan product transactions, but this is due to the significant level of support provided by experienced teams that can address production challenges. . . . Data repository and platform deficiencies impact the ability to produce accurate and timely performance and risk information for internal use and external disclosures.[10]

Processes are also important. Each organization's culture should include a mandate for each person to surface major negative information promptly when it appears. As at successful firms that weathered the crisis, top managers need to insist that they hear bad news from their own people before they find out from others.

Polling stakeholders such as customers, vendors, and counterparties can open lines of communication so that people are willing to surface information early about changes in the environment or other potential risks that managers need to be aware of. Indeed, one can argue that a major mistake of financial firms in the crisis was that they had failed to ensure themselves access to strong capable government regulators who might have served as a source of feedback before the crisis broke.

7. Understand the Nature of Risks; Some Involve Trade-offs, others must be Mitigated, and yet others must be Accepted; when Appropriate use Pilot Programs or other Tests

For financial firms, some risks, such as credit risk or (for many firms) interest-rate risk, are inherent in the lending business. Credit risk is the risk that a borrower will not repay the money to the lender. Interest rate risk involves the impact of potential changes in interest rates on the valuation of assets or liabilities of the firm. Credit risk can be mitigated, for example, by requiring a borrower to take out mortgage insurance that protects the lender against default. Financial firms get paid to take credit or interest rate risk in their business.

Other risks require investments by a firm. These include operational risk—the risk that a firm cannot manage its business effectively. To address operational risk, a firm (or a government agency) must invest in systems with the capacity to carry out its activities without failing. Protecting against cyber attack is an important part of dealing with operational risk, especially as firms migrate increasing amounts of their business to more sophisticated information systems and cloud computing.[11]

Another such risk is liquidity risk, or the risk that the market will dry up and that firms will not be able to roll over their maturing obligations or to sell assets at other than a fire-sale price. Some state and local governments suffered from liquidity risk when the financial markets froze and they could not roll over their expiring debt. Many of the affected localities had tried to save on interest costs by borrowing short-term and continuously rolling over their debt. This worked until the markets froze and they were left with the need to pay off their debt holders without being able to fund themselves at low rates.

Reputational risk was another problem for financial firms and their management. This kind of risk, if anything, is even more critical to government agencies than private firms. In the aftermath of the financial crisis, executives of major financial firms found themselves hauled before the Senate Permanent Subcommittee on Investigations or the House Committee on Oversight and Government Reform.

Especially with operational or reputational risks in mind, it sometimes behooves an organization to pilot an activity to determine its ability to carry out the necessary operations and also with respect to reactions of stakeholders or the public to the pilot. This would have been a wise course as firms sought to service increasing volumes of troubled mortgages without having had the capacity needed to do so properly. As always, good sources of information can be critical in assessing such a pilot and deciding whether or not or how to go to scale.

RESPONSE

8. Respond Without Panic; Especially in a Complex Crisis, Look
in Multiple Directions

In a crisis one needs to look in multiple directions. Major financial firms that thought they had shed exposure to the subprime mortgage market, for example, sometimes found that the exposure existed in unexpected forms, such as when the firm was funding large accumulations of mortgages that it had planned to package into mortgage securities. Other firms did shed their mortgage exposures in time, but failed to note their exposures to other forms of vulnerable assets such as commercial real estate or leveraged loans. And some firms dealt well with financial aspects of the crisis but neglected to pay attention to reputational risk until significant transactions became the subject of congressional hearings and SEC scrutiny.

There is a theory of the financial crisis that suggests that major financial firms had lost their older cohort of leaders and staff who had weathered earlier financial crises. As these experienced people retired, people succeeded them who had come into their professional lives in a relatively benevolent financial period. When warning signs mounted in the run-up to the financial crisis, the older managers and staff might have recognized the signs of excess leverage, diminishing credit standards, and—above all—risking the entire firm on the untested assumption that home prices always would go up, or at least remain stable. But many of these people had left their positions for retirement. In the liquidity crisis, when firms saw their sources of funding panic and retreat, seasoned treasurers and CFOs were able to improvise more effectively if they had past experiences—say from the more limited crisis of 1998—to draw upon.

Moreover, risks can materialize in unexpected combinations. The financial crisis, as explained in chapter 2, was a two-step process of first taking credit losses and then facing market panic and disappearance of liquidity. Once there is a crisis, many things can go wrong at once. Firms such as Wachovia, which acquired Golden West, and Bank of America, which acquired Countrywide, and JPMorgan, which acquired WaMu, suddenly experienced unprecedented demand for capacity to service and resolve troubled mortgages. The problem rapidly expanded as firms and government agencies discovered shortcomings in paperwork required to foreclose under state law on homes with defaulted mortgages.

THE POWER OF CONSTRUCTIVE DIALOGUE

There is a bright side to these lessons: Adopting the approaches proposed here can help organizations to improve their decision making not merely to help avoid black swan events, but also to improve company performance more generally. Robust decision making, active checking for vulnerabilities, improved information flow, and building organizational resilience all can improve the results that firms deliver every day, and not just in a crisis.

That leads to the most fundamental difference between firms that weathered the financial crisis and those that failed: The successful firms all understood the need for integrated decision making that took account of upsides and downsides of proposed actions and of the firm's condition at any point in time. Leaders of failed firms simply didn't get it. They either pursued market share or other league table rankings, essentially without regard to risks, or they failed to manage their firms well enough to be able to understand their potential exposures to downside risks.

This leads in turn to a major question: What can be done to improve governance and risk management at firms that simply don't get it?

Imparting the model of success to other firms

Return again to Alan Greenspan's statement of regret that so many firms failed to protect their own interests or the interests of their owners. If policy makers are to infuse large complex financial institutions with one specific improvement, it should be to require a process of constructive dialogue whenever they make major decisions. It would be a great help to the financial system to enhance the capability of supervisors to provide useful feedback to firms that lack adequate governance and risk management. The feedback would come in two forms: (1) testing of the quality of governance and risk management at each large complex financial institution and requiring improvements, and (2) as Citi's Charles Prince requested of Treasury Secretary Paulson in 2008, imposition of limitations on risky lines of business.

Consider the advantages of requiring large complex financial institutions to adopt regular processes of constructive dialogue. First, this is something that supervisors can monitor. Supervisors can routinely request information from major financial firms about:

1. Examples of constructive dialogue between the CEO and the board of directors and show how input from the board affected final decisions on major matters.
2. Examples of constructive dialogue between the CEO and top management and show how input from an engaged top management team affected final decisions on major matters.

3. Examples of constructive dialogue between those who wanted to engage in activities or close a deal or change concentration limits or other risk limits and the chief risk officer, and show how input from the chief risk officer affected the final decisions.

Essentially, supervisors would be weighing in on behalf of often-neglected parts of the decision process vis-à-vis the CEO and revenue producing units to ensure that their voices were properly heard and considered.

Second, supervisors need to back up the review of decision making with a review of the flow of information to decision makers, especially including risk-related information that often was inadequate or neglected by unsuccessful firms in making their decisions. It is a sign of dysfunction either when top management lacks important information that is known farther down in the organization, or when organizational "silos" prevent important information from flowing across different parts of the organization. Supervisors need to interview across the organization and up and down the organizational hierarchy to pick up these trouble signs.

Third, each of these reviews of the presence of constructive dialogue for major decisions and the timely availability of appropriate information to all of the decision makers can be conducted regardless whether a firm has taken losses. The focus on constructive dialogue, and whether it is effective or not in shaping decisions, allows supervisors to address otherwise nebulous governance and risk management issues without waiting for losses as a sign of vulnerability. Once the focus is on the processes a firm uses to make important decisions, supervisory agencies can design metrics for examiners to apply.

Fourth, insisting on effective constructive dialogue can improve the performance and efficiency of large complex financial institutions. By focusing on the effectiveness of the process in shaping decisions, supervisors can avoid imposing costs on firms that might occur if a supervisor insisted on a specific form of risk management—for example, whether the risk function should be embedded in business units or separate—that went against the firm's culture. To some extent, supervisors also can avoid getting into difficult issues such as evaluating whether particular directors are qualified enough to sit on the board of a large complex financial institution.

Fifth, devoting supervisory attention to effective constructive dialogue can create incentives for management to improve the quality of board members and risk staff as a way to improve the quality of constructive dialogue.

Sixth, by developing a systematic focus on constructive dialogue and information flow, supervisors can help to insulate themselves from the kind of political pressure that can accrue if supervisors were insisting on something that the firm alleges would cost it money and lose deals, such as happened when supervisors sought to object to specific activities that seemed to be generating substantial revenues in the years before the crisis. The supervisor is objecting to the lack of balanced input rather than needing to try to prove that the deal itself was risky. Similarly, while a supervisor would not generally try to inject itself into a decision whether or not to acquire a firm, such as the Wachovia acquisition of Golden West, and at what price, the supervisor would be on firmer ground in assessing the quality of decision making and whether or not constructive dialogue was effective in making the decision.

The suggestion here is that supervisory attention to the need for constructive dialogue is more of a fulcrum than a panacea. It gives supervisors a better place from which to apply leverage when they try to reduce vulnerabilities and increase safety and soundness of an institution, especially in boom years when it seems that no one can make a bad decision.

A Call for Statesmen

Needed, of course, would be support from statesmen in the financial industry who are willing to take a longer-term view and support a stronger mandate and greater capacity for financial supervisors. In mid-2011 such a statesman-like position appeared during the controversy about the Consumer Financial Protection Bureau (CFPB) established by Dodd-Frank. Even while partisan warfare had broken out over implementation of the CFPB, Richard K. Davis, chairman and CEO of US Bancorp, told a banking conference that banks shouldn't "overreact" to creation of the CFPB. As Bloomberg reported:

> "The original mandate of the CFPB was a good one, which is disclosure, transparency, clarity," Davis said. "I love all of that, and I think they are making some progress there."
>
> Davis urged bankers to accept the new regulator although "we should push back when they are overreaching." Davis added that he advised that approach regardless of who becomes the bureau's first director.
>
> "I think we probably ought to embrace it and move forward and work with whomever is in that position," Davis said.[12]

It would behoove the chairman of the Federal Reserve Board, backed by other top federal officials, to try to cultivate such statesmen among major financial institutions. The financial crisis reveals a record of financial institutions actively lobbying for short-term benefits that were against their own best interests. The classic case was the way that Fannie Mae and Freddie Mac fought for years against more capable supervision even though this might have saved them from making bad decisions in 2005–2007 that destroyed the companies.

The question then becomes whether and to what extent large complex financial institutions are willing to strengthen the mandate and capacity of their supervisors. The political influence of financial institutions over structure and effectiveness of supervisory organizations has already been noted, especially in chapter 7. Resistance of major financial firms to implementation of key parts of Dodd-Frank, including derivatives rules and strong capital requirements for large complex financial institutions, has also been growing.[13] Outgoing FDIC Chairwoman Sheila Bair, against whose agency firms have directed some of their criticisms, said that "I see a lot of amnesia setting in now," concerning the need for increased prudential requirements.[14] On the other hand, as effects of the crisis continue to weigh on our financial system and the economy, financial statesmen may be increasingly easy to find.

By contrast to some prudential requirements that major firms may see as cutting into their revenues and profits, supervisory emphasis on effective constructive dialogue is arguably a help to management and longer-term returns. Increasing firms' ability to weigh upside profitability against downside risk is, as Sydney Finkelstein and his colleagues point out, a recipe for improved decision making that can help firms and their leaders increase their performance.

They report that "we quickly found there are an awful lot of bad decisions out there! Indeed, in unfamiliar circumstances, such as businesses entering new markets . . ., flawed decisions abound."[15] Building constructive dialogue into decision making at major financial firms can help firms improve their capacity to navigate uncertain cyclical financial markets and reduce the tendency to make bad decisions such as Fannie Mae, Freddie Mac, Lehman, Bear, and many others made at just the wrong time in the years after 2004.

Well-managed firms also have a stake in improving decision making at their weaker competitors. The Financial Crisis Inquiry Commission estimated that CDOs that included mortgage securities as collateral—the primary toxic asset that helped to precipitate the crisis—amounted to only about $700 billion total.[16] The total number of subprime mortgages amounted to perhaps twice that, depending on the definition one uses for subprime.[17] This occurred in a market that, at year-end 2008, amounted to about $25 trillion of domestic private nonfinancial debt outstanding.

In other words, CDOs amounted to about three percent of debt outstanding and—almost but not quite by themselves—managed to bring down the entire financial system to the point where private firms and government officials feared another Great Depression. There were two reasons for this. First, when complex opaque CDO securities accumulated in concentrated holdings by highly leveraged financial firms and securitization vehicles, these holdings were large enough to threaten the institutions' financial viability. Second, recall that the crisis was a two-step process: Losses from CDOs and other toxic assets began to materialize and, because they were unexpected, financial panic ensued. It was panic and a liquidity crisis rather than actual writing off of losses that brought many firms down.

One can argue that even successful firms—and especially survivors Goldman Sachs and Morgan Stanley—that had to convert to bank holding companies to withstand the panic lost much of the entrepreneurial latitude that they had enjoyed before the crisis. Moreover, as the economy sank into recession, millions of mortgages that were not subprime suddenly became delinquent or defaulted in serious numbers. This hit successful firms such as JPMorgan Chase and Wells Fargo, as well as the others.

The financial crisis continues to take its toll. At this writing in late 2011, unemployment hovers around nine percent, and a total of perhaps ten million households in the United States will be foreclosed on. People have lost immense amounts of money in their retirement plans and other investments. The financial sector continues to shrink, and the United States sees itself increasingly vulnerable as a debtor nation.

In other words, the financial crisis was a serious problem for successful firms as well as the others. Successful firms have a major stake in improving decision making, and injecting constructive dialogues into the processes of their weaker competitors. They have a stake in increasing the mandate and capacity of supervisory organizations to provide high quality feedback to improve the decision making of all large complex financial institutions. Without effective supervisors, there is no way to provide the needed feedback to financial firms that suffer from infirmities that this book has sought to highlight.

Strengthening Supervision

If there were sufficient political support, then a series of reforms suggest themselves that arguably would be in the long-term interests of large financial firms. Consider why supervisory actions failed to prevent or overcome shortcomings in governance and risk management at many firms and then possible improvements.

Perhaps the most serious shortcoming in the current supervisory structure was the organizational imperative caused by allowing institutions to shop for the most congenial federal or state regulator. This can be overcome, but the rules must change. For example, one could require that all large complex financial institutions be supervised and regulated by the Office of the Comptroller of the Currency for banks and by the Federal Reserve for holding companies. In the case of major insurance companies (an especially powerful political constellation), a new federal supervisor ultimately should supervise safety and soundness of these institutions as a part of the move to federal chartering that leading insurance companies increasingly see as beneficial; the Fed should supervise the holding companies.

A second problem was the prevailing deregulatory and market-oriented mood among political level regulators. The financial crisis dissipated that particular enthusiasm, at least for the moment. The new Office of Financial Research (OFR), established by Dodd-Frank in the Treasury Department, provides one possibility for dealing with boom times. Tracking changes in leverage, asset prices, outstanding indebtedness as a fraction of GDP, and other key variables can at least put policy makers and supervisors on notice that extra watchfulness is needed.

Instead of focusing on quantitative factors alone, the OFR should also try to carry out a monitoring and warning function. If this is not a suitable role for the office itself, then it would be important to establish a financial system safety board similar to the National Transportation Safety Board, but focusing on systemic matters (what economists call "macro-prudential" supervision) rather than on problems of individual institutions that can best be left to supervisory agencies (and "micro-prudential" supervision).[18] For example, the new organization should monitor nonquantifiable factors such as changes in legal covenants that could signal that investors are getting complacent.

Third, supervisors fear that prudent rules could drive financial services from the regulated banking sector to the largely unregulated shadow banking sector. Dodd-Frank already addresses much of this issue. It directs the Federal Reserve to designate systemically important financial institutions (SIFIs), whatever their organizational form, and to supervise them and impose prudential requirements. This will avoid many of the problems of Fed-Lite and ensure that the Fed can and should review nonbank affiliates of holding companies, as well as nonbank firms such as Countrywide.

That said, there is no doubt that some financial services will flee from regulated firms to less-regulated or unregulated firms. Some financial services also will flee from countries with meaningful prudential regulation to those without. To some extent effective supervision of large complex financial institutions will help create protection against some of the worst aspects of this tendency. That is because well-supervised firms will come with a cachet that indicates their creditworthiness as counterparties. This seal of approval appears to be a major reason why the decision of Switzerland to impose greater capital requirements than other countries may be increasing rather than diminishing the attractiveness of Switzerland as a place for banks to do business.

Fourth, cognitive regulatory capture continues to be a major problem and needs to be addressed directly. Analysts recognize the pattern in many different areas of government-private sector relations. As chapter 1 notes, they have evolved the idea of principled intimacy to deal with it. Supervisors need to be close enough to firms to obtain useful information while remaining separate in their culture and outlook.

Part of the solution is to revitalize the cultures of regulators, and especially the relationship of political level leadership of the regulatory agencies and their senior professional staff. Another important problem relates to the organizational fault line that appears to impede relations of supervisors at the Federal Reserve Board with supervisory staff at the regional Federal Reserve banks. The Federal Reserve Board needs to revisit the terms of its delegation of supervisory responsibilities to the district Reserve banks so that it will automatically chair cross-cutting supervisory teams such as Governor Bies sought to create for large financial institutions, increase the size of Board supervisory staff, and enhance the mandate and capacity of Board staff to participate with Reserve Bank staff in examinations and other direct interactions with supervised institutions. More active involvement of Board staff can help overcome impediments to the Board knowing what is happening on the ground, and also will improve the ability of supervisors to resist the intellectual blandishments of cognitive regulatory capture.

Fifth, there is the ability of supervised firms to call upon political support in a dispute with a supervisor. Transparency would seem to be a useful tool for reducing the capacity of supervised institutions to exert untoward influence on supervisors. It would be helpful for a congressional oversight committee to call upon the Government Accountability Office to provide reports to Congress, based on confidential interviews with supervisors and firms, as to the extent that political influence rather than professional judgment has affected the contents of particular reports of examination and the application of remedial measures for large complex financial institutions.

It also would be good to question the tradition that bank supervisors have of keeping their examination reports confidential. Supervisors could redact proprietary information, as the Office of Federal Housing Enterprise Oversight did when publishing annual examination findings about Fannie Mae and Freddie Mac, but the regular publication of examination findings on large complex financial institutions could have a salutary effect in improving the incentives of supervisors to get it right in their reports.

Ultimately, a cultural norm needs to be established that limits the seemliness of approaching political-level officials to challenge the propriety of supervisory actions. This can come only when the quality of supervisory assessments and proposed remedies is widely regarded being as very high. The institution of an ombudsman's office, such as the FDIC has had for many years, can help to provide a forum where a mutually respectful constructive dialogue between supervisory staff and financial firm officials can take place. To be effective, these reviews should seek to improve processes rather than assign blame to particular supervisors. Feedback can be a gift for both supervisors and financial firms.

Other factors are related to the capacity of supervisors to supervise large complex financial institutions, and especially to the legitimacy of feedback from supervisors in the eyes of senior officers of major firms. There are immense gaps in compensation between supervisory agencies and supervised firms, and these may reflect themselves in differences in skill levels between supervisors and firms—and, if unmanaged, even resentment and envy by some supervisors. Compensation for supervisors never will compete in economic terms with compensation available at large complex financial institutions. The key is to infuse the supervisory corps with leadership, training, and support systems so that they can develop a culture of supervisory competence that earns respect from the financial world. If some LCFIs are indeed too big to manage, stronger and more comprehensive off-site monitoring systems can help supervisors to draw the attention of a firm's leadership to weak elements in the organization. The examples of AIG Financial Products, CDO operations of many Wall Street firms, and mortgage origination activities at numerous firms come to mind here.

A variety of organizational approaches are possible. The key is to achieve a balance of experienced supervisors who have seen all types of behavior in all types of economic environments with younger people, who come for a few years and bring the latest skills and capabilities to the supervisory agency or instrumentality. As senior supervisors noted in interviews, leaders of supervisory teams must have people skills and not just professional capability if they are to succeed. That said, compensation must be high enough to ensure that supervisors can send their children to college and that they do not need to excessively stretch to do so.

Another issue relates to information asymmetries between supervisors and supervised institutions. Even if they do not have the full depth of expertise available to large complex financial institutions, supervisors have the capacity to render useful judgments about firms and their risk exposures. One technique, described earlier, relates to the power of simple questions. Where is the firm making its money? How much capital is allocated to major lines of business? What off-balance sheet exposures exist?

The Federal Reserve's stress-test capital assessment (SCAP) program used data from financial firms and then double-checked that data with input from approximately 150 supervisory staff. Supervisory staff benchmarked the firms' estimates against their portfolio characteristics, and then determined the amount of capital each firm would need to withstand two sets of adverse scenarios.[19] The point here is not whether the SCAP tests were too generous or not, as some have suggested, but rather that it is possible for experienced staff to undertake analyses of multiple large institutions and check their information against one another.

There is also the venerable approach of transactions testing: How well do the firm's transactions correspond to information about those transactions that is made available to senior management? How easy is it for managers to query the firm's systems to obtain real time information on business matters that are their responsibility?

And it is possible for supervisors to obtain information from firms in the industry. A strong supervisory culture can build on itself. If large complex financial institutions believe that supervisors are capable and trustworthy, then it may be possible to elicit information from financial firms about risky practices at their competitors.

Moreover, supervisors need the resources to hire financial and technical experts to help assess complex issues such as derivative transactions, measures of risk exposure, and the myriad of other complex matters that must be addressed in understanding the business of a large financial institution. Limits on the ability of firms to shop for the most congenial regulator can allow supervisors more latitude to invest in the expertise they need to inform their judgments. In the end, the culture of supervision will need to change.

This is especially important given the high rate of financial innovation in recent years designed to arbitrage capital and other regulations. Innovations deserve scrutiny, and again, there is the power of simple questions. One retired official of the Israel Central Bank described financial firms approaching a senior supervisor with information about a complex new financial product. The supervisor spent much time trying to understand the product and its features and concluded, similar to Edmund Clark at TD Bank, that he simply didn't understand why the product was needed. The supervisor discouraged firms from investing in the product and saved the supervised financial firms considerable money from losses that they otherwise would have suffered.

Again, the point is to provide feedback in a useful form. Federal Reserve Bank supervisors dealt with capital arbitrage devices such as Lehman's repo 105 end-of-quarter transactions simply by monitoring capital ratios daily rather than every three months. This is not to say that all complexities can be addressed with simple questions. Supervisors need access to knowledgeable experts both in the industry and as contractors to the supervisory organization, and they themselves will need to undertake continuous training to keep up with financial innovations and their practical implications for individual firms and for the financial services industry.

Supervisors also should raise questions relating to governance and risk management: What are examples of vulnerabilities that the firm has corrected based on input from a risk officer? Did the board know? Has the board challenged major management decisions? What happened? As can be seen from analyses of governance issues presented in chapter 4, for example, based on the work of Nestor Advisors, it is possible to assess the strength of a board and its relationship to the risk management function of the firm.

These improvements can build the capacity of supervisors to provide feedback to large complex financial institutions and thereby improve the quality of decisions. Supervisors can be a constant voice for a longer-term perspective than firms, with their susceptibility to league tables and other measures of short-term success, would undertake on their own. In addition, as Citi's Charles Prince argued, supervisors can set a floor on unsafe and unsound practices. A stronger mandate can allow supervisors to act early to limit potentially dangerous activities that the industry itself recognizes as risky.

Prince was right: Only supervisors can stop the race to the bottom. Improved governance, management, and organization in both private firms and government supervisors are needed to restore the ability of private companies, in Greenspan's words, to protect their own shareholders and the equity in their firms.

10 }

Governance and Management

BEYOND THE FINANCIAL CRISIS

Leaders must visibly and tangibly engage in promoting and recognizing safe behaviors, to clearly communicate to all employees and contractors that safety is not a priority but a core value. Priorities can change with the business environment. Core values do not.

—MARVIN ODUM, PRESIDENT, SHELL

The culture of safety starts with leadership, because leadership drives behavior and behavior drives culture. Leaders influence culture by setting expectations, building structure, teaching others, and demonstrating stewardship.

—REX TILLERSON, CHAIRMAN AND CEO, EXXONMOBIL

While this book focuses on lessons of the financial crisis for governance and risk management of major financial firms, the lessons apply to management broadly, and not merely to risk management. Incorporating a sound sense of risk-reward trade-offs is good business; risk management is merely half of the equation. In the end, JPMorgan Chase, Goldman Sachs, Wells Fargo, and TD Bank were better-managed firms than many of their competitors; strong risk management was only a part of managerial quality more generally.

Moreover, organization, governance, and management lessons from the crisis apply to firms other than major financial firms. Firms are becoming more complex, and not only in the financial sector. The Boston Consulting Group surveyed over one hundred listed companies in the United States and Europe and found that "over the past 15 years, the amount of procedures, vertical layers, interface structures, coordination bodies, and decision approvals needed in each of these firms has increased by anywhere from 50 percent to 350 percent."[1]

Managing complex and complicated organizations is difficult at best; the governance literature applies broadly, and not just to financial firms.[2] The duty of a board (whether of a financial or nonfinancial firm) to provide respectful and constructive feedback to management is an established principle in the governance literature. The business literature on more effective decision making does not focus only on executives in financial firms.[3] When a disaster occurs, postmortem reports often are filled with lessons about culture, the need to balance production against risks, regulatory laxity, and the special problems caused by new complex technologies.[4]

Consider the basic lesson of governance and management from this book: Feedback is a gift. Without soliciting and accepting feedback from knowledgeable people, an executive can make serious mistakes. The point of feedback is to raise questions that prompt the gathering of more information so that major decisions, when they are made, reflect a robust understanding of the context and implications.

Potential sources of feedback for an executive include the board of directors, an engaged management team that brings views from across the organization to bear on decisions, the chief risk officer and other company officials responsible for risk management, and a government regulator or supervisor. Ultimately, this book argues, a well-managed firm engages regularly in a process we call constructive dialogue, between those who support a major decision and those who may have misgivings.

Consider the following examples relating to risks when a firm produces goods or services other than financial services. The following discussion is based on secondary resources without access to the extensive interviews and detailed information that was available for financial firms from the Financial Crisis Inquiry Commission. Yet even with that limitation, it seems that lessons of this book from the financial crisis generalize quite well to these other contexts.

As happened with the financial crisis, the best documentation becomes available after a costly failure. Firms that made expensive mistakes include the BP oil spill in the Gulf of Mexico; Massey Mining Company, which experienced multiple preventable fatal accidents and was acquired in 2011; and PG&E and the fatal San Bruno, California, gas pipeline explosion. Also relevant are hospital medical errors and the absence of constructive dialogue in a variety of settings, and the Challenger space shuttle disaster. Interesting counterpoints are companies that are said to have superior risk management, such as Shell and ExxonMobil.

In chapter 3 it was seen that successful financial firms possessed (1) discipline and long-term perspective, (2) robust communications and information systems, (3) the capacity to respond effectively to early warning signs, and (4) a process of constructive dialogue between business units and risk managers. Each of the successful firms applied these according to its distinctive culture, while unsuccessful firms lacked most of these attributes. This can be generalized; while practices of successful firms have not been as well documented in other sectors, the experiences of BP, Massey Mining, and PG&E would seem to fit the pattern of unsuccessful firms in the financial sector.

The Petroleum Industry

1. BP OIL COMPANY

On April 20, 2010, a BP exploratory deep sea rig blew up, killing 11 people, injuring 17 others, and releasing almost five million barrels of oil—about 206 million gallons—into the Gulf of Mexico from BP's Macondo well. When BP finally capped the leak two months later, the company had spent about $6 billion on cleanup and pledged another $20 billion to a fund for restitution to people and businesses harmed by the spill. The BP oil spill was the worst environmental disaster in US history, compared, for example, to the 1989 *Exxon Valdez* oil spill that released 10.8 million gallons of oil—about 5 percent of the Gulf oil spill.

A federal joint investigation team found that although "at the time of the blowout, BP had a number of carefully documented policies and practices addressing drilling operations, change management, safety and risk management," these policies and procedures had been largely disregarded.[5] The Deepwater Commission found that "as of April 20, BP and the Macondo well were almost six weeks behind schedule and more than $58 million over budget," and the oil rig was under pressure to finish its work.[6] According to the joint investigation team:

> The Panel found that in the weeks leading up to the blowout on April 20, the BP Macondo [oil rig] team made a series of operational decisions that reduced costs and increased risk. The Panel did not find any explicit statements by BP personnel that any of these decisions were made as part of a conscious cost/risk trade-off. . . . Moreover, the Panel found no evidence that the cost-cutting and time-saving decisions were subjected to the various formal risk assessment processes that BP had in place.[7]

BP used a contractor, Transocean, to operate the oil rig itself. The National Commission on the BP Deepwater Horizon Oil Spill and Offshore Drilling (Deepwater Commission) reported on a survey that Transocean conducted of its shore employees and rig crews some weeks before the disaster, revealing that "some 46 percent of crew members surveyed felt that some of the workforce feared reprisals for reporting unsafe situations, and 15 percent felt that there were not always enough people available to carry out work safely."[8]

BP used another contractor, Halliburton, to cement the well into place. The Deepwater Commission found that Halliburton and BP's management processes failed to ensure that the cement was adequately tested, even though the companies recognized the need for such testing. Because BP and Halliburton crews failed to communicate adequately with one another, managers made decisions without understanding the context or significance of choices they made to save time and money:

> None of BP's (or the other companies') decisions . . . appear to have been subject to a comprehensive and systematic risk-analysis, peer-review, or management of change process. The evidence now available does not show that the BP team members (or other companies' personnel) responsible for these decisions conducted any sort of formal analysis to assess the relative riskiness of available alternatives.[9]

BP's regulator in the Gulf, the Minerals Management Service (MMS), was a federal agency with the dual mission of leasing drilling rights and collecting revenues from oil companies, and also regulating their safety. The Deepwater Commission found MMS to be a weak agency, writing that it provided "safety regulation on a starvation diet":

> Over time, MMS increasingly fell short in its ability to oversee the offshore oil industry. The agency's resources did not keep pace with industry expansion into deeper waters and industry's related reliance on more demanding technologies. And, senior agency officials' focus on safety gave way to efforts to maximize revenue from leasing and production.[10]

MMS was a weak regulator because industry wanted it that way:

> At the time of the Macondo blowout—almost 20 years after its original proposal—MMS had still not published a rule mandating that all operators have plans to manage safety and environmental risks. The agency's efforts to adopt a more rigorous and effective risk-based safety regulatory regime were repeatedly revisited, refined, delayed, and blocked alternatively by industry or skeptical agency political appointees. MMS thus never achieved the reform of its regulatory oversight of drilling safety consonant with practices that most other countries had embraced decades earlier.[11]

BP had a long history of safety-related problems. In 2005, a fire and explosion at a BP refinery in Texas City killed 15 workers and injured 180 others. This was the worst US industrial accident since 1990. In its review, the Chemical Safety Board, a federal agency, found that "many of the safety problems that led to the March 23, 2005, disaster were recurring problems that had been previously identified in audits and investigations," and concluded that "the disaster at Texas City had organizational causes, which extended beyond the [directly affected] unit, embedded in the BP refinery's history and culture."[12]

At the request of the Chemical Safety Board, BP formed an independent panel to investigate underlying causes of the Texas City mishap. The panel looked at BP in some depth. It reported that:

> BP tended to have a short-term focus, and its decentralized management system and entrepreneurial culture have delegated substantial discretion to U.S. refinery plant managers without clearly defining process safety expectations, responsibilities, or accountabilities. . . . BP has not demonstrated that it has effectively held executive management and refining line managers and supervisors, both at the corporate level and at the refinery level, accountable for process safety performance.[13]

The panel concluded that "BP did not effectively incorporate process safety into management decision-making."[14]

BP is a case study in the lessons of this book. The company failed to respond effectively to feedback, even from repeated disasters. The regulator was weak. Lower level employees working for Transocean, BP's contractor, feared reprisals if they reported safety violations, and, as the independent panel found after the Texas City explosion, the company lacked constructive dialogue between process safety and the company's production goals.

2. COUNTERPOINTS: EXXONMOBIL AND SHELL

The Deepwater Commission took testimony from two oil companies that it considered to have superior safety records and asked them about their risk management practices. CEOs of both companies, ExxonMobil and Shell, told the commission that they have designed safety and risk systems and rules and processes and embedded them in the company's culture.[15] As the Deepwater Commission observed, a "safety culture means doing the right thing even when no one is watching."[16]

Both companies strengthened their risk cultures after experiencing serious setbacks. For ExxonMobil, the experience was the *Exxon Valdez* oil spill; for Shell it was a combination of events, including a public controversy over the company's decision to sink a decommissioned oil storage buoy, the *Brent Spar*, in the North Atlantic and another controversy over the company's human rights record in dealing with the government of Nigeria.

ExxonMobil chairman and CEO Rex Tillerson told the Deepwater Commission that the *Exxon Valdez* was a wake-up call. "Companies must develop a culture in which the value of safety is embedded in every level of the workforce, reinforced at every turn, and upheld above all other considerations," he told the Deepwater Commission. ExxonMobil adopted the Operations Integrity Management System (OIMS), an eleven-point set of elements designed to identify hazards and manage risks. ExxonMobil uses OIMS to manage its diverse set of organizations, and contractors, operating around the globe: "Through OIMS, ExxonMobil monitors, benchmarks, and measures all aspects of our safety performance. Its structure and standards are shared and communicated the world over."[17]

For Tillerson, OIMS is a constantly improving process, starting with leadership from the top and permeating the organization. OIMS applies regular reviews, designed, Tillerson told the Deepwater Commission, not to find fault with people, but to ensure continuous process improvement. Constant improvement rather than a static set of rules is needed because a high-technology industry such as oil extraction is constantly evolving: "What we have come to understand is the traditional metrics are all lagging indicators."[18]

In a company brochure, Tillerson explains that OIMS seeks to "promote and maintain a work environment in which each of us accepts personal responsibility for our own safety and that of our colleagues, and in which everyone actively intervenes to ensure the safety, security and wellness of others."[19]

Shell's president Marvin Odum told the Deepwater Commission about his company's Health, Safety, and Environment (HSE) Management System, consisting of eight elements including clear and firm rules for both Shell employees and contractors, and application of an approach known as the "safety case," requiring a clear plan to manage major risks before engaging in major activities.

Odum also stressed that risk management—the HSE system in Shell's case—must be integral to the company culture: "Leaders must visibly and tangibly engage in promoting and recognizing safe behaviors, to clearly communicate to all employees and contractors that safety is not a priority but a core value. Priorities can change with the business environment. Core values do not."[20]

Employees play a key role in implementing the HSE system:

> At Shell, intervention or the stop work rule is another overarching principle. Every employee and contractor in the Shell site has the right and the obligation to intervene and stop work if it feels unsafe. We ensure everyone knows about it, and we reward those who do it. It's a key part of our job planning, and it works.[21]

Shell also enlists feedback from outside the company. In 2009, the company invited DuPont to administer a safety and culture survey in the Shell drilling organization, comparing the company to others across the world: "While we ranked world-class overall, improvement areas were identified."[22]

Feedback is essential to making the system work: "The mindset must be one of always seeking feedback and identifying gaps, with the ultimate goal of ensuring safety is built into every aspect of the way we do work."[23]

Tillerson and Odum both contended that attention to safety and mitigation of risks enhanced their company's bottom line rather than detracting from it. While an individual work stoppage because of a safety alert might cost money in the moment, overall the companies found risk management to be profitable and sustainable.

The two company leaders also said that they supported strong capable government supervision. Tillerson believes that the industry should educate supervisors on technological developments so that supervisors can ask the right questions:

> As to the regulator, it is a significant challenge for the regulator to have people at competency levels commensurate with where the industry is technologically. . . . They may not be capable of formulating the precise response, and that may not be necessary. But they need to be capable enough to say, I see a risk, it's not clear how it's being managed, and say to us, how are you addressing that? And that's enormously important to us as an industry. In my view, we want a competent regulator. They are part of risk management system.
>
> They are part of redundancy in the system that can test, are the risks being managed. So they don't have to be capable necessarily of designing all the elements of the deepwater drill program. But they do have to have significant technical competency to recognize that there is a risk exposure in this operation. We're going to make sure the risk has been addressed by asking the right questions.[24]

Odum agreed, saying that "the industry needs a robust, expertly staffed, and well-funded regulator that can keep pace with and augment industry's technical expertise. A competent and nimble regulator will be able to establish and enforce the rules of the road to assure safety without stifling innovation and commercial success."[25]

On the other hand, it was not clear that the CEOs would be willing to pay to support a more capable regulator. According to Odum, "I do think the funding should come from the Federal government. I mean, I think, to be fairly blunt, there's a very strong stream of resources that come from the industry to the government that I think part of that should be directed towards supporting [supervisory] agencies."[26]

In summary, BP's culture discouraged constructive dialogue or a balance of risks and rewards taking account of both sides of the equation. By contrast, leaders of ExxonMobil and Shell both articulated the need for good information flow across the organization and prompt and effective feedback to decision makers from multiple directions, in reviews, from peers, from other companies, and, potentially at least, from a regulator capable of asking the right questions.

Other Examples

Consider three other nonfinancial examples: (1) Massey Mining Company, (2) the Pacific Gas and Electric Company (PG&E) natural gas pipeline explosion in San Bruno, California, and (3) the serious incidence of hospital medical errors in the United States. Again, the clear theme emerges that constructive dialogue should become an integral part of a firm's management of risk-reward trade-offs. While the pattern of failure is striking across these quite different examples, further research is needed to fill out the picture with counter-examples of companies or hospitals with positive cultures and approaches to decision making in these lines of business.

1. MASSEY MINING COMPANY

On April 5, 2010, a catastrophic methane gas explosion in the Upper Big Branch (UBB) mine owned and operated by the Massey Mining Company killed 29 miners. This was the nation's worst mining incident in forty years. Investigations revealed serious safety shortcomings at the mine and in the company generally. The company reported 2010 after-tax expenses connected with the explosion of $115 million, and a loss for the year of $166.6 million, compared to net income of $104.4 million the year before. A competitor, Alpha Natural Resources, acquired Massey and Massey chairman and CEO Don Blankenship resigned in 2011, albeit on generous terms.

Massey had a history of mining accidents and fatalities. The company had a total of twenty-three fatalities in the years 2000–2009, tied for the most fatalities of any coal company, and amassed thousands more safety violations than any other coal company in the period. The West Virginia Governor's Independent Investigation Panel on the disaster reported that since 1997, the UBB mine itself "had experienced at least three major methane-related events. . . . All took place in longwall mining sections [where the 2010 explosion also occurred]. . . . Upper Big Branch management elected to consider each methane outburst or explosion as an anomaly."[27]

Massey emphasized production to the detriment of other goals such as safety:

> All bosses appeared to know the "Six Key Numbers" of interest to upper management—the continuous miner load rate, shuttle car haul rate, feeder dump rate, roof bolt per row rate, average cut depth and linear foot per continuous miner. There is nothing on the daily forms that reflects measures of safety, such as pounds of rock dust applied by machine or linear feet of accumulated float coal dust removed.[28]

The company did not welcome feedback and, indeed, had a track record of intimidation vis-à-vis regulators, the West Virginia judicial system, and its employees. Citing examples of "intimidation of workers," the governor's panel found that "there is ample evidence through testimony that miners were discouraged from stopping production for safety reasons. Workers said that those who questioned safety conditions were told to get on with production."[29]

Joseph Main, US Assistant Secretary of Labor for Mine, Safety, and Health, told a Senate subcommittee that "a number of current and former Massey employees have publicly stated that miners at Upper Big Branch who reported hazards to the company or MSHA risked losing their jobs, sacrificing pay, or suffering other adverse actions."[30]

Massey also discouraged feedback from regulators. Analyzing failure of the federal Mine Safety and Health Administration (MSHA) to prevent the UBB disaster despite numerous serious violations, the governor's panel found Massey to be deliberately contentious:

> Some companies, Massey among them, relish the opportunity to challenge inspectors' enforcement actions by disputing findings and arguing about what the law requires. Massey's Vice President for Safety Elizabeth Chamberlin reportedly took a violation written by an inspector, looked at her people and said, "Don't worry, we'll litigate it away." . . . As one long-time MSHA official told investigators, "Massey trains our inspectors better than we do." He meant that the way inspectors are treated during inspections at Massey mines impacts the enforcement attitude of the inspectors.[31]

In the end, prodding by MSHA was not enough. The Governor's Panel suggests that MSHA as well as Massey Mining underwent a pattern of "normalization of deviance" such as that Diane Vaughan found in the Challenger disaster:

> The ultimate failure of MSHA at UBB, however, was the agency's inability to see the entire picture, the inability to connect the dots of the many potentially catastrophic failures taking place at the mine—especially the operator's failure to properly ventilate the mine, to control methane, to apply sufficient amounts of rock dust. The failure to consider the previous methane outbursts when addressing the current ventilation woes points to a disconnect which suggests the whole picture is not being considered by MSHA's enforcement.[32]

Massey's behavior toward West Virginia state officials, backed up by the company's political influence in the state, was even harsher than its treatment of MSHA inspectors.[33] In a particularly prominent effort (concerning a private contract dispute rather than mine safety), Massey sought to overturn an unfavorable judicial verdict in a $50 million case by donating generously to a candidate for election to become chief justice of the West Virginia Supreme Court. The successful candidate won election to his position after receiving $3 million from Massey—more than he received from any other source—and then, when Massey appealed the case to the state Supreme Court, ruled to overturn the verdict against Massey. In 2009 the United States Supreme Court reversed the decision, and ordered the successful judicial candidate to recuse himself from deciding the case.[34]

In short, Massey Mining emphasized production, neglected risk management except as a slogan, accumulated and fought against numerous citations from regulators, and intimidated employees, regulators, and others from providing feedback to the company, thereby causing numerous avoidable fatalities and injuries.

2. PACIFIC GAS AND ELECTRIC COMPANY

On September 9, 2010, an old 30-inch-diameter natural gas pipeline ruptured in San Bruno, California, releasing natural gas into a residential neighborhood. The gas explosion killed eight people, injured many more, destroyed 38 homes and damaged 70, forcing an evacuation of the area. PG&E took 95 minutes to stop the flow of gas.

The National Transportation Safety Board (NTSB) investigated and found that: "the accident was clearly preventable . . . PG&E's inadequate pipeline integrity management program failed to identify, detect, and remove the substandard pipe segments before they ruptured."[35]

The California Public Utilities Commission, responsible for regulating pipeline safety in California, convened an independent review panel. The panel's final report flagged issues similar to those seen in reports of other independent commissions after other disasters.

Management emphasized financial performance rather than the imperative of managing a safe gas pipeline infrastructure. Thus, "in the high level corporate goals material which was presented to the panel . . . the company did not include any goals for safety as part of its long-term aspirations. It did include an aspiration for financial performance, however."[36]

The panel found that PG&E had a "dysfunctional culture," and pointed to five elements of the culture that impeded attention to pipeline integrity and operational management more generally:

1. Excessive layers of management, sometimes amounting to nine levels between front-line employees and the CEO, so that "the management that is setting the direction is distant from those who know the business the best," and difficulty in communicating across silos in the company,

2. A "large presence of telecommunications, legal and finance executives in top leadership positions, and the under representation of engineers and professionals with significant operating experience in the natural gas utility industry,"

3. Strategy-setting that appears more oriented to media relations than to actual implementation,

4. Failure to keep up with technological developments and lack of understanding of the company's practices compared to superior practices of others in the industry, and

5. Overemphasis on financial performance and neglect of operational safety and performance such that others in the organization are discouraged from challenging the priorities put in place by top management.[37]

PG&E lacked the ability to collect or understand implications of data relating to gas pipeline operations, and provided erroneous information to the NTSB when it began to investigate the San Bruno explosion. As the independent panel reported:

> PG&E provided erroneous data because of a lack of: (1) robust data and document information management systems to archive historical data, and (2) processes to capture emerging information about the underground gas transmission system . . . Threat identification and analysis of pipeline segments are limited by quality and accuracy of data and information.[38]

The panel concluded that PG&E's "lack of an overarching effort to centralize diffuse sources of data hinders the collection, quality assurance and analysis of data to characterize threats to pipelines as well as to assess the risk posed by the threats on the likelihood of a pipeline's failure and consequences."[39]

PG&E also was limited by the capabilities of its staff: "We did not observe a coherent planning process to assure the system was being maintained and modernized with any urgency. In particular, the resource complement of qualified and experienced engineers and other professionals was limited."[40]

The California Public Utilities Commission (CPUC) was completely unequipped to provide effective oversight of PG&E, the quality of its risk management, or actual risks relating to pipeline operations. NTSB Chairman Deborah A. P. Hersman reported that the NTSB investigation "revealed that for years, PG&E exploited weaknesses in a lax system of oversight [and] regulators that placed a blind trust in the companies that they were charged with overseeing to the detriment of public safety."[41]

Both the CPUC and PG&E emphasized compliance rather than more sophisticated supervision:

> The technology for utility operations and the regulations regarding safe utility operations are constantly changing. It is challenging for the staff to keep up with all of these changes, particularly as training opportunities diminish. . . . Given these realities, it is understandable the staff's "comfort zone" in its oversight is to be prescriptive. The utilities, in turn, reinforce this compliance-oriented mindset because it reduces the ambiguity of regulation for them. While staff is conscientious, there are many forces that drive towards a "check the boxes" type of regulatory enforcement.[42]

The result, the panel found was that whether or not PG&E "was technically compliant with the letter of the regulations . . . we seriously question whether PG&E has embraced the spirit of the pipeline integrity regulations."[43]

The CPUC's Utilities Safety and Reliability Branch (USRB), responsible for supervising safety, was limited by a tiny staff and few funds for travel or training. The panel found that the gas section of CPUC's Utilities Safety and Reliability Branch (USRB) had a staff of only eighteen people to oversee the three major gas utilities in California and audit their operations for compliance with federal pipeline safety regulations on 11,000 miles of transmission pipeline, as well as almost 2,350 miles of transmission pipeline in high consequence areas for which it was to perform in-depth audits of pipeline integrity. In addition, the staff also was charged with inspecting the small propane systems and distribution systems of over 3,200 mobile home operators every five years.[44] The agency had, the Panel reported, a "victim mentality."[45]

Supervisory staff also seemed to lack the necessary skills:

> There is no evidence the USRB [has] the skills to perform quality analysis of risk management choices, either at an enterprise level or at the technical level specific to Pipeline Integrity Management. The CPUC collectively does not appear to have the skills necessary to perform an in-depth appraisal of any such analyses that might be offered by the operators.[46]

In short, the CPUC seemed to lack ability to ask and pursue basic questions to indicate whether or not a regulated utility was dealing properly with the substantial risks involved in transmitting gas or electric power for long distances through California's communities and neighborhoods.

3. HOSPITAL MEDICAL ERRORS

Hospital medical errors provide a useful example of the costs of a rigid culture that discourages constructive dialogue. While precise numbers concerning medical errors are hard to discover, evidence from organizations such as the Institute of Medicine is alarming. In November 2010, the Office of Inspector General of the Department of Health and Human Services published a report suggesting that perhaps one out of seven Medicare beneficiaries discharged from hospitals had experienced an adverse event involving patient harm. Physician reviewers determined that perhaps 44 percent of these were preventable.[47] In response, the Agency for Healthcare Research and Quality concurred that "adverse events continue to affect hospital patients at an alarming rate."[48]

According to research, "ineffective communication among healthcare providers is one of the leading causes of medical error and patient harm."[49] One cause of ineffective communication—the failure of physicians to obtain important information from nurses—relates directly to the issue of constructive dialogue:

> Communication breakdowns have long been cited as a root cause in almost every sentinel event reported to The Joint Commission's Sentinel Event Database and as the leading root cause in a majority of cases studied since 1996. Hierarchy differences, conflicting roles, ambiguity in responsibilities, and power struggles can all lead to communication failures that compromise patient safety and quality of care.[50]

Intimidation and other disruptive behaviors contribute significantly to medical errors and preventable adverse outcomes. When it occurs, intimidation derives from the institutional setting and cultural norms:

> There is a history of tolerance and indifference to intimidating and disruptive behaviors in health care. . . . Systemic factors stem from the unique health care cultural environment, which is marked by pressures that include increased productivity demands, cost containment requirements, embedded hierarchies, and fear of or stress from litigation. These pressures can be further exacerbated by changes to or differences in the authority, autonomy, empowerment, and roles or values of professionals on the health care team, as well as by the continual flux of daily changes in shifts, rotations, and interdepartmental support staff.[51]

Fortunately, improved communication across the medical provider hierarchy, and particularly between doctors and nurses, may be improving. While there continue to be reports of bullying of nurses by doctors, Ken Stanton, a healthcare administrator and a nurse, reports that,

> There is a lot less bullying now than there used to be. Over the past 10–20 years, I have found physicians to be much more collegial and cooperative than in earlier years. I think it has happened for several reasons—physicians are being trained to be collegial; the majority of physicians now are virtual employees of medical groups, with peer review and an organizational mentality in place of an independent mentality; and they get lots of feedback.[52]

GOVERNANCE AND RISK MANAGEMENT AFFECT GOVERNMENT AS WELL

Lessons of governance and risk management apply to governmental organizations as well as private firms. While the legal framework and organizational imperatives of government agencies differ from those of private companies, higher level lessons such as the need to build constructive dialogue into decision making and the risks of not doing so apply to all organizations, and not merely private firms.[53] This was apparent from the NASA experience with both the Challenger and the Columbia space shuttle disasters (and, as the Columbia accident investigation board reported, in many ways "the parallels are striking" in culture, management, and impediments to employee feedback between the two events).[54] Besides the regulatory failures seen in the financial sector and in other contexts, government has seen emergence of its own expensive black swan events, including Hurricane Katrina, the massive 2010 Gulf oil spill, homeland security events such as September 11, and the Great Recession that resulted from the financial crisis. All of these occurred within a single decade.[55]

Conclusion

Issues of complacency, flawed incentives, poor communication across organizational hierarchies and silos, and failure to encourage high quality supervision and feedback from regulators extend beyond the financial crisis to other firms in other sectors at other times. While costs of such organizational and management failures are substantial, there are signs that progress is being made. As evidence mounts that successful firms and people bear these costs, and not just the firms that make expensive mistakes, it is time for leaders in both the private and public sector to take the initiative to promote higher quality organizational design and management—not only to reduce risks for firms that might fail, but also to improve the institutions upon which all of us depend for our safety and economic well being.

TABLE OF ACRONYMS

ABCP   – asset-backed commercial paper
ABS   – asset backed security
ABX   – Associates Business Xchange index
AIG   – American International Group
AIGFP   – American International Group-Financial Products
AMLF   –Asset-Backed Commercial Paper Money Market Mutual Fund
          Liquidity Facility
ARM   – adjustable rate mortgage
CDO   – collateralized debt obligation
CDS   – credit default swap
CEO   – chief executive officer
CFC   – Countrywide Financial Corporation
CFO   – chief financial officer
CFPB   – Consumer Financial Protection Bureau
CFTC   – Commodity Futures Trading Commission
CIO   – chief information officer
COO   – chief operating officer
CPFF   – Commercial Paper Funding Facility
CPUC   – California Public Utilities Commission
CRE   – commercial real estate
CRO   – chief risk officer
CSE   – Consolidated Supervised Entity program
ED   – US Department of Education
EESA   – Emergency Economic Stabilization Act of 2008
EPD   – early payment default
ERM   – enterprise risk management
FCIC   – Financial Crisis Inquiry Commission
FDIC   – Federal Deposit Insurance Corporation
FDICIA – FDIC Improvements Act
FFIEC   – Federal Financial Institutions Examination Council
FHA   – Federal Housing Administration
FHFA   – Federal Housing Finance Agency
FOMC   – Federal Open Market Committee
FRBNY   – Federal Reserve Bank of New York
FSA   – Financial Services Authority

FSB	– Federal Savings Bank
FSOC	– Financial Stability oversight Council
GAAP	– Generally Accepted Accounting Principles
GAO	– Government Accountability Office
GDP	– gross domestic product
GLBA	– Gramm-Leach-Bliley Act
GS	– Goldman Sachs
GSE	– government sponsored enterprise
HERA	– Housing and Economic Recovery Act
HSE	– Health, Safety, and Environment Management System
HUD	– US Department of Housing and Urban Development
ICBA	– Independent Community Bankers of America
JPMC	– JPMorgan Chase
LCFI	– large complex financial institution
LEH	– Lehman Brothers
LTV	– loan-to-value ratio
MAC	– Material Adverse Change
MBS	– mortgage backed security
MH	– manufactured housing
MIS	– management information system
MMIFF	– Money Market Investor Funding Facility
MMS	– Minerals Management Service
MSHA	– Mine Safety and Health Administration
NA	– National Association
NAPA	– National Academy of Public Administration
NASA	– National Aeronautics and Space Administration
NTSB	– National Transportation Safety Board
OCC	– Office of the Comptroller of the Currency
OECD	– Organization for Economic Cooperation and Development
OFHEO	– Office of Federal Housing Enterprise Oversight
OIMS	– Operations Integrity Management System
OMB	– Office of Management and Budget
OTC	– over-the-counter
OTS	– Office of Thrift Supervision
PDCF	– Primary Dealer Credit Facility
RMBS	– residential mortgage backed security
SCAP	– stress-test capital assessment program
SEC	– Securities and Exchange Commission
SIV	– structured investment vehicle
SRO	– self-regulatory organization
SSG	– Senior Supervisors Group
TAF	– Term Auction Facility
TALF	– Term Asset-Backed Securities Lending Facility

TARP   – Troubled Asset Relief Program
TSLF   – Term Securities Lending Facility
UBB   – Upper Big Branch mine
USRB   – CPUC Utilities Safety and Reliability Branch
VaR   – Value at Risk

NOTES

Preface

1. Jon S. Corzine, Statement before the House Committee on Agriculture, December 8, 2011 ("I was stunned when I was told on Sunday, October 30, 2011, that MF Global could not account for many hundreds of millions of dollars of client money . . . I had little expertise or experience in those operational aspects of the business").

2. Aaron Lucchetti and Julie Steinberg, "Corzine Rebuffed Internal Warnings on Risks," *Wall Street Journal*, December 6, 2011; and Ben Protess and Azam Ahmed, "MF Global's Risk Officer Said to Lack Authority," *New York Times*, December 14, 2011.

3. Azam Ahmed, Ben Protess, and Suzanne Craig, "A Romance with Risk that Brought on a Panic," *New York Times*, December 11, 2011.

4. Azam Ahmed and Ben Protess, "As Regulators Pressed Changes, Corzine Pushed Back, and Won," *New York Times*, November 3, 2011.

5. They are available at http://fcic.law.stanford.edu/.

6. "Perhaps the most effective advocate for safety and soundness regulation has been a private individual: Thomas Stanton . . . Stanton's 1991 book *State of Risk* and his personal lobbying were influential in the legislative process leading to the passage of the [1992 Federal Housing Enterprises Financial Safety and Soundness Act]." Koppell, Jonathan G. S., *The Politics of Quasi-Government*, Cambridge: Cambridge University Press, 2003, p. 107.

Chapter 1

1. Wessel, David, "Inside Dr. Bernanke's E. R.: As Obama Considers Reappointing the Fed Chairman, a Look at How He Took on More Power," *Wall Street Journal*, July 24, 2009.

2. Blinder, Alan S. and Mark Zandi, *How the Great Recession was Brought to an End*, monograph, July 27, 2010. The Blinder/Zandi forecast of spending on TARP turned out to be high; as it happened, the government made money on TARP in the end.

3. Congressional Oversight Panel, "A Review of Treasury's Foreclosure Prevention Programs," December Oversight Report, December 14, 2010, p. 4 ("8 to 13 million foreclosures expected by 2012").

4. Bricker, Jesse, Brian Bucks, Arthur Kennickell, Traci Mach, and Kevin Moore, "Surveying the Aftermath of the Storm: Changes in Family Finances from 2007 to 2009," working paper, Board of Governors of the Federal Reserve System, March 2011; Office of Management and Budget, *Budget of the United States for Fiscal Year 2011*, February 1, 2010, p. 7.

5. Ibid., "Surveying the Aftermath of the Storm."

6. US Census Bureau, *Income, Poverty, and Health Insurance Coverage in the United States: 2010*, September 2011.

7. Alan Greenspan, testimony before the House Committee on Oversight and Government Reform, hearing transcript, "The Financial Crisis and the Role of Federal Regulators," October 23, 2008, p. 33.

8. Senate Permanent Subcommittee on Investigations, Committee on Homeland Security and Governmental Affairs, Final Report, *Wall Street and the Financial Crisis: Anatomy of a Financial Collapse*, April 13, 2011, pp. 9–10.

9. Craig, Susanne, and Peter Lattman, "Goldman's Shares Tumble as Blankfein Hires Top Lawyer," *New York Times*, August 22, 2011.

10. Taleb, Nassim Nicholas, *The Black Swan: The Impact of the Highly Improbable*. New York: Random House, 2007.

11. On design of organizations that carry out public purposes, see, e.g., Thomas H. Stanton, "Moving Toward More Capable Government: A Guide to Organizational Design," chapter 1 in Stanton, Thomas H. ed., *Meeting the Challenge of 9/11: Blueprints for Effective Government*, M. E. Sharpe Publishers, 2006.

12. See, generally, Thomas H. Stanton, "Nonquantifiable Risks and Financial Institutions: The Mercantilist Legal Framework of Banks, Thrifts and Government-Sponsored Enterprises," chapter 3 in Stone, Charles and Anne Zissu, eds., *Global Risk Based Capital Regulations*, Vol. 1, Burr Ridge and New York: Irwin, 1994.

13. Financial Crisis Inquiry Commission, hearing transcript, June 30, 2010, p. 151.

14. Rex Tillerson, Chairman and CEO, ExxonMobil, testimony before the National Commission on the BP Deepwater Horizon Oil Spill and Offshore Drilling, Fifth Meeting, Day Two, *Transcript of Proceedings*, November 9, 2010, p. 248.

15. Lang William W. and Julapa A. Jagtiani, "The Mortgage and Financial Crises: The Role of Credit Risk Management and Corporate Governance," *Atlantic Economic Journal*, 2010, vol. 38, pp. 295–316.

16. Vaughan, Diane, *The Challenger Launch Decision: Risky Technology, Culture, and Deviance at NASA*, Chicago: University of Chicago Press, 1996.

17. FCIC interview with Richard Syron, formerly Freddie Mac, August 31, 2010; FCIC interview with Madelyn Antoncic, formerly Lehman Brothers, July 14, 2010.

18. See, e.g., Sparrow, Malcolm, *The Regulatory Craft: Controlling Risks, Solving Problems, and Managing Compliance*, Washington, D.C.: Brookings Institution Press, 2000.

19. Financial Crisis Inquiry Commission, *Final Report of the Financial Crisis Inquiry Commission*, 2011, p. xviii.

20. Pollock, Alex J., "Introduction to a Conference on Improving Mortgage Disclosure," American Enterprise Institute, June 15, 2007.

21. Ibid., citing Federal Trade Commission, "Improving Consumer Mortgage Disclosures: An Empirical Assessment of Current and Prototype Disclosure Forms," Bureau of Economics Staff Report by James M. Lacko and Janis K. Pappalardo, June 2007.

Chapter 2

1. Bernanke, Ben S. "The Global Saving Glut and the U.S. Current Account Deficit," Homer Jones Lecture, St. Louis, Missouri, April 14, 2005.

2. Council of Economic Advisers, *2011 Economic Report of the President*, February 2011, p. 90.

3. Pierre-Olivier Gourinchas, "U.S. Monetary Policy, 'Imbalances' and the Financial Crisis," remarks prepared for the Financial Crisis Inquiry Commission Forum, Washington, D.C., February 26–27, 2010, pp. 24–25.

4.See, e.g., FCIC *Final Report*, p. 260: "Even before the mass downgrades of CDOs in late 2007, a triple-A tranche of a CDO had a 1 in 10 chance of being downgraded within 5 years of its original rating."

5. Cresci, Gregory. "Merrill, Citigroup Record CDO Fees Earned in Top Growth Market," *Bloomberg*,August30,2005,availableatwww.bloomberg.com/apps/news?pid=10000103&sid=a. FcDwfi.ZG4&;refer=us, C:\Documents and Settings\Thomas H. Stanton\Local Settings\ Temp\Temporary Directory 2 for Stanton Copyedited Files.zip\<a href=accessed June 4, 2011.

6.Ibid.

7. Posner, Kenneth A. and Mita Nambiar, "U.S. Mortgage Finance: The American Dream Industry, 2002–2020," Morgan Stanley Equity Research Industry report, February 5, 2002, p. 8.

8.Federal Deposit Insurance Corporation. "Subprime Lending: Supervisory Guidance for Subprime Lending," March 1, 1999.

9.Subcommittee on Financial Institutions and Consumer Credit and Subcommittee on Housing and Community Opportunity, House Committee on Financial Services, "Protecting Homeowners: Preventing Abusive Lending While Preserving Access to Credit," Joint Hearing, Statement of Robert C. Couch, Chairman, Mortgage Bankers Association, November 5, 2003.

10. LaCour-Little, Michael and Jing Yang, monograph, *Taking the Lie Out of Liar Loans*, June 23, 2009, p. 1.

11. Gorton, Gary B., *Slapped by the Invisible Hand: The Panic of 2007*, Oxford: Oxford University Press, 2010, p. 67, citing a report from Bank of America.

12. Ibid. p. 74.

13. See, e.g., Brevoort, Kenneth P. and Cheryl R. Cooper, The Urban Institute, "Foreclosure's Wake: The Credit Experiences of Individuals Following Foreclosure," paper presented at the 47th Annual Conference on Bank Structure and Competition, Federal Reserve Bank of Chicago, May 4, 2011.

14. Rosner, Josh, "Housing in the New Millennium: A Home Without Equity Is Just a Rental With Debt," *GrahamFisher*, June 29, 2001.

15. Belsky Eric S. and Nela Richardson, "Understanding Boom and Bust in the Nonprime Mortgage Market," Harvard Joint Center for Housing Studies, September 2010, p. 38.

16. Ibid.

17. Ibid, p. 39.

18. *Commonwealth v. Fremont Investment & Loan*, 452 Mass. 733, 897 N. E. 2d 548 (2008).

19. *The People of the State of California v. Countrywide Financial Corporation, et al.*, Case No. LC081846, First Amended Complaint, July 17, 2008, paragraph 69, p. 16.

20. Residential Assets Security Corporation, "Home Equity Mortgage Asset-Backed Pass-Through Certificates," Series 2004-KS12, Depositor, Registration File No.: 333-108868, December 22, 2004, p. 185.

21. Federal Trade Commission, "Improving Consumer Mortgage Disclosures: An Empirical Assessment of Current and Prototype Disclosure Forms," Bureau of Economics Staff Report by James M. Lacko and Janis K. Pappalardo, June 2007.

22. LaCour-Little, Michael, Eric Rosenblatt, and Vincent Yao, "Home Equity Extraction by Homebuyers: 2000–2006," unpublished manuscript, January 18, 2009, p. 16.

23. Bush, George W., President of the United States. Remarks on Signing the American Dream Downpayment Act, December 16, 2003.

24. National Association of Realtors, *Daily Real Estate News*, "HUD Secretary Urges Homeownership as 2005 Resolution."

25. "Credit default swaps greased the CDO machine in several ways. First, they allowed CDO managers to create synthetic and hybrid CDOs more quickly than they could create cash CDOs. Second, they enabled investors in the CDOs (including the originating banks, such as Citigroup and Merrill) to transfer the risk of default to the issuer of the credit default swap (such as AIG and other insurance companies). Third, they made correlation trading possible. As the FCIC survey revealed, most hedge fund purchases of equity and other junior tranches of mortgage backed securities and CDOs were done as part of complex trading strategies. As a result, credit default swaps were critical to facilitate demand from hedge funds for the equity or other junior tranches of mortgage-backed securities and CDOs. Finally, they allowed speculators to make bets for or against the housing market without putting up much cash." Financial Crisis Inquiry Commission, *Final Report of the Financial Crisis Inquiry Commission*, 2011, p. 195.

26. Gorton, *Slapped by the Invisible Hand*, p. 44.

27. Ibid.

28. Washington Mutual, "Higher Risk Lending Strategy, 'Asset Allocation Initiative,' Board of Directors, Finance Committee Discussion," January 2005, p. B1.2, available from the Permanent Subcommittee on Investigations, Senate Committee on Homeland Security and Governmental Affairs.

29. Ibid.

30. United States Bankruptcy Court, Southern District of New York, In re Lehman Brothers Holdings, Inc., "Report of Anton R. Valukas, Examiner," Section III.A. 1: Risk, p. 4 (footnotes omitted), March 11, 2010.

31. Acharya, Viral V., Thomas Cooley, Matthew Richardson, and Ingo Walter, "Manufacturing Tail Risk: A Perspective on the Financial Crisis of 2007–09," *Foundations and Trends in Finance*, volume 4, 2010.

32. United States Bankruptcy Court, Southern District of New York, In re Lehman Brothers Holdings, Inc., "Report of Anton R. Valukas, Examiner," Section III.A. 1: Risk, March 11, 2010, pp. 95–96 (footnotes omitted).

33. Bagehot, Walter. *Lombard Street*, London: Henry S. King and Company, 1873, p. 78, quoted in Pollock, Alex J. *Boom & Bust: Financial Cycles and Human Prosperity*, New York: AEI Press, 2011, p. 69.

34. Federal Reserve Bank of New York, "Summary of Supervisory Activity and Findings, JPMorgan Chase & Co.," April 15, 2008.

35. Buffett, Warren "Chairman's Letter, 2001," Berkshire Hathaway.

36. Bernanke, Ben S. "The Subprime Mortgage Market," speech at the Federal Reserve Bank of Chicago's 43rd Annual Conference on Bank Structure and Competition, Chicago, Illinois, May 17, 2007.

37. Gorton, *Slapped by the Invisible Hand*.

38. FCIC interview with John Mack, Morgan Stanley, November 2, 2010.

39. This timeline is excerpted from a more extensive timeline prepared by the Federal Reserve Bank of St. Louis, available at www.stlouisfed.org/timeline/timeline.cfm, accessed September 1, 2011. In the interests of brevity, major items have been omitted. These include market developments, monetary policy actions of the Federal Open Market Committee, and actions of other federal agencies.

40. Financial Crisis Inquiry Commission, *Final Report of the Financial Crisis Inquiry Commission*, 2011, p. xvii.

41. Ibid., p. 430.

Chapter 3

1. Another firm, Deutsche Bank, weathered the crisis but was hit by significant losses after that, particularly on its leveraged loans and commercial real estate loans. See, Standard & Poor's, *Deutsche Bank AG*, October 2, 2009; and Kurbjuweit, Dirk, Armin Mahler and Christoph Pauly, "Deutsche Bank Chief Weakened by Heavy Losses," *Spiegel Online*, January 20, 2009.

2. Federal Reserve Bank of New York, "Summary of Supervisory Activity and Findings, JPMorgan Chase & Co.," April 15, 2008.

3. Ibid.

4. Deutsch, Clayton G. "Building the Global Bank: An Interview with Jamie Dimon," *The McKinsey Quarterly*, 2006, no. 4.

5. *Business Week*, "Dimon's Grand Design: Jamie Dimon is Bracing for Another Tough Year at JPMorgan. But Now He Has a $1.1 Billion Plan to Revive the Nation's No. 2 Bank. An Inside Look," March 28, 2005.

6. JPMorgan Chase, "2006 Letter to Shareholders."

7. See, e.g., Der Hovanseian, Mara, "JPMorgan: The Bank of Technology; The financial giant is making investments in info tech and expects to reap huge awards," *Business Week*, June 19, 2006; Deutsch, "Building the Global Bank"; Lashinsky, Adam. "Riders on the Storm [Wells Takeover of Wachovia]," Fortune Magazine via CNNMoney.com, April 20, 2009.

8. Hintze, John, "Top 10 CIOs on Wall Street: Duncan Rawls, JPMorgan Chase," *Securities Technology Monitor*, November 4, 2010.

9. Walker, Russell, "Fortune Favours the Well-Prepared," op-ed, *Financial Times*, January 29 2009. The communications are described in Tully, Shawn, "Jamie Dimon's Swat Team; How J. P. Morgan's CEO and His Crew are Helping the Big Bank Beat the Credit Crunch," *Fortune*, September 2, 2008.

10. Tully, "Jamie Dimon's Swat Team."

11. Dan Sparks, former head of the Goldman mortgage trading desk, told Commission staff, "The firm was not a bank. Use of the balance sheet was very carefully guarded." FCIC interview with Dan Sparks, Goldman Sachs, June 16, 2010.

12. Goldman Sachs, "Goldman Sachs: Risk Management and the Residential Mortgage Market," April 23, 2010, p. 5 (footnote omitted).

13. Ibid.

14. Anderson, Jenny, and Landon Thomas, Jr. "Goldman Sachs Rakes in Profit in Credit Crisis," *New York Times*, November 19, 2007.

15. Goldman Sachs, "Fall 2008 Narrative," undated.

16. Creswell, Julie and Ben White. "Wall Street, R. I. P.: The End of an Era, Even at Goldman," *New York Times*, September 28, 2008.

17. Allison, Herbert M. (2011), *The Megabanks Mess*. Kindle Edition.

18. Senate Permanent Subcommittee on Investigations, "Wall Street and the Financial Crisis: The Role of Investment Banks," hearing, transcript.

19. Securities and Exchange Commission, Consent Order of Defendant Goldman Sachs & Co., paragraph 3, p. 2.

20. Chan, Sewell, and Louise Story "Goldman Pays $550 Million to Settle Fraud Case," *New York Times*, July 15, 2010.

21. See, e.g., Seidman, Dov. *How: Why How We Do Anything Means Everything . . . in Business (and in Life)*, Hoboken: John Wiley & Sons, 2007.

22. *New York Times*, "Goldman Sachs Group Inc.," available at http://topics.nytimes.com/top/news/business/companies/goldman_sachs_group_inc/index.html?scp=1-spot&sq=goldman%20sachs&st=cse, accessed March 21, 2011.

23. Goldman Sachs, *Report of the Business Standards Committee: Executive Summary*.

24. Allison, *The Megabanks Mess*.

25. Stanford Graduate School of Business, "Wells Fargo and Norwest: Merger of Equals (B)," October 11, 2004, p. 2.

26. Ryssdal, *Kai*. "Conversations from the Corner Office: Wells Fargo & Company President and CEO John Stumpf," June 10, 2008.

27. FCIC interview with John Stumpf, Wells Fargo, September 23, 2010.

28. Ryssdal, Kai. "Conversations from the Corner Office: Wells Fargo & Company President and CEO John Stumpf," June 10, 2008.

29. FCIC interview with John Stumpf, September 23, 2010.

30. *New York Times*, "Wells Fargo & Company," January 20, 2011.

31. Clark, W. Edmund. "President and CEO's Message," *TD Bank Financial Group 2005 Annual Report*, Toronto Dominion Bank, 2006, p. 6.

32. Sydney Morning Herald, Bloomberg, "The bank that said 'No' to subprime debt," May 27, 2008.

33. Ibid.

34. Clark, Edmund. National Bank 2010 Financial Services Conference, presentation, TD Bank Financial Group, March 30, 2010

35. See, e.g., Der Hovanseian, "JPMorgan: The Bank of Technology"; Deutsch, "Building the Global Bank"; Lashinsky, "Riders on the Storm [Wells Takeover of Wachovia]."

36. Knight, Frank. *Risk, Uncertainty, and Profit*, Boston: Houghton Mifflin, 1921.

37. FCIC interview with Eugene Ludwig, former Comptroller of the Currency, September 2, 2010.

38. Walker, Russell. "Fortune Favours the Well-Prepared," op-ed, *Financial Times*, January 29 2009.

39. Allison, *The Megabanks Mess*.

40. Fannie Mae, "Single Family Guarantee Business: Facing Strategic Crossroads." June 27, 2005.

41. Fannie Mae, "Fannie Mae Strategic Plan 2007–2011 'Develop Segments—Develop Breadth,'" undated, approximately end of June 2007; Freddie Mac, "Freddie Mac's Business Strategy," Board of Directors Meeting, March 2–3, 2007. Emphasis omitted.

42. Testimony of James B. Lockhart, Federal Housing Finance Agency, to the FCIC, April 9, 2010.

43. Duhigg, Charles. "At Freddie Mac, Chief Discarded Warning Signs," *New York Times*, August 5, 2008; United States Bankruptcy Court, Southern District of New York, *In re Lehman Brothers Holdings, Inc.*, "Report of Anton R. Valukas, Examiner," Section III.A.1: Risk, p. 4 (footnotes omitted), March 11, 2010.

44. Davidson, Andrew, "The Financial Crisis: a Failure of American Enterprise," monograph, February 2011, p. 5.

45. Federal Housing Finance Agency, *Report to Congress 2008*, May 18, 2009, pp. 110, 127.

46. McGinty, Thomas, Kate Kelly and Kara Scannell, "Debt 'Masking' Under Fire," *Wall Street Journal*, April 21, 2010, p. A-1.

47. On the impact of growth on internal controls at Fannie Mae and Freddie Mac, see, e.g., Stanton, Thomas H. "The Life Cycle of the Government-Sponsored Enterprise: Lessons for Design and Accountability," *Public Administration Review*, September/October 2007.

48. The problem was larger than merely the absence of a common information system; there was also the problem of data. "Some groups also mentioned the absence of a group-wide database, a lack of uniformity and timeliness in collected data, and data access and quality issues . . . as other hindrances to identifying and consolidating exposures across risks and business units." Bank for International Settlements, Joint Forum, Working Group on Risk Assessment and Risk-Capital Concentration, "Cross-sectoral review of group-wide identification and management of risk concentrations," January 9, 2008 version.

49. See, e.g., Dash, Eric and Julie Creswell, "Citigroup Saw No Red Flags Even as it Made Bolder Bets," *New York Times*, November 23, 2008.

50. Financial Crisis Inquiry Commission, *Final Report of the Financial Crisis Inquiry Commission*, 2011, pp. 321–22 (footnote omitted).

51. Senate Permanent Subcommittee on Investigations, Committee on Homeland Security and Governmental Affairs, Final Report, *Wall Street and the Financial Crisis: Anatomy of a Financial Collapse*, April 13, 2011, p. 87 (footnote omitted).

52. Ibid.

53. Testimony of Charles Prince, Citigroup, to the FCIC, April 8, 2010, transcript, pp. 3–4.

54. The author is grateful to Albert Crego of the FCIC staff for this insight.

55. FCIC interview with Anurag Saksena, June 22, 2010.

56. American International Group. *Form 10-K for the fiscal year ended December 31, 2007*, p. 28, pp. 33, 4.

57. Testimony of Robert Rubin to the FCIC, Hearing Transcript, April 8, 2010, pp. 16–17.

58. Another potential signal about the low value of the super-senior tranches came from the low returns that they generated. See Tett, Gillian, *Fool's Gold*, New York: The Free Press, 2009, p. 126, with respect to JPMorgan: "One solution was simply to park the super-senior on J. P. Morgan's books, but [JPMorgan official Bill]Winters didn't like that. . . . Winters thought it was just a bad idea to let assets pile up on the balance sheet . . . The returns on super-senior were far too low to justify holding it in any appreciable volume."

59. Davidson, Andrew, Anthony Sanders, Lan-Ling Wolff, and Anne Ching, *Securitization: Structuring and Investment Analysis*, Hoboken, N.J.: Wiley Finance, 2003, p. 381.

60. See, e.g., Fannie Mae, "Quarterly Risk Assessment YE 2002," memorandum from Adolfo Marzol to Timothy Howard and Dan Mudd, February 6, 2003, February 6, 2003 ("Conseco—We were wise to limit our participation to basically AAA paper. But, we might have benefitted significantly from a credit officer focused on that business, perhaps enabling us to identify earlier the changing nature of the market and weaknesses in rating agency analysis").

61. Fannie Mae, Memorandum from Adolfo Marzol to Dan Mudd. "Private Label Securities," March 2, 2005, draft. (emphasis added).

62. FCIC Interview with Scott McCleskey, formerly Moody's Investors Service, April 16, 2010.

63. McCleskey, Scott, letter to the US Securities and Exchange Commission, March 12, 2009.

64. Stephen B. Ashley, Chairman, Remarks, Fannie Mae Senior Management Meeting, June 27, 2006 (emphasis added).

65. Countrywide Financial Corporation. *Form 10-K for the fiscal year ended December 31, 2005*, pp. 39–40. Because Countrywide securitized many mortgage loans and sold them, the volume of originations was significantly greater than the volume of loans on its balance sheet.

66. Countrywide, *Fixed Income Investor Forum*, February 28, 2006.

67. Financial Crisis Inquiry Commission, *Final Report of the Financial Crisis Inquiry Commission*, 2011, p. 89.

Chapter 4

1. Basel Committee on Banking Supervision, *Principles for enhancing corporate governance*, Consultative document, March 2010, pp. 5–6. The text from the Basel document is specifically oriented towards banks:
From a banking industry perspective, corporate governance involves the allocation of authority and responsibilities, i.e. the manner in which the business and affairs of a bank are governed by its board and senior management, including how they:
- set the bank's strategy and objectives;
- determine the bank's risk tolerance/appetite;
- operate the bank's business on a day-to-day basis;
- protect the interests of depositors, meet shareholder obligations, and take into account the interests of other recognised stakeholders; and
- align corporate activities and behaviour with the expectation that the bank will operate in a safe and sound manner, with integrity and in compliance with applicable laws and regulations.

2. Alex Pollock aptly cites Walter Bagehot in this regard: "All which the best board of directors can really accomplish is to form a good decision on the points which the manager presents to them and perhaps on a few others which one or two zealous members of their body may select for discussion. A meeting of fifteen or eighteen persons is wholly unequal to the transaction of more business than this. . . . Not only would a real supervision of a large business by a board of directors require much more time than the board would consent to occupy in meeting, it would also require much more time and much more thought than the individual directors would consent to give. . . . Directors of a company cannot attend principally and anxiously to the affairs of a company without neglecting their own business." Alex J. Pollock, "What Should Society Want from Corporate Governance?" *Financial Services Outlook*, American Enterprise Institute, February 2006, citing Bagehot, Walter. *Lombard Street*, London: Henry S. King and Company, 1873, p. 126.

3. Finkelstein, Sydney, Jo Whitehead, and Andrew Campbell, *Think Again: Why Good leaders Make Bad Decisions and How to Keep it From Happening to You*, Boston: Harvard Business Press, 2010. The author is grateful to Desi Duncker of the Commission staff for first pointing me to this book.

4. Clark, Edmund, "Corporate Transparency and Corporate Accountability—Today's Table Stakes for Senior Executives," remarks to the Executive Women's Alliance Conference, Vancouver, July 12, 2004.

5. Myners, Paul, "Reform of Banking Must Begin in the Boardroom," letter, *Financial Times*, April 24, 2008.

6. Basel Committee on Banking Supervision, *Principles for Enhancing Corporate Governance*, consultative document, March 2010, passim.

7. Allison, Herbert M. (2011), *The Megabanks Mess*, Kindle Edition

8. Nestor Advisors, *Governance in Crisis: A Comparative Study of Six US Investment Banks*, April 2009, p. 7.

9. Tully, Shawn, "Jamie Dimon's Swat Team; How J. P. Morgan's CEO and His Crew are Helping the Big Bank Beat the Credit Crunch," *Fortune*, September 2, 2008.

10. Ibid.

11. Nestor Advisors, *Governance in Crisis: A Comparative Study of Six US Investment Banks*, April 2009, pp. 6–7.

12. Ibid., p. 15.

13. "Risk Management at Goldman Sachs: Presentation to the McKinsey Advisory Committee," February 20, 2007, p. 6.

14. FCIC interview with Dan Sparks, Goldman Sachs, June 16, 2010.

15. United States Bankruptcy Court, Southern District of New York, *In re Lehman Brothers Holdings, Inc.*, "Report of Anton R. Valukas, Examiner," March 11, 2010, vol. 1, risk, pp. 55–56.

16. Nestor Advisors, *Governance in Crisis: A Comparative Study of Six US Investment Banks*, April 2009, p. 5.

17. This text is quoted directly from the OECD Principles of Corporate Governance, appendix to *Using the OECD Principles of Corporate Governance: A Boardroom Perspective*, 2008.

18. Macey, Jonathan R. *Corporate Governance: Promises Kept, Promises Broken*, Princeton, N. J.: Princeton University Press, 2008, chapter 4.

19. Nestor Advisors, Ltd, *Governance in Crisis: A Comparative Case Study of Six U.S. Investment Banks*, 2009, p. 12 (footnote omitted).

20. Sonnenfeld, Jeffrey A., "What Makes Great Boards Great," *Harvard Business Review*, September 2002, pp. 106–13, p. 106.

21. Finkelstein, Sydney, *Why Smart Executives Fail, and What you Can Learn From Their Mistakes*, New York: Portfolio, 2003.

22. Paul Myners is only one of many observers who make scathing observations about the composition of many financial institution boards: "The typical bank board resembles a retirement home for the great and the good: there are retired titans of industry, ousted politicians and the occasional member of the voluntary sector," letter, "Reform of banking must begin in the boardroom." *Financial Times*, April 24, 2008.

23. Walker, David, *A Review of Corporate Governance in UK Banks and Other Financial Industry Entities: Final Recommendations*, November 26, 2009, p. 12. Walker was tasked by the UK Prime Minister "to review corporate governance in UK banks in the light of the experience of critical loss and failure throughout the banking system."

24. Nestor Advisors, *Governance in Crisis: A Comparative Study of Six US Investment Banks*, April 2009, p. 1.

25. United States Bankruptcy Court, Southern District of New York, *In re Lehman Brothers Holdings, Inc.*, "Report of Anton R. Valukas, Examiner," March 11, 2010, p. 184, footnotes omitted.

26. *In Re Citigroup Inc. Shareholder Derivative Litigation*, Delaware Court of Chancery, 964 A. 2d 106 (2009), at 123.

27 Finkelstein, Sydney, *Why Smart Executives Fail, and What you Can Learn From Their Mistakes*, New York: Portfolio, 2003, pp. 251–52.

28. Clark, Edmund, "Corporate Transparency and Corporate Accountability—Today's Table Stakes for Senior Executives," remarks to the Executive Women's Alliance Conference, Vancouver, July 12, 2004.

29. FCIC interview with Mark Olson, former Federal Reserve Governor, October 4, 2010.

30. Financial Crisis Inquiry Commission, hearing transcript, June 30, 2010, p. 151.

31. FCIC interview with Charles Prince, Citigroup, March 17, 2010, pp. 72–74.

32. UBS AG, *Shareholder Report on UBS's Write-Downs*, April 18, 2008, p. 40.

33. Nestor Advisors, *Governance in Crisis: A Comparative Study of Six US Investment Banks*, April 2009, p. 4; Stanford Rock School of Business. "Lehman Brothers: Peeking Under the Board Façade" June 4, 2010.

34. Committee for Economic Development, "Restoring Trust in Corporate Governance: Six Essential Tasks of Boards of Directors and Business Leaders," January 2010, p. 14, discusses the short term outlook of institutional investors and states that "the average holding period for equities is now less than a year."

35. Walker, *A Review of Corporate Governance in UK Banks and Other Financial Industry Entities*, p. 71.

36. Beltratti, Andrea and René M. Stulz. "Why Did Some Banks Perform Better during the Credit Crisis? A Cross-Country Study of the Impact of Governance and Regulation," European Corporate Governance Institute, Working Paper No. 254/2009, July 2009, pp. 2–3.

37. Allison, *The Megabanks Mess*.

38. Ibid.

39. Freddie Mac, Freddie Mac's Business Strategy, Board of Directors Meeting, March 2–3, 2007, pp. 3–4.

40. Ibid., p. 79.

41. Jerome S. Fons, Testimony before the Committee on Oversight and Government Reform, United States House of Representatives, October 22, 2008. See also Statement of Richard Michalek, Former VP/Senior Credit Officer, Moody's Investors Service, Submitted to Permanent Subcommittee on Investigations, Committee on Governmental Affairs, United States Senate, April 23, 2010; and Statement of Eric Kolchinsky Before The Senate Permanent Subcommittee on Investigations, April 23, 2010.

42. Stanton, Thomas H., *Government-Sponsored Enterprises: Mercantilist Companies in the Modern World*, Washington, D. C.: AEI Press, 2002, pp. 83–84.

43. Heineman, Ben W. Jr., "Executive Compensation: Let's Look at Fund Managers' Pay, Too," *HBR Now*, July 30, 2009.

44. Goldman Sachs, *2006 Annual Report*, p. 65. The same statement appears in the *2007 Annual Report*, p. 77.

45. United States Bankruptcy Court, Southern District of New York, *In re Lehman Brothers Holdings, Inc.*, "Report of Anton R. Valukas, Examiner," March 11, 2010, vol. 1, p. 3, footnotes omitted.

46. FCIC interview with Thomas Fontana, Citigroup, August 13, 2010.

47. Financial Crisis Inquiry Commission, hearing transcript, April 8, 2010, p. 87.

48. Johnson, Simon and James Kwak, *13 Bankers: The Wall Street Takeover and the Next Financial Meltdown*, New York: Pantheon, 2010.

49. FCIC interview with Lew Ranieri, July 30, 2010, Part 1.

50. Quoted in Arthur E. Wilmarth, Jr., "Controlling Systemic Risk in an Era of Financial Consolidation," p. 16, footnote 25.

51. FCIC interview with Edward DeMarco, FHFA Director, March 18, 2010, Memorandum for the Record.

52. FCIC Financial Crisis Inquiry Commission, hearing transcript, June 30, 2010, p. 141.

53. FCIC interview with Charles Prince, Citigroup, March 17, 2010, pp. 26–28. On the regulatory settlement with Citi that occurred before Prince became CEO, see, Federal Trade Commission, "Citigroup Settles FTC Charges Against the Associates Record-Setting $215 Million for Subprime Lending Victims," September 19, 2002.

54. Memorandum to Members of the Permanent Subcommittee on Investigations, "Wall Street and the Financial Crisis: The Role of High Risk Loans," April 13, 2010, available from the Permanent Subcommittee on Investigations, Senate Committee on Homeland Security and Governmental Affairs, pp. 14–15.

55. Jackson, Howell E. and Laurie Burlingame, "Kickbacks or Compensation: The Case of Yield Spread Premiums," *Stanford Journal of Law, Business and Finance*, vol. 12, no. 2, Spring 2007, pp. 289–361, pp. 291–92.

56. Antje Berndt, Burton Hollifield, and Patrik Sandas, "The Role of Mortgage Brokers in the Subprime Crisis," April 2010.

57. Ibid.

58. Financial Crisis Inquiry Commission, hearing transcript, April 8, 2010, p. 51.

59. FCIC interview with Joseph St. Denis, formerly AIG, Memorandum for the Record, April 23, 2010.

60. Acharya, Viral V., Thomas Cooley, Matthew Richardson and Ingo Walter, "Manufacturing Tail Risk: A Perspective on the Financial Crisis of 2007–09," forthcoming, *Foundations and Trends in Finance*, volume 4, 2010.

61. Bebchuk, Lucian A. and Holger Spamann, "Regulating Bankers' Pay," discussion paper No. 641, Harvard John M. Olin Center for Law, Economics, and Business, October 2009 revision.

62. Hilzenrath, David S. "Chief Says Freddie Won't Raise Capital; Mortgage Financer Cites Responsibility to Shareholders, Won't Increase Loan Capacity," *Washington Post*, March 13, 2008, p. D4.

63. Nestor Advisors, *Governance in Crisis: A Comparative Study of Six US Investment Banks*, April 2009, p. 17.

64. Bebchuk, Lucian A. Alma Cohen, and Holger Spamann, "The Wages of Failure: Executive Compensation at Bear Stearns and Lehman 2000–2008," discussion paper No. 657, Harvard John M. Olin Center for Law, Economics, and Business, February 2010 revision.

65. FCIC interview with Joseph St. Denis, formerly AIG, Memorandum for the Record, April 23, 2010.

66. Senate Permanent Subcommittee on Investigations, Hearing on *Wall Street and the Financial Crisis: The Role of High Risk Home Loans*, April 13, 2010, Exhibit 64.

67. *Liquidated: An Ethnography of Wall Street*, p. 290.

68. Craig, Suzanne, "At Goldman, Partners Are Made, and Unmade," *New York Times*, September 12, 2010. See also FCIC interview with David Viniar, Goldman Sachs, June 16, 2010.

69. See, e.g., *Business Week*, "The Leadership Factory: Paulson is Just the Latest Product of Goldman's Public Service Culture," June 12, 2006.

70. FCIC Interview of Brian R. Leach, Citigroup, March 4, 2010.

71. Source quoted on condition of confidentiality.

72. FCIC interview with David Viniar, Goldman Sachs, June 16, 2010.

73. Paul, Weiss, Rifkind, Wharton & Garrison LLP, *Report to the Special Review Committee of the Board of Directors of Fannie Mae*, 2006, p. 456.

74. Office of Federal Housing Enterprise Oversight, *Report on the Special Examination of Freddie Mac*, 2003, p. 91.

75. For example, in 1996 the Congressional Budget Office reported: "In keeping with its fiduciary responsibility to shareholders and its own financial interests, the management of the housing GSEs has devoted a significant (but undisclosed) portion of the enterprises' resources to countering—or hedging—that political risk. . . . Fannie Mae, in particular, makes no secret of its attempts to influence federal policy toward the GSEs as a means of controlling political risk. . . . Significantly, too, Fannie Mae explicitly includes the contribution to preserving its 'franchise' when evaluating the performance of executive staff." Congressional Budget Office, *Assessing the Public Costs and Benefits of Fannie Mae and Freddie Mac*, 1996, pp. 36–37 (footnotes omitted).

76. Testimony of Patricia Lindsay, New Century Financial Corporation, to the FCIC, April 7, 2010.

77. FCIC interview with former Lehman Chief Risk Officer Madelyn Antoncic, July 14, 2010; FCIC interview with former Lehman Global Head of Risk Management Christopher O'Meara, July 17, 2010.

78. Tabe, Henry, *The Unraveling of Structured Investment Vehicles: How Liquidity Leaked Through SIVs*, UK: Thoth Capital, 2010, pp. 54–55.

79. Senior Supervisors Group, "Notes on Senior Supervisors' Meetings with Firms, Citigroup, Inc.," November 19, 2007, p. 21.

80. FCIC interview with former Lehman Chief Risk Officer Madelyn Antoncic, July 14, 2010; FCIC interview with former Global Head of Risk Management Christopher O'Meara, July 17, 2010.

81. For Deutsche Bank, see FCIC interview with Patrick McKenna, Deutsche Bank, August 2, 2010.

Chapter 5

1. Hiemstra, Stephen W., "An Enterprise Risk Management View of Financial Supervision," *Enterprise Risk Management Institute International*, October 2007.

2. Also helpful is the brief summary of leading risk management practices that the consulting firm Oliver Wyman prepared for Bear Stearns in 2008. The summary is especially attractive in the way that it treats risk management as a performance-oriented process and not merely a paper exercise. Oliver Wyman, "Bear Stearns Management Committee: Risk Governance Diagnostic Recommendations and Case for Economic Capital Development," February 5, 2008, slide # 5.

3. Notes on Senior Supervisors' Meetings with Firms, "Citigroup, Inc.," November 19, 2007, p. 2.

4. Here the FCIC staff interview with David Wong, Treasurer of Morgan Stanley, October 15, 2010, is informative.

5. The market panics of August 2007 and September 2008 reflected dynamics of bank runs in the days before deposit insurance. Coping with such a run required imagination, discipline, and luck. For the story of a bank's success in coping with a bank run during the Great Depression, see Eccles, Marriner S., *Beckoning Frontiers: Public and Personal Recollections*, New York: Knopf, 1951, chapter 2.

6. Power, Michael, "Organizational Responses to Risk: The Rise of the Chief Risk Officer," chapter 5 in Hutter, Bridget M. and Michael Power, eds., *Organizational Encounters with Risk*, Cambridge: Cambridge University Press, 2005, pp. 147–48.

7. Buiter, Willem, Lessons from the North Atlantic Financial Crisis, revised May 28, 2008.

8. FCIC interview with Madelyn Antoncic, July 14, 2010. The approach articulated by Dr. Antoncic is similar to the idea of "principled intimacy" that former police official Malcolm Sparrow has defined. See Sparrow, Malcolm K., *The Regulatory Craft: Controlling Risks, Solving Problems, and Managing Compliance*, Washington, D.C.: Brookings Institution Press, 2000, p. 177.

9. Senior Supervisors Group, *Risk Management Lessons from the Global Banking Crisis of 2008*, p. 2.

10. Rossi, Clifford V., "Anatomy of Risk Management Practices in the Mortgage Industry: Lessons for the Future," Research Institute for Housing America and Mortgage Bankers Association, May 2010, p. 46.

11. Senior Supervisors Group, *Risk Management Lessons from the Global Banking Crisis of 2008*, p. 4.

12. Enrico Dallavecchia, email to Michael Williams (COO), July 16, 2007. Typographical errors in original.

13. "Facilitating development of certain biases toward risk management are the differences in information content between business, risk and finance units. Risk management functions provide estimates of uncertain outcomes such as expected losses or stress capital for example. Business and finance managers typically rely on deterministic models and outcomes such as market share, production, and revenue growth." Rossi, "Anatomy of Risk Management Practices in the Mortgage Industry," p. 46.

14. Financial Crisis Inquiry Commission, *Final Report of the Financial Crisis Inquiry Commission*, 2011, pp. 181–82.

15. Federal Reserve Bank of New York, "Summary of Supervisory Activity and Findings, Citigroup, Inc.," transmitted April 15, 2008, p. 4.

16. Ho, Karen, *Liquidated: An Ethnography of Wall Street*, Durham: Duke University Press, 2009, p. 322.

17. Kevin M. Blakely, Testimony, Senate Committee on Banking, Housing and Urban Affairs, Subcommittee on Securities, Insurance, and Investment, June 19, 2008, p. 19.

18. FCIC interview with John G. Stumpf, Chairman and CEO, Wells Fargo, September 23, 2010.

19. FCIC interview with Michael Loughlin, Chief Risk Officer, Wells Fargo November 23, 2010.

20. FCIC interview with Dan Sparks, Goldman Sachs, June 16, 2010.

21. Kevin M. Blakely, testimony, Senate Committee on Banking, Housing and Urban Affairs, Subcommittee on Securities, Insurance, and Investment, June 19, 2008, p. 7.

22. Yale School of Management, "Pay, Risk, and Stewardship: Private Sector Architecture for Future Capital Markets," Policy Briefing No. 5, consultative draft, 2009, p. 19. One thinks here too of Bagehot's observation: "The business of banking ought to be simple; if it is hard, it is wrong. The only securities which a banker, using money that he may be asked at short notice to repay, ought to touch, are those which are easily saleable and easily intelligible." Walter Bagehot, *Lombard Street*, London: Henry S. King and Company, 1873, pp. 244–45.

23. Golub Bennett W. and Conan C. Crum, "Risk Management Lessons Worth Remembering From the Credit Crisis of 2007—2009," p. 16. Golub and Crum are Vice Chairman and Chief Risk Officer, and Associate, Risk & Quantitative Analysis, respectively, at Black-Rock, Inc.

24. A story along these lines comes from Cambridge Massachusetts, about the student who placed twenty-five items on the conveyor belt for the grocery store express checkout lane where customers were limited to a maximum of eight items. Asked the checkout clerk: "Are you from MIT and you can't read, or are you from Harvard and can't count?"

25. FCIC interview with David Viniar, Goldman Sachs, June 16, 2010.

26. CRMPG III, *Containing Systemic Risk: The Road to Reform*, report, August 6, 2008, p. 84.

27. Bank for International Settlements, Joint Forum, Working Group on Risk Assessment and Risk-Capital Concentration, "Cross-sectoral review of group-wide identification and management of risk concentrations," January 9, 2008 version, p. 35.

28. Deutsch, Clayton G., "Building the global bank: An interview with Jamie Dimon," *The McKinsey Quarterly*, 2006, no. 4.

29. Douglas Webster, communication to the author, December 2, 2011.

30. Committee of Sponsoring Organizations of the Treadway Commission, *Enterprise Risk Management—Integrated Framework, Executive Summary*, September 2004, p. 1.

31. Ibid.

32. For a collection of essays considering ERM and the financial crisis, see, Society of Actuaries, the Casualty Actuarial Society and the Canadian Institute of Actuaries, "Risk Management: The Current Financial Crisis, Lessons Learned and Future Implications," published by the Enterprise Risk Management Institute International ("ERM-II"), 2008.

33. An excellent overview of ERM is found in John Fraser and Betty J. Simkins, editors, *Enterprise Risk Management*, 2010.

34. Tim Ryan, "American International Group, Inc. Meeting Notes," PwC, February 6, 2008.

35. "Citigroup chief stays bullish on buyouts," *Financial Times*, July 9, 2007.

36. See, e.g., "ICGN Corporate Risk Management Principles," p. 7.

37. Senior Supervisors Group, *Risk Management Lessons from the Global Banking Crisis of 2008*, p. 4.

38. Kevin M. Blakely, testimony, Senate Committee on Banking, Housing and Urban Affairs, Subcommittee on Securities, Insurance, and Investment, June 19, 2008, p. 11.

39. Lewis, Michael. *The Big Short*, New York: Norton, 2010, p. 257. For example, New York City financial companies paid bonuses in 2008 totaling over $17 billion despite taking substantial losses. White, Ben. "What Red Ink? Wall Street Paid Hefty Bonuses," *New York*

Times, January 29, 2009; Office of the New York State Comptroller, "New York City Securities Industry Bonus Pool," February 23, 2010.

40. FCIC interview with Brian R. Leach, Citigroup Chief Risk Officer, March 4, 2010.

41. Senior Supervisors Group, *Risk Management Lessons from the Global Banking Crisis of 2008*, p. 26.

42. FCIC Interview of Brian R. Leach, March 4, 2010.

43. Senior Supervisors Group, *Risk Management Lessons from the Global Banking Crisis of 2008*, p. 26.

44. Viral Acharya sees the publication of covenant provisions as a major advantage of placing derivatives contracts onto exchanges; the market then can respond as firms see how other firms have adjusted their approaches to collateral management. Comments at the 47th Conference on Bank Structure and Competition, Federal Reserve Bank of Chicago, May 5, 2011.

45. Office of the Comptroller of the Currency (OCC), *Supervisory Guidance on Model Risk Management*, OCC Bulletin 2011—12, April 4, 2011.

46. Adapted from Basel Committee on Banking Supervision, *Principles for Sound Liquidity Risk Management and Supervision*, September 2008, p. 1.

47. Golub, Bennett W. and Conan C. Crum. "Risk Management Lessons Worth Remembering From the Credit Crisis of 2007—2009," p. 25.

48. Lang William W. and Julapa Jagtiani, "The Mortgage and Financial Crisis: The Role of Credit Risk management and Corporate Governance," *Atlantic Economic Journal*, 2010 p. 16.

49. FCIC interview with Dan Sparks, Goldman Sachs, June 16, 2010.

50. Lang and Jagtiani, "The Mortgage and Financial Crisis," pp. 12–13.

51. Nocerra, Joe, "Risk Mismanagement," *New York Times Magazine*, January 4, 2009.

52. PwC, AIG's external auditor, told CEO Martin Sullivan, CFO Steven Bensinger and Director of Internal Audit Michael Roemer in a meeting on November 29, 2007, "the fact that FP and AGF in late 2005 were reducing their exposure to subprime while AIG Investment and UGC were increasing theirs—seemed to show a lack of cross AIG evaluation of risk exposure to a sector" and combined with other items "raised control concerns around risk management which could be a material weakness." PwC, notes of November 29, 2007 Meeting.

53. FCIC hearing transcript, June 30, 2010, pp. 154–57.

54. See, e.g., Seidman, Dov. *How: Why How We Do Anything Means Everything . . . in Business (and in Life)*, Hoboken, N. J.: Wiley, 2007.

55. Bank for International Settlements, Joint Forum, Working Group on Risk Assessment and Risk-Capital Concentration, "Cross-Sectoral Review of Group-Wide Identification and Management of Risk Concentrations," January 9, 2008 version, p. 31.

56. Quoted in Creswell, Julie and Vikas Bajaj, "$3.2 Billion Move by Bear Stearns To Rescue Fund," *New York Times*, June 23, 2007.

57. Davis, Gerald F., *Managed by the Markets: How Finance Re-Shaped America*, Oxford and New York: Oxford University Press, 2009, pp. 122–24.

Chapter 6

1. Herring Richard and Jacopo Carmassi. "The Corporate Structure of International Financial Conglomerates: Complexity and its Implications for Safety and Soundness," chapter 8 in Berger, Allen N., Phillip Molyneux and John O. S. Wilson, eds, *The Oxford Handbook of Banking*, Oxford: Oxford University Press, 2010, figure 8.2.

2. Allison, Herbert M. (2011). *The Megabanks Mess*. Kindle Edition.

3. Herring Richard and Jacopo Carmassi, "The Corporate Structure of International Financial Conglomerates: Complexity and its Implications for Safety and Soundness," chapter 8 in Berger et al., eds, *The Oxford Handbook of Banking*, figure 8.1.

4. US Government Accountability Office, "Troubled Asset Relief Program, Status of Government Assistance Provided to AIG," GAO-09-975, September 2009, p. 5; American International Group. *Form 10-K for the fiscal year ended December 31, 2007*, p. 7.

5. US Government Accountability Office, "Troubled Asset Relief Program, Status of Government Assistance Provided to AIG," GAO-09-975, September 2009, pp. 6–7.

6. The author respectfully differs with the definition of "shadow banking" adopted by economists at the Federal Reserve Bank of New York. They include GSEs as part of the shadow banking sector while the present author considers GSEs more to resemble banks and thrifts in their legal structures, for reasons presented in Stanton, Thomas H., "Nonquantifiable Risks and Financial Institutions: The Mercantilist Legal Framework of Banks, Thrifts and Government-Sponsored Enterprises," in *Global Risk Based Capital Regulations*, edited by Professors Charles Stone and Anne Zissu, 1994, and Stanton, Thomas H., *Government Sponsored Enterprises: Mercantilist Companies in the Modern World*, 2002.

7. Financial Crisis Inquiry Commission, *Final Report of the Financial Crisis Inquiry Commission*, 2011, p. 317.

8. Daniel Mudd, testimony before the House Committee on Oversight and Government Reform, hearing, "The Role of Fannie Mae and Freddie Mac in the Financial Crisis," December 9, 2008.

9. Financial Crisis Inquiry Commission, *Final Report of the Financial Crisis Inquiry Commission*, 2011, p. 41.

10. Stanton, "Nonquantifiable Risks and Financial Institutions," pp. 90–91.

11. While smaller institutions did not cause the financial crisis, smaller banks and thrifts went through a similar process. They increasingly lost market share to larger institutions and unregulated securitization conduits for mortgages and other financial assets. The result, the FCIC staff were told, is that smaller FDIC-insured institutions have increasing concentrations of risk in commercial real estate, including acquisition, development, and construction loans, and smaller commercial loans, all of which are cyclical businesses and make the institutions vulnerable to a downturn such as occurred after the crisis broke. The lack of good investments for many smaller banks was likely a cause of their investment in GSE preferred stock that lost its value when Fannie Mae and Freddie Mac went into conservatorship. See Office of Inspector General, Department of the Treasury, *Material Loss Review of National Bank of Commerce*, OIG-09-042, August 6, 2009, ("All things considered, we believe that NBC acted in good faith when it invested in the GSE securities. Additionally, we have no reason to fault OCC's supervision of the institution as it relates to NBC's investment practices. Current law and regulatory standards permit banks to purchase GSE securities without limitation").

12. Office of the Comptroller of the Currency, "Observations—Allowance Process and Methodology," August 2008 (last revised September 8, 2008), p. 3.

13. Wilmarth, Arthur, "The Transformation of the U.S. Financial Services Industry, 1975–2000: Competition, Consolidation, and Increased Risks," *University of Illinois Law Review*, vol. 2002, pp. 215–476, 2002.

14. Bank of England, *Financial Stability Report*, April 2007, p. 38.

15. FCIC interview with Brian R. Leach, Citigroup, March 4, 2010.

16. FCIC interview with David Viniar, Goldman Sachs, June 16, 2010.

17. Ibid.

18. Ibid.

19. Tabe, Henry, *The Unraveling of Structured Investment Vehicles: How Liquidity Leaked Through SIVs*, UK: Thoth Capital, 2010, chapter 8.

20. FCIC interview with Anurag Saksena, Chief Enterprise Risk Officer, Freddie Mac, June 22, 2010.

21. Ibid.

22. Koppell, Jonathan G. S., *The Politics of Quasi-Government Hybrid Organizations and the Dynamics of Bureaucratic Control*, Cambridge: Cambridge University Press, 2003, p. 101.

23. Vise, David A., "The Money Machine: How Fannie Mae Wields Power," *Washington Post*, January 16, 1995, p. A14.

24. Paul A. Volcker, letter to Fannie Mae CEO David O. Maxwell, March 6, 1990, published in the "Second Roundtable Hearing on the Safety and Soundness of Fannie Mae and Freddie Mac," Subcommittee on Housing and Urban Affairs, Senate Committee on Banking, Housing and Urban Affairs, August 2, 1990; FCIC interview with Paul Volcker, October 11, 2010.

25. Stiglitz, Joseph E. Jonathan M. Orszag and Peter R. Orszag, "Implications of the New Fannie Mae and Freddie Mac Risk-based Capital Standard," *Fannie Mae Papers*, March 2002 ("The paper concludes that the probability of default by the GSEs is extremely small. Given this, the expected monetary costs of exposure to GSE insolvency are relatively small—even given very large levels of outstanding GSE debt and even assuming that the government would bear the cost of all GSE debt in the case of insolvency").

26. See, e.g., Pearce James E. and James C. Miller III, "Fannie Mae and Freddie Mac: Their Funding Advantage and Benefits to Consumers," Proceedings, the 37th Annual Conference on Bank Structure and Competition, Federal Reserve Bank of Chicago, May 2001 ("Our analysis shows that the current arrangement benefits consumers much more than any funding advantage received by Freddie Mac and Fannie Mae").

27. See, e.g., Freddie Mac, *Financing America's Housing: The Vital Role of Freddie Mac*, 1996 ("Numerous government studies have concluded that the risk of insolvency is minuscule. Sound management and adequate capital protect taxpayers and enable the companies to continue providing public benefits. The industry's toughest, most dynamic risk-based capital requirements and an exclusive regulator—two initiatives taken by Congress in 1992— essentially eliminate any taxpayer risk"), p. ii.

28. FCIC interview with former Senator and former HUD Secretary Mel Martinez, September 28, 2010.

29. Center for Responsive Politics, "Finance/Insurance/Real Estate."

Chapter 7

1. Coffee, John C. Jr. and Hilary A. Sale, "Redesigning the SEC: Does the Treasury have a Better Idea?" University of Iowa Legal Studies Research Paper, December 2008, p. 9.

2. Comptroller of the Currency, News Release, "Comptroller Calls Preemption a Major Advantage of National Bank Charter," February 12, 2002.

3. Superintendent Julie Dickson, Office of the Superintendent of Financial Institutions Canada (OSFI), "Too focused on the rules; the importance of supervisory oversight in

financial regulation," remarks to the Heyman Center on Corporate Governance, New York, March 16, 2010.

4. See e.g., Richards, Lori A., "Strengthening Examination Oversight: Changes to Regulatory Examinations," speech, June 17, 2009.

5. Scott M. Polakoff, Acting Director, Office of Thrift Supervision, "Lessons Learned in Risk Management Oversight at Federal Financial Regulators," testimony, Committee on Banking, Housing and Urban Affairs, Subcommittee on Securities, Insurance, and Investment, United States Senate, March 18, 2009.

6. "Federal Reserve Bank of New York: Report on Systemic Risk and Supervision," Discussion Draft, August 18, 2009, p. 2.

7. Ibid., p. 5.

8. Ibid., p. 2.

9. Financial Services Authority (UK), *The Turner Review: A Global Response to the Global Banking Crisis*, March 2009, p. 88.

10. A Report to the Minister for Finance by the Governor of the Central Bank, *The Irish Banking Crisis Regulatory and Financial Stability Policy, 2003–2008*, May 31, 2010, p. ii.

11. Alan Greenspan. "Statement by Alan Greenspan, Chairman, Board of Governors of the Federal Reserve System before the Committee on Banking, Housing, and Urban Affairs, US Senate, March 2, 1994. (Statements to Congress) (Transcript)." *Federal Reserve Bulletin.* May 1, 1994.

12. Ibid.

13. Ibid.

14. Statement of Senator Gramm at the signing ceremony for the GLBA: "We are here today to repeal Glass-Steagall because we have learned that government is not the answer. We have learned that freedom and competition are the answers. We have learned that we promote economic growth and we promote stability by having competition and freedom. I am proud to be here because this is an important bill; it is a deregulatory bill. I believe that that is the wave of the future, and I am awfully proud to have been a part of making it a reality." Senator Phil Gramm, Chairman, Senate Committee on Banking, Housing and Urban Affairs, statement, November 12, 1999.

15. See, e.g., Alan Greenspan, "H. R. 10 and financial modernization: Functional Regulation," testimony, Subcommittee on Finance and Hazardous Materials, Committee on Commerce, US House of Representatives, April 28, 1999. ("The holding company structure—especially for the new activities—also has the significant benefit of promoting effective supervision and the functional regulation of different activities. The holding company structure, along with the so-called 'Fed-lite' provisions in H. R. 10, focuses on and enhances the functional regulation of securities firms, insurance companies, insured depository institutions and their affiliates by relying on the expertise and supervisory strengths of different functional regulators, reducing the potential burdensome overlap of regulation, and providing for increased coordination and reduced potential for conflict among functional regulators.")

16. Meyer, Laurence H., Federal Reserve Governor, "The Implications of Financial Modernization Legislation for Bank Supervision," Washington, D. C., December 15, 1999.

17. FCIC interview of Eugene A. Ludwig, September 2, 2010.

18. Richard Spillenkothen, "Notes on the performance of prudential supervision in the years preceding the financial crisis by a former director of banking supervision and regulation at the Federal Reserve Board (1991 to 2006)," May 31, 2010, p. 15.

19. FCIC interview of Eugene A. Ludwig, September 2, 2010.

20. Office of the Comptroller of the Currency, "PWG Working Group on Supervision, Questionnaire," August 11, 2009, p. 14.

21. Office of Thrift Supervision, "Response to the Questionnaire on Supervision Compiled by OTS," August 11, 2009, p. 11, p. 16.

22. FCIC interview of Eugene A. Ludwig, September 2, 2010.

23. See, e.g., Federal Reserve Board, *The Federal Reserve System: Purposes and Functions*, June 2005, pp. 1 and 59 ("The Federal Reserve has supervisory and regulatory authority over a wide range of financial institutions and activities. It works with other federal and state supervisory authorities to ensure the safety and soundness of financial institutions, stability in the financial markets, and fair and equitable treatment of consumers in their financial transactions").

24. FCIC interview with Janet Yellen, Vice Chair of the Federal Reserve Board, November 15, 2010.

25. FCIC interview with Sabeth Siddique, formerly Federal Reserve Board, October 25, 2010.

26. Federal Reserve Board, "Federal Reserve Supervision and Regulation Cost and Staffing."

27. FCIC interview with Sabeth Siddique, October 25, 2010.

28. Bernanke's comments can be found on the Fed website: Ben S. Bernanke, "The Subprime Mortgage Market," speech at the Federal Reserve Bank of Chicago's 43rd Annual Conference on Bank Structure and Competition, Chicago, Illinois, May 17, 2007.

29. Labaton, Stephen, "The Reckoning: Agency's '04 Rule Let Banks Pile Up New Debt," *New York Times*, October 3, 2008.

30. US Securities and Exchange Commission, Office of Inspector General, Office of Audits, *SEC's Oversight of Bear Stearns and Related Entities: the Consolidated Supervised Entities Program*, Report No. 446-A, September 25, 2008, p. 19.

31. Personal communication, October 27, 2011.

32. Christopher Cox, Chairman, US Securities and Exchange Commission, "Testimony Concerning the Role of Federal Regulators: Lessons from the Credit Crisis for the Future of Regulation," hearing, Committee on Oversight and Government Reform, United States House of Representatives, October 23, 2008.

33. Ibid.

34. US Securities and Exchange Commission, Office of Inspector General, Office of Audits, *SEC's Oversight of Bear Stearns and Related Entities: the Consolidated Supervised Entities Program*, p. ix.

35. FCIC interview with Harvey Goldschmid, former SEC Commissioner, April 8, 2010.

36. Christopher Cox, Chairman, U.S. Securities and Exchange Commission, "Testimony Concerning the Role of Federal Regulators: Lessons from the Credit Crisis for the Future of Regulation," hearing, Committee on Oversight and Government Reform, United States House of Representatives, October 23, 2008.

37. FCIC interview with Janet Yellen, Vice Chair of the Federal Reserve Board, November 15, 2010.

38. Ibid.

39. Ibid.

40. Ibid.

41. Interview with Mark Olson, former Federal Reserve Governor, October 4, 2010.

42. FCIC interview with Harvey Goldschmid, former SEC Commissioner, April 8, 2010.

43. Testimony of Armando Falcon, Office of Federal Housing Enterprise Oversight, to the FCIC, April 9, 2010,p. 3.

44. Ibid., p. 7.

45. Subcommittee on Financial Institutions and Consumer Credit of the House Committee on Financial Services, "A Review Of Regulatory Proposals on Basel Capital and Commercial Real Estate," hearing, September 14, 2006, p. 7.

46. Ibid, p. 21.

47. Ibid, p. 24.

48. Ibid, p. 37.

49. House Committee on Financial Services, Press Release, "Frank And Bachus React To Guidance On Commercial Real Estate Lending," December 6, 2006.

50. Sandra Thompson, Director, Division of Supervision and Consumer Protection, Federal Deposit Insurance Corporation, Statement on The Current State of Commercial Real Estate Finance and Its Relationship to the Overall Stability of the Financial System before the Congressional Oversight Panel, Washington, DC, February 4, 2011.

51. Ibid.

52. American Bankers Association, letter to the bank supervisors, "Re: Proposed Interagency Guidance on Nontraditional Mortgage Products," March 29, 2006.

53. Federal Reserve Board, "Supervised Assets Under The Federal Reserve System's Supervisory Umbrella," and "Federal Reserve Supervision and Regulation Cost and Staffing."

54. FCIC interview with Joseph Gonzalez, Office of Thrift Supervision, May 7, 2010.

55. Financial Crisis Inquiry Commission, *Final Report of the Financial Crisis Inquiry Commission*, 2011, p. 351.

56. Federal Reserve Bank of New York, "Report on Systemic Risk and Bank Supervision," discussion draft, August 18, 2009, p. 3.

57. Richard Spillenkothen, "Notes on the performance of prudential supervision in the years preceding the financial crisis by a former director of banking supervision and regulation at the Federal Reserve Board (1991 to 2006)," May 31, 2010, p. 7

58. Ibid.

59. Interview with Roger Cole, formerly Federal Reserve Board, August 2, 2010.

60. Federal Reserve Bank of New York, "Report on Systemic Risk and Bank Supervision," discussion draft, August 18, 2009, p. 5.

61. Ibid.

62. Federal Reserve Bank of New York, "Summary of Supervisory Activity and Findings, Citigroup, Inc.," transmitted April 15, 2008.

63. US Government Accountability Office, Orice M. Williams, *Financial Regulation: Review of Regulators' Oversight of Risk Management at a Limited Number of Large, Complex Financial Institutions*, testimony, GAO-09-499T, March 18, 2009.

64. Federal Reserve Bank of New York, "Report on Systemic Risk and Bank Supervision," discussion draft, August 18, 2009, p. 5.

65. Interview with Roger Cole, formerly Federal Reserve Board, August 2, 2010.

66. Ibid.

67. Federal Reserve Bank of New York, "Report on Systemic Risk and Bank Supervision," discussion draft, August 18, 2009, p. 7.

68. FCIC interview with Roger Cole, formerly Federal Reserve Board, August 2, 2010.

69. FCIC interview with Sabeth Siddique, formerly Federal Reserve Board, October 25, 2010.

70. Federal Reserve Bank of New York, "Report on Systemic Risk and Bank Supervision," discussion draft, August 18, 2009, p. 6.

71. Ibid.

72. Office of Comptroller of the Currency, *Comptroller's Handbook: Large Bank Supervision*, May 2001, p. 3.

73. US Treasury and Federal Deposit Insurance Corporation, Offices of Inspector General, *Evaluation of Federal Regulatory Oversight of Washington Mutual Bank*, April 2010, p. 20.

74. Ibid. p. 29.

75. James Vanasek, testimony before the Senate Permanent Subcommittee on Investigations, hearing on "Wall Street and the Financial Crisis: The Role of High-Risk Home Loans," April 13, 2010, p. 39.

76. Ibid., p. 40.

77. Siddique's findings are reviewed in Financial Crisis Inquiry Commission, *Final Report of the Financial Crisis Inquiry Commission*, 2011, p. 20.

78. FCIC interview with Susan Bies, former Federal Reserve Governor, October 25, 2010.

79. Association of Inspectors of the Bank of Spain, letter to the Second Vice Chairman of the Government and Minister of the Economy & Finance, May 26, 2005 ("In summary, we, the Inspectors of the Bank of Spain, do not share the complacent attitude of the Governor of the Bank of Spain with respect to the growing accumulation of risks in the Spanish banking system resulting from the anomalous evolution of the national real estate market during the seven years of his mandate, nor do we agree completely with him on the causes in our opinion, of the unsustainable behavior of real estate prices in Spain, nor on the means to adopt to change the situation to make it acceptable. The well-intentioned optimism of the Governor, far from comforting us, makes us worry").

80. Office of the Comptroller of the Currency, "PWG Working Group on Supervision, Questionnaire," August 11, 2009, p. 12, available on the FCIC permanent website.

81. FCIC interview with Ronald Marcus, Office of Thrift Supervision, July 23, 2010.

82. See, respectively, Committee for Economic Development, *Restoring Trust in Corporate Governance: The Six Essential Tasks of Boards of Directors and Business Leaders*, policy brief, January 2010; and Senior Supervisors Group, *Observations on Risk Management Practices during the Recent Market Turbulence*, March 6, 2008.

83. See, FCIC interview with Charles Prince, Citigroup, Transcript, March 17, 2010, pp. 126–27.

84. Federal Reserve Bank of New York, "Report on Systemic Risk and Supervision," Discussion Draft, August 18, 2009, p. 15.

85. This dynamic was first presented in the author's testimony before the Senate Banking Committee in a hearing on *The Safety and Soundness of Government Sponsored Enterprises*, October 31, 1989, p. 41, pointing out that increases in stringency of capital requirements and government supervision for thrift institutions after the savings and loan debacle would drive many billions of dollars of mortgages from the portfolios of savings and loan associations to Fannie Mae and Freddie Mac because their capital standards and government oversight were much weaker.

86. George L. Harrison, Governor of the Federal Reserve Bank of New York, testimony before the Senate Committee on Banking and Currency, hearing on "Operation of the National and Federal Reserve Banking Systems," January 20, 1931, p. 66.

87. FCIC interview with former Governor Susan Bies, October 11, 2010.

88. Bonocore, Joe, Corporate Treasurer, JPMorgan Chase & Co, Comments at the 47th Conference on Bank Structure and Competition, Federal Reserve Bank of Chicago, May 6, 2011, slide no. 2.

89. FCIC interview with Lord Adair Turner, Financial Services Authority (UK), November 30, 2010.

90. See, e.g., Braithwaite, Tom, Brooke Masters and Jeremy Grant, "Financial Regulation: A Shield Asunder," *Financial Times*, May 19, 2011.

91. See, e.g., the classic work by Kenneth Culp Davis, *Discretionary Justice: A Preliminary Inquiry*, Champaign: University of Illinois Press, 1969.

92. Sloan, Steven. "Fannie CEO Details Issues with GSE Bill," *American Banker*, June 5, 2008.

93. Pierce, James L. *The Future of American Banking*, Yale University Press, 1991, pp. 99–100.

Chapter 8

1. See, e.g., Olson, James S. *Saving Capitalism: The Reconstruction Finance Corporation and the New Deal, 1933–1940*, Princeton: Princeton University Press, 1988, chapter 2, "The Emergency Banking Act of 1933."

2. Jones, Jesse H. *Fifty Billion Dollars: My Thirteen Years with the RFC (1932–1945)*, New York: MacMillan, 1951, p. 21.

3. Federal Deposit Insurance Corporation, *History of the Eighties—Lessons for the Future*, Volume 1, chapter 2, "The LDC Debt Crisis," p. 207.

4. Quoted ibid., p. 208.

5. Ibid., p. 210.

6. Walter Bagehot, *Lombard Street: A Description of the Money Market*, London: Henry S. King and Company, 1873.

7. Ibid., p. 197.

8. American Enterprise Institute, "A Conversation with President Bush," Transcript, December 18, 2008.

9. Eugene A. Ludwig, William Taylor Memorial Lecture, International Conference of Banking Supervisors, Brussels, September 25, 2008.

10. Ibid.

11. Stephen Labaton, "Leading Senator Pushes New Plan to Oversee Banks," *New York Times*, September 20, 2009.

12. *Congressional Record*, May 12, 2010, p. S 3573 (daily edition).

13. Carmen M. Reinhart and Kenneth S. Rogoff, *This Time is Different: Eight Centuries of Financial Folly*, 2009, p. xxv.

14. American International Group, Form 10-K, *Annual Report for the fiscal year ended December 31, 2007*, p. 33.

15. Federal Deposit Insurance Corporation, *History of the Eighties: Lessons for the Future*, Volume I, chapter 10, "Banking Problems in the Northeast," Washington, DC, 1997, p. 338.

16. Gretchen Morgenson, "The Reckoning: Behind Insurer's Crisis, Blind Eye to a Web of Risk," *New York Times*, September 27, 2008.

17. Max H Bazerman, Kimberly P Morgan, and George F Loewenstein, "The Impossibility of Auditor Independence." *Sloan Management Review;* Summer 1997; vol. 38, no. 4, pp. 89–94.

18. Ibid., p. 91.

19. Ibid.

20. Lawrence J. White, "The Credit Rating Agencies: How Did We Get Here? Where Should We Go?"

21. Minsky, Hyman P., *Stabilizing an Unstable Economy*, New Haven: Yale University Press, 1986, p. 281.

22. Henry T. C. Hu and Bernard Black, "Debt, Equity, And Hybrid Decoupling: Governance and Systemic Risk Implications," June 15, 2008 draft.

23. Louise Story, Landon Thomas Jr. and Nelson D. Schwartz, "Wall St. Helped to Mask Debt Fueling Europe's Crisis," *New York Times*, February 14, 2010.

24. Stephen B. Ashley, Chairman, Remarks, Fannie Mae Senior Management Meeting, June 27, 2006.

25. FCIC Final Report, pp. 105 and 108.

26. FCIC Final Report, p. 105.

27. Center for Responsive Politics, "Finance/Insurance/Real Estate."

28. Kaufmann, Daniel, "Corruption, Governance and Security: Challenges For the Rich Countries and the World," chapter in the *Global Competitiveness Report 2004/2005*, Washington, D. C.: World Bank Institute.

29. Testimony of Robert Rubin to the FCIC, Hearing Transcript, April 8, 2010, p. 109. See also Hearing Transcript, pp. 123–4.

30. Ibid., pp. 109–10.

31. "Protecting Homeowners: Preventing Abusive Lending While Preserving Access to Credit," Hearing, Subcommittee on Financial Institutions and Consumer Credit and Subcommittee on Housing and Community Opportunity, House Committee on Financial Services, November 5, 2003, Opening Statement of Subcommittee Chairman Robert Ney, p. 2.

32. "Protecting Homeowners: Preventing Abusive Lending While Preserving Access to Credit," Hearing, Subcommittee on Financial Institutions and Consumer Credit and Subcommittee on Housing and Community Opportunity, House Committee on Financial Services, November 5, 2003, statement of Margot Saunders, National Consumer Law Center, p. 63.

33. Federal Deposit Insurance Corporation, "Risk Management Manual of Examination Policies."

34. Ibid.

35. Interview with former Senator and former HUD Secretary Mel Martinez, September 28, 2010, at 0:53.

36. Cargill, Thomas F., and Gillian G. Garcia, *Financial Reform of the 1980s*, Stanford: Hoover Institution Press, 1985, p. 38.

37. Kopecki, Dawn, "Dimon Challenges Bernanke in Wall Street Bid to Tame Regulators," Bloomberg News, June 9, 2011.

38. Timothy Geithner, Treasury Secretary, to the International Monetary Conference, June 6, 2011.

Chapter 9

1. Board of Governors of the Federal Reserve System, "The Supervisory Capital Assessment Program: Design and Implementation," April 24, 2009, p. 2.

2. Tully, Shawn, "Jamie Dimon's Swat Team; How J. P. Morgan's CEO and His Crew are Helping the Big Bank Beat the Credit Crunch," *Fortune*, September 2, 2008.

3. Policy and Impact Committee of the Committee for Economic Development, "Restoring Trust in Corporate Governance: The Six Essential Tasks of Boards of Directors and Business Leaders," January 2010.

4. Finkelstein, Sydney, Jo Whitehead, and Andrew Campbell, *Think Again: Why Good Leaders Make Bad Decisions and How to Keep it From Happening to You*, Boston: Harvard Business Press, 2008.

5. Moore, Heidi N., "Wachovia-Golden West: Another Deal From Hell?" *Wall Street Journal*, July 22, 2008; Dash, Eric, "Wachovia Reports $23.9 Billion Loss for Third Quarter, *New York Times*, October 23, 2008; de la Merced, Michael J., "Regulators Approve Wells Fargo Takeover of Wachovia," *New York Times*, October 10, 2008; Subramanian, Guhan and Nithyasri Sharma, "Citigroup-Wachovia-Wells Fargo," case study, Harvard Law School, June 10, 2010.

6. See JPMorgan Chase, *Annual Report 2008*, p. 10; Sidel, Robin, David Enrich, and Dan Fitzpatrick, "WaMu Is Seized, Sold Off to J. P. Morgan, In Largest Failure in U.S. Banking History," *Wall Street Journal*, September 26, 2008; Dash, Eric, and Andrew Ross Sorkin, "Government Seizes WaMu and Sells Some Assets," *New York Times*, September 26, 2008.

7. Compare Yang, Jia Lynn, "J. P. Morgan, FDIC tangle over responsibility for WaMu liabilities," *Washington Post*, November 10, 2010, with JPMorgan Chase Annual Report for the Year 2010.

8. Office of Federal Housing Enterprise Oversight, *Report of the Special Examination of Freddie Mac*, 2003, p. 139.

9. Office of the Comptroller of the Currency (OCC), *Supervisory Guidance on Model Risk Management*, OCC Bulletin 2011–12, April 4, 2011, p. 3.

10. Office of Federal Housing Enterprise Oversight, "Fannie Mae Report of Annual Examination 2006," p. 8.

11. Stanton, Thomas H., "Defending Cyberspace: Protecting Individuals, Government Agencies and Private Companies Against Persistent and Evolving Threats," monograph, Johns Hopkins University, July 2008.

12. Dougherty, Carter, "US Bancorp's Davis Warns Against Overreaction to Consumer Bureau," *Bloomberg*, June 13, 2011.

13. See, e.g., Kopecki, Dawn, "Dimon Challenges Bernanke in Wall Street Bid to Tame Regulators," *Bloomberg*, June 9, 2011.

14. Sorkin, Andrew Ross, "Two Views on Bank Rules: Salvation and Jobkillers," *New York Times*, June 13, 2011.

15. Finkelstein, Sydney, Jo Whitehead, Andrew Campbell, *Think Again: Why Good leaders Make Bad Decisions and How to Keep it From Happening to You*, Boston: Harvard Business Press, 2010, p. xi.

16. Financial Crisis Inquiry Commission, *Final Report of the Financial Crisis Inquiry Commission*, 2011, p. 129.

17. See, e.g., Lang William W. and Julapa Jagtiani, "The Mortgage and Financial Crises, The Role of Credit Risk Management and Corporate Governance," *Atlantic Economics Journal*, vol. 38, pp. 295–316, p. 296, July 10, 2010.

18. The functions of such an organization are discussed in Stanton, Thomas H. "Creating a Financial System Safety Board," *The American Interest*, autumn, September/October 2009.

19. Board of Governors of the Federal Reserve System, "The Supervisory Capital Assessment Program: Design and Implementation," April 24, 2009, p. 2.

Chapter 10

1. Morieux, Yves. "Smart Rules: Six Ways to Get People to Solve Problems Without You," Spotlight on Managing Complex Organizations, *Harvard Business Review*, September 2011, pp. 2–9, at p. 4; see also Sargut, Gökçe and Rita Gunther McGrath, "Learning to Live with Complexity," Spotlight on Managing Complex Organizations, *Harvard Business Review*, September 2011.

2. See, e.g., Committee for Economic Development, "Restoring Trust in Corporate Governance: Six Essential Tasks of Boards of Directors and Business Leaders," January 2010; Sonnenfeld, Jeffrey A., "What Makes Great Boards Great," *Harvard Business Review*, September 2002, pp. 106–13; and Heineman, Ben, *High Performance with High Integrity*, Harvard Business Press, 2008, to name but a few.

3. See, e.g., Finkelstein, Sydney, *Why Smart Executives Fail, and What you Can Learn From Their Mistakes*, New York: Portfolio, 2003; Finkelstein, Sydney, Jo Whitehead, and Andrew Campbell, *Think Again: Why Good Leaders Make Bad Decisions and How to Keep it From Happening to You*, Boston: Harvard Business Press, 2008.

4. See, e.g., National Commission on the BP Deepwater Horizon Oil Spill and Offshore Drilling, *Deep Water: The Gulf Oil Disaster and the Future of Offshore Drilling, Report to the President*, January 2011; B. P. US Refineries Independent Safety Review Panel. Report, January 2007; Governor's Independent Investigation Panel [West Virginia]. *Upper Big Branch: The April 5, 2010, Explosion: A Failure of Basic Coal Mine Safety Practices*, May 2011; Kaufmann, Daniel and Veronika Penciakova, "Japan's Triple Disaster: Governance and the Earthquake, Tsunami and Nuclear Crises," The Brookings Institution, March 16, 2011; and Vaughan Diane, *The Challenger Launch Decision: Risky Technology, Culture, and Deviance at NASA*, Chicago: University of Chicago Press, 1996.

5. Bureau of Ocean Energy Management, Regulation and Enforcement (formerly the Minerals Management Service of the US Department of the Interior, MMS), *Report Regarding the Causes of the April 20, 2010, Macondo Well Blowout*, September 14, 2011, p. 176. The Joint Investigation Team consisted of officials from the Bureau and the Coast Guard.

6. National Commission on the BP Deepwater Horizon Oil Spill and Offshore Drilling, *Deep Water: The Gulf Oil Disaster and the Future of Offshore Drilling*, Report to the President, January 2011, p. 2.

7. Joint Investigation Team report, p. 176.

8. National Commission on the BP Deepwater Horizon Oil Spill and Offshore Drilling. *Deep Water: The Gulf Oil Disaster and the Future of Offshore Drilling*, Report to the President, January 2011, p. 224.

9. Ibid., pp. 123–25.

10. Ibid., pp. 72 and 68.

11. Ibid., p. 71.

12. US Chemical Safety and Hazard Investigation Board. *Refinery Explosion And Fire (15 Killed, 180 Injured), BP, Texas City, Texas, March 23, 2005*, Investigation Report No. 2005-04-I-TX, March 2007, pp. 142–3.

13. BP US Refineries Independent Safety Review Panel. *The BP U.S. Refineries Independent Safety Review Panel Report*, January 2007, p. xii.

14. Ibid.

15. National Commission on the BP Deepwater Horizon Oil Spill and Offshore Drilling, Fifth Meeting, Day Two, *Transcript of Proceedings*, November 9, 2010.

16. National Commission on the BP Deepwater Horizon Oil Spill and Offshore Drilling. *Deep Water: The Gulf Oil Disaster and the Future of Offshore Drilling*, Report to the President, January 2011, p. 218.

17. National Commission on the BP Deepwater Horizon Oil Spill and Offshore Drilling, Fifth Meeting, Day Two, *Transcript of Proceedings*, November 9, 2010, p. 252.

18. Ibid., p. 266.

19. ExxonMobil Corporation. *Operations Integrity Management System*, "Chairman's Message," undated, p. 3.

20. National Commission on the BP Deepwater Horizon Oil Spill and Offshore Drilling, Fifth Meeting, Day Two, *Transcript of Proceedings*, November 9, 2010, p. 282.

21. Ibid., p. 283.

22. Ibid., pp. 284–5.

23. Ibid., p. 285

24. Ibid., pp. 276–7.

25. Ibid., p. 287.

26. Ibid., p. 305.

27. Governor's Independent Investigation Panel [West Virginia], *Upper Big Branch*, p. 78.

28. Ibid. p. 96.

29. Ibid., p. 100.

30. Testimony of Joseph A. Main before the Senate Subcommittee on Labor, Health and Human Services, and Education, and Related Agencies, Committee on Appropriations, Hearing, "Investing In Mine Safety: Preventing Another Disaster," May 20, 2010, p. 8.

31. Governor's Independent Investigation Panel [West Virginia], *Upper Big Branch*, p. 77.

32. Ibid., p. 83.

33. Ibid., p. 85.

34. United States Supreme Court, *Caperton et al. v. A. T. Massey Coal Co., Inc.*, decided June 8, 2009.

35. National Transportation Safety Board. "NTSB cites Pacific Gas & Electric (PG&E) and government oversight in fatal California pipeline rupture," August 30, 2011.

36. Independent Review Panel. *Report of the Independent Review Panel San Bruno Explosion*, Prepared For California Public Utilities Commission, Revised Copy, June 24, 2011, p. 50.

37. Ibid., pp. 16–17.

38. Ibid. p. 62.

39. Ibid., p. 8.

40. Ibid., p 10.

41. National Transportation Safety Board, "NTSB cites Pacific Gas & Electric (PG&E) and Government Oversight in Fatal California Pipeline Rupture," August 30, 2011.

42. Independent Review Panel. Report of the Independent Review Panel San Bruno Explosion, Prepared For California Public Utilities Commission, Revised Copy, June 24, 2011, p. 98.

43. Ibid., p. 9.

44. Ibid., p. 22.

45. Ibid., p. 24.

46. Ibid., p. 100.

47. Department of Health and Human Services, Office of Inspector General, "Adverse Events in Hospitals: National Incidence Among Medicare Beneficiaries," OEI-06-09-00090, November 2010, pp. i–ii.

48. The agency's letter is found ibid., pp. 62–3.

49. Dingley C, Daugherty K, Derieg MK, Persing R., "Improving Patient Safety Through Provider Communication Strategy Enhancements," in Henriksen, K., Battles, J. B., Keyes, M. A., and Grady, M. L., eds., *Advances in Patient Safety: New Directions and Alternative Approaches* (Vol. 3, Performance and Tools), Agency for Healthcare Research and Quality, August 2008.

50. Nadzam, Deborah M., "Nurses' Role in Communication and Patient Safety," *Journal of Nursing Care Quality*, Vol. 24, No. 3, 2009, pp. 184–88, at p. 184; see also Dingley et al., "Improving Patient Safety Through Provider Communication Strategy Enhancements."

51. The Joint Commission, "Behaviors that Undermine a Culture of Safety," *Sentinel Event Alert*, Issue 40, July 9, 2008.

52. See Brown, Theresa. "Physician, Heel Thyself," *New York Times*, May 7, 2011; Ken Stanton quote from personal communication to the author, September 2, 2011.

53. For an illustrative past example of dissonance and impeded information flows from front-line officials to senior levels of a government agency, see, e.g., Richard Feynman's account of his experiences interviewing politically attuned officials at NASA compared to what he learned from engineers: Feynman, Richard P., *What do You Care What Other People Think?* part 2, "Mr. Feynman Goes to Washington: Investigating the Space Shuttle Challenger Disaster," 1988.

54. Columbia Accident Investigation Board, *Report Volume I*, August 2003, p. 130.

55. For a public sector agenda to try to monitor and anticipate the impact of such events, see, e.g., Stanton, Thomas H. "Improving Managerial Capacity of the Federal Government: A Public Administration Agenda for the Next President," *Public Administration Review*, November/December 2008, pp. 1027–36.

REFERENCES

Materials Gathered and Produced by the Financial Crisis Inquiry Commission

The permanent FCIC website is found at http://fcic.law.stanford.edu. All of the materials cited below, including FCIC interviews, documents made public by the FCIC, and FCIC reports, testimony, and hearing transcripts, are available on the website, which is fairly easy to navigate. The search function is robust and helpful in locating interviews and documents.

FCIC INTERVIEWS

FCIC interview with Brian R. Leach, Citigroup, March 4, 2010

FCIC interview with Charles Prince, Citigroup, March 17, 2010

FCIC interview with Edward DeMarco, Federal Housing Finance Agency, Memorandum for the Record, March 18, 2010

FCIC interview with Harvey Goldschmid, former SEC Commissioner, April 8, 2010

FCIC Interview with Scott McCleskey, formerly Moody's Investors Service, April 16, 2010

FCIC interview with Joseph St. Denis, formerly AIG, Memorandum for the Record, April 23, 2010

FCIC interview with Joseph Gonzalez, Office of Thrift Supervision, May 7, 2010

FCIC interview with David Viniar, Goldman Sachs, June 16, 2010

FCIC interview with Anurag Saksena, Freddie Mac, June 22, 2010

FCIC interview with Madelyn Antoncic, formerly Lehman Brothers, July 14, 2010

FCIC interview with Christopher O'Meara, formerly Lehman Brothers, July 17, 2010

FCIC interview with Ronald Marcus, Office of Thrift Supervision, July 23, 2010

FCIC interview with Lew Ranieri, July 30, 2010

FCIC interview with Roger Cole, formerly Federal Reserve Board, August 2, 2010

FCIC interview with Patrick McKenna, Deutsche Bank, August 2, 2010

FCIC interview with Thomas Fontana, Citigroup, August 13, 2010

FCIC interview with Richard Syron, formerly Freddie Mac, August 31, 2010

FCIC interview with Eugene Ludwig, former Comptroller of the Currency, September 2, 2010

FCIC interview with John G. Stumpf, Wells Fargo, September 23, 2010

FCIC interview with Mel Martinez, former Senator and former HUD Secretary, September 28, 2010

FCIC interview with Mark Olson, former Federal Reserve Governor, October 4, 2010

FCIC interview with Paul Volcker, former Federal Reserve Chairman, October 11, 2010

FCIC interview with David Wong, Morgan Stanley, October 15, 2010

FCIC interview with Sabeth Siddique, formerly Federal Reserve Board, October 25, 2010

FCIC interview with Susan Bies, former Federal Reserve Governor, October 25, 2010

FCIC interview with John Mack, Morgan Stanley, November 2, 2010

FCIC interview with Janet Yellen, Vice Chair of the Federal Reserve Board, November 15, 2010

FCIC interview with Michael Loughlin, Wells Fargo, November 23, 2010

FCIC interview with Lord Adair Turner, Financial Services Authority (UK), November 30, 2010

DOCUMENTS MADE PUBLIC BY THE FCIC

Antje Berndt, Burton Hollifield, and Patrik Sandas, "The Role of Mortgage Brokers in the Subprime Crisis," April 2010

Bank for International Settlements, Joint Forum, Working Group on Risk Assessment and Risk-Capital Concentration, "Cross-sectoral review of group-wide identification and management of risk concentrations," January 9, 2008 version

Bank for International Settlements, Joint Forum, Working Group on Risk Assessment and Risk-Capital Concentration, "Cross-Sectoral review of group-wide identification and management of risk concentrations," January 9, 2008 version

Countrywide, *Fixed Income Investor Forum*, February 28, 2006

Enrico Dallavecchia, email to Michael Williams (COO), July 16, 2007

Fannie Mae, "Quarterly Risk Assessment YE 2002," memorandum from Adolfo Marzol to Timothy Howard and Dan Mudd, February 6, 2003

Fannie Mae, "Single Family Guarantee Business: Facing Strategic Crossroads." June 27, 2005

Fannie Mae, "Fannie Mae Strategic Plan 2007–2011 'Develop Segments—Develop Breadth,'" undated, approximately end of June 2007

Fannie Mae, Memorandum from Adolfo Marzol to Dan Mudd. "Private Label Securities," March 2, 2005

Federal Reserve Bank of New York, "Report on Systemic Risk and Supervision," Discussion Draft, August 18, 2009

Federal Reserve Bank of New York, "Summary of Supervisory Activity and Findings, JPMorgan Chase & Co.," April 15, 2008

Federal Reserve Bank of New York, "Summary of Supervisory Activity and Findings, Citigroup, Inc.," transmitted April 15, 2008

Federal Reserve Bank of New York, "Summary of Supervisory Activity and Findings, Citigroup, Inc.," transmitted January 14, 2009

Federal Reserve Board, "Federal Reserve Supervision and Regulation Cost and Staffing"

Federal Reserve Board, "Supervised Assets Under The Federal Reserve System's Supervisory Umbrella"

Freddie Mac, Freddie Mac's Business Strategy, Board of Directors Meeting, March 2–3, 2007

Office of the Comptroller of the Currency, "PWG Working Group on Supervision, Questionnaire," August 11, 2009

Office of the Comptroller of the Currency, "Observations—Allowance Process and Methodology," August 2008 (last revised September 8, 2008)

Office of Thrift Supervision, "Response to the Questionnaire on Supervision Compiled by OTS," August 11, 2009

Oliver Wyman, "Bear Stearns Management Committee: Risk Governance Diagnostic Recommendations and Case for Economic Capital Development," February 5, 2008

PwC, notes of a meeting to discuss Super Senior valuations and collateral disputes November 29, 2007

"Risk Management at Goldman Sachs: Presentation to the McKinsey Advisory Committee," February 20, 2007

Richard Spillenkothen, "Notes on the performance of prudential supervision in the years preceding the financial crisis by a former director of banking supervision and regulation at the Federal Reserve Board (1991 to 2006)," May 31, 2010

Senior Supervisors Group, "Notes on Senior Supervisors' Meetings with Firms, Citigroup, Inc.," November 19, 2007

Stephen B. Ashley, Chairman, Remarks, Fannie Mae Senior Management Meeting, June 27, 2006

FCIC REPORTS, TESTIMONY, HEARING TRANSCRIPTS

Financial Crisis Inquiry Commission, *Final Report of the Financial Crisis Inquiry Commission*, 2011

Financial Crisis Inquiry Commission, hearing transcript, April 8, 2010

Financial Crisis Inquiry Commission, hearing transcript, June 30, 2010

Pierre-Olivier Gourinchas, "U.S. Monetary Policy, 'Imbalances' and the Financial Crisis," Remarks prepared for the Financial Crisis Inquiry Commission Forum, Washington DC, February 26–27, 2010

Testimony of Patricia Lindsay, New Century Financial Corporation, to the FCIC, April 7, 2010

Testimony of Charles Prince, Citigroup, to the FCIC, April 8, 2010

Testimony of Robert Rubin, Citigroup, to the FCIC, April 8, 2010

Testimony of Armando Falcon, Office of Federal Housing Enterprise Oversight, to the FCIC, April 9, 2010

Testimony of James B. Lockhart, Federal Housing Finance Agency, to the FCIC, April 9, 2010

Books

Allison, Herbert M. *The Megabanks Mess*, Amazon: Kindle eBook, 2011

Bagehot, Walter. *Lombard Street*, London: Henry S. King and Company, 1873

Berger, Allen N., Phillip Molyneux and John O.S. Wilson, eds, *The Oxford Handbook of Banking*, Oxford: Oxford University Press, 2010

Cargill, Thomas F. and Gillian G. Garcia. *Financial Reform of the 1980s*, Stanford: Hoover Institution Press, 1985

Davidson, Andrew, Anthony Sanders, Lan-Ling Wolff, and Anne Ching. *Securitization: Structuring and Investment Analysis*, Hoboken, N.J.: Wiley Finance, 2003

Davis, Gerald F. *Managed by the Markets: How Finance Re-Shaped America*, Oxford: Oxford University Press, 2009

Davis, Kenneth Culp. *Discretionary Justice: A Preliminary Inquiry*, Champaign: University of Illinois Press, 1969.

Eccles, Marriner. *Beckoning Frontiers*, New York: Knopf, 1951

Feynman, Richard P. *What do You Care What Other People Think?* New York: Norton, 1988

Finkelstein, Sydney, Jo Whitehead, and Andrew Campbell. *Think Again: Why Good leaders Make Bad Decisions and How to Keep it From Happening to You*, Boston: Harvard Business Press, 2010

Finkelstein, Sydney. *Why Smart Executives Fail, and What you Can Learn From Their Mistakes*, New York: Portfolio, 2003

Gorton, Gary B., *Slapped by the Invisible Hand: The Panic of 2007*, Oxford: Oxford University Press, 2010

Heineman, Ben W. *High Performance with High Integrity*, Boston: Harvard Business Press, 2008

Henriksen K, J. B. Battles, M. A. Keyes, and M. L. Grady, eds. *Advances in Patient Safety: New Directions and Alternative Approaches* (Vol. 3, Performance and Tools), Washington, D.C.: Agency for Healthcare Research and Quality, August 2008

Ho, Karen. *Liquidated: An Ethnography of Wall Street*, Durham, N.C.: Duke University Press, 2009

Hutter, Bridget M., and Michael Power, eds. *Organizational Encounters with Risk*, Cambridge: Cambridge University Press, 2005

Johnson, Simon and James Kwak. *13 Bankers: The Wall Street Takeover and the Next Financial Meltdown*, New York: Pantheon, 2010.

Jones, Jesse H. *Fifty Billion Dollars: My Thirteen Years with the RFC (1932–1945)*, New York: MacMillan, 1951

Knight, Frank. *Risk, Uncertainty, and Profit*, Boston: Houghton Mifflin, 1921

Koppell, Jonathan G. S. *The Politics of Quasi-Government*, Cambridge: Cambridge University Press, 2003

Lewis, Michael. *The Big Short*, New York: Norton, 2010

Macey, Jonathan R. *Corporate Governance: Promises Kept, Promises Broken*, Princeton, N.J.: Princeton University Press, 2008

Minsky, Hyman P. *Stabilizing an Unstable Economy*, New Haven: Yale University Press, 1986.

Olson, James S. *Saving Capitalism: The Reconstruction Finance Corporation and the New Deal, 1933–1940*, Princeton, N.J.: Princeton University Press, 1988

Pierce, James L. *The Future of American Banking*, New Haven: Yale University Press, 1991

Pollock, Alex J. *Boom & Bust: Financial Cycles and Human Prosperity*, New York: AEI Press, 2011

Reinhart, Carmen M., and Kenneth S. Rogoff. *This Time is Different: Eight Centuries of Financial Folly*, Princeton, N.J.: Princeton University Press, 2009

Seidman, Dov. *How: Why How We Do Anything Means Everything . . . in Business (and in Life)*, Hoboken, N.J.: Wiley, 2007

Sparrow, Malcolm. *The Regulatory Craft: Controlling Risks, Solving Problems, and Managing Compliance*, Washington, D.C.: Brookings Institution Press, 2000

Stanton, Thomas H. *Government-Sponsored Enterprises: Mercantilist Companies in the Modern World*, Washington, D.C.: AEI Press, 2002

Stanton, Thomas H. ed. *Meeting the Challenge of 9/11: Blueprints for Effective Government*, Armonk, NY: M.E. Sharpe Publishers, 2006

Stone, Charles and Anne Zissu, eds. *Global Risk Based Capital Regulations*, Vol. 1, New York: Irwin, 1994.

Tabe, Henry. *The Unraveling of Structured Investment Vehicles: How Liquidity Leaked Through SIVs*, Chatham, Kent, UK: Thoth Capital, 2010

Taleb, Nassim Nicholas. *The Black Swan: The Impact of the Highly Improbable*. New York: Random House, 2007

Tett, Gillian. *Fool's Gold*, New York: The Free Press, 2009

Vaughan, Diane. *The Challenger Launch Decision: Risky Technology, Culture, and Deviance at NASA*, Chicago: University of Chicago Press, 1996

Journals

Acharya, Viral V. Thomas Cooley, Matthew Richardson and Ingo Walter. "Manufacturing Tail Risk: A Perspective on the Financial Crisis of 2007–09," *Foundations and Trends in Finance*, volume 4, no. 4, pp. 247–325, 2010

Bazerman, Max H. Kimberly P Morgan, and George F Loewenstein. "The Impossibility of Auditor Independence." *Sloan Management Review*, vol. 38, no. 4, pp. 89–94, Summer 1997

Deutsch, Clayton G. "Building the Global Bank: An Interview with Jamie Dimon," *The McKinsey Quarterly*, no. 4, pp. 51–59, November 2006.

Jackson Howell E. and Laurie Burlingame. " Kickbacks or Compensation: The Case of Yield Spread Premiums," *Stanford Journal of Law, Business and Finance*, vol. 12, no. 2, pp. 289–361, Spring 2007.

Lang William W. and Julapa A. Jagtiani. "The Mortgage and Financial Crises: The Role of Credit Risk Management and Corporate Governance," *Atlantic Economic Journal*, vol. 38, no. 3, pp. 295–316, September 2010.

Morieux, Yves. "Smart Rules: Six Ways to Get People to Solve Problems Without You," Spotlight on Managing Complex Organizations, *Harvard Business Review*, pp. 2–9, September 2011.

Nadzam, Deborah M. "Nurses' Role in Communication and Patient Safety," *Journal of Nursing Care Quality*, vol. 24, no. 3, pp. 184–88, 2009.

Sargut, Gökçe and Rita Gunther McGrath. "Learning to Live with Complexity," Spotlight on Managing Complex Organizations, *Harvard Business Review*, September 2011.

Sonnenfeld, Jeffrey A. "What Makes Great Boards Great," *Harvard Business Review*, pp. 106–13, December 2002.

Stanton, Thomas H. "Creating a Financial System Safety Board," *The American Interest*, vol. 5, no. 1, pp. 26–30, September/October, 2009.

Stanton, Thomas H. "Improving Managerial Capacity of the Federal Government: A Public Administration Agenda for the Next President," *Public Administration Review*, vol. 68, no. 6, pp. 1027–36, November/December 2008.

Stanton, Thomas H. "The Life Cycle of the Government-Sponsored Enterprise: Lessons for Design and Accountability," *Public Administration Review*, vol. 67, no. 5, pp. 837–45, September/October 2007.

Wilmarth, Arthur E. "The Transformation of the U.S. Financial Services Industry, 1975–2000: Competition, Consolidation, and Increased Risks," *University of Illinois Law Review*, vol. 2002, no. 2, pp. 215–476.

Periodicals

Anderson, Jenny, and Landon Thomas, Jr. "Goldman Sachs Rakes in Profit in Credit Crisis," *New York Times*, November 19, 2007

Ahmed, Azam, and Ben Protess, "As Regulators Pressed Changes, Corzine Pushed Back, and Won," *New York Times*, November 3, 2011.

Ahmed, Azam, Ben Protess, and Suzanne Craig, "A Romance with Risk that Brought on a Panic," New York Times, December 11, 2011.

Braithwaite, Tom, Brooke Masters, and Jeremy Grant. "Financial Regulation: A Shield Asunder," *Financial Times*, May 19, 2011

Brown, Theresa. "Physician, Heel Thyself," op-ed, *New York Times*, May 7, 2011

Business Week. "Dimon's Grand Design: Jamie Dimon is bracing for another tough year at JPMorgan. But now he has a $1.1 billion plan to revive the nation's No. 2 bank. An inside look," March 28, 2005

Business Week. "The Leadership Factory: Paulson is just the latest product of Goldman's public service culture," June 12, 2006

Chan, Sewell, and Louise Story. "Goldman Pays $550 Million to Settle Fraud Case," *New York Times*, July 15, 2010

Craig, Susanne, and Peter Lattman. "Goldman's Shares Tumble as Blankfein Hires Top Lawyer," *New York Times*, August 22, 2011

Craig, Suzanne. "At Goldman, Partners Are Made, and Unmade," *New York Times*, September 12, 2010

Cresci, Gregory. "Merrill, Citigroup Record CDO Fees Earned in Top Growth Market," Bloomberg, August 30, 2005, www.bloomberg.com/apps/news?pid=10000103&;sid=a. FcDwf1.ZG4&refer=us, accessed June 4, 2011

Creswell, Julie and Ben White. "Wall Street, R.I.P.: The End of an Era, Even at Goldman," *New York Times*, September 28, 2008

Creswell, Julie and Vikas Bajaj. "$3.2 Billion Move by Bear Stearns To Rescue Fund," *New York Times*, June 23, 2007

Dash, Eric and Julie Creswell. "Citigroup Saw No Red Flags Even as it Made Bolder Bets," *New York Times*, November 23, 2008.

Dash, Eric, and Andrew Ross Sorkin. "Government Seizes WaMu and Sells Some Assets," *New York Times*, September 26, 2008

Dash, Eric. "Wachovia Reports $23.9 Billion Loss for Third Quarter," *New York Times*, October 23, 2008

de la Merced, Michael J. "Regulators Approve Wells Fargo Takeover of Wachovia," *New York Times*, October 10, 2008

Der Hovanseian, Mara. "JPMorgan: The Bank of Technology; The financial giant is making investments in info tech and expects to reap huge awards," *Business Week*, June 19, 2006

Dougherty, Carter. "US Bancorp's Davis Warns Against Overreaction to Consumer Bureau," *Bloomberg*, June 13, 2011

Duhigg, Charles. "At Freddie Mac, Chief Discarded Warning Signs," *New York Times*, August 5, 2008

Financial Times. "Citigroup Chief Stays Bullish on Buyouts," July 9, 2007

Heineman, Ben W. Jr. "Executive Compensation: Let's Look at Fund Managers' Pay, Too," *HBR Now*, July 30, 2009

Hilzenrath, David S. "Chief Says Freddie Won't Raise Capital; Mortgage Financer Cites Responsibility to Shareholders, Won't Increase Loan Capacity," *Washington Post*, March 13, 2008, p. D4

Hintze, John. "Top 10 CIOs on Wall Street: Duncan Rawls, JPMorgan Chase," *Securities Technology Monitor*, November 4, 2010

Kopecki, Dawn. "Dimon Challenges Bernanke in Wall Street Bid to Tame Regulators," *Bloomberg News*, June 9, 2011

Kurbjuweit, Dirk, Armin Mahler, and Christoph Pauly. "Deutsche Bank Chief Weakened by Heavy Losses," *Spiegel Online*, January 20, 2009, available at www.spiegel.de/international/business/0, 1518, 602415,00.html, accessed April 25, 2011

Labaton, Stephen. "Leading Senator Pushes New Plan to Oversee Banks," *New York Times*, September 20, 2009

Labaton, Stephen. "The Reckoning: Agency's '04 Rule Let Banks Pile Up New Debt," *New York Times*, October 3, 2008

Lashinsky, Adam. "Riders on the Storm," Fortune Magazine via CNNMoney.com, April 20, 2009, Available at http://money.cnn.com/2009/04/19/news/companies/lashinsky_wells.fortune/index.htm.

Lucchetti, Aaron, and Julie Steinberg. "Corzine Rebuffed Internal Warnings on Risks," *Wall Street Journal*, December 6, 2011.

McGinty, Thomas, Kate Kelly and Kara Scannell. "Debt 'Masking' Under Fire," *Wall Street Journal*, April 21, 2010, p. A-1

Moore, Heidi N. "Wachovia-Golden West: Another Deal From Hell?" *Wall Street Journal*, July 22, 2008.

Morgenson, Gretchen. "The Reckoning: Behind Insurer's Crisis, Blind Eye to a Web of Risk," *New York Times*, September 27, 2008

Myners, Paul. "Reform of Banking Must Begin in the Boardroom," letter, *Financial Times*, April 24, 2008

National Association of Realtors, *Daily Real Estate News*, "HUD Secretary Urges Homeownership as 2005 Resolution," available at www.realtor.org/RMODaily.nsf/pages/News2005011102?OpenDocument, accessed April 26, 2011

New York Times, "Goldman Sachs Group Inc.," available at http://topics.nytimes.com/top/news/business/companies/goldman_sachs_group_inc/index.html?scp=1-spot&sq=goldman%20sachs&st=cse, accessed March 21, 2011

New York Times, "Wells Fargo & Company," available at http://topics.nytimes.com/top/news/business/companies/wells_fargo_and_company/index.html, accessed March 23, 2011

Nocerra, Joe. "Risk Mismanagement," *New York Times Magazine*, January 4, 2009

Protess, Ben, and Azam Ahmed. "MF Global's Risk Officer Said to Lack Authority," *New York Times*, December 14, 2011.

Sidel, Robin, David Enrich and Dan Fitzpatrick. "WaMu Is Seized, Sold Off to J.P. Morgan, In Largest Failure in U.S. Banking History," *Wall Street Journal*, September 26, 2008

Sloan, Steven. "Fannie CEO Details Issues with GSE Bill," *American Banker*, June 5, 2008

Sorkin, Andrew Ross. "Two Views on Bank Rules: Salvation and Jobkillers," *New York Times*, June 13, 2011

Story, Louise, Landon Thomas Jr., and Nelson D. Schwartz. "Wall St. Helped to Mask Debt Fueling Europe's Crisis," *New York Times*, February 14, 2010

Sydney Morning Herald, Bloomberg, "The Bank That Said 'No' to Subprime Debt," May 27, 2008, available at www.smh.com.au/business/the-bank-that-said-no-to-subprime-debt-20080527-2ihd.html, accessed March 21, 2011

Tully, Shawn. "Jamie Dimon's Swat Team; How J.P. Morgan's CEO and His Crew are Helping the Big Bank Beat the Credit Crunch," *Fortune*, September 2, 2008

Vise, David A. "The Money Machine: How Fannie Mae Wields Power," *Washington Post*, January 16, 1995, p. A1

Walker, Russell. "Fortune Favours the Well-Prepared," op-ed, *Financial Times*, January 29, 2009

Wessel, David. "Inside Dr. Bernanke's E.R.: As Obama Considers Reappointing the Fed Chairman, a Look at How He Took on More Power," *Wall Street Journal*, July 24, 2009

White, Ben. "What Red Ink? Wall Street Paid Hefty Bonuses," *New York Times*, January 29, 2009

Yang, Jia Lynn. "J.P. Morgan, FDIC Tangle Over Responsibility for WaMu Liabilities," *Washington Post*, November 10, 2010

Congressional Hearings, Reports, Documents

TESTIMONY, HEARINGS, AND STATEMENTS

Kevin M. Blakely, testimony before the Senate Committee on Banking, Housing and Urban Affairs, Subcommittee on Securities, Insurance, and Investment, June 19, 2008. Available at http://banking.senate.gov/public/index.cfm?FuseAction=Files. View&FileStore_id=2b95d716-ece9-4015-a5da-5f33031d7dce, accessed January 29, 2012.

Jon S. Corzine, testimony before the House Committee on Agriculture, December 8, 2011, available at http://agriculture.house.gov/pdf/hearings/Corzine111208.pdf, accessed January 29, 2012.

Senator Chris Dodd, statement, *Congressional Record*, May 12, 2010, p. S 3573 (daily edition)

Jerome S. Fons, Testimony before the Committee on Oversight and Government Reform, October 22, 2008. Available at http://oversight-archive.waxman.house.gov/documents/20081022102726.pdf, accessed January 29, 2012.

Senator Phil Gramm, Chairman, Senate Committee on Banking, Housing and Urban Affairs, statement, November 12, 1999, available at http://banking.senate.gov/prel99/1112gbl.htm, accessed September 15, 2011

Alan Greenspan, "Statement by Alan Greenspan, Chairman, Board of Governors of the Federal Reserve System before the Committee on Banking, Housing, and Urban Affairs, U.S. Senate, March 2, 1994. (Statements to Congress) (Transcript)." *Federal Reserve Bulletin*. May 1, 1994, www.thefreelibrary.com/_/print/PrintArticle. aspx?id=15428220, accessed May 17, 2011

Alan Greenspan, testimony before the House Committee on Oversight and Government Reform, hearing transcript, "The Financial Crisis and the Role of Federal Regulators," October 23, 2008. Available at http://democrats.oversight.house.gov/images/stories/documents/20081024163819.pdf, accessed January 29, 2012.

Alan Greenspan, "H.R. 10 and financial modernization: Functional Regulation," testimony, Subcommittee on Finance and Hazardous Materials, Committee on Commerce, U.S. House of Representatives, April 28, 1999. Available at http://www.federalreserve. gov/boarddocs/testimony/1999/19990428.htm, accessed January 29, 2012.

George L. Harrison, Governor of the Federal Reserve Bank of New York, testimony before the Senate Committee on Banking and Currency, hearing, "Operation of the National and Federal Reserve Banking Systems," January 20, 1931. Available at http://fraser. stlouisfed.org/docs/meltzer/senope31.pdf, accessed January 29, 2012.

House Committee on Financial Services, Press Release, "Frank and Bachus React to Guidance on Commercial Real Estate Lending," December 6, 2006. Available at http:// democrats.financialservices.house.gov/pr12062006.shtml, accessed January 29, 2012.

Eric Kolchinsky, statement before the Permanent Subcommittee on Investigations, United States Senate, April 23, 2010. Available at http://www.hsgac.senate.gov/subcommittees/ investigations/hearings/wall-street-and-the-financial-crisis-the-role-of-credit-rating-agencies, accessed January 29, 2012.

Richard Michalek, FormerVP/Senior Credit Officer, Moody's Investors Service, statement to the Permanent Subcommittee on Investigations, Committee on Governmental Affairs, United States Senate, April 23, 2010. Available at http://www.hsgac.senate.gov/ subcommittees/investigations/hearings/wall-street-and-the-financial-crisis-the-role-of-credit-rating-agencies, accessed January 29, 2012.

Daniel Mudd, testimony before the House Committee on Oversight and Government Reform, hearing, "The Role of Fannie Mae and Freddie Mac in the Financial Crisis," December 9, 2008. Available at http://oversight-archive.waxman.house.gov/docu-ments/20081209103231.pdf, accessed January 29, 2012.

Scott M. Polakoff, Acting Director, Office of Thrift Supervision, "Lessons Learned in Risk Management Oversight at Federal Financial Regulators," testimony, Committee on Banking, Housing and Urban Affairs, Subcommittee on Securities, Insurance, and Investment, United States Senate, March 18, 2009. Available at http://banking.senate. gov/public/index.cfm?FuseAction=Files.View&FileStore_id=01eef8f1-59c5-4678-8860-486cebb44112, accessed January 29, 2012.

Senate Committee on Banking, Housing, and Urban Affairs, "Safety and Soundness of Government Sponsored Enterprises," hearing, October 31, 1989.

Senate Permanent Subcommittee on Investigations, "Wall Street and the Financial Crisis: The Role of High Risk Home Loans," hearing, April 13, 2010. Available at http://www. gpo.gov/fdsys/pkg/CHRG-111shrg57319/html/CHRG-111shrg57319.htm; exhibits available at http://www.hsgac.senate.gov/imo/media/doc/Financial_ Crisis/041310Exhibits.pdf?attempt=2, accessed January 29, 2012.

Senate Permanent Subcommittee on Investigations, "Wall Street and the Financial Crisis: The Role of Investment Banks," hearing, transcript available at http://hsgac.senate.gov/ public/index.cfm?FuseAction=Hearings.Hearing&Hearing_ID=f07ef2bf-914c-494c-aa66-27129f8e6282, accessed July 18, 2011

Senate Subcommittee on Labor, Health and Human Services, and Education, and Related Agencies, Committee on Appropriations, "Investing in Mine Safety: Preventing Another Disaster," hearing, May 20, 2010. Available at http://www.gpo.gov/fdsys/pkg/ CHRG-111shrg56690/html/CHRG-111shrg56690.htm, accessed January 29, 2012.

Subcommittee on Financial Institutions and Consumer Credit and Subcommittee on Housing and Community Opportunity, House Committee on Financial Services, "Protecting Homeowners: Preventing Abusive Lending While Preserving Access to Credit," Joint Hearing, November 5, 2003. Available at http://www.gpo.gov/fdsys/ pkg/CHRG-108hhrg92983/html/CHRG-108hhrg92983.htm, accessed January 29, 2012.

Subcommittee on Financial Institutions and Consumer Credit of the House Committee on Financial Services, "A Review Of Regulatory Proposals on Basel Capital and

Commercial Real Estate," hearing, September 14, 2006. Available at http://archives.
financialservices.house.gov/pdf/ArchiveHearing/109-120.PDF, accessed January 29,
2012.

Sandra Thompson, Director, Division of Supervision and Consumer Protection, Federal
Deposit Insurance Corporation, Statement on The Current State of Commercial Real
Estate Finance and Its Relationship to the Overall Stability of the Financial System
before the Congressional Oversight Panel, Washington, DC, February 4, 2011. Available
at http://www.gpo.gov/fdsys/pkg/CHRG-112shrg65083/pdf/CHRG-112shrg65083.pdf,
accessed January 29, 2012.

James Vanasek, testimony before the Senate Permanent Subcommittee on Investigations,
hearing on "Wall Street and the Financial Crisis: The Role of High-Risk Home Loans,"
April 13, 2010. Available at http://www.hsgac.senate.gov/subcommittees/investigations/
hearings/wall-street-and-the-financial-crisis-the-role-of-high-risk-home-loans,
accessed January 29, 2012.

COMMITTEE REPORTS

Senate Permanent Subcommittee on Investigations, Committee on Homeland Security
and Governmental Affairs, Final Report, *Wall Street and the Financial Crisis: Anatomy
of a Financial Collapse*, April 13, 2011. Available at http://www.hsgac.senate.gov/imo/
media/doc/Financial_Crisis/FinancialCrisisReport.pdf?attempt=2, accessed January
29, 2012.

Memorandum to Members of the Permanent Subcommittee on Investigations, "Wall
Street and the Financial Crisis: The Role of High Risk Loans," April 13, 2010, available
from the Permanent Subcommittee on Investigations, Senate Committee on Homeland
Security and Governmental Affairs, available at http://hsgac.senate.gov/public/_files/
Financial_Crisis/041310Exhibits.pdf, accessed March 20, 2011

CONGRESSIONAL REPORTS

Congressional Budget Office, *Assessing the Public Costs and Benefits of Fannie Mae and
Freddie Mac, 1996*

Congressional Oversight Panel, "A Review of Treasury's Foreclosure Prevention
Programs," December Oversight Report, December 14, 2010

U.S. Government Accountability Office, "Financial Regulation: Industry Trends Continue
to Challenge the Federal Regulatory Structure," GAO-08-32, October 2007

U.S. Government Accountability Office, Orice M. Williams, "Financial Regulation: Review
of Regulators' Oversight of Risk Management at a Limited Number of Large, Complex
Financial Institutions," testimony, GAO-09-499T, March 18, 2009

U.S. Government Accountability Office, "Troubled Asset Relief Program, Status of
Government Assistance Provided to AIG," GAO-09-975, September 2009

Documents Released in Connection with Congressional Hearings

Washington Mutual, "Higher Risk Lending Strategy, 'Asset Allocation Initiative,' Board of
Directors, Finance Committee Discussion," January 2005, p. B1.2, available from the
Permanent Subcommittee on Investigations, Senate Committee on Homeland Security
and Governmental Affairs, available at http://hsgac.senate.gov/public/_files/
Financial_Crisis/041310Exhibits.pdf, accessed March 20, 2011

Paul A. Volcker, letter to Fannie Mae CEO David O. Maxwell, March 6, 1990, published in the "Second Roundtable Hearing on the Safety and Soundness of Fannie Mae and Freddie Mac," Subcommittee on Housing and Urban Affairs, Senate Committee on Banking, Housing and Urban Affairs, August 2, 1990, pp. 142–52.

Reports, Letters, Monographs, Conferences

REPORTS AND LETTERS

American Bankers Association. Letter from the American Bankers Association to the bank supervisors, March 29, 2006, "Re: Proposed Interagency Guidance on Nontraditional Mortgage Products," Available at http://www.aba.com/NR/rdonlyres/DC65CE12-B1C7-11D4-AB4A-00508B95258D/42556/grnontradmortgage06.pdf, accessed January 29, 2012.
American International Group. Form 10-K for the fiscal year ended December 31, 2007
BP U.S. Refineries Independent Safety Review Panel. *The BP U.S. Refineries Independent Safety Review Panel Report*, January 2007
Buffett, Warren."Chairman's Letter, 2001," Berkshire Hathaway, available at www.berkshirehathaway.com/letters/2001pdf.pdf, accessed March 20, 2011
Center for Responsive Politics, "Finance/Insurance/Real Estate" (1) available at www.opensecrets.org/industries/background.php?cycle=2010&;ind=F, accessed April 28, 2011
Center for Responsive Politics. "Finance/Insurance/Real Estate" (2) available at www.opensecrets.org/industries/indus.php?ind=F, accessed April 28, 2011
Clark, W. Edmund. "President and CEO's Message," *TD Bank Financial Group 2005*
Committee for Economic Development. "Restoring Trust in Corporate Governance: Six Essential Tasks of Boards of Directors and Business Leaders," January 2010
Committee of Sponsoring Organizations of the Treadway Commission. *Enterprise Risk Management—Integrated Framework, Executive Summary*, September 2004
Countrywide Financial Corporation. Form 10-K for the fiscal year ended December 31, 2005
CRMPG III [Counterparty Risk Management Policy Group]. *Containing Systemic Risk: The Road to Reform*, report, August 6, 2008, available at www.crmpolicygroup.org/, accessed April 21, 2011
Federal Reserve Bank of St. Louis. Financial Crisis Timeline, available at www.stlouisfed.org/timeline/timeline.cfm, accessed September 1, 2011
Freddie Mac, *Financing America's Housing: The Vital Role of Freddie Mac*, 1996
Goldman Sachs, "Fall 2008 Narrative," undated
Goldman Sachs, "Goldman Sachs: Risk Management and the Residential Mortgage Market," April 23, 2010
Goldman Sachs, *2006 Annual Report*
Goldman Sachs, *2007 Annual Report*
Goldman Sachs, *Report of the Business Standards Committee: Executive Summary*, available at www2.goldmansachs.com/our-firm/business-standards-committee/executive-summary.html, accessed March 23, 2011.
Hiemstra, Stephen W. "An Enterprise Risk Management View of Financial Supervision," *Enterprise Risk Management Institute International*, research report, October 2007,

JPMorgan Chase, "2006 Letter to Shareholders."

JP Morgan Chase Annual Report for the Year 2008

JP Morgan Chase Annual Report for the Year 2010

McCleskey, Scott. Letter to the U.S. Securities and Exchange Commission, March 12, 2009

Nestor Advisors, *Governance in Crisis: A Comparative Study of Six US Investment Banks*, April 2009

Paul, Weiss, Rifkind, Wharton & Garrison LLP, *Report to the Special Review Committee of the Board of Directors of Fannie Mae*, 2006

Posner Kenneth A. and Mita Nambiar, "U.S. Mortgage Finance: The American Dream Industry, 2002–2020," MorganStanley Equity Research Industry report, February 5, 2002

Rosner, Josh, "Housing in the New Millennium: A Home Without Equity Is Just a Rental With Debt," GrahamFisher, June 29, 2001

Rossi, Clifford V. "Anatomy of Risk Management Practices in the Mortgage Industry: Lessons for the Future." Research Institute for Housing America and Mortgage Bankers Association, May 2010

Russonello, Giovanni, "Massey had Worst Mine Fatality Record Even Before April Disaster," American University School of Communication, Investigative Reporting Workshop, November 23, 2010

Ryssdal, Kai. "Conversations from the Corner Office: Wells Fargo & Company President and CEO John Stumpf," June 10, 2008, available at http://marketplace.publicradio.org/display/web/2008/06/10/corneroffice_stumpf_transcript/, accessed March 23, 2011

Standard & Poor's, *Deutsche Bank AG*, October 2, 2009

Stiglitz, Joseph E., Jonathan M. Orszag and Peter R. Orszag, "Implications of the New Fannie Mae and Freddie Mac Risk-based Capital Standard," *Fannie Mae Papers*, March 2002

The Joint Commission, "Behaviors that Undermine a Culture of Safety," *Sentinel Event Alert*, Issue 40, July 9, 2008

Toronto Dominion Bank, *Annual Report*, 2006

UBS AG, *Shareholder Report on UBS's Write-Downs*, April 18, 2008

Monographs

American Enterprise Institute, "A Conversation with President Bush," transcript, December 18, 2008

Bebchuk Lucian A. and Holger Spamann. "Regulating Bankers' Pay," discussion paper No. 641, Harvard John M. Olin Center for Law, Economics, and Business, October 2009 revision

Bebchuk, Lucian A., Alma Cohen, and Holger Spamann. "The Wages of Failure: Executive Compensation at Bear Stearns and Lehman Brothers 2000–2008," discussion paper no. 657, Harvard John M. Olin Center for Law, Economics, and Business, February 2010 revision

Belsky Eric S., and Nela Richardson. "Understanding Boom and Bust in the Nonprime Mortgage Market," Harvard Joint Center for Housing Studies, September 2010, available at www.jchs.harvard.edu/publications/finance/UBB10-1.pdf, accessed April 26, 2011

Beltratti, Andrea and René M. Stulz. "Why Did Some Banks Perform Better during the Credit Crisis? A Cross-Country Study of the Impact of Governance and Regulation," European Corporate Governance Institute, Working Paper No. 254/2009, July 2009, available at www.law.columbia.edu/null/download?&;exclusive=filemgr. download&file_id=154789, accessed March 20, 2011

Blinder, Alan S. and Mark Zandi. *How the Great Recession was Brought to an End*, monograph, July 27, 2010. Available at http://www.suu.edu/faculty/berri/End-of-Great-Recession.pdf, accessed January 29, 2012.

Buiter, Willem (2008). Lessons from the North Atlantic Financial Crisis, revised May 28, 2008, available at www.newyorkfed.org/research/conference/2008/rmm/buiter.pdf

Coffee, John C. Jr. and Hilary A. Sale. "Redesigning the SEC: Does the Treasury have a Better Idea?" University of Iowa Legal Studies Research Paper, December 2008

Golub, Bennett W. and Conan C. Crum. "Risk Management Lessons Worth Remembering From the Credit Crisis of 2007–2009," available at http://papers.ssrn.com/sol3/papers. cfm?abstract_id=1508674, accessed 06-14-2010

Hu, Henry T. C., and Bernard Black. "Debt, Equity, And Hybrid Decoupling: Governance and Systemic Risk Implications," June 15, 2008 draft, available at http://ssrn.com/abstract=1084075

Kaufmann, Daniel and Veronika Penciakova. "Japan's Triple Disaster: Governance and the Earthquake, Tsunami and Nuclear Crises," The Brookings Institution, March 16, 2011

LaCour-Little, Michael and Jing Yang. *Taking the Lie Out of Liar Loans*, monograph, June 23, 2009. Available at http://www.fhfa.gov/webfiles/15048/website_lacour.pdf, accessed January 29, 2012.

LaCour-Little, Michael, Eric Rosenblatt, and Vincent Yao. "Home Equity Extraction by Homebuyers: 2000–2006," unpublished manuscript, January 18, 2009

Pollock, Alex J. "What Should Society Want from Corporate Governance?" *Financial Services Outlook*, American Enterprise Institute, February 2006

Society of Actuaries, the Casualty Actuarial Society and the Canadian Institute of Actuaries. "Risk Management: The Current Financial Crisis, Lessons Learned and Future Implications," published by the Enterprise Risk Management Institute International ("ERM-II"), 2008

Stanford Graduate School of Business. "Wells Fargo and Norwest: Merger of Equals (B)," October 11, 2004. Available at http://charlottechamber.com/clientuploads/Survive_Thrive/norwestfargo.pdf, accessed January 29, 2012.

Stanford Rock School of Business. "Lehman Brothers: Peeking Under the Board Façade" June 4, 2010. Available at http://papers.ssrn.com/sol3/papers.cfm?abstract_id=1678044, accessed January 29, 2012.

Stanton, Thomas H. "Defending Cyberspace: Protecting Individuals, Government Agencies and Private Companies Against Persistent and Evolving Threats," monograph, Johns Hopkins University, July 2008. Available at http://advanced.jhu.edu/bin/g/z/Defending_Cyberspace.pdf, accessed January 29, 2012.

Subramanian, Guhan and Nithyasri Sharma. "Citigroup-Wachovia-Wells Fargo," case study, Harvard Law School, June 10, 2010

White, Lawrence J. "The Credit Rating Agencies: How Did We Get Here? Where Should We Go?" available at www.ftc.gov/be/seminardocs/091112creditratingagencies.pdf, accessed June 4, 2011

Wilmarth, Arthur E. Jr., "Controlling Systemic Risk in an Era of Financial Consolidation," 2002, available at www.imf.org/external/np/leg/sem/2002/cdmfl/eng/wilmar.pdf, accessed March 19, 2011

Yale School of Management. "Pay, Risk, and Stewardship: Private Sector Architecture for Future Capital Markets," Policy Briefing No. 5, consultative draft, 2009

Conferences

Acharya, Viral. Comments at the 47th Conference on Bank Structure and Competition, Federal Reserve Bank of Chicago, May 5, 2011

Bonocore, Joe, Corporate Treasurer, JPMorgan Chase & Co. Comments at the 47th Conference on Bank Structure and Competition, Federal Reserve Bank of Chicago, May 6, 2011

Brevoort, Kenneth P. and Cheryl R. Cooper. The Urban Institute, "Foreclosure's Wake: The Credit Experiences of Individuals Following Foreclosure," paper presented at the 47th Annual Conference on Bank Structure and Competition, Federal Reserve Bank of Chicago, May 4, 2011

Clark, Edmund. National Bank 2010 Financial Services Conference, presentation, TD Bank Financial Group, March 30, 2010

Clark, Edmund. "Corporate Transparency and Corporate Accountability—Today's Table Stakes for Senior Executives," remarks to the Executive Women's Alliance Conference, Vancouver, July 12, 2004

Ludwig, Eugene A. William Taylor Memorial Lecture, International Conference of Banking Supervisors, Brussels, September 25, 2008

Pearce, James E., and James C. Miller III. "Fannie Mae and Freddie Mac: Their Funding Advantage and Benefits to Consumers," proceedings, the 37th Annual Conference on Bank Structure and Competition, Federal Reserve Bank of Chicago, May 2001

Pollock, Alex J. "Introduction to a Conference on Improving Mortgage Disclosure," American Enterprise Institute, June 15, 2007, available at www.aei.org/docLib/20070615_PollockIntro.pdf, accessed June 23, 2011

Government Documents

Bernanke, Ben S. "The Subprime Mortgage Market," speech at the Federal Reserve Bank of Chicago's 43rd Annual Conference on Bank Structure and Competition, Chicago, Illinois, May 17, 2007.

Board of Governors of the Federal Reserve System. "The Supervisory Capital Assessment Program: Design and Implementation," April 24, 2009

Board of Governors of the Federal Reserve System. Federal Reserve Statistical Releases H.4.1 for December 28, 2006; December 27, 2007; and December 29, 2008

BP U.S. Refineries Independent Safety Review Panel. *The BP U.S. Refineries Independent Safety Review Panel Report*, January 2007

Bricker, Jesse, Brian Bucks, Arthur Kennickell, Traci Mach, and Kevin Moore, "Surveying the Aftermath of the Storm: Changes in Family Finances from 2007 to 2009," Working paper, Board of Governors of the Federal Reserve System, March 2011

Bureau of Ocean Energy Management, Regulation and Enforcement (formerly the Minerals Management Service of the US Department of the Interior—MMS). *Report Regarding the Causes of the April 20, 2010, Macondo Well Blowout*, September 14, 2011

Bush, George W., President of the United States. Remarks on Signing the American
Dream Downpayment Act, December 16, 2003, available at www.presidency.ucsb.edu/
ws/index.php?pid=64935, accessed March 20, 2011.

Columbia Accident Investigation Board. *Report Volume I*, August 2003

Comptroller of the Currency. News release, "Comptroller Calls Preemption a Major
Advantage of National Bank Charter," February 12, 2002

Council of Economic Advisers. 2011 *Economic Report of the President*, February 2011

Department of Health and Human Services, Office of Inspector General. "Adverse Events
in Hospitals: National Incidence Among Medicare Beneficiaries," OEI-06-09-00090,
November 2010

Department of the Treasury, Office of Inspector General. *Material Loss Review of National
Bank of Commerce*, OIG-09-042, August 6, 2009

Federal Deposit Insurance Corporation. "Risk Management Manual of Examination
Policies," accessed at www.fdic.gov/regulations/safety/manual/section3-2.html, (last
updated 2005), accessed June 6, 2011

Federal Deposit Insurance Corporation. "Subprime Lending: Supervisory Guidance for
Subprime Lending," March 1, 1999, available at www.fdic.gov/regulations/laws/
rules/5000-5100.html, accessed March 20, 2011

Federal Deposit Insurance Corporation. *History of the Eighties: Lessons for the Future*,
Washington, D.C., 1997

Board of Governors of the Federal Reserve System. *The Federal Reserve System: Purposes
and Functions*, June 2005

Federal Housing Finance Agency, *Report to Congress 2008*, May 18, 2009

Federal Trade Commission. "Citigroup Settles FTC Charges Against the Associates
Record-Setting $215 Million for Subprime Lending Victims," September 19, 2002,
available at www.ftc.gov/opa/2002/09/associates.shtm, accessed June 13, 2011

Federal Trade Commission. "Improving Consumer Mortgage Disclosures: An Empirical
Assessment of Current and Prototype Disclosure Forms," Bureau of Economics Staff
Report by James M. Lacko and Janis K. Pappalardo, June 2007

Geithner, Timothy, Secretary of the Treasury. Address to the International Monetary
Conference, June 6, 2011

Governor's Independent Investigation Panel [West Virginia]. Upper Big Branch: *The April
5, 2010, Explosion: A Failure of Basic Coal Mine Safety Practices*, 2011

Independent Investigation Panel, Upper Big Branch: *The April 5, 2010, Explosion: A Failure
of Basic Coal Mine Safety Practices*, Report to the Governor [West Virginia], May 2011

Independent Review Panel. *Report of the Independent Review Panel San Bruno Explosion*,
prepared for California Public Utilities Commission, revised copy, June 24, 2011

Meyer, Laurence H., Federal Reserve Governor. "The Implications of Financial Modernization Legislation for Bank Supervision," Washington, D.C. December 15, 1999

National Commission on the BP Deepwater Horizon Oil Spill and Offshore Drilling. *Deep
Water: The Gulf Oil Disaster and the Future of Offshore Drilling*, Report to the President, January 2011

National Commission on the BP Deepwater Horizon Oil Spill and Offshore Drilling. Fifth
Meeting, Day Two, *Transcript of Proceedings*, November 9, 2010

National Transportation Safety Board. "NTSB Cites Pacific Gas & Electric (PG&E) and
Government Oversight in Fatal California Pipeline Rupture," August 30, 2011

Office of Comptroller of the Currency (OCC). *Comptroller's Handbook: Large Bank
Supervision*, May 2001

Office of the Comptroller of the Currency (OCC). *Supervisory Guidance on Model Risk Management*, OCC Bulletin 2011–12, April 4, 2011.

Office of Federal Housing Enterprise Oversight. *Fannie Mae Report of Annual Examination*, 2006

Office of Federal Housing Enterprise Oversight. *Report of the Special Examination of Freddie Mac*, 2003

Office of the New York State Comptroller. "New York City Securities Industry Bonus Pool," February 23, 2010, available at, www.osc.state.ny.us/press/releases/feb10/bonus_chart_2009.pdf, accessed April 21, 2011

Richards, Lori A. "Strengthening Examination Oversight: Changes to Regulatory Examinations," speech, June 17, 2009, www.sec.gov/news/speech/2009/spch061709lar.htm, accessed May 17, 2011

U.S. Census Bureau. *Income, Poverty, and Health Insurance Coverage in the United States: 2010*, September 2011

U.S. Chemical Safety and Hazard Investigation Board. *Refinery Explosion And Fire (15 Killed, 180 Injured), BP, Texas City, Texas, March 23, 2005*, Investigation Report No. 2005-04-I-TX, March 2007

U.S. Securities and Exchange Commission, Office of Inspector General, Office of Audits. *SEC's Oversight of Bear Stearns and Related Entities: the Consolidated Supervised Entities Program*, Report No. 446-A, September 25, 2008

U.S. Treasury and Federal Deposit Insurance Corporation, Offices of Inspector General, *Evaluation of Federal Regulatory Oversight of Washington Mutual Bank*, April 2010

Legal Documents

Commonwealth v. Fremont Investment & Loan, 452 Mass. 733, 897 N.E. 2d 548 (2008).

In Re Citigroup Inc. Shareholder Derivative Litigation, Delaware Court of Chancery, 964 A.2d 106 (2009)

Residential Assets Security Corporation, "Home Equity Mortgage Asset-Backed Pass-Through Certificates," Series 2004–KS12, Depositor, Registration File No.: 333–108868, December 22, 2004, p. 185, available at www.sec.gov/Archives/edgar/data/932858/000095013604004579/file001.htm

Securities and Exchange Commission, Consent Order of Defendant Goldman Sachs & Co., available at www.sec.gov/litigation/litreleases/2010/consent-pr2010-123.pdf, accessed July 18, 2011

The People of the State of California v. Countrywide Financial Corporation, et al., Case No. LC081846, First Amended Complaint, July 17, 2008

United States Bankruptcy Court, Southern District of New York, *In re Lehman Brothers Holdings, Inc.*, "Report of Anton R. Valukas, Examiner," March 11, 2010, available at http://lehmanreport.jenner.com/VOLUME%201.pdf, accessed March 29, 2011.

United States Supreme Court, *Caperton et al. v. A.T. Massey Coal Co., Inc.*, decided June 8, 2009

International

A Report to the Minister for Finance by the Governor of the Central Bank, *The Irish Banking Crisis: Regulatory and Financial Stability Policy*, 2003–2008, May 31, 2010

Association of Inspectors of the Bank of Spain, letter to the Second Vice Chairman of the Government and Minister of the Economy & Finance, May 26, 2005

Bank of England, *Financial Stability Report*, April 2007

Basel Committee on Banking Supervision, *Principles for Enhancing Corporate Governance*, Consultative document, March 2010

Basel Committee on Banking Supervision, *Principles for Sound Liquidity Risk Management and Supervision*, September 2008

Walker, David. *A Review of Corporate Governance in UK Banks and Other Financial Industry Entities: Final Recommendations,"* November 26, 2009, available at, www.ecgi. org/codes/documents/walker_review_261109.pdf, accessed March 15, 2011

Financial Services Authority (UK), *The Turner Review: A Global Response to the Global Banking Crisis*, March 2009

Kaufmann, Daniel. "Corruption, Governance and Security: Challenges For the Rich Countries and the World," chapter in the *Global Competitiveness Report 2004/2005*, Washington, DC: World Bank Institute, 2004, available at http://web.worldbank.org/WBSITE/EXTERNAL/WBI/EXTWBIGOVANTCOR/0,contentMDK:20788416~isCURL:Y~menuPK:1976979~pagePK:64168445~piPK:64168309~theSitePK:1740530,00.html, accessed May 16, 2009

Senior Supervisors Group, *Observations on Risk Management Practices during the Recent Market Turbulence*, March 6, 2008

Senior Supervisors Group, *Risk Management Lessons from the Global Banking Crisis of 2008*

Superintendent Julie Dickson, Office of the Superintendent of Financial Institutions Canada (OSFI), "Too Focused on the Rules; The Importance of Supervisory Oversight in Financial Regulation," remarks to the Heyman Center on Corporate Governance, New York, March 16, 2010

Using the OECD Principles of Corporate Governance: A Boardroom Perspective, 2008, available at www.oecd.org/dataoecd/20/60/40823806.pdf, accessed March 15, 2011

INDEX